Women Reading
William Blake

Edited by

Helen P. Bruder

First published 2007 by
PALGRAVE MACMILLAN
Houndmills, Basingstoke, Hampshire RG21 6XS and
175 Fifth Avenue, New York, N.Y. 10010
Companies and representatives throughout the world

PALGRAVE MACMILLAN is the global academic imprint of the Palgrave
Macmillan division of St. Martin's Press, LLC and of Palgrave Macmillan
Ltd. Macmillan® is a registered trademark in the United States, United
Kingdom and other countries. Palgrave is a registered trademark in the
European Union and other countries.

ISBN-13: 978-1-4039-9704-3 hardback
ISBN-10: 1-4039-97047 hardback

This book is printed on paper suitable for recycling and made from fully
managed and sustained forest sources.

A catalogue record for this book is available from the British Library.

Library of Congress Cataloging-in-Publication Data
Women reading William Blake / edited by Helen P. Bruder.
    p.   cm.
    Includes bibliographical references and index.
    ISBN 1-4039-9704-7 (cloth)
    1. Blake, William, 1757–1827 – Criticism and interpretation.
2. Blake, William, 1757–1827 – Characters – Women.   3. Women in
literature.   4. Gender identity in literature.   5. Sex role in
literature.   6. Feminist literary criticism.   I. Bruder, Helen P.
PR4147.W66 2007
821'.7–dc22   2006047262

10   9   8   7   6   5   4   3   2   1
16   15   14   13   12   11   10   9   8   7

Printed and bound in Great Britain by
Antony Rowe Ltd, Chippenham and Eastbourne

For my Dad,
'I hate scarce smiles I love laughing' (E 585)

Contents

List of Illustrations   x

List of Abbreviations   xi

Notes on Contributors   xii

Introductory Note   xv

 1 'The Bread of sweet Thought & the Wine of Delight': Gender,
   Aesthetics and Blake's 'dear Friend Mrs Anna Flaxman'   1
   Helen P. Bruder

 2 Peeking over the Garden Wall   12
   Tracy Chevalier

 3 Blake, Literary History and Sexual Difference   16
   Claire Colebrook

 4 Transgender Juvenilia: Blake's and Cristall's *Poetical Sketches*   26
   Tristanne Connolly

 5 'The right stuff in the right hands': Anne Gilchrist and
   The Life of William Blake   35
   Shirley Dent

 6 William Blake's Lavaterian Women: Eleanor, Rowena
   and Ahania   44
   Sibylle Erle

 7 Blake's Golden Chapel: the Serpent Within and Those Who
   Stood Without   53
   Eugenie R. Freed

 8 How To Nearly Wreck Your Life By Living Blake   62
   Addie Stephen

 9 Aesthetic Agency? Enitharmon in Blake's *Europe*   70
   Nancy Moore Goslee

10 'No Earthly Parents I confess': the Clod, the Pebble and
   Catherine Blake   78
   Germaine Greer

11 The Impact of Feminism on Blake Studies in Japan   91
   Yoko Ima-Izumi

12 Blake's Mary and Martha on the Mount of Olives: Questions
    on the Watercolour Illustrations of the Gospels   100
    Mary Lynn Johnson

13 The Trimurti Meet the Zoas: 'Hindoo' Strategies in the Poetry
    of William Blake   109
    Kathryn Sullivan Kruger

14 Towards an Ungendered Romanticism: Blake, Robinson and
    Smith in 1793   118
    Jacqueline M. Labbe

15 William Blake and Romantic Women Poets: 'Then what have
    I to do with thee?'   127
    Harriet Kramer Linkin

16 'Endless Their Labour': Women in Blake's Illuminated Works
    and in the British Workforce   137
    Catherine L. McClenahan

17 Sentiment, Motherhood and the Sea in Gillray and Blake   148
    Cindy McCreery

18 Framing Eve: Reading Blake's Illustrations   159
    Jennifer Davis Michael

19 Lucid Dreaming/Lucid Reading: Notes on Sleepers in
    Blake's *Songs*   170
    Gerda S. Norvig

20 Valkyries and Sibyls: Old Norse Voices of Female Authority in
    Blake's Prophetic Books   179
    Heather O'Donoghue

21 Re-Deeming Scripture: My William Blake Revisited   189
    Alicia Ostriker

22 The Gender of Los(s): Blake's Work in the 1790s   200
    Tilottama Rajan

23 The 'Secret' and the 'Gift': Recovering the Suppressed
    Religious Heritage of William Blake and Hilda Doolittle   209
    Marsha Keith Schuchard

24 A Kabbalistic Reading of *Jerusalem*'s Prose Plates   219
    Sheila A. Spector

25 Brittannia Counter Britannia: How *Jerusalem* Revises Patriotism 228
    June Sturrock

26 Blake: Sex and Selfhood   237
    Irene Tayler

27 Blake Moments   247
    Janet Warner

28 Blake, Sex and Women Revisited   254
    Brenda Webster

29 The Strange Difference of Female 'Experience'   261
    Susan J. Wolfson

30 Baillie and Blake: at the Intersection of Allegory and Drama   270
    Julia M. Wright

Index   279

List of Illustrations

12.1   William Blake, *The Hymn of Christ and the Apostles*
       (private collection, copyright Agnews, London/Bridgeman
       Art Library)   101

15.1   Mary Tighe, watercolour sketch for the final page of 1803
       manuscript copy of her *Psyche*, prepared for the Ladies of
       Llangollen (National Library of Wales, Aberystwyth/Llyfrgell
       Genedlaethol, Cymru)   131

17.1   James Gillray, *The Nancy Packet* (British Museum, London,
       object no. 1862,0712.296)   150

17.2   William Blake, *Little Tom the Sailor* (British Museum,
       London, object no. 1868,0808.13497)   152

18.1   William Blake, *The Creation of Eve* (Museum of Fine
       Arts, Boston)   163

18.2   William Blake, *The Creation of Eve: 'And She shall be
       called Woman'* (Metropolitan Museum of Art, New York)   165

18.3   William Blake, *Eve Tempted by the Serpent* (Victoria and
       Albert Museum, London)   166

Thanks to these institutions for their kind permission to reproduce the images.

List of Abbreviations

Unless otherwise noted, references to the works of Blake come from *The Complete Poetry and Prose of William Blake*, edited by David V. Erdman, newly revised edition (Garden City: Anchor/Doubleday, 1988). References in form (E) refer to page numbers in that volume.

FZ   *The Four Zoas*
M   *Milton a Poem in 2 Books*
J   *Jerusalem The Emanation of The Giant Albion*

Much of Blake's visual art can be viewed, free of charge, at the Blake Archive website: www.blakearchive.org. References to works consulted there are referenced (BA), where relevant followed by plate/line reference.

BQ   *Blake: An Illustrated Quarterly*

Notes on Contributors

Helen P. Bruder, independent scholar, wrote *William Blake and the Daughters of Albion* (1997) and the 'Gender' chapter in the *Palgrave Guide to Advances in William Blake Studies* (2006). She is currently working on the journals and letters of Blake's friend, Ann Flaxman.

Tracy Chevalier has written five novels, including *Burning Bright*, which is about William Blake (to be published March 2007), as well as the bestselling *Girl with a Pearl Earring*. She is American and lives in London.

Claire Colebrook, Professor of Modern Literary Theory at the University of Edinburgh, is the author, most recently, of *Gender* (2004) and *Deleuze: a Guide for the Perplexed* (2005).

Tristanne Connolly, Assistant Professor of English at St Jerome's, University of Waterloo, is the author of *William Blake and the Body* (2002).

Shirley Dent, press officer for the Institute of Ideas, organized 'What is poetry for?' a debate at the Battle of Ideas festival, 2005. She is co-author with Jason Whittaker of *Radical Blake: Afterlife and Influence 1827–2000* (2002).

Sibylle Erle, who teaches at Birkbeck, University of London and is an Associate Lecturer for the Open University, works on Blake, Lavater and European Romanticism.

Eugenie R. Freed is Research Fellow in English, University of the Witwatersrand, Johannesburg, SA; her work on medieval and Renaissance literature influences her Blake studies.

Nancy Moore Goslee, Professor of English at the University of Tennessee, is finishing a book on Shelley's manuscript notebooks that owes much to her study of Blake's composite arts. A recent essay on Shelley's *Discourse on the Manners of the Ancient Greeks* also deals with inter-arts comparisons.

Germaine Greer, renowned academic, writer, broadcaster. Professor Greer's many scintillating publications include *The Female Eunuch* (1970), *The Obstacle Race* (1979), *Slip-shod Sibyls* (1995), *The Whole Woman* (1999) and *The Boy* (2003).

Yoko Ima-Izumi is Professor of English and Film Studies, University of Tsukuba, Japan, and author, recently, of *Blake's Re-Vision of the Female* (2001) and *Film Syntax: Shot Analysis of Japanese Film* (2004).

Mary Lynn Johnson, Special Assistant (Emerita), President's Office, University of Iowa, is co-editor of *Blake's Poetry and Designs* (2nd edn, 2006).

Kathryn Sullivan Kruger is the author of *Weaving the Word: the Metaphorics of Weaving and Female Textual Production* (2001) and a volume of poetry, *Solstice* (2001).

Jacqueline M. Labbe, Professor of English, University of Warwick, is author of *Charlotte Smith: Romanticism, Poetry and the Culture of Gender* (2003) and editor of Smith's poems for *The Works of Charlotte Smith* (forthcoming 2007).

Harriet Kramer Linkin, Professor of English at New Mexico State University, has published widely on Romantic-era writers, and is the editor of *The Collected Poems and Journals of Mary Tighe* (2005).

Catherine L. McClenahan, of the English Department, Indiana University of Pennsylvania, writes on Blake, gender and politics, most recently on Erin and the United Irish.

Cindy McCreery, Lecturer in History at the University of Sydney, Australia, is the author of *The Satirical Gaze: Prints of Women in Late Eighteenth-century England* (2004).

Jennifer Davis Michael, who teaches English at the University of the South (Sewanee), is the author of *Blake and the City* (forthcoming 2006).

Gerda S. Norvig, formerly Professor of English at the University of Colorado, has written about Blake in *Dark Figures in the Desired Country* (1993) and 'Female Subjectivity and the Desire of Reading in(to) Blake's *Book of Thel*' (1998).

Heather O'Donoghue, Reader at the University of Oxford, and Professorial Fellow at Linacre College, is the author, most recently, of *Old Norse-Icelandic Literature: a Short Introduction* (2004), and *Skaldic Verse and the Poetics of Saga Narrative* (2005).

Alicia Ostriker, Professor Emerita of English at Rutgers University, is the author of *Vision and Verse in William Blake* and of essays on Blake and sexuality, and is editor of the Penguin *Complete Poems of William Blake*.

Tilottama Rajan, Canada Research Chair, University of Western Ontario, is the author, most recently, of *Deconstruction and the Remainders of Phenomenology: Sartre, Derrida, Foucault, Baudrillard* (2002), and *Idealism without Absolutes: Philosophy and Romantic Culture* (2004).

Marsha Keith Schuchard is the author of *Restoring the Temple of Vision: Cabalistic Freemasonry and Stuart Culture* (2001) and *Why Mrs. Blake Cried: William Blake and the Sexual Basis of Spiritual Vision* (2006).

Sheila A. Spector, independent scholar, is the author of *'Glorious incomprehensible': the Development of Blake's Kabbalistic Language* and *'Wonders Divine': the Development of Blake's Kabbalistic Myth* (both 2001).

Addie Stephen, who teaches in the Goucher College MFA Program, is the author of twelve books.

June Sturrock, Emerita Professor of English, Simon Fraser University, Canada, has edited *Jane Austen's Mansfield Park* (2001).

Irene Tayler, Professor Emerita of Literature, MIT, is the author of *Blake's Illustrations to the Poems of Gray* (1971).

Janet Warner, retired Professor of English, York University, Toronto, passed away during the production of this volume. Her last work is a novel, *Other Sorrows, Other Joys: the Marriage of Catherine Sophia Boucher and William Blake* (2003). She also wrote *William Blake and the Language of Art* (1984).

Brenda Webster, critic, translator, novelist, and president of PEN West, is the author of eight books, most recently a novel, *The Beheading Game*.

Susan J. Wolfson, Professor of English, Princeton University, has a chapter on Blake in *Formal Charges* (1998). *Borderlines: the Shiftings of Gender in British Romanticism* is forthcoming 2006.

Julia M. Wright, Canada Research Chair in European Studies, Dalhousie University, is the author or editor of several volumes, including *Ireland, India and Nationalism in Nineteenth-century Literature* (forthcoming).

Introductory Note: 'look over the events of your own life . . .' (E 617)

Helen P. Bruder

It seems to me that readers are entitled to discover from an Introduction not only what a book is about but also why it was produced. This note, briefly, answers that question. I mused over which design to use for this collection's cover in the dark peace of Duke Humfrey's Library in Oxford. Though my family have lived in the city for years we're definitely town not gown, so when, in 1987, I scraped into Oxford Poly's English course I hardly knew such spiritual interiors existed. I'd not dreamt I'd inhabit them and I had never heard of William Blake. Finding him and beginning those studies was a miraculous stroke of good fortune, and this abounded as our liaison unfurled. I was blessed with a pair of wonderful Blake teachers, Paul O'Flinn and Colin Pedley, who shared their different passions for his art and together gave me a love of history and historical detail. The times themselves were also auspicious. UK campus life in the 1980s was marked by truculence and rebelliousness; which nursed my girlish fantasy that feminism was academically essential and universally desired. More modestly, timing was lucky in other ways too. The polytechnic began to offer higher degrees and I was among the first batch of eager postgraduate students. Better still, I was fortunate enough to receive a British Academy grant to fund my research. I was actually given money to sit and think. Imagine that. I am unashamed to say that studying Blake utterly changed my life, and though I have no wish to generalise about how *Women* are or should be *Reading William Blake* it's certainly true that acknowledging, explicitly, the unusually passionate response he tends to provoke is a striking feature of this volume (indeed his influence can be emotionally incendiary – hence the need for one contributor to appear anonymously).

The joyful recognition that I felt on reading Blake was, sadly, not often experienced during the hours I spent yawning over Blake criticism – much of which I found alienating and tiresome. The work itself was not a problem. I knew the value of graft and sometimes even invented feats for myself – such as copying out his epics, in full, by hand, in a physical attempt to absorb something of their meaning. Indeed in twenty years of study I've never minded labouring over Blake, because I've always felt that his works are hard because what he is trying to say is hard, and moreover that he communicates as lucidly as the content's complexity (especially when sexual) will allow. This was not the case – I suspected – with many of his esteemed critics, who did not seem to *want* to be understood, at least not by outsiders. It wasn't just their assumptions of prior knowledge. Having received almost no literary education in the 'too dim for "O" levels' class of a segregated comprehensive (a half-hour film about Macbeth was the sum total of our schooling in Shakespeare, for instance) I did find the more densely allusive studies rather intimidating. But on the other hand my upbringing among Bible-believing Christians meant that (for good and ill) Blake's most beloved sourcebook was almost as deep in my blood as in his. So the problem wasn't just blithe, 'educated', assumptions – offputting as they could be. It was something less precise, but more pernicious. A pervasive sense that Blake's art was tricky and special stuff, suitable only for a special (clearly elite) audience. This idea, that Blake rightly belongs to a select coterie of distinguished initiates, has a long lineage (see Chapter 5) but it struck me then (as now) as complete anathema. Experience, Blake's touchstone, convinced. After all, I wasn't part of a cultured clique, yet I'd been able to 'get' something of what he was saying – and what's more, I'd been tempted to turn interpreter precisely because of Blake's brazen egalitarianism. His inclusive 'every's flew off the page: 'every human bosom . . . soul . . . perfection . . . heart' (E 338, 350, 147, 114), 'every species . . . beast . . . herb . . . flower . . . plant' (E 392, 14, 189, 495, 319), 'Every scatterd Atom . . . every thing that breathes . . . every Generated Body . . . Every Divine Member' (E 121, 375, 123, 153), 'every Nation of the Earth . . . every Earth in the wide universe' (E 159, 403), 'Every child . . . female . . . man' (E 7, 220, 13), 'every face . . . voice . . . tongue' (E 26, 27, 487), 'every thing that lives is holy!' (E 51). Wow! My feeling then (which teaching deepened) was that what Blake creates – with his cast of weirdly-named characters, his topsy-turvy cosmic geography, his logic defying syntax (and so on and so on and so on) – is a democracy of confusion. *Every*one is baffled, at the beginning, and beyond, and it's heartening to note that Blake himself didn't shilly-shally over who'd 'crack' him: 'I am happy to find a Great Majority of Fellow Mortals . . . can Elucidate My Visions' (Letter to Trusler, E 703). His would-be patron the 'Revd Dr' Trusler felt himself uniquely qualified to pronounce, but Blake would have none of it. Why? Because, 'There is a vast Majority on the side of Imagination' (E 703). I still remember the thrill I felt when Paul showed us these indignantly democratic letters (16/23 August 1799 E 701–3). Equally memorable is the birth of my belief that the least Blake's expositors should do is to write in ways accessible to that 'vast Majority'. Usually, of course, we don't, and it's one of *Women Reading William Blake*'s two structuring aims to make amends. Blake's 250th birthday (2007) will provoke much curiosity, and it's a dear wish that the intrigued will find writing here which is not only illuminating but (rarer still) enjoyable. Various aspects of the book's composition engender optimism. All the articles are concise, which enables the inclusion of a uniquely wide range of voices. Many of the writers come from outside Blake studies, and the cast is international and spans generations. There's also little pretence of academic anonymity (see especially chapters 7, 8, 11, 21, 22, 26–30). The collection is peppered, too, with new insights into Blake's biography (especially chapters 1, 2, 5, 10, 15, 23, 26) and visual art (especially chapters 9, 10, 12, 17, 18). We're also blessed with fascinating contributions from two authors who command the interest of millions, Tracy Chevalier and Germaine Greer. So, at the very least, *not* just another exclusive academic compendium.

The other miraculously sustaining context for my study of Blake took shape in the early 1990s, when I found myself working with a bevy of female colleagues. We were different ages, with very different specialisms, interests and dispositions but shared an enthusiastic commitment to feminism and feminist research. It was a uniquely sustaining environment in which to study and write (not to mention relax and be gay) and, perhaps even more incredibly, most of our institutionally secure male colleagues had sufficient integrity and dispassion to realise that our agendas were not quirky fads but, rather, evidence of a paradigm shift too profound (or as we then thought, inexorable) to be ignored. Coming from that mileu it was inevitable that I would find the elitism, gender bias and sometimes outright sexism endemic to Blake studies very, very alarming. Later in the 1990s I wrote an angry book about the interpretative consequences of such conservative attitudes (1997) and though much had – thankfully – changed when I returned to review the rich vein of gender studies now in print (2006)[1] it remains sadly the case that when collections, surveys and guides – which aim to chart the critical terrain and tell us who Blake was and where Blake studies are going – are published women's judgements are universally underrepresented. Over the last twenty years around a dozen collected volumes have appeared. Women scarcely make up a quarter of the writers included – often less than 20 per cent – with the only book approaching sexual equity being the single work which has a woman amongst its editors.[2] In the 1980s there were, perhaps, some practical reasons for this imbalance but to find it replicated in overviews published this century is shocking: from that undergraduate staple *The Cambridge Companion to William Blake* (2003), which finds space for only three women among its 14 contributors and none for chapters on queer or gender scholarship, to the loftier reaches aimed at by a *Studies in Romanticism* twentieth anniversary Blake special (2002), which felt it achieved a 'manifesto-like' critical quality by (again) including only the thoughts of male seers (it remains a moot point whether the admission of a young woman, to elicit their prophetic insights, represents much progress).[3] Obviously, this book's other governing aim is to overturn such prejudices. It isn't a feminist collection, in the sense of there being a prescribed political agenda, and we all know (often from bitter experience) that the equation female = feminist does not add up. Further, it's possible that some contributors would reject the label, though others – famously – would not. What clearly *is* a feminist gesture is my bringing together of generations of female writers on Blake, with the aim of restoring and celebrating an important but neglected critical heritage. It has been a privilege to work with the women whose writings provoked and inspired me, and this collection's other unequivocally feminist intention is to fiercely rebut the common caricature which suggests that female scholars' regard for and gravititation toward gender issues necessarily involves a narrowing of intellectual focus and a reduction of academic merit. This richly diverse compendium shows quite the reverse, and though it is too early to chart trends (and I'd frankly prefer others to discern for themselves) quickly tracing some significant contours is a useful way to conclude. There is a keen interest in Blake's female literary contemporaries, in that other Romanticism (chapters 1, 4, 14, 15, 30). There's also a fascination with exploring spiritual traditions – 'Hindoo' (13), Norse (20), Moravian (23), Kabbalistic (24) – as well as in looking again at Christian iconography (12). The collection's historical enthusiasm is deepened by other, varied, contextualising work: informed by the Napleonic wars writers re-view patriotism (25) and the sea (17). Neglected women workers are also brought into focus (16). It is interesting too to see how many women have found that Blake inspires their own creativity. It is wonderful to hear the thoughts of internationally acclaimed writers – fictional (2) and poetic (21) – and of other creators too (7, 8, 13, 27, 28). Of course that knottiest of questions is addressed, from many perspectives, as well: for Blake's sexual politics see especially chapters 3, 8, 16, 22, 26, 28, 29. There's also an attempt to get beyond the usual North American/UK dominance, with contributions which look at European (6), Japanese (11) and South African (7) contexts for Blake and Blake studies. And no book is complete without a fresh look at his popular *Songs* (19).

These are some of the shapes I see, and it seems safe to risk a bald assertion too – namely that it's fascinating how different Blake (like all men) looks in the company of women – critical and contemporary. Many of the cherished myths about him carry a whiff of testosterone – hot radical, flinty outsider, strong poet, penetrating visionary – and while there's some truth here, we might remember that he was also a man who worked at home, with his wife, who exhibited his works in very modest, family settings and who – while producing the luminously great art we love – was mindful that, 'the light is better in our kitchen'.[4] What might be termed the domestic Blake – interested in 'every pot & vessel & garment' (E 157) – hasn't been beaten into the mix much of late, and this collection reminds us why he should be. I'll venture another assertion too. These writings show, un-ambiguously, that the scale of Blake's worries about sexual identity, creativity, power, fantasy, violence, relationships, spirituality (and on and on) dictates that these subjects cannot be shut in a 'gender studies box'. They are inescapable and inflect every significant aspect of his work. They are, in fact, the grit in Blake's oyster, and though it's debatable whether a pearl appears, their abrasive dominance is not. Any collection which fails to acknowledge this fails its subject, miserably.

I would, though, hate to conclude on a negative note, and my opening quotation explains why: 'look over the events of your own life & if you do not find that you have both done ... miracles & lived by such you do not see as I do' (E 617). More than anything it's an intimation of the miraculous which Blake brought alive for me, and this book only exists because of miracles, of so many kinds.

Most particularly, miracles of generosity from all the contributors – with especial thanks to Sibylle Erle and Jean Freed for stimulating conversation, Irene Tayler for appraising my barbaric (or not!) prose, Janet Warner and Kathryn Kruger for sharing their creative work, Susan Wolfson for chasing details, and to many others as well for their kindness during my recent illness. Above all I want to thank Tristanne Connolly, who ensured this book's safe delivery. A heroic indexer, saintly IT consultant, sage scholar, tireless enthusiast and – despite all the work – a barrel of laughs. Thank you, truly. Thanks, too, to Barbara Slater, Paula Kennedy and Helen Craine at Palgrave, who smoothed our path considerably. My gratitude also to the generous collector Susanne Sklar.

My friends, as ever, pitched in wonderfully. Sara Mattingley was a word processing star. Siân Gaines and Paula Booth (so) generously took care of much essential business. Ann Ross encouraged me throughout, and Jennie Cockram provided an invaluable delivery service! Cheers to you all.

I also want to thank the healers who got me back on my feet again, and thinking. Appreciation – beyond words, really – to Jo Hanstead, Lin Paris, Kate O'Donovan of course ('Unseen descending, weigh my light wings' (E 5), I won't forget) – and an ocean of gratitude to Seka Nikolic.

My family, too, crafted their own brand of miracles, 'the bricks, well wrought affections ... And well contrived words, firm fixing, never forgotten' (E 155).

Notes

1. *William Blake and the Daughters of Albion* (Basingstoke: Macmillan, 1997); *Palgrave Advances in William Blake Studies*, ed. Nicholas M. Williams (Basingstoke: Palgrave, 2006), 132–66.

2. *Blake, Politics, History*, ed. Jackie Di Salvo et al. (New York: Garland Publishing, 1998).
3. *The Cambridge Companion to William Blake*, ed. Morris Eaves (Cambridge: Cambridge University Press, 2003); *Studies in Romanticism* 41, 2 (Summer 2002), 143–348, xxi. Also *Palgrave Advances*, two out of 13 contributors.
4. Letter to Henry Banes, 25/11/1825, in *BQ* 39, 1 (Summer 2005) cover.

1

'The Bread of sweet Thought & the Wine of Delight': Gender, Aesthetics and Blake's 'dear Friend Mrs Anna Flaxman' (E 709)

Helen P. Bruder

Just before the Blakes left London, on their only significant trip together, they took the unusual step of collaboratively producing a letter to Ann Flaxman. Catherine provided the prose,[1] William the verse (a flavour of which is given above). It's a noteworthy epistle, not least because Catherine emerges from it as an image-maker in her own right – conjuring a picture of London as 'the terrible desart' (sic) and encapsulating their journey as an airy 'migration the Swallows call us fleeting past our window' (E 708). It is unique, too, because it contains Catherine's only textual account of a companionable moment from the Blakes' long life together, 'O how we delight in talking of the pleasure we shall have in preparing you a summer bower' (E 708). William Blake happily discussing holiday laundry with his wife: it's not an image of the artist we're used to considering these days, but it will be my argument that just as Catherine's homely vignette revealed for Ann the currently neglected domestic Blake, so the artistic gems William produced for Ann's enjoyment reveal the ease he felt with aesthetic forms which (like bedmaking) have habitually been gendered feminine. Obviously the clearest evidence for this potentially far-reaching argument are those 116 exquisite watercolour 'Drawings' (Spring.1) – designed, in the words of their original recipient, to illuminate the poems of Thomas Gray, which despite their sublime themes are extraordinarily beautiful – and the verses for Ann with which Blake enwrapped them.[2]

These designs are arguably the most delightful of all Blake's works and those unfamiliar with his symbols, preoccupations and contexts can readily enjoy them. Initially it seemed that critics too might be enthusiastic: when the first widely available facsimile appeared Geoffrey Keynes (1971) hailed it as the Blake Trust's 'most important publication' (viii). The designs were proudly shown to the public in both the UK (Tate) and USA (Yale). Those who subsequently devoted themselves to consolidating Blake's canonical and institutional status, however, had little time for his *Gray* and it's my

1

aim to explore the ways in which this is connected to its feminine status as a private entertainment, commissioned on modest terms by a friend, and designed specifically to please the tastes of (to quote one contemporary) an 'amiable and accomplished . . . a most cheerful intelligent woman'.[3] Ann Flaxman was also a highly reflexive scholar, and one comment she makes about the motivation behind her desire to 'gain a knowledge of the Arts & a power of describing what I see of them' is illuminating, for the wish that her memorandums express with justice 'the Love I have for them & the Pleasure I receive in viewing those that are truly fine' (24.b)[4] is central to an understanding of feminine aesthetics. The axiomatic role of attraction and affection; the desire to share artistic impulses, driven by aesthetic pleasure and the intimation that fine appreciation can foster sociability are quintessentially feminine convictions; moreover, it helps to keep a sense of these gendered aesthetics in mind when we begin to consider the trouble caused for critics by the intimate lines of verse (Inscription and Dedication) with which Blake topped and tailed the collection:

> Around the Springs of Gray my wild root weaves
> Traveller repose & Dream among my leaves.
>
> Will. Blake   (Spring.2)

To Mrs Ann Flaxman

> A Little Flower grew in a lonely vale
> Its form was lovely but its colours. pale
> One standing in the Porches of the Sun
> When his Meridian Glories were begun
> Leapd from the steps of fire & on the grass
> Alighted where this little flower was
> With hands divine he movd the gentle Sod
> And took the Flower up in its native Clod
> Then planting it upon a Mountains brow
> 'Tis your own fault if you dont flourish now
>
> William Blake   (Elegy.12)

I will explore Blake's vivid personifications later, but what must first be noted is the beguiling tone of 'Will's' poetic invitation and his warm wish to make playful, amusing contact. All in all these lines lack poetic sobriety, let alone prophetic grandeur, and clearly ill fit the work they frame for inclusion into masterful narratives of Blake's vision – which begins to explain his *Gray's* critical neglect. The only grandee of Blake studies to give it sustained attention, Keynes (1971), actually attempted to classify the Inscription as 'impersonal' (4) but his comments on the Dedication introduce what became a common strategy: conceding intimacy while simultaneously shifting Blake's motivation from the giving of feminine pleasure to the dispensing of masculine instruction. He finds, 'the spirit of Blake's creative powers introducing Ann Flaxman's delicate perceptions to a greater appreciation of poetry and design on the mountain of the double genius of Blake and Gray' (5). Some may see more scurrilous meanings gather around such twin peaks but a joyless, schoolmasterly precedent was thus set and though Irene Tayler's landmark study (1971) made its educational comments mildly (161), the other major treatment of Blake's *Gray* argues for a most alarming form of manly didacticism. Frank Vaughan (1996) presents an artist irritably frustrated by 'Nancy's slowness or resistance to learn from William Blake' (17). His appellations are revealing (Nancy being an affectionate name used only by intimates) but what I take serious issue with is the material Vaughan chooses as 'evidence' to advance his case, for the letters Ann Flaxman wrote to friends in praise of Blake's *Night Thoughts'* designs and in anticipation of his *Gray* (16 March 1796–November 1797) should be treasured as rare and insightful contemporary celebrations of Blake's talents.[5] Vaughan, though, claims they reveal that she was 'puzzled' and 'coped by incorporating him into the stereotypic image of the wild, natural genius' – for her, he alleges, Blake was 'rudely or arbitrarily inspired' (16). Peter Ackroyd (1995) also besmirched Ann's perceptions, claiming she 'overlooked' Blake's 'real genius' to 'characterise' him in 'conventionally sentimental terms' (204). The ignorance these assertions reveal about the depth of William and Ann's relationship and about the profundity of her interest in art and inspiration will soon become clear, but what must be strongly contested from the outset is their distortion of her artistic assessment, for though pitifully few of his peers were willing to prize Blake's 'Strong & Singular Imagination' (1797) or joy in him as one 'whose genius soars above all rule' (1796) without raising some doubts about his sanity, Ann Flaxman was, unequivocally, and attention to her unique significance is long overdue.

Not all critics, of course, contend that Blake felt anger towards the 'passive, orthodox . . . feminine mind' (106) that Vaughan believes she represented. By contrast G.E. Bentley (2001) finds a cordially 'tactful compliment' peeping through the Dedication (177). What remains baffling, though, is the notion that shared floral allusions imply William is responding to Ann's epistolary description of his genius, which is surely impossible since the letters which conveyed it were personal correspondence, one of which never even reached its addressee, let alone a third party like Blake. Which is not to say that Ann Flaxman's many other, less private, writings had no role in the genesis of Blake's *Gray,* or are irrelevant in our interpretations. Quite the contrary, for her essays, notes, correspondence, memorandums, notebooks and (especially) travel journals are a precious store which has been passed over by generations of scholars.[6] The literary output of less signifi-cant male associates has of course been repeatedly trawled and though I have insufficient space fully to illustrate my polemic, it is undoubtedly true that her neglected writings have a unique power to dispel the perplexed sexism which has gathered around *Gray*'s personal, and arguably feminised, Inscription and Dedication.

Of especial relevance is the opening section of Ann Flaxman's *Journey to Rome*, written during the Flaxmans' stay on the continent (1787–94), which describes their eventful trip in witty and arresting detail. It remains unpublished, but was designed to be circulated and to appeal to 'the partiality of those friends into whose hands it may fall' (1). Hands like Blake's? As the volume started doing its rounds William and Ann had been acquainted for over ten years and during the Flaxmans' stay abroad he was undoubtedly in her thoughts, for example when William's birthday approached, Ann asked her sister-in-law for news of him (20/11/1793).[7] One can reasonably speculate that Blake was amongst the friends sorely missed by the Flaxmans, for the decade after their return was one of unprecedented closeness. The spaciousness of the Blakes' Lambeth house and garden enabled easeful entertaining – which we know the Flaxmans enjoyed – and this period (1794–1805) saw the production by Blake not only of feminine private work such as *Gray*, but of collaboration on womanly public works too: in 1799, for example, Blake engraved a gargantuan Britannia for Flaxman's Naval Pillar.[8] These were also the years of his most intense patronage by John and Ann's close friend William Hayley, which included engraving work for an edition of his 'Ladys book', *The Triumphs of Temper* (1803), after 'New Original Designs' by Maria Flaxman, and for another volume with feminine appeal, Hayley's milky and tearful, *Ballads . . . Founded on Anecdotes Relating to Animals* (1802).[9] This was sometimes a stormy decade too but pleasure in the company of the female-enriched Flaxman family remained a constant. Blake, for example, especially notes their 'kind affection' after his acquittal for treason (14/1/1804, E 740) and, tellingly, when piqued that John hasn't 'had the time or grace to call on me' we hear nonetheless that 'Mrs Flaxman & her Sisters' had visited and continually encouraged his artistic labours (23/2/1804, 18/12/1804, E 742, 758). As Blake put it, a grievance with her husband was one thing but 'Should that make a difference betwixt me & Thee' (E 507)? The answer was evidently no and if affections are taken seriously, and the women in Blake's milieu treated as more than wifely emanations, it is clear that the Inscription's invitation 'to repose & Dream' is addressed to one, very literal, 'Traveller': the friend Blake described as 'a good connoisseur in engraving' (E 758), Ann Flaxman, recently returned from Italy – Blake's 'Envied Storehouse of Intellectual Riches' (E 581) – with a sheaf of impressions to share.

His saucy invitation, then, to dreamy slumber is especially tantalising, both because it gestures towards the cheeky sensuality which infuses the *Gray* designs and because it implies that Blake was familiar with the references to recumbent pleasure which pepper the opening pages of Ann's *Journey*. Very early, when the Flaxmans were still in France, she sighs 'in the midst of the Garden we were lull'd to sleep by the murmuring of the Cascades & when we wak'd we were delighted with the surrounding View' (5.b) and, again, after a delicious night spent under 'silk hangings' in Florence, 'we slept that night in Paradise' (29.b). Just ripples of connection? Certainly, but if their relationship is valued, many more become apparent, especially if we jettison that dogmatic seriousness. As we've seen, it conjures a gendered judgmentalism between them which female critics have long been wary of. Years ago Margaret Ruth Lowery (1949) illuminated the 'happy friendship' (289) the pair enjoyed – it starts, for heaven's sake, with Ann's exuberant 'I rejoice for Blake' (1783) and as it closes she's still (1816) prepared to 'put up with' her friend's 'odd humours'[10] – and part of its vibrancy derives from sociability and a sense of fun. I know laughter isn't encouraged in Blake studies but these are, as Mona Wilson noted even earlier (1927), 'more humourous than any of Blake's other work' (97) so it is frankly unavoidable here – not least because Ann's journal, described with light self-mockery as 'an Uninteresting Detail of a journey to Rome' (1), is a hoot and the same archly feminine spirit animates Blake's Dedication to its author.

Comedy, though sniffed at, is *the* interpretative key, and the associated volume which gives the best clue to how we should read Blake's lines is John Flaxman's illustrated poem, *The Knight of the Blazing Cross* which he gave to his wife on her birthday as a token of 'Fifteen Happy Years passed in Your Society' (29).[11] In 1796 Ann received Flaxman's *Knight*; in 1797, Blake's *Gray*. Much could be said about Flaxman's charming book, which well demonstrates Cunningham's gendered aesthetic reminder, 'Though master of its purest lines, he was still more the sculptor of sentiment than of form ... in household or domestic things Flaxman shone unrivalled'[12]; but for now I'll hone in on *The Knight*'s provocative, at times cartoonish, personifications. As a boy John strode through the parks of London, faux sword in hand, eyes vigilant for distressed damsels. This image became a family joke, and years later we find him both invoking and deflating masculine heroism – for while there are straight depictions of the Knight undergoing 'trials of Virtue' (29) his stride and horsemanship become burlesque (37), while his breastplate morphs into a pair of stunning, Madonna-esque, nipples (59, 63). These sketches were 'produced at Your desire' (29) and it is easy to see Ann's feminising tastes emerging in *The Knight*'s giggly undercurrents. Its females are equally slippery. Ostensibly emblems of vulnerability and temptation, or chaste representatives of heavenly assistance and reward (55–7), the most arresting design, nonetheless, is an elaborate ascending pyramid of naked, serpentine women: the 'Blue-eyed Sisters of the deep' who 'pouring out their watery treasure/Perform thy will' (65).

The Knight betokens an enviably complex union, but what's most revealing in the context of Blake's Dedication to *Gray* is Flaxman's ready use of hyperbolic and humorous self-representation, and his playful deployment of sexy and sexual stereotypes. The social currency of such images (John's half-sister Mary Ann, for example, pictures in poetry her brother using 'Minerva's Casque, to make his stews'[13]) – in fact unlocks Blake's otherwise bizarre depiction of the diffident John as a fiery figure 'standing in the Porches of the Sun' and the equally dissonant portrait of the cosmopolitan Ann as 'A little Flower . . . in a lonely Vale'. By the late 1790s Blake and his friends were close enough to indulge in this kind of coy, referential fun and, importantly, seem happy, like so many of their female poetic peers, for art to be an instrument of convivial communication and personalised entertainment: this *is* occasional verse. Arguably Blake takes the gender joke a shade further, straining the active male/passive female opposition beyond credence (as he so often does) but what is of most interest is the feminised function and flavour of Blake's lines, and the fact that he makes an allusion to the Flaxmans' continental trip within this comic context. The arduous journey catalogued by Ann figures here as the leaping John's swift removal of his little flower to the giddy height of a 'Mountains brow' – an ironic allusion which is intriguing because it strongly suggests that Blake knew of and enjoyed her wonderfully amusing account of the pair's sexually segregated travails over some formidable foreign peaks. Ann Flaxman's lengthy Alpine interlude is an engaging and eloquent mix of fashionable pictur-esque aesthetics, genuinely delighted appreciation of the sublime scenery – 'Rocks whose Summits reach'd the Clouds' (18.b) – and potted local history, which has echoes throughout Blake's *Gray*, where landscape is given unusual significance. What evidently most amused Blake, though, is her account of the females' assisted passage over Mount Denis (first on orna-mented mules, then in a rustic sedan) while the men soldiered over on foot – and paid for it later, waking she says with 'Legs of Lead' (21). Space pre-vents adequate quotation, but a quintessential and tonal connection is easily established: 'in this manner were we convey'd . . . by two chairmen who no doubt found our weight more than our worth; It cost *us* a deal of Mirth, & *them* a deal of Labour' (20). So this is how Flaxman's 'Flower' fared when lifted from her 'native Clod', and given this web of jovial allusions Blake's concluding sentiment – ''Tis your own fault if you don't flourish now' – isn't a mannish jibe but rather an arch jest. I suspect William knew first-hand how well Ann flourished on her *Journey to Rome* and I'll conclude by suggesting a few ways in which the *Gray* designs speak both to and of the writer and her travels.

A generic tribute is present, I think, in the female scribes which Blake includes (with book in Adversity.4 and scroll in Poesy.2), in the potent energy (Poesy.12) and wrapt contemplation (Spring.4) of his muses, and in the expressive power gifted to other literary women, like the 'mighty mother' who beams over Ann Flaxman's favourite, Shakespeare (Poesy.9). The feminised art-form with a more direct connection, though, is music – Ann's passion. The first two pages of her *Journey* contain three references to her voice – 'my Talent for singing . . . was my best Friend' (2) – and it is possible that this melody-maker's features are sketched upon the face of the elegant woman, with lyre, who dominates 'The Progress of Poesy' (Poesy.3). Other elaborations extend the compliment: there is no textual precedent for the decorative songbird (Music.2), scarcely more for the trumpeting females who represent fame (Music.1 / 10), nor for the luminescent band who, with flutes and tabors, seem to emblematise (Poesy.5) one of Ann's theoretical contentions about musical sound.[14] The few critics who have considered the designs tend to hail their heroic bards, but it is worth noting that Blake's artistic females are accompanied by less heroic male poets too: Gray himself is a hunched figure, orthopaedically so by the end (Elegy.1); the penman of 'A Long Story' a begowned effete, who scares children & farmyard animals (.6) and must submit to womanly judgement (.10 / 11) and Blake also subjects himself to a female epitaph writer: 'DOST THOU ART' her finger reminds him (Elegy.8). Images likely to resonate with a woman who spent much time amongst (visionary) artists?

Other designs speak of Ann Flaxman's directly expressed aesthetic tastes. One striking theme in her memorandums is the pleasure derived from the contemplation of male bodies: among the 'very fine Casts' at the Academy in Milan Ann selects, 'a fawn snapping his fingers & a sitting Mercury, this last is exquisitely beautiful' (25); at the Palazzo Sampieri, Bologna 'my favourites were a douce of beautiful Boys by Albani' (28); in the Duke's Gallery, Florence she remembers 'with satisfaction a drunken or rather a muddled fawn' and a Bacchanalian 'Group', and from a further chamber 'a Ganymede restor'd by Cellini & a beautiful Cupid'. Evidently 'the Cabinet de l'amour' (33) was delightful and Ann Flaxman's linguistic choices are significant, for her repeated description of these figures as beautiful represents a requisitioning of a firmly gendered aesthetic concept in the service of her heterosexual female gaze – an act of possession Blake gladly accepted and indeed extravagantly indulged across his *Gray*. To many eyes, including I suspect their original recipient's (who mused over their being 'wantonly shewn to anybody'[15]) it offers a pageant of male allurement. Launched by a peek-a-boo portrait of erectile splendour (Spring.1) this flight of feminine fancy takes in: eager naked youths (Spring.3 / 6); rough (Poesy.7) and soft (Eton. 1/2/3/5/9/10) boys – some caught at toilette (Odin.7) or sportively unclad (Eton.4); a winsome cupid among girls (Poesy.5) plus a stageshow of costumed lovelies: a moody moonlit scholar (Music.5), soulful (Elegy.2 / 9 / 10) and frock-coated (Story. 10 / 11) poets, heart-torn widowers (Bard.10 / Epitaph.2), a trio of huge-handed labourers, worthy of D.H. Lawrence (Elegy.5 / 6 / 7), a table of affectionate conversationalists (Owen.2) and last but not least a stable of dashing knights and nobles (the most chisel-jawed: Adversity.3 / Sisters.10 / Odin.3 / 4 / 9). Ann noted that Venetian 'Ladies of Quality . . . form little evening parties to sup on men'.[16] William, it seems, gladly fed such appetites.

A feminine sensibility is also evident in the designs' curiously detailed interiors. On leaving England Ann sadly bid 'Farewell now to Comfortable Parlours' (3.b), examples of which William sketches for her – complete with birdcage (Story.7), card table (Story.12) and ornate fireplace (Epitaph.2). She also gave a feminine twist to gendered architecture, describing the Gothic steeple of Milan cathedral as 'so very light & Elegant' (24.b) – a revisionary strategy repeated by Blake through the whimsical work of 'fairy hands' on the severe vaulted arches of 'An Ancient Pile' (Story.3). The two similarly share an enthusiasm for fabrics and fashion. Ann's was both technical (noting with interest silk manufacture at Lyon (17.b) and 'how exact they die their Worsted' (13) at Gobelins) and aesthetic. Indeed European fashion is one of her major themes: from the finery of coachmen in Milan (25.b), to the 'chip hats' (26) worn by peasants in Parma (see Elegy.5), through the class divisions of dress in Florence (31) – a city which provoked unusually fierce comment, 'the Ladies of Fashion are furious to imitate the English fashions but as the English all pass through France . . . & of Course get themselves Frenchified, the Florentines can never get at the true English mode' (35). If only there were time to pursue the politics of dress and Blake's sensitive rendering of inflected style, but it is valuable just to note the four, somewhat incongruous, sartorial shifts of his Fatal Sisters[17] (.1 / 5 / 7+8 / 9) and the loving detail apparent in 'A Long Story' – both in the astonishing millinery of the female jury (.10 / 11) and in the couture donned (.5 / 7 / 8) by that 'brace . . . rustling in their silks and tissues' (66).

These are revelations to those schooled in the 'Intense! naked!' (E 53) Blake of critical masculinism and it is fitting to close with a vivid variant of the other, domestic, Blake ushered in by an indisputably feminine art form, purveyed by Flaxman's employer Wedgwood:[18] decorative ceramics. The vase in which the catwoman Selima drowns in 'Ode on the Death of a Favourite Cat' is an example of modish chinoiserie (.3) which proved popular with female consumers; though the poem's moral is pettishly chauvinistic: lest reminded 'Nor all that glisters, gold' (52) women's venially capricious appetites will, like any housecat's lust for fish, prove fatal. Blake had little truck with stereotypes of feline femininity – with his most catty female also being his most externally constrained (.1): her laced bodice is tight, her neck-tied shawl equally binding. What perhaps animates these wonderful designs is an intimation that woman are victims of such notions (.5) who can nonetheless see beyond the fluffy ruffles imposed upon them to the human form beneath (.3). And Blake's play with ideas about felines, females and liberation is given delicious bite when we consider it alongside Ann Flaxman's passionate account of the captive cats she saw at Versailles. The palace, with its 'filthy' rooms and smelly sausage stalls (10), is briskly passed through but she dwells at length on the fate of the 'fine Persian cats' (see Cat.2) who 'were for Man's Caprice depriv'd of Nature's right' (10.b). The confinement of the other animals is less distressing but 'poor Puss', caged amid her prey, appears 'like Tantalus . . . prevented from gratifying what the strongest temptations are constantly exciting' (11). Ann's cat craves pheasant; William's fish. But both are unfairly trapped and this scintillating link is tightened when we see how his designs apparently answer her protests. Hearing the cat's pitiful mewing, Ann concludes, 'she Sighs for Liberty' (10.b), whereupon William diverges from Gray's verse to give his catwoman a ninth life[19] in which to obtain her freedom: there can be no better portrait of orgasmic relief than the open-mouthed female sighing above the waves in the poem's final illumination (.6).

This chapter is just a volley in my campaign to establish Ann Flaxman's significance, but I hope it has shown how lamentable it is that the *Gray* watercolours haven't stood alongside Blake's *Night Thoughts* designs and *The Four Zoas* as, in all senses, big works, fundamental to our appreciation of the transitional Blake. And, additionally, that this can in part be accounted for by masculinist assumptions and constructions of the artist which gloss over his feminine (and camp) enthusiasms, while denying women any positive formative role in the development of Blake's aesthetic values. Viewing Blake's artistic circles Robert Essick (1991), for example, sees only female competitors or feminine corruption. Should any doubts remain, why not consider this question. If there had been a long-standing male friend of Blake who had weighed, while in Italy, the comparative merits of Florentine and Venetian art (calling 'St Marks . . . bad Gothic'[20]), and who had written detailed accounts of the artists Blake railed against (including that 'soft and effeminate demon' (E 548) Correggio), and who had 'felt' himself 'quite in M. Angelo's opinion when I view'd . . . the gates of Paradise' (32) while touring the Duomo in Florence, and who had a passion for Christian art, comparative religion and the writings of Dante, *and* who was in the unique position of receiving over one hundred personally tailored poetic illuminations would – (deep breath) – 'his' fascinating corpus have remained unstudied for so long? There's only one truthful answer. William named Ann a 'scholar' (E 740). He conveyed 'Italian Letters' (E 742) on her behalf to William Hayley. John said of his wife, 'She is my Dictionary'.[21] Surely the consultative role Ann Flaxman played in Blake's artistic thinking must be explored? Some may not be comfortable pondering the opinions of a contemporary who likened Blake's works to jewels and flowers ('the meadows queen' indeed) but anxious gender prejudice should not eclipse the perceptions of a woman who, unlike any of those men who have doubted her, actually knew the artist for over thirty years.

Notes

1. Gilchrist finds the letter 'characteristic . . . of Blake' and decides 'the husband is obviously the author' (126). Actually the tone, syntax and imagery of the prose are strikingly atypical.

2. All *Gray* and Gray quotations and references, verbal and visual, are from Tayler, short titles and accompanying picture numbers also refer to this volume. The work is now available in electronic form at BA.
3. Cunningham, Vol. III, 290, 351.
4. Ann Flaxman quotations come from her unpublished *Journal to Rome* or *Journey to Rome* (both titles are in ink on the cover) BL. Add. 39, 787 unless otherwise stated.
5. BL.Add. 39, 780, f. 212 (1796), BL. Add. 39, 790, f. 3–4 (1797) and reproduced in *Blake Records* (1796) 69, (1797) 80.
6. The only substantial treatment is Stevens's, ' "Putting to rights . . ." '.
7. BL. Add. 39, 780, ff. 61–62; 62b.
8. Ann's sister Maria Denman told Gilchrist, 'As a girl she had . . . reverenced Blake' during family visits to Hercules Buildings, Lambeth; she 'observed . . . with some emotion "One remembers, even in age, the kindness of such a man" ', (307, 323). Critics quickly noted this 'woman large enough to graze a couple of goats in her lap', quoted by Cunningham (323).
9. Hayley's classification in letter to John Flaxman (7 August 1803) in *Blake Records*, 157. Blake tells his brother James (30 January 1803) that he is sending '5 copies of N4 of the Ballads for Mrs Flaxman' and two more for 'Mrs Chetwynd' (E 727).
10. In letters to her husband: BL. Add. 39, 780, f. 157 (early 1780s); f. 364, 364b (July 1816).
11. Reproduction of *The Knight* in *Flaxman, Blake, Coleridge . . .* (27–73). Subsequent references are to this edition.
12. Cunningham (362, 319). See too his account of *Knight* (312–20) and of Flaxman's other invention, *The Casket* (332–7).
13. BL. Add. 39, 789, f. 116.
14. Her 'Essay on the Arts Commonly Call'd Imitative' distinguishes 'Common sound' from 'Musical sound', the latter is 'like a Circle which is an intire [sic] figure though it is generated by a multitude of Points flowing, at equal distances round a Common Centre', BL. Add. 39, 790, ff. 113–18; 115–16b. Blake's poem for Ann is 'a song to you' (E 708). Another huge, unexplored, affinity.
15. Letter to her husband, BL. Add. 39, 780, f. 263 (September 1805). Uncharacteristically Ann was loath to loan Blake's *Gray* to a sick (male) friend, keen to collect his artwork.
16. BL. Add. 39, 790, 162.
17. Gray's Preface describes 'twelve gigantic figures resembling women' (110). Blake opts for 'Three Fatal Sisters' (Bard.4). Ann's closeness to her sister Maria and sister-in-law, Mary Ann (both artists) produced many contemporary references to a sisterly trio. It may (also?) inform Blake's moony triple state, Beulah and other conceptions of 'Three-fold Wonder: feminine: most beautiful' (E 224).
18. Wedgwood was Flaxman's main employer, 1773–87. Wedgwood's cash and contacts – along with Ann's resolution 'we must work and economise' – made their Rome trip possible (Smiles, 195–227, 204). During this period Blake forged his friendship with the Flaxmans and themes which John treated for Wedgwood – such as (1782) Blind Man's Buff (211) – reappear (1783) in Blake's *Poetical Sketches* (E 421–3). There is not enough space here to discuss womens' roles in the production of that volume but Blake's female patrons, from Harriet Mathew to the Countess of Egremont (E 552–66), warrant consideration.
19. Gray 'Eight times . . . She mew'd to ev'ry wat'ry God' (51), Blake 'Nine times' (Cat.2).

20. BL. Add. 39, 790, 159b.
21. Cunningham (352).

References

Ackroyd, Peter, *Blake* (London: Sinclair-Stevenson, 1995).
Bentley, G.E., *The Stranger from Paradise* (New Haven and London: Yale University Press, 2001).
Bentley, G.E., *Blake Records* (New Haven: Yale University Press, 2004).
Cunningham, Allan, *The Lives of the Most Eminent British Artists, Sculptors and Architects*, 2 vols (London: John Murray, 1830).
Essick, Robert, 'William Blake's "Female Will" and its Biographical Context', *Studies in English Literature*, 31(1991), 615–30.
Gilchrist, Alexander, *The Life of William Blake* (London: Everyman, 1982), first published 1863.
Keynes, Geoffrey, *William Blake's Watercolour Designs for the Poems of Thomas Gray* (London: Trianon Press and William Blake Trust, 1971).
Lowery, Margaret Ruth, 'Blake and the Flaxmans', in *The Age of Johnson* (New Haven: Yale University Press, 1949), pp. 282–9.
Morris, H.N., *Flaxman, Blake, Coleridge . . .* (London: New Church Press, 1915).
Smiles, Samuel, *Josiah Wedgwood* (London: John Murray, 1894).
Stevens, Bethan, ' "Putting to rights some of the wrecks": Nancy Flaxman's Contribution to the Italian Journey', in *Flaxman, Master of the Purest Line* (London: John Soane Museum, 2003), pp. 19–24.
Tayler, Irene, *Blake's Illustrations to the Poems of Gray* (Princeton, NJ: Princeton University Press, 1971).
Vaughan, Frank A., *Again to the Life of Eternity: William Blake's Illustrations to the Poetry of Thomas Gray* (London: Associated Universities Presses, 1996).
Wilson, Mona, *The Life of William Blake* (St Albans: Granada, 1978), first published 1927.

2

Peeking over the Garden Wall

Tracy Chevalier

William Blake is one of those celebrated figures that educated people like to think they know and understand. Many contemporary artists claim to be influenced by him, though when you look at their work – often abstract, certainly not figurative, nor painted nor engraved – there is little to suggest any affinity. Tate Collection Blake curator Robin Hamlyn, who certainly does know and understand Blake, told me that what artists are actually attracted to is not his technique, but his life as a misunderstood artist who pursues his own vision despite the consequences. Certainly it must be a comfort to penniless artists and poets whose work is ignored to think that Blake is now one of Britain's best known and most admired artists/poets – albeit 200 years too late to be much use to him.

Questioned closely, most artists would admit to never having picked up a burin, printed their own books, made works combining words and images, or drawn long-limbed people with clear musculature outlined under flowing clothes. Nor would poets be able to say that they wrote book-length poems peopled with a world of characters representing different parts of the human psyche. If we're honest, we don't know Blake well at all; most British people have sung 'Jerusalem' at weddings or recited 'The Tyger' at school, but few could say what either is really about.

Apart from those poems, William Blake seems to be best known to the British public for the story told about him and his wife Catherine while they were living at 13 Hercules Buildings in Lambeth, south London. According to Alexander Gilchrist, Blake's first biographer, the Blakes' friend Thomas Butts said he visited William and Catherine one day and found them sitting naked in their garden, reciting Milton's *Paradise Lost*. 'Come in!' Blake is meant to have said. 'It's only Adam and Eve, you know!'

This act of freedom and daring, innocence and experience – not to mention the shock it must have given the neighbours – seems to have tickled the fancy of many. When I mention that I'm writing a novel about Blake, as often as not people chuckle and murmur, 'Naked in his garden!' or 'Adam and Eve!' It was one of the things that drew me to Blake too. What must it have been like, I thought, to be a neighbour of Blake's, with such shenanigans going on in the garden next door? That indeed is what I decided to write about; the novel's working title is *Blake's Neighbours*, though the final product will doubtless require something punchier.

Blake scholars have effectively demolished the Adam and Eve story as apocryphal. In his definitive Blake biography, G.E. Bentley Jr relegates it to a footnote and calls it a 'silly story'. But it is one of those stories that sticks, whether scholars denounce it or not. The public likes it. It humanises Blake, for one thing. So much of his work is dark, uneasy, and too personal a vision to be either relevant or comprehensible, for us as for his contemporaries. Moreover, much of his life was a misery of poverty and misunderstanding; it is frankly a relief to hear of the Blakes involved in an incident worthy of a French farce, and hard to give up even on the advice of po-faced scholars. Besides, it is just possible that Thomas Butts did interrupt them, *in flagrante delicto*, as might happen on a fair day when a man and woman have a summer house at their disposal in their garden. Butts might have been mortified to walk in on them. On the other hand, he might have found it irresistible gossip, making it respectable by throwing the cloak of Milton over it. Considered in that light, it is not so improbable an incident.

I have decided not to give up the anecdote. Indeed, I begin the novel with it, devising my own theory for how such a myth could have evolved. My reasoning is that, though it may not have happened, there is something about Blake that makes people want to tell and believe such stories. No smoke without fire, in other words.

We know only a little about either Blake's neighbours or his garden. Some of the neighbours are colourful in their own right. The oversized, charismatic circus owner Philip Astley lived at Hercules Hall, a mansion in a field at the back of the Blakes' garden. Next door at 14 Hercules Buildings lived his son John Astley, an equestrian performer who rode his horse around the circus ring while standing on his head or sitting backwards in a chair with a glass of wine. Slender, elegant, alcoholic and a ladies' man, he must have run a lively house. On the other side at 12 Hercules Buildings was a Miss Rachael Pelham, unknown but for her name. Nonetheless, in the novel she holds her own against both Astleys and Blakes, and does her share of peeking into the Blakes' garden to compare her grapevine to theirs.

As for the Blakes' Eden, their Lambeth garden, we now know its dimensions, thanks to the detective work of Blake scholar Michael Phillips, who is writing a biography of Blake during his Lambeth years: it was 110 feet long and 18 feet wide, with a privy and an ash pit. From contemporary descriptions we know it had a grapevine and a fig tree, possibly given to the Blakes by their friend, the painter George Romney. I have always imagined the garden as a little wild and unkempt, with the part nearest the house ankle-high grass and the back overgrown with brambles, thistles, and nettles. Blake was a man of ideas, and I thought that he and Catherine would have preferred to focus their energy on making those ideas concrete rather than on gardening.

However, I realised recently that I had fallen into the familiar trap of romanticising Blake when Michael Phillips gently pointed out to me that Catherine Blake came from a family of kitchen gardeners in Battersea, and would have known how to cultivate much of their Lambeth patch to feed them. So much for my overgrown Eden. Phillips' feet-on-the-ground approach to Blake's life and work will do much to demystify him. After all, Blake may have been a visionary, but he also spent hours and hours bent over copper plates, scraping thousands of tiny lines for engravings. Such gruelling work does not make a man discuss angels in the trees all the time, but rather sit in exhaustion in his garden and simply watch the light on the wall, or his wife hoeing, or a caterpillar crawling up his grapevine.

It is this focus on Blake in daily life, as a working man living amongst working people, which appeals to me. I may have no idea what the Four Zoas really represent, or what Blake is trying to articulate in *Visions of the Daughters of Albion*, but I can relate to someone who sits in a room on his own and writes or engraves for much of the day. I can walk where he walked (or at least follow the routes using detailed maps of the period), gaze (via illustrations of the time) at the views he gazed at, try my hand at a printing press (thanks once again to Michael Phillips) just as Blake did, and try to see him as his neighbours would have. This approach aims to strip away the miasma of his feverish imagination and return him to the daily practice of living. That is why so much of the book takes place within a few hundred yards of his house. It keeps him – and me – from straying too far from a local, focused milieu.

Even weeded of its romantic wildness, however, the Blakes' long back garden is still for me a place of mystery and revelation, a staging post midway between the private and the public. It would have been walled, and in principle no one would see what was going on there. Blake could sing his poems, look at his engravings in bright daylight, argue with friends over the revolutionary happenings in France, talk to his dead brother Robert, and make love to his wife, ostensibly without any witnesses. In reality, however, his neighbours could see into his garden from their first-floor windows, or stand on garden benches and look over the wall. In their own gardens they could hear the Blakes if they were angry or upset or happy enough for their voices to carry beyond neighbourly boundaries.

Neighbours have peculiar relationships, sharing the intimacy that comes from proximity, tempering it with a studied disinterest in order to preserve privacy. However, Blake's neighbours must have known something of him: seen and heard his huge star-handled printer in use in his front room; noted the stream of erudite visitors from across the river; maybe even studied copies of the books he illustrated. They would have noted that he didn't attend church; that he didn't keep a servant, though he had a house big enough for one; that he had no children; that he sometimes walked along talking to someone when there was no one there to talk to. They would have suspected he had radical leanings and continued to support the French revolution long after many were frightened off by the violence and the execution of the French royal family; however, they probably wouldn't have engaged him about his views. Neighbours don't in general discuss politics or religion. They need to get along, or at least agree to disagree. Blake was not the sort to be so agreeable; best to stick with discussing the weather with him.

But he was unlikely to have talked to his neighbours about anything, much less contentious issues. Indeed, he doesn't seem to have been particularly interested in other people. Blake rarely painted or sketched anyone real; he preferred his own creations. As he put it so strongly, 'Natural objects always did and now do weaken, deaden and obliterate imagination in me'! The daily, petty concerns of his neighbours would have been meaningless to him. Blake was far more engaged in his own imaginary world.

Would the neighbours have been interested in Blake, though? I suspect they couldn't help but be. At a time when life amongst the working people of Lambeth was unvaried, if not monotonous, any difference was bound to play out as entertainment. And where better a stage than Blake's garden, where private life gets its first airing in public? If, for instance, Blake and his wife were canoodling in their garden, what would a neighbour boy and girl make of the sight? That is what I have tried to imagine, bringing Blake to life on a local level – and in the process making him less remote and more relevant.

Note

This chapter was first published in an abbreviated form in the catalogue for CLOUD&VISION, an exhibition at the Museum of Garden History, London (Summer 2005).

3
Blake, Literary History and Sexual Difference

Claire Colebrook

In this chapter I will argue that Blake's poetry, with its explicit figures of sexual binaries and its apocalyptic imagery, provides a new way for feminist criticism to approach the politics of literary history. Despite the fact that Blake's *Jerusalem* concludes with the re-incorporation of the female emanation and thus indicates an ethics of unity, integrity and inclusive recognition, there are other aspects of Blake's corpus (including both its material form and its more difficult allusions) which indicate an ethics of positive difference, one in which male and female are not interacting, mutually productive complements, but non-relational contraries, each opening up a perceptive world. Such an ethics – which I will approach through *Milton* – opens a new thought of literary history, in which the past is not material for incorporation and renewal; the past can always remain unactualised, unproductive and without relation.

Milton is already a poem *about* literary history. Apart from the explicit figure of Milton's return to earth and his entry into Blake's foot – in contrast with the usual figure of cerebral inspiration – the poem is dominated by figures of re-appropriating wasted labour. The work is about loss in a general sense, but it is also possible to read the opening sections regarding the division of labour that results in a loss of fruition and production as a figure for the detached relation we bear to sense and meaning. There are certain images central to Blake's poetics – ranging from the apocalyptic figures of harvests, winepresses, inscription and destruction to the seeming mystery of the female body – that are also images of reading. The idea of a shift from a fallen world in which signs are repeated in an empty and reified manner to a world that is immediate and fully given is central to the apocalyptic tradition, where the fires and furnaces of the apocalypse burn away distance and opacity to reveal the world as it is, infinite (Wittreich, 1975). But it is precisely this apocalyptic tradition that Blake's *Milton* stages and complicates.

For Blake, questions of reading and history are already intertwined with questions of sexual difference. His figures of the Fall – the diremption of spectre and emanation – and his figures of redemption are sexual; but they are also literary. The alien other – the sexually threatening female body – is both unreadable, mysterious and seductively lulling *and* a threat to the self in so far as she accuses and creates an allegorical distance from fulfilment:

> Now comes the night of Enitharmon's joy!
> Who shall I call? Who shall I send?
> That Woman, lovely Woman! may have dominion?
> Arise O Rintrah thee I call! & Palamabron thee!
> Go! tell the human race that Womans love is Sin!
> That an Eternal life awaits the worms of sixty winters
> In an allegorical abode where existence hath never come:
> Forbid all Joy, & from her childhood shall the little female
> Spread nets in every secret path.
>
> (*Europe*, 5: 1–9; E 62)

By contrast, the redeemed world no longer requires interpretation, schema or conceptual mediation; everything shines by its own inner light, and is liberated from any overarching single law.

> In Great Eternity, every particular Form gives forth or Emanates
> Its own peculiar Light, & the Form is the Divine Vision
> And the Light is his Garment This is Jerusalem in every Man
>
> (*J*, 54: 1–3; E 203)

Redeemed life allows for intrinsic difference, where life is neither read nor interpreted through some preconceived set of categories, just as fallen life is always dominated by *relative* difference: woman is a pale shadow or copy of man, and her merely negative difference stands as the figure for a world in which everything is compared to everything else but nothing is allowed to be as it is, in itself.

The question of literary history and life for Blake is always already gendered, for it is precisely gender that can stand both as a figure of relative difference and for positive difference. On the one hand, it is the 'Shadowy Female' who has garments 'woven of sighs & heart broken lamentations' and who will have 'Writings . . . That every Infant that is born upon the Earth shall read /And get by rote as a hard task of a life of sixty years' (*M*, 18; E 111). On the other hand, it is Jerusalem who resists study, interpretation and the reduction of all that is to one knowable law: 'Then spoke Jerusalem O Albion! my Father Albion / Why wilt thou number every little fibre of my Soul / Spreading them out before the Sun like stalks of flax to dry?' (*J*, 22: 19–21; E 167). Further, the reduction of the soul to what is self-evident and fully actual is directly aligned by Blake with the destruction of the female emanation: 'Those who devour his soul, are taken into his bosom! / To destroy his Emanation is their intention' (*J*, 36: 17–18; E 182).

This distinction between mere negation and contraries has long been recognised as central to Blake's work, but Blake's specific language of contraries has its poetic prehistory. Milton dealt explicitly with the question of contraries in his prose works. In *Doctrine and Discipline of Divorce* Milton argues that incompatible partners in marriage should not be forced to remain together. To support this argument he invokes a notion of cosmological harmony defined through the concept of contraries:

> there is indeed a twofold Seminary or stock in Nature, from whence are deriv'd the issues of love and hatred distinctly flowing through the whole masse of created things, and . . . Gods doing is ever to bring the due likenesses and harmonies of his works together, except when out of the two contraries met to their own destruction, he moulds a third existence, and that . . . is error, or some evil Angel.
>
> (Milton, 1953–1982: 272)

Milton goes on to state that a refusal to act in accordance with either the natural attraction for like to meet with like or the repulsion of contraries is 'against the fundamental law book of nature' (272). It is when different forces, which are themselves innocent, are mistakenly coupled that evil emerges. Evil is not something present and created by God, but follows from an improper coupling. In the case of *Paradise Lost*, when a perfectly divine female form is uncoupled from 'manly' virtue and combined with aspirations to knowledge and mastery, true reason is deflected from its proper aim. This deflection of reason from itself is, for Milton, *the* problem of evil: if man is rational and created in God's image then he must have the *potential* to be good, but this potential may also fail to realise itself. This occurs when reason remains within itself – remains indifferent – and fails to make a proper and fruitful coupling. Milton's clearest expression of this distinction between evil and virtuous couplings is given figurally, in *Paradise Lost*, in the emergence of Sin from Satan's head.

Sin springs from Satan's head, but not through any decided act or willed production; and it is just this lack of conscious decision that characterises Sin's non-being. Sin and evil are not positive created qualities but failures that occur when the mind does not act on its own power, does not take command of itself. After Sin's emergence, Satan becomes enamoured of his female 'emanation' who, though initially abhorrent, becomes narcissistically appealing: 'Thy self in me they perfect image viewing / Becamest enamoured, and such joy thou took'st / With me in secret' (*Paradise Lost*, 2.763–5). Sin then gives birth to Death whose 'life' is divided between consumption and rape, for he is perpetually raping his own mother, whose womb is then continually gnawed at by the 'yelling monsters' to whom she has given birth: 'Before mine eyes in opposition sits / Grim Death my son and foe, who sets them on, / And me his parent would full soon devour / For want of other prey, but that he knows / His end with mine involved' (*Paradise Lost*, 2.803–7). Evil is self-consumption, incest and the circulation of sameness without progress, production or any true difference; everything is already fully given and can yield nothing other than the 'same dull round' (E 2).

By contrast, the loving relation between Adam and Eve in Paradise is not the mere coupling of bodies, for the other body is – for both Adam and Eve – an expression of a divine life different and distinct from their own. The two contrasting scenes of self-consuming evil and other-directed love in *Paradise Lost* are part of a larger poetic project that privileges images of outward expansion, connection, difference and fecundity over images of involution, redounding, repetition, consumption and inertia. The contrasting figures of redundant difference and fecund difference express an ethic of life that is at the heart of *Paradise Lost* and which is both repeated and challenged in Blake's *Milton*. The opposition between good and evil becomes, through this literary and aesthetic figuration, no longer a simple moral binary or opposition between two terms, but a logic of life in which evil is essentially parasitic, derivative and other than what really and truly *is*. If a being refuses its essence – refuses its determination and specificity or refuses to actualise its proper potential – then it moves not toward actualisation or expression of God as being, but away from expression to indefiniteness, formlessness and chaos, to non-production and non-being. Evil is the negation of life, not another value within life but the refusal of life as the refusal of being or what *is*.

God could not create *non*-being, but by creating a potential *for* the realisation of form there is also the possibility that such form or reason might *not* realise itself. Reason is, for Milton, not a set of rules for obedience but a capacity for Adam (and then Eve) to recognise what one ought to become in order to realise one's proper being. By contrast, evil remains within itself, turns back upon itself and neither progresses nor genuinely differs. God is love, life, expression, and the desire for each being not simply to remain what it already is but to flow towards its proper and higher potential. Evil is therefore not something created or admitted by God; it is non-creation, or the failure of life to become other than it already is.

Both Milton's and Blake's Satan are enslaved by a terror and denial of what is not reflective of, or reducible to, their own being. The theme of life-denying self-mirroring dominates Blake's earliest figures of sexual difference (in *Visions of the Daughters of Albion*, plate 6). Blake rejects images of the female as either a passive reflection of the male or as a merely natural body; the redeemed emanation is neither a double nor an aspect of oneself. In redeemed relations each aspect strives in its own being, and realises its own potential – neither remaining what it already is, nor reduced to an equivalence of all other forms.

The Fall, in *Milton*, occurs when there is a redistribution and division of labour. Rather than each of Albion's sons maintaining his own activity Satan takes over Palamabron's harrow, and does so through seeming pity and mildness (7: 5–15; E 486). The division of labour occurs with the idea of every man's equivalence, and this idea is dressed up in the seeming virtue of a pity and friendship that would ease the burden of one's fellow man, creating a greater efficiency. Like Milton, Blake's clear criticisms of capitalist 'man' – a self who has no definition other than that which is achieved quantitatively through labour and power – is grounded in a deeper metaphysic and aesthetic of differentiating life. Whereas capital or purely quantitative conceptions of being and value will reduce everything to so much equivalent force, and will thereby deaden life by reducing it to a single inhuman and unthinking system that determines all difference in advance, redeemed life grants each being its proper power and place. Enlightenment man reduces difference to a general and exchangeable form, allowing only for the fallen 'hermaphroditic: male & female' or 'Female hidden in a Male' (*M*, 14[15]: 39; 40: 20; E 108, 141). The self that must be annihilated in Blake's prophecies is the inwardness of the Cartesian cogito, a self that simply *is* in its certainty and is therefore the negation of dynamic difference. In *Milton* this critical insight is articulated by Milton to Ololon, after Ololon has already suspected that it is the 'Femin[in]e portions' of Enlightenment thinkers that destroy religion, only to replace religion with another 'Phantasm' (*M*, 40: 9–11; E 141). In the new Natural Religion there can be no difference or event outside the one law of calculation. The modern 'selfhood' is therefore the negation of difference, a point from which all being can be measured and all difference mastered. It is only when Ololon sees herself as man's *contrary* that she sees a way beyond the 'Void Outside of Existence' (41: 35–7; E 143). Redemption occurs when the feminine is neither a difference in degree (the generic male-female) nor radically other. Only when the man of reason or universal selfhood is destroyed will productive difference emerge:

> There is a Negation, & there is a Contrary:
> The Negation must be destroy'd to redeem the Contraries.
> The Negation is the Spectre, the Reasoning Power in Man:
> This is a false Body, an Incrustation over my Immortal
> Spirit
>
> (*M*, 40: 31–6; E 142)

Redemption occurs when each potential is restored to realising its own life, no longer suffering from the indistinction, equivalence and uniformity of a single system. The biological difference of the false body must be annihilated to give way to spiritual difference: in *Milton* these two types of body (natural and spiritual) are expressed in two modes of sexual difference. In the natural, rational, vegetative false body of mere matter, sexual difference is biological and differentiates an otherwise general 'man', yielding the 'Female hidden in Male' which is also 'Religion hidden in War' precisely because spirit is reduced to so much warring, competing and opposed force. But in the redeemed body, sexual difference is essential and actively productive. In the final plates of *Milton* Ololon descends to become a garment that clothes the body of Jesus, and this garment is made up of script. Whereas fallen difference is the war of all against all and the chaotic and violent opposition of competing equivalent units, redeemed difference is radically *distinct*. And for both Blake and Milton there is no greater distinction than that between letter and spirit.

If we see the letter as mere matter or body, we fall into literalism, believing that to repeat the mere word is to repeat all, and that to receive the word is to know all. These are the 'blind mouths' of Milton's *Lycidas* which reiterate and repeat the letter without the spirit, sense or life of the law; and for Blake, also, it is the fallen viewpoint of experience that sees all at once in a fully comprehending gaze without sense of depth or resonance. But if we see the letter and the spirit as contraries, then we recognise – as both Blake and Milton did – that there is no God or divine life without the body or the letter, but that divinity cannot be reduced to the letters through which it is expressed. A redeemed and divine poetics attends to the difference between script and word, just as a redeemed sexual relation notes the difference between the body of the other and the soul of which that body is an expression. Accordingly, in the conclusion of *Milton* Blake will contrast the 'Sexual Garments' that 'Hid[e] the Human Lineaments' (41: 25–6; E 142) – a surface that conceals distinction – with the garment of Ololon which is 'Written within & without in woven letters: & the Writing / Is the Divine Revelation in the Litteral expression: / A Garment of War' (42: 13– 15; E 143). The dynamic sexual relation, in which each body strives according to its own difference is therefore a figure for redeemed life in general, where each being strives to realise its inner virtue. Life strives to take on form; it is never mere body, matter or inert stuff.

Milton is dominated not only by images of Los and his anvil, Palamabron and his harrow, Enitharmon and her weaving, but also of Milton and his sculpting of a formed body for Urizen. Traditionally, matter without form – mere nature awaiting spirit – is associated with the female body; form, differentiation or bringing potentiality into *act* is associated with masculine insemination (Colebrook, 24). Blake's conclusion to *Milton* seems to repeat this traditional gendered binary. Ololon is the matter or body, the outward clothing and the 'Litteral expression' that is subtended by the spirit of 'One Man Jesus the Saviour. wonderful!' (42: 11; E 143). Only with this restored sexual relation that will overcome the selfhood that wars against all that is not itself, is life opened up to further creation. Once again it seems that forming, marking, delimiting and forging is privileged over a state of passivity, rest and receptivity. *Milton* concludes not with a state but with an infinitive, a potentiality *to act*: 'To go forth to the Great Harvest & Vintage of the Nations' (43: 1; E 144).

By privileging act, formation, distinction and production Blake does seem to elevate the traditionally masculine image of form-giving and self-creation over the feminised values of indistinction and passivity. However, Blake is also critical of the gender binary that simply opposes male to female. *Milton* presents processes of internalisation, projection, mirroring and divisive accusation which complicate the idea that one can simply divide good from evil, repetition from production. Blake repeats the image of Sin springing from Satan's own self. The accusing Satan, who in plate 7 produced fallen chaos by taking on Palamabron's specific labour, results from Sin not only springing from Satan's breast, but also turning back and hiding within his brain:

> I weeping hid in Satan's inmost brain.
> But when the Gnomes refus'd to labour more, with blandishments
> I came forth from the head of Satan, back the Gnomes recoil'd.
> And call'd me Sin, and for a sign portentous held me.
>
> (*M*, 12: 36–9; E 106)

After the Fall, Leutha takes on the responsibility for Satan's divisive triumph. Satan has created one individualist law: 'Satan, making to himself Laws from his own identity. / Compell'd others to serve him in moral gratitude and submission / Being call'd God:setting himself above all that is called God' (11: 10–12; E 104). This, explains Leutha, is because she entered 'the doors of Satan's brain night after night' and 'stupefied the masculine perceptions / And kept only the feminine awake' (12: 5–6; E 105). Whereas Milton's Satan corrupts Eve by suggesting that she can be a queen of all with reference to no authority other than herself, Blake has Satan seduced by a jealous female who effeminates Satan. The struggle of *Milton* is this struggle to overcome that false sexual division in which the female is indifference and jealousy at war with the other's difference. The epic strives to move towards a sexual difference in which each being can shine by its own inner light. Such difference can only be achieved in a shift from a logic of transcendence, where 'man' or the 'selfhood' seems to determine everything in advance, to a logic of immanence where no power provides the law for any other and each being establishes its own relations from itself: 'The nature of infinity is this: That every thing has its / Own Vortex' (15: 21–2; E 109).

Milton is not only a text within literary history that includes sexual difference as one of its themes; it is a text about literary history expressed through a drama of sexual difference. Milton has to descend from his transcendent height, enter the poet's body, and re-encounter his female others (15–17: 45–3; E 110).

The scene can be read as a repairing or restoring of the ethical sexual relation that Milton's historical prejudices precluded him from adopting. There is, it has been argued, a real radical Milton whose spirit was belied by the residues of received tradition (Wittreich, 1987). Milton wrote in 'fetters' when he wrote of God, still labouring under received texts; but this apparent blindness can be redeemed if we read beyond the letter of Milton to the animating spirit. We can do so – we can read the *real* Milton – through Blake; for the later poet releases the radical spirit from the cloth of received law. In terms of literary history, Blake is therefore the active realisation or coming to fruition of what was only potential in Milton. Blake brings Milton's radicalism to fruition, sloughing off all those aspects in Milton's work that were the result of received tradition. Blake therefore gives life to the text and the past, refusing all that has lost its relation to animation, refusing any text that has now become priestly law and no longer poetic creation. This notion of giving life to the past is depicted in Blake as giving a (male) living body to the (female) garment and text. Milton is no longer a voice from the past but a force entering Blake's strolling body, while the literal text – as female body – becomes finally a garment that clothes the 'One Man' or saviour.

But if we take seriously the body and work of Blake's text then things are not so simple. There is, depicted within *Milton*, a traditional sexual opposition between the active, forming, progressive and creative living body on the one hand, and the inert, non-relational, vegetative isolated natural body on the other. The fallen body is surrounded by a sea of time and space, condemned to peering out at its world through 'chinks' in its cavern, while the redeemed body is no longer an object within time and space, but is the opening to infinity: there is not a subject *who* perceives, looking out *from* his body. Rather, the world is a perceiving, interacting, pulsing life, with each body being a single pulsation or moment of eternity. Thus Blake's work would seem to endorse a textual vitalism, such that all signs, texts and matter might be referred back to and connected with their originating life. And this would be accompanied by a sexual vitalism: as long as the feminine is understood as an alien, threatening, fallen and unproductive harlot or whore there can be no productive life, but if the feminine is incorporated in a fruitful and dynamic contrary then sexual difference will be the opening to new life and renovated perception (*M*, 31: 45–9; E 131).

However, there is a contrary reading of binaries in Blake's work. Here, against notions of transparency, communication, universal sense and the realisation or arrival at unity, there is the insistence on what remains without relation, production or justification. The later prophetic books emphasise both a forgiveness without justification or recompense and an ethic of self-annihilation, in which mastery, inclusion, comprehension and incorporation are sacrificed. We might recall here Leutha's act, in *Milton*, of taking on responsibility for an act that she has not authored. While the feminine in its non-productive aspect can be demonised in the figure of the harlot, or a sexuality not oriented towards production, Blake does not necessarily oppose this to an emanation which would reflect, expand and complement the man of form, reason and limit. What is most radical in Blake's work, for sexual politics, is the suggestion of the non-relational. Although Blake presents printing, forging, delimiting and bounding as activities of revivification, there are nevertheless images in his prophecies, especially *Milton*, of a self-annihilation that abandons the introjection, interpretation and redemption of that which cannot be put to work, made to perform or rendered active. The contrary, here, is not an otherness that exists in fruitful production and interaction but that remains unmastered: 'Before Ololon Milton stood & perceivd the Eternal Form / Of that mild Vision; wondrous were their acts by me unknown / Except remotely' (40: 1–3; E 141).

The figure of sexual difference in Blake's work is itself a problem of difference, and the sense and ethics of difference. On the one hand the figure of gender is manifestly interpretable, drawing on apocalyptic, natural, Miltonic and scientific concepts of relation, production and force – as though male and female were exemplary images through which the very process and sense of life might be understood. And so we would read Blake as arguing for the necessary complementarity of male and female, reason and imagination, limit and unbounded, order and difference. On the other hand, there is another figure of sexual difference: two bodies who no longer mirror, complement or complete each other. The female emanation is neither the fallen whore/harlot nor the pastoral counterpart to the forging male imagination. She stands as an alluring but incomprehensible resistance to relation, and resistance to time as forward movement and revelation. Blake's work incorporates these two images of difference – the female as activating emanation, and the female as a seductive and dreamy rest from life – but his text also demands this tension of sexual difference. For interpretation, reading and the practice of literary history is always both the desire to comprehend, incorporate and bring the text to life, alongside the necessary resistance, singularity and non-relation of the text: for it is only the fact that a text is never fully alive, never fully present or presentable, that allows for the interpretive and reading relation. This relation is both sexual, a relation of desire, and sexually different – a desire that can never incorporate its desired.

Bibliography

Colebrook, C., *Gender* (London: Palgrave, 2003).

McGann, J., *Byron and Romanticism* (Cambridge: Cambridge University Press, 2002).

Milton, J., *Complete Prose Works: Volume Two*, ed. Don M. Wolfe (New Haven, CT: Yale University Press, 1953–1982).

Milton, J., *Paradise Lost*, ed. Alastair Fowler (London: Longman, 1968).

Wittreich, J.A. (ed), *Milton and the Line of Vision* (Wisconsin: University of Wisconsin Press, 1975).

Wittreich, J.A., *Feminist Milton* (Ithaca: Cornell UP, 1987).

4

Transgender Juvenilia: Blake's and Cristall's *Poetical Sketches*

Tristanne Connolly

A poet, age 25, printed a first collection of verse entitled *Poetical Sketches*. Written earlier, these youthful productions combined derivativeness – particularly from the poets of sensibility – and experimentation with irregular versification and diction. The book opened with a series of verses personifying seasons and times of day, and subsequent contents ranged from dramatic narratives to astute psychological portraits and maturely complex love poems. It found readers in the intellectual circles of its patron, along with some friends of the poet, but its reception history is obscure, as few copies survive. The poet published no other letterpress book of poetry.

The parallels between the *Poetical Sketches* by William Blake (1783) and Ann Batten Cristall (1795) could be coincidences. Sha's list of representative works on sketching reveals the title was not uncommon.[1] Wu finds 'some of [Cristall's] characters have names that sound a shade Blakean – Eyezion, Thelmon, Carmel', but qualifies, 'Macpherson is another likely influence here'.[2] The strongest ties between Blake and Cristall are Mary Wollstonecraft and Joseph Johnson. In 1790–91, Blake illustrated Wollstonecraft's translation of *Elements of Morality* and her *Original Stories from Real Life*, published by Johnson.[3] In 1788, Cristall, as a schoolteacher, met Everina Wollstonecraft, and through her, Mary; both would subscribe to her book (Wu, 271). Wollstonecraft corresponded with Cristall's brother Joshua, who studied under James Barry at the Royal Academy in 1792, and from 1805 was a prominent member (and later president) of the Watercolour Society, which included Varley and Linnell. Joshua also tried his hand at engraving, as did Cristall's sister Elizabeth.[4] In 1795, when Johnson published Cristall's book, Blake was still engraving for him, and in the two previous years, may have advertised and exhibited his illuminated books (though probably not *Poetical Sketches*) in Johnson's shop.[5] But since both *Poetical Sketches* claim to be juvenilia, no inter-influence could have occurred before the poems were written.

Still, their affinities allow us to see Blake, in his first poetic production as a young man, in comparison with Cristall, in hers, as a young woman.

Both *Poetical Sketches* challenge developmental readings of juvenilia: Cristall's is her only book, and Blake's later work takes a different form.[6] Leslie Robertson contests the traditional model of juvenilia as 'apprenticeship' and suggests play as an alternative.[7] Yet play is also developmental: its escapist 'model situations' are channelled into learning 'to master reality by experiment and planning' (294). I would suggest, as another analogy, adolescent experimentation with sexual identities and partners. How this might unfold for late eighteenth-century adolescents is suggested by marriage plot novels: some initial straying is involved in learning to fulfil gender roles, and consideration of various suitors is necessary to find a suitable match, but such promiscuities are only forgivable if they end in mature correctness.

In Blake's *Poetical Sketches*, this pattern is epitomised by the 'Song', 'How sweet I roam'd' (E 412–13): the speaker wanders from field to field, 'taste[s] all the summer's pride', is enticed by the 'prince of love', and ends up in a 'golden cage'. The poem enacts, and resists, the standard progression, apparently condemning the culmination as humiliating imprisonment. But McGowan observes, 'the captured spirit seems to be thriving'.[8] Does the song then endorse happy patriarchal slavery, or the kinky pleasure of BDSM? Though narrating enclosure, the poem eludes moral judgement. Crucially, the speaker cannot be pinned as masculine or feminine, freeing the scenario, and the poetic voice, from any finalised gender or orientation.

Both Blake and Cristall refuse to 'settle down'. They try on the voice of the other gender, or create gender-ambiguous speakers.[9] They play with courtship, probing the limitations of heterosexual conformity and trying out different kinds of partnership. They test whether masculinity and femininity can be escaped entirely, and adolescent experimentation (both sexual and poetic) extended indefinitely. By constantly shifting personae and relationships, they literally do not make anything of themselves.

From the beginning of each book, the poet's gender is alternately indicated and obscured. On Blake's title page, the author is an androgynous 'W.B.'[10] The following page confirms masculinity with a scattering of 'his' and 'he'. Yet the apologies of the 'Advertisement' (E 846) are standard rhetoric for introductions to women's poetry: demure double negatives ('less unfit'), tentativeness about 'meet[ing] the public eye', acknowledgement of 'irregularities and defects' and the corresponding appeal to 'originality', displacement of responsibility for publication on to well-meaning 'friends'. This could be lower-class rather than feminine deference, but both come together in the conventional assurance that the poet is not being lured from proper duties by pretensions to poetry. 'His talents being wholly directed to the attainment of excellence in his profession' is the excuse for lack of revision. Yet professional excellence, closed to women and beyond the humble artisan, injects the formula with masculinity and ambition. The introduction categorises Blake's gender and class, and reveals he is not contained by either.

How much control Blake had over the production of *Poetical Sketches* is uncertain. J.T. Smith's account credits the Reverend Mathew with writing the 'Advertisement' and, with Flaxman, arranging publication.[11] Phillips, considering Smith's inaccuracies, argues for Flaxman as the author, and Peterfreund, for Blake himself.[12] However, Smith emphasizes that Harriet Mathew was the motivator; wouldn't this make her a more likely writer of the 'Advertisement' than her husband? Phillips finds both John and Ann Flaxman actively involved in distributing *Poetical Sketches*. If that is a strong argument for John writing the 'Advertisement', it also applies to Ann. That the copy with additional handwritten poems is traced to her might suggest special interest in the volume.[13] *Poetical Sketches* may also have had a woman printer (again possibly working with her husband): Bentley tentatively suggests Jane Matthews, a relative of the Flaxmans.[14]

So much potential female involvement in Blake's first book of poetry would be a formative patronage experience. It could be seen as sowing seeds for later insecurity and antagonism, along the lines of Essick's 'Female Will' argument. But Blake kept copies of *Poetical Sketches* and gave them to close friends until the end of his life. The title page and preface, whether orchestrated by Blake or a patron, could perform a positive rather than demeaning feminisation. The number of poems readable as female-voiced suggests that, if Blake perceived women artists and 'feminised' aesthetics as increasingly dominant, as Essick argues, he may have wanted not to beat them but join them. 'W.B.' gives the impression of a modest woman poet protecting her honour and privacy through anonymity. The 'Advertisement', though, reasserts masculinity and precludes any completely convincing female impersonation. Through feminine rhetorical convention, and possibly the pen of a woman patron, Blake is cast as a man of feminised aesthetics, as he later sees Hayley.[15] This enables him to take on feminine voices and attributes by choice, among the many personae that follow in the *Sketches* (some starkly masculine, as in the military patriotism of *King Edward the Third* and 'A War Song to Englishmen').

On Cristall's title page,[16] the masculine presences multiply. In the centre is a picture, by her brother, of one of her male characters, Holbain, and below it (in contrast to 'W.B.'s title page without publisher) 'J Johnson' also appears. The ornate, swirling lettering could be considered feminine decoration, but the ostentatious self-advertisement could be construed as masculine assertiveness. Labbe emphasises that Cristall proudly gives her full name:[17] not two but three, as she includes her mother's maiden name, a female presence counterbalancing the male presences, and asserting the matrilineal in contrast to the masculine poetic inheritance claimed in her preface. She also avoids indicating her own marital status and effacing her individuality: she is not 'Miss Cristall'.

While the title page inscribes Ann's femininity with her name, the preface is in the first person. It could be considered a more masculine introduction than Blake's. Labbe notes the characteristics of women's prefaces which do not appear in Cristall's: for instance, instead of blaming 'friends' for publication, Cristall confesses 'a strong motive' both mysterious and irresistible (275).[18] Labbe sees Cristall using expectations of helplessness to get away with unruliness in female roles and poetry. I would add that Cristall plays on juvenilia as undeveloped, even embarrassing, to slide by the promiscuity, erotic and poetic, of her verses. They are 'juvenile productions' on 'subjects' which 'are not always such as, on maturer reflection, I should have chosen, had they been originally intended for publication'. Older and wiser, she nonetheless opens her adolescent fantasies to public view, though when written they were private. Cristall also links poetic and sexual experimentation. 'The seeds scattered in my mind were casual; the productions spontaneous and involuntary' – sowing wild oats, casual sex, accidental fertility. 'Those who have ever felt the warm influence of the muse, must know that her inspirations are flattering and seductive; that she often raises the heart with vanity, and then overwhelms it with fears.' Poetry does not respectfully woo, but deceptively seduces, and Cristall responds in the imprudent and mercurial manner of a teenager; or, less anachronistically, a young woman dangerously close to becoming a fallen woman (like the seventeen-year-old Marianne in *Sense and Sensibility*). Though the muse's behaviour is equally rakish and coquettish, she is specified as feminine, unlike Cristall who unsexes herself, not only by using first person, but also by trying on the role of a man and/or a lesbian, as the beloved of a woman muse.

Cristall comments, conventionally, on her limited knowledge of tradition. She admits, 'with the ancient poets . . . my acquaintance has been but small' and through translations, but asserts, 'I can only say that what I have written is genuine, and that I am but little indebted either to ancient or modern poets' (275). She is detached from tradition by choice, not necessity, breaking with 'modern' vernacular poetry as well. Yet, she places herself among contemporaries, selecting a non-traditional tradition. As 'modern poets who have succeeded without treading too closely in [the] steps' of the 'great masters', she names Robert Burns and her patron George Dyer. She puts herself in masculine poetic company. Dyer is so much an 'old boy' that he wrote a history of Cambridge, and inspired the portrait of the scholar in Lamb's 'Oxford in the Vacation'. And if Burns stands for the rustic, self-educated poet, Cristall could have named a female precursor in Yearsley; if chosen for his nationality (Cristall was Scottish on her father's side), she could name Joanna Baillie.

The title pages and introductions set the stage for poetry spoken in gender-ambiguous voices. Blake's opening poems are in the first person, usually collective plural: the speaker's identity is subsumed in a group. Speaking for all the people of the land, the voice need not have a gender of its own; or, it can contain the genders of all those it represents. The speaker need not have a defined sexual orientation either, since her/his desire is the desire of the group: 'let our winds / Kiss thy perfumed garments; let us taste / Thy morn and evening breath' (E 408). The 'dewy locks' of Spring (and similarly, Summer's 'flourishing hair'; E 409) could indicate feminine personification, if it weren't a borrowed description of the bridegroom in the Song of Solomon. However, the Song of Solomon is a model for both Blake and Cristall of alternating male and female voices, and its lush, erotic natural imagery can be ambiguous: perfumes, as well as luxuriant hair, are associated with both man and woman. Spring is never given a gendered pronoun. Spring's beloved, the land, is, but only after three stanzas of overwhelming collectivity. Imagery may hint Spring is masculine, if 'scatter thy pearls / Upon our love-sick land' is read, with Hilton, as ejaculation.[19] But such an onanistic and orgiastic relationship prevents classification of Spring and the land in normative heterosexual roles.

The poetic voice, as Cristall's collection commences, is not a group representative, but a detached observer who describes the dalliances of others, and frequently allows their voices to take over. Each poem centres on one character, alternating boy-girl: Eyezion, Rosamonde, Lysander, Gertrude, Henry. Masculine and feminine mix within the characters as well. In 'Before Twilight' (276–9), Eyezion, the 'light poet of the spring', is effeminate, not only because he is an alter-ego of the female author of these 'light effusions' ('Preface' 275).[20] He says, glamorously, 'Love in wanton ringlets curled / My tresses, passion to excite'. Again long hair blurs gender: he has Eve's *Paradise Lost* hairstyle, 'wanton ringlets wav'd / As the Vine curls her tendrils', but though 'Before Twilight' is all about 'amorous delay', 'Subjection' has nothing to do with it (4: 306–11). Neither lover takes a categorically male-dominant or female-subordinate position. As Labbe finds, Eyezion's beloved Viza is unfemininely forward, ending the poem with the invitation, 'Expect me on the dewy lawn'. And Eyezion's curls, though borrowed from Eve, are not like a clinging vine, but grow organically from his active, tempestuous 'current of creative mind'. They become phallicised, and emblematic of his gender transgression, when linked with the arrows associated with Eyezion throughout the poem: 'Unzoned I shot, and o'er each limit strained; / Around in airy circles whirled / By a genius infinite'.

While Blake's season poems personify nature, the 'Song', 'Love and harmony combine' (E 413–14), naturalizes persons, and the result is, temporarily, an escape from gender, which apparently does away with separation altogether. The treelike lovers' 'souls intwine', 'branches mix' and 'roots together join': they are physically and spiritually united within themselves, and with each other. The natural imagery does not allow deduction of their genders, or moral pronouncement on their relationship.[21] The intertwining trees could be a vegetative version of man and woman becoming one flesh in socially sanctioned marriage; or, a reference to Tristan and

Iseult, adulterous lovers together in death as the trees planted on their graves reach out to each other. Allusion to courtly love highlights the image's idealism and 'romantic' impossibility. Intertwined roots and branches would stunt real trees, but would that mean illicit romance, or virtuous marriage, or both, were damaging to natural growth? Both lovers have 'roots', suggesting a third alternative, a male-male relationship (latent in the male corners of the courtly love triangle). In the third stanza, the beloved bears 'golden fruit', and the speaker 'flowers fair'. These cannot be conclusively labelled male and female, metaphorically by shape, or scientifically by classification. (As Darwin's 'Loves of the Plants' would later dramatise, mapping plant reproduction on human sexuality involves some distortion, and promiscuity, on both sides.) Between flowers and fruit there is continuity rather than opposition: the lovers combine on a continuum. The first gendered pronoun appears in the second-last stanza, with the turtle and her offspring: 'There she sits and feeds her young / Sweet I hear her mournful song'. With gender come procreation and bittersweet sorrow; previously, it was 'joys' in the branches 'singing sweet'. With gender also comes inequality: the male bird sleeps, and sports and plays as the prince of love does with the caged winged singer in 'How sweet I roam'd'. Remembering both poems might depict male-male relationships, the male bird could be unconnected with the female turtledove, suggesting that (male) same-sex relationships, without sexual reproduction, are where 'love' is found. 'There is love: I hear his tongue': the male bird embodies love. However, that line is printed 'I hear her tongue'. If read as 'her', then love is associated with the mother bird rather than the carefree male, who then seems to come from nowhere, deprived of identity and relationship. Blake hand-corrected *Poetical Sketches'* typos, but not consistently: he amends 'her' to 'his' in only two copies (E 847). The gender of love varies depending on the version, ensuring that the lovers' identities remain flexible, and judgement on their relationship remains suspended.

In 'To a Lady on the Rise of Morn' (329–30), natural imagery lets Cristall suggest, but avoid committing to the gender of the first-person speaker. The title specifies the beloved as female; heterosexual assumptions would require Cristall to take on a male voice. But whereas Blake uses the apparent opposition of flowers and fruit to reveal that the lovers' genders are continuous, Cristall does not attribute different natural imagery to each lover; instead, she floods the poem with symbols of female sexual excitement.

The lady is addressed as 'blossom of the spring', specifically allying flowers with femininity, and playing on 'spring': the season which inspires love, and the running waters brought by spring thaw. That a 'blossom of the spring' is thus an aroused and wet flower is reiterated in the image of 'dews of morn', the entreaty to 'Pursue the trickling rills', and the call, 'I wait thee on the thawing mountains, / Where spring dissolves the lingering fountains'. Cristall's exclusive, reiterative use of streams, showers, hills, and flowers creates an emphatically female world. Under the weight of imagery, the possibility of a male speaker is reduced to a thin disguise. 'Oh trace with me the opening flowers' is an invitation to mutual masturbation in a landscape of female pleasure. If it were the ladylike pastime of sketching from nature, drawing would be more likely than tracing a previous image. These ladies copy no given model. Instead, they touch nature directly. And if 'traced', the flowers must have been hidden: as in the pursuit of trickling rills, a great part of the pleasure is in exploring, finding and revealing. The flowers, and the lovers, might be made vulnerable by 'opening', but Cristall dismisses this in the next line, which asks, or commands, 'Brave the sharp breeze, damp dews, and vernal showers!' The main purpose of the poem, inviting the 'lady' to be unladylike and roam freely, unprotected against the weather, recalls Wollstonecraft's arguments on women's unnatural weakness: 'Most men are sometimes obliged to bear with bodily inconveniences, and to endure, occasionally, the inclemency of the elements; but genteel women are, literally speaking, slaves to their bodies, and glory in their subjection.'[22] In Cristall's poem, the call to the lady to expose herself to (and in) the great outdoors, melts into a song of liberty. Cristall imagines an escape from feminine indolence which doesn't require being more masculine, or sacrificing sensuality. Wollstonecraft attacks stereotypical femininity's pendulum-swings between sweet attractiveness and cruel tyranny by insisting they are not natural. Cristall, in contrast, makes Nature personify feminine fickleness: 'Wild various Nature strews her charms, / And storms surround her mildest calms'. The next line, 'Oh to her frowns let us superior be', could be an exhortation to stoical rationality, but it enables plunging into nature in all its instability. 'Wild various' celebrates unruliness and difference as natural, as in Wollstonecraft as well: 'most of the women, in the circle of my observation, who have acted like rational creatures, or shewn any vigour of intellect, have accidentally been allowed to run wild – as some of the elegant formers of the fair sex would insinuate' (155). Wollstonecraft has educators disapprove of running wild, while for Cristall nature herself frowns. Being superior to Nature's frowns implies resisting the stereotypes 'she' embodies in the poem, lassitude and fickleness, but also, in 'brav[ing] the sharp breeze', embracing positive versions of those qualities, sensuality and variety. It re-echoes with a lesbian reading: the lovers will rise above any disapproval of their 'unnatural' union, as they roam in a naturally various landscape.

For T.S. Eliot, Blake's 'early poems show what the poems of a boy of genius ought to show, immense power of assimilation. Such early poems are not, as usually supposed, crude attempts to do something beyond the boy's capacity; they are, in the case of a boy of real promise, more likely to be quite mature and successful attempts to do something small.'[23] Comparison with Cristall's *Poetical Sketches* not only answers the begged question, 'What should the poems of a girl of genius show?'[24] It also reveals that Blake's poems, though quintessentially adolescent, are not *boy*ish enough to warrant Eliot's triple repetition. Both poets assimilate, but not just tradition; they ingeniously assimilate the other gender, taking on, and blending, male and female voices at will. Is it going beyond a boy's capacity to occasionally pretend to be a girl?

Notes

My thanks to Jacqueline Labbe for generously sharing her work on Cristall and responding to mine, to Steve Clark for incisive, energetic dialogue, and to K.V. Johansen for a 'fantastically' affirming reading.

1. Richard Sha, *The Visual and Verbal Sketch in British Romanticism* (Philadelphia: University of Pennsylvania Press, 1998), 196–207.
2. Duncan Wu, *Romantic Women Poets* (Oxford: Blackwell, 1997), 271.
3. Robert N. Essick, 'William Blake's "Female Will" and its Biographical Context', *Studies in English Literature 1500–1900*, 31 (1991), 615–30, 620.
4. Basil Taylor, *Joshua Cristall (1768–1847)* Exhibition, February–April 1975, Victoria and Albert Museum (London, 1975), 13–14; Richard and Samuel Redgrave, *A Century of British Painters* (New York: Phaidon, 1947), 195; John Lewis Roget, *History of the Old Watercolour Society*, 2 vols (London: Longmans, Green & Co, 1891; reprint, Antique Collectors' Club, Clopton, Woodbridge, Suffolk, 1972), 1: 187–8.
5. Keri Davies, 'Mrs. Bliss: a Blake Collector of 1794', in *Blake in the Nineties*, eds Steve Clark and David Worrall (Basingstoke: Macmillan, 1999), pp. 212–30, 217, 226.
6. On developmental readings of *Poetical Sketches* see Robert F. Gleckner, *Blake's Prelude* (Baltimore: Johns Hopkins University Press, 1982), 2–3 and Thomas Vogler, 'Troping the Seasons: Blake's Helio-Poetics and the "Golden Load"', in *Speak Silence*, ed. Mark L. Greenberg (Detroit: Wayne State University Press, 1996), pp. 105–52, 105–6.
7. Leslie Robertson, 'Changing Models of Juvenilia: Apprenticeship or Play?' *English Studies in Canada*, 24 (1998), 291–8, 291.
8. James McGowan, 'The Integrity of the *Poetical Sketches*', *Blake Studies* 8 (1979), 121–44, 133.
9. Warren Stevenson, *Romanticism and the Androgynous Sublime* (London: Associated Universities Press, 1996) contends the 'most successful' poems in Blake's *Poetical Sketches* have androgynous speakers, in contrast to 'perfunctory references . . . by a lovesick, presumably male, speaker to his "black eyed maid"' (24). For Blake's trying on of various rhetorical and poetic rather than gender voices, see Vogler (111) and Geoffrey Hartman, 'Blake and the Progress of Poesy', in *Beyond Formalism* (New Haven: Yale University Press, 1970), 193–205.
10. In G.E. Bentley Jr, *William Blake's Works in Conventional Typography* (Delmar: Scholars' Facsimiles, 1984), 7.
11. In G.E. Bentley Jr, *Blake Records* (Oxford: Clarendon, 1969), 456.
12. Michael Phillips, 'William Blake and the "Unincreasable Club"', *Bulletin of the New York Public Library*, 80 (1976–7), 6–18, 7–9; Stuart Peterfreund, 'The Problem of Originality and Blake's *Poetical Sketches*', in *Speak Silence* 71–103, 71.
13. See Bentley, *Conventional Typography*, 1–2.
14. Bentley, 'John Flaxman and the Mathew Clan', *Bulletin of the New York Public Library*, 67 (1963), 443–54, 453–4.

15. Flaxman sent Hayley a copy of *Poetical Sketches*, commenting that Blake's 'education will plead sufficient excuse to your Liberal mind for the defects of his work
& there are few so able to distinguish & set a right value on the beauties as
yourself' (*Blake Records*, 27–8).
16. Reproduced in Sha, 125.
17. Jacqueline M. Labbe, 'The Seductions of Form in the Poetry of Cristall and
Smith', in *Romanticism and Form*, ed. Alan Rawes (Basingstoke: Palgrave Macmillan, 2006) (forthcoming).
18. References to Cristall are taken from Wu.
19. Nelson Hilton, *Literal Imagination* (Berkeley, CA: California University Press,
1983), 267.
20. Eyezion is one of a series of bard-figures of both genders, including Thelmon
and Arla. Viza's response to Eyezion is also a self-reference by Cristall to juvenilia
and identity formation: 'Who sang so early and so sweet?'
21. William Crisman, in 'Songs Named "Song" and the Bind of Self-Conscious Lyri-
cism in Blake' (*ELH: A Journal of English Literary History*, 61 (1994), 619–33, also
sees 'an experimental effort to circumvent both entrapment and entrapping',
but argues 'a concern for sociability informs the choice of love narrative for the
series, since courtship, marriage, and family establish the basis of community'
(625–6). This conservative view of community endorses 'sociability' without
questioning what kind.
22. *A Vindication of the Rights of Woman*, in *The Vindications*, ed. D.L. Macdonald
and Kathleen Scherf (Peterborough: Broadview, 1997), 99–343, 156.
23. T.S. Eliot, 'William Blake', in *Selected Essays* (London: Faber & Faber, 1951),
317–22, 318.
24. Southey insists, 'Her verses are very incorrect, and the literary circle say she has
no genius, but she has genius' (in Wu, 274).

5

'The right stuff in the right hands': Anne Gilchrist and *The Life of William Blake*

Shirley Dent

William Blake's best-known biographer, Alexander Gilchrist, recorded in his diary a conversation he had with Thomas Carlyle concerning the completion of *The Life of William Blake*:

[From Alexander Gilchrist's diary, dated 28th December 1859]

Carlyle again asked me about the Blake; what I was doing with it. I stated that I had delivered his letter to Chapman, but was giving my MS. a last revisal before sending it in. He talked of the difficulties of a book, of getting it done, of reducing chaos to order.

(Anne Gilchrist, 74)

The Gilchrist 1863 biography is still the starting point for almost anybody researching the life of William Blake. However it is a book born of very particular kinds of chaos that came to be ordered in very particular kinds of way. One element of chaos that was specific to the 1863 biography is that the author of *The Life of William Blake*, Alexander Gilchrist, died from scarlet fever before he had completed the manuscript. The task of finishing the biography was taken up by those who already had fingers in *The Life of William Blake* editorial pie, specifically the Rossetti brothers, Dante Gabriel and William Michael. However, it was Alexander Gilchrist's widow, Anne, who is credited by William Michael Rossetti as the chief editor of *The Life of William Blake*: 'Mrs Gilchrist has edited it, and (if I may be permitted to say so) very efficiently.'[1]

This nod to the forgotten female editor – not without the patronising pat of 'and not a bad or inefficient job either' from W.M. Rossetti – is intriguing. Anne Gilchrist as editor is a compelling image: the dutiful widow working away at the nitty-gritty of bringing order to manuscript chaos, pushed out of the limelight by showy Pre-Raphaelite élan and a sanctified dead husband.

It would be wrong, however, to see Anne Gilchrist as a loyal dupe who was elbowed out by the editorial bonhomie of a male-dominated Victorian literary establishment. Anne Gilchrist knew her own mind when it came to the posthumous editing of *The Life of William Blake*:

> In regard to the additional chapter, I earnestly thank Mr. Rossetti and yourself. If it ought to be done, assuredly his and yours are the hands to which I would gratefully intrust the task. But I think you will not find it hard to forgive me a little reluctance that *any* living tones should blend with that voice which here speaks for the last time on earth. I will not however, sacrifice the interests of the book to this feeling. Perhaps we are not yet in a position to decide with certainty what is best. When I have incorporated all additional matter contained in the notes, we shall be better able to do so.
>
> (*Anne Gilchrist*, 124)

From this letter at least it would appear that Anne Gilchrist is the person calling the editorial shots, in however diplomatic a fashion.

Anne was also very much at the heart of another role that the Pre-Raphaelite brethren played in the nineteenth-century Blake revival. The group that clustered around Gilchrist's *The Life of William Blake* was very concerned with creating a constituency for Blake's works, a defined readership. But this was not based on their love and appreciation of Blake's work alone. My argument is that the Gilchrist coterie was concerned to tie potential Blake readership into a tight-knit circle of exclusivity. Undoubtedly there was a sense of sharing an appreciation of Blake with the reader, with Gilchrist's *Life*'s stated editorial claim being 'to quicken the reader's insight and enjoyment'.[2] But there is a strong sense throughout the Gilchrist/Pre-Raphaelite reclamation of William Blake and his works in the 1860s and 1870s that you have to be a special sort of person to appreciate William Blake with a special sort of sensitivity.

Algernon Charles Swinburne takes the 'special' status of the Blake reader to absurd extremes and talks of the potential audience for Blake's works in terms of cultish ordination:

> It should have been preserved, certainly, but strictly for the inspection of esoteric Blakists – never to be exposed to the eyes of Saducees, neo-phytes, weak brethren, – worshippers in the court of the Gentiles; whose faith may (not improbably) be shaken by its perusal, and their poor souls in consequence eternally lost; which result I do think you were bound in common Blakian charity (He would have said Christian, but I won't) to take into consideration. Speaking from the severely orthodox (not to say High Church or even Ultra-montane) point of view which I humbly presume the *first* (apostolic or patristic) commentator on *Jerusalem* has a

right to take, I cannot but say I would rather this book had remained in the Apocrypha than been inscribed in the canon – that is, in the roll of those books 'which whosoever believeth not, without doubt' etc. etc.[3]

Not every mid-nineteenth-century commentator is as evangelical in their apostolic devotion to Blake's more esoteric works. But the Gilchrist/Pre-Raphaelite circle certainly felt not just an ownership of William Blake and his works but a guardianship. One of their chief concerns was to guard against the 'wrong' sort of reader. What a reader was buying into when they opened *The Life of William Blake* was a beautifully packaged invitation to realise a sympathy that was beyond the common reader:

> These are no everyday volumes; they have a high beauty, both substantial and artistic – are fit for a place of honour on the drawing-room table and on the library shelf. Those mental haschish-eaters [sic] who form the bulk of the 'reading public' will, perhaps, not care for them much; but they will find their own public, and the name and genius of William Blake will, by their help, become known to thousands, and no longer remain as the almost private treasure of a small and scattered band of enthusiasts.[4]

The idea of the *sympathetic* reader is very important to the Gilchrist interpretation of William Blake's life and works. Very early in *The Life of William Blake* we are told that to appreciate William Blake requires an almost innate quality, that 'one must almost be born with a sympathy for it' (*Life*, 2). Anne Gilchrist uses the idea of a special sympathy between reader and author to pay homage to her husband and in this way she locks the reader's response into an emotional rather than critical or rational register:

> He desired always to treat his subject exhaustively; as a critic to enter into close companionship with his author or painter; to stand hand in hand with him, seeing the same horizon, listening, pondering, absorbing. No subtlest shade of meaning, no shifting hue of beauty should escape him or his reader if he could help it.
>
> ('Memoir', *Life*, 1880, II, 369)

Anne's abilities as a literary critic and editor are not in doubt and are not really the question at the heart of this chapter. The double bind that Anne consciously or unconsciously presents us with in the emphasis she and the other Gilchrist collaborators place on the empathetic reader is this: you have to be part of it to get it and to get it you have to be part of it. The Gilchrist collaborators seem to suggest that to read William Blake's work requires a private response that cannot be taught, what might almost be called an aesthetic intelligence. This aesthetic intelligence places an emphasis not on what the reader is reading but on the type of reader, on *who* the reader is. This reader is a private individual – and the private is important here – of particular cultivation and culture. Anne Gilchrist plays an important role in developing this sense of the reader, both in *The Life of William Blake* and in the instructive comparison of her essay on Walt Whitman, 'A Woman's Estimate of Walt Whitman'. She builds a sense of the ideal reader through focusing on a sense of domestic refinement in which private communion with an author flourishes.

The focus on the sentimental and domestic in relation to William Blake's life was not new to Gilchrist's *The Life of William Blake*. Following Allan Cunningham's poetic licence in 'inventing' Blake's death-bed speech,[5] Blake's life and death became sentimental grist to the mill of Victorian domesticity. Felicia Hemans's domestic rendering of the death-bed scene focused on the presence of Catherine Blake, her 'extraordinary character and the painfulness of her situation'.[6] Hemans poetic interpretation set a precedent for the domestic Blake in the 1840s and 1850s: ranging from Pamela Chandler's interpretation of 'A Cradle Song' presented as a saccharine moment within childhood, in which a little girl sings to her baby sister a poem she has learnt from William Blake's *Songs of Innocence*, to Mary Howitt's inclusion of Blake's 'Eccohing [sic] Green' in the *Pictorial Calender of the Seasons* (under the new title 'A Summer Evening on a Village Green'), where 'text, illustrations and context all emphasize the theme to which the Howitts devoted so much of their lives, the celebration of a vanishing (or vanished) rural England'.[7]

The Life of William Blake melds a sense of domestic family life to the private and the personal, manifested in the *personality* of poet and biographer alike. The domestic underpins and informs the private throughout Gilchrist's *The Life of William Blake*. Gossip and anecdotes about the poet's life act out his personality: from the twee tale of Catherine placing the empty plate in front of Blake to remind him to get out working again to the rather raunchier Adam and Eve in the bower of bliss apocrypha. The Gilchrist/Pre-Raphaelite coterie all had a belief in the idea of the *personality* of the poet as a conduit for a special relationship with the aesthetically intelligent reader. Once part of this special relationship, the reader not only has a relationship with the personality of the dead poet, but, by extension, with fellow acolytes: a 'brotherhood of believers'. They believed, to paraphrase Richard Sennett, in the *The Life of William Blake* as a fantasy in which they could form a community of fellow minds through sharing a collective personality, albeit a dead one.[8]

Death and personality are what Anne Gilchrist, in a manner of speaking, plays on and with, in her relationship with *The Life of William Blake*. Although we tend to think of the Pre-Raphaelite brotherhood as the boys who brought about the mid-century revival of William Blake, Anne is the linchpin in fostering an aura of intimacy, of intense personal investment, with *The Life of William Blake*. In a letter written to a relative in 1863 Anne Gilchrist describes the labour of love that the *Life* became after Alexander Gilchrist's death:

> That beloved task [the Blake] kept my head above water in the deep sea of affliction, and now it is ended I sometimes feel like to sink – to sink, that is, into pining discontent – and a relaxing of the hold upon all high aims. I find it so hard to get on at anything beyond the inevitable daily routine, deprived of that beloved and genial Presence, which so benignantly and tenderly fostered all good, strengthening the hands, cheering the heart, quickening the intellect even.
>
> *(Anne Gilchrist*, 142)

There is an uncanny sense in reading this letter that the 'beloved and genial Presence' Anne speaks of may be either the ghostly presence of Alexander Gilchrist or the posthumous (in a double sense) biography, *The Life of William Blake*. Anne's words reflect Ruskin's comments on the book in *Sesame and Lilies*: 'But a book is written, not to multiply the voice merely, not to carry it merely, but to preserve it.'[9] The fraying of the dividing line between personal life and literary project seems to be par for the course as far as the Gilchrist collaborators go. This is Dante Gabriel Rossetti writing to Anne Gilchrist in 1862, following the death of Elizabeth Siddal:

> Whenever it may be necessary to be thinking about the 'Life of Blake,' I hope you will let me know; as my brother is equally anxious with myself, and perhaps at the present moment better able to be of any service in his power. While writing this, I have just read your letter again, and again feel forcibly the bond of misery which exists between us; and the unhappy right we have of saying to each other what we both know to be fruitless.
>
> *(Anne Gilchrist*, 122)

Anne's special status as literary widow enabled her to preserve the idea of personality in *The Life of William Blake* through the idea of an intimate, special relationship. In writing at least, the part she plays in the Blake revival is pitch perfect: she is the watchful gatekeeper at a double mausoleum. She uses that private, personal voice of grief to cement the literary project that was the creation of the book, *The Life of William Blake*. The idea of the book as a place of personal and private affirmation rather than as a public expression of an author's ideas is important here.

Samuel Palmer wrote to Anne Gilchrist on 27 June 1862:

> The copy [of *The Marriage of Heaven and Hell*] I saw was highly finished. Blake had worked so much and illuminated so richly, that even the type seemed as if done by hand.

The ever-fluctuating colour; the spectral pigmies [sic] rolling, flying, leaping among the letters; the ripe bloom of quiet corners; the living light and bursts of flame; the spires and tongues of fire, vibrating with the full prism, made the page seem to move and quiver within its boundaries; and you lay the book down tenderly, as if you had been handling something which was alive. As a picture has been said to be something between a thing and a thought, so, in some of these type books over which Blake had long brooded with his brooding fire, the very paper seems to come to life as you gaze upon it – not with a mortal but an indestructible life, whether for good or evil.[10]

Palmer talks of the book as a live thing, a world unto itself. But he circumscribes the life of the book within a personal life, describing the *Life* as belonging to Anne Gilchrist (*Anne Gilchrist*, 143–5). At the same time as *The Life of William Blake* is described as 'an indestructible life', Palmer also describes the *Life* as an 'imperishable monument'. The life of the book is trapped within a very personal narrative.

Anne Gilchrist's vision of what a book is, how a book may mean and convey meaning, is evident in her correspondence with Walt Whitman:

& the Book that is so dear – my life-giving treasure . . .
Your book does indeed say all – book that is not a book, for the first time a man complete, godlike, august, standing revealed the only way possible . . .[11]

The book becomes here, almost literally, the man. Walt Whitman appreciated Anne Gilchrist's critical understanding of the unexpurgated *Leaves of Grass* saying that she had an understanding 'better and fuller and clearer than anyone else'.[12] 'A Woman's Estimate of Walt Whitman' is a heartfelt work of criticism. To read this essay is to be immersed in an immediate and intelligent response to a great poet's work. But the essay's main argument – that Whitman's robust (by Victorian standards) references to the body and sex signal a frankness and directness that are part and parcel of the poetry's 'kindling, vitalising power' and 'fearless and comprehensive dealing with reality' (*Woman's Estimate*, 349) – comes with caveats. And these caveats are to do with the sort of reader who should be exposed to this 'kindling, vitalising power'.

William Michael Rosetti gave Anne Gilchrist a complete version of *Leaves of Grass* after she expressed enthusiasm for Rossetti's edited version, in which he had expunged the offensive passages. Her response to these poems, originally written as letters to Rossetti, became 'A Woman's Estimate of Walt Whitman', published in *The Radical* in 1870. In the introduction to the essay published in *The Radical*, Rossetti is at pains to emphasise that not only is this the expression of a woman but that this woman is both cultivated and respected: 'The most valuable, I say, because this is the expression of what *a woman* sees in Whitman's poems, – a woman who has read and thought much, and whom to know is to respect and esteem in every relation, whether of character, intellect, or culture' (*Woman's Estimate*, 345). Anne Gilchrist acknowledges Rossetti's trust in handing the poems to her in the essay: 'I think it was very manly and kind of you to put the whole of Walt Whitman's poems into my hands; and that I have no other friend who would have judged them and me so wisely and generously' (*Woman's Estimate*, 346). Rossetti's 'manly' action fits into Anne's rhetorical positioning throughout the essay of herself as a female reader. The actual title of the essay makes it clear that Anne is not just any reader but a female reader. But she is not just any female reader either. She is a female reader reading within the privileged, refined space of the domestic and private. There is virtue, as Anne says, in the homely:

> All occupations, however homely, all developments of the activities of man, need the poet's recognition, because every man needs the assurance that for him also the materials out of which to build up a great and satisfying life lie to hand, the sole magic in the use of them, all of the right stuff in the right hands.
>
> (*Woman's Estimate*, 352)

But although there is undeniably a gender specificity about Anne Gilchrist's essay – she talks about wives and mothers learning through Whitman to rejoice in the grandeur and beauty of sex – this is not just about the female reader. It is about how notions of gender roles help to create the idea of a private reader who should be privileged – morally and aesthetically – in what they read. Anne Gilchrist's sense of the reader is very much about the 'right stuff in the right hands'. Even in praising Whitman's universality, it is clear that a strong sense of hierarchy runs through Anne's liberalism:

> If he feared to stretch out the hand, not of condescending pity, but of fellowship, to the degraded, criminal, foolish, despised, knowing that they are only laggards in the 'great procession winding along the roads of the universe' . . . how could he roll the stone of contempt off the heart as he does and cut the strangling knot of the problem of inherited viciousness and degradation?
>
> (*Woman's Estimate*, 351)

Anne is a critical tease and an editorial prig. Whereas she suggests all sorts of literary vigour and frankness in her assessment of *Leaves of Grass*, adopting the persona of the private gentlewoman speaking to like-minded gentlefolk in personal correspondence, her role as the editor of *The Life of William Blake* is one of moral guardianship to the point of censorship. How do we square this circle of sensuous defender of Whitman's unexpurgated poetry and behind-the-scenes slasher of Blake's racier lines? Anne presents it as a case of mediation between the raw truth and power of Blake's works and the moral propriety of the age, this 'propriety' represented by the morally upright and potentially indignant publisher, Macmillan. In the midst of this moral cauldron, Anne presents herself as the angel of the editorial hearth. She calms and soothes ruffled feathers behind the scenes, privately holding together the public propriety of the enterprise and 'tenderly and indulgently' dealing with the big boys' artistic and editorial tantrums:

> I am afraid you will be vexed with me that I was afraid to adopt entirely that most vigorous and admirable little bit a propos of the 'Daughters of Albion.' But it was no use to put in what I was perfectly certain Macmillan (who reads all the Proofs) would take out again. I am certain of this from past experiences – but I would have *tried it* at an earlier stage; but as that sheet has been twice set up – and has now kept us at a standstill for three weeks, I did not think it right to do so: I therefore 'reduced the subject' to still less – to a very shadowy condition indeed – but left enough, I trust, for the cause of truth and honesty. It might be well perhaps to mention to Mr Swinburne, if he is so kind as to do what was proposed, that it would be perfectly useless to attempt to handle this side of Blake's writings – that Mr. Macmillan is far more inexorable against any shade of heterodoxy in morals than religion – and that in fact, poor 'flustered propriety' would have to be most tenderly and indulgently dealt with.
>
> (*Anne Gilchrist*, 127–8)

Swinburne dismissed Anne's reticence here as that of a 'virtuous editor' being 'abjectly afraid' of 'any handling of the hot cinder or treading on the quagmire' ('Letter to William Michael Rossetti', 6 October 1862, in *Swinburne Letters*, Vol. I, 60). But this moral editing is not about an editor's belief that the poet's works are in and of themselves immoral. It is about a sense of the private, privileged reader as opposed to a common reader. Although Anne presents her own censorship as a pre-emptive strike against Macmillan's moral outrage, it is obvious that for her the publication of William Blake's works is tightly bound up with propriety. Propriety here means correctness as understood and owned (the word retaining some of its original meaning) by private individuals who are members of a privileged class. This is about correct readers rather than common readers: the 'right stuff in the right hands'. If any criticism should be made of Anne Gilchrist it is this one: as a woman described by Whitman as 'a picked woman, profound, noble, sacrificing' who 'saw clearly when almost everyone else was interested in raising the dust'[13] it is a pity that she did not have the same sort of estimate of her audience that she did of the poets she criticised and edited.

Frequently cited works

Anne Gilchrist	*Anne Gilchrist: Her Life and Writings,* ed. H.H. Gilchrist, with a prefatory notice by W.M. Rossetti (London: T. Fisher Unwin, 1887).
Woman's Estimate	Anne Gilchrist, 'A Woman's Estimate of Walt Whitman', *The Radical* (Boston, May 1870), Vol. 7.
Life	Alexander Gilchrist, *The Life of William Blake* (London: Macmillan, 1863).
Life, 1880	Alexander Gilchrist, *The Life of William Blake* (London: Macmillan, 1880).

Notes

1. 'To the Editor of the *Reader'*, in *Reader,* 11 (7 November 1863), 544.
2. Letter: Anne Gilchrist to Dante Gabriel Rossetti, 2 May 1863, in *Anne Gilchrist,* 138.
3. Letter to William Michael Rossetti, 30 October 1874, in *The Swinburne Letters,* ed. Cecil Y. Lang, 6 vols (New Haven, CT: Yale University Press, 1959), Vol. II, 348.
4. Anon., 'Review', in *Reader,* 11 (7 November 1863), 529.
5. Allan Cunningham, 'Life of Blake', in *Lives of the Most Eminent British Painters, Sculptors, and Architects,* 2, 6 vols (London: John Murray, 1830).
6. Paula R. Feldman, 'Felicia Hemans and the Mythologizing of Blake's Death', in *BQ,* 27:3 (1993–94), 69–72, 69. Feldman's essay reproduces Felicia Hemans's poem, 'The Painter's Last Work. – A Scene', in full, as it was originally published in *Blackwood's Edinburgh Magazine,* June 1832.
7. H.B. de Groot, 'R.H. Horne, Mary Howitt and a Mid-Victorian Version of "The Ecchoing [sic] Green"', in *Blake Studies,* 4:1 (1971), 81–88, 82.
8. Richard Sennett, *The Fall of Public Man* (London: Penguin, 2002), 262, first published 1977.
9. John Ruskin, *Sesame & Lilies, The Two Paths, & The King of the Golden River* (London: J.M. Dent, 1907), 8.
10. A.H. Palmer, *The Life and Letters of Samuel Palmer, Painter & Etcher* (London: Seeley & Co. Ltd., 1892), 243.
11. Anne Gilchrist to Walt Whitman, 4 July 1874 and 27 November 1871, *The Letters of Anne Gilchrist and Walt Whitman,* ed. Thomas B. Harned (London: T. Fisher, 1920), 112 and 68 respectively.
12. *The Letters of Anne Gilchrist and Walt Whitman,* ed. Thomas B. Harned (Garden City, New York, 1918), 67.
13. Elizabeth Porter Gould, *Anne Gilchrist and Walt Whitman* (Philadelphia, 1900), 53.

6
William Blake's Lavaterian Women: Eleanor, Rowena and Ahania

Sibylle Erle

The faces of kings and queens are always integral to our beliefs about their characters as well as the character of their reigns. Blake's interest in face reading has been linked by a number of Blake scholars to the publication of Johann Caspar Lavater's *Essays on Physiognomy* (1789; 1789–98). This chapter will discuss how Blake encoded the characters of Edward I, Vortigern, Urizen and, in particular, those of their female companions, Eleanor, Rowena and Ahania. Blake made four engravings for *Essays on Physiognomy*[1] and extensively annotated Lavater's *Aphorisms on Man* (1788). Lavater tended to move beyond stereotypes in analyses of individuals, but overall his conception of woman was very traditional. When defining female virtue, he insisted, that through woman man became whole:

> They [women] are not a foundation, upon which something is built, but the gold, silver, precious stone, wood, hay, stubble that can be built upon the male foundation. They are leavening to the male character – or, better yet: oil for the vinegar of manhood. Man alone is only half a man – or at least only half a human being – a king without a kingdom. Only through man is she [woman], whether standing or walking, the female aware of her femininity – but also only through the female is man what he can be and ought to be. Therefore it is not good for human beings to be alone.[2]

Blake's engagement with Lavater's view of sexual relationships can be traced back to *Aphorisms on Man*. Lavater starts with 'A great woman not imperious, a fair woman not vain, a woman of common talents not jealous, an accomplished woman, who scorns to shine – are four wonders.' Blake responds: 'let the men do their duty & the women will be such wonders, the female life lives from the light of the male. see a mans female dependants you know the man' (E 596). The idea that woman is eventually subsumed in Blake's myth is nothing new.[3] A discussion of Blake's Lavaterian women will test how far a gender-scenario of female dependence informed the relationship of three royal couples whose bodies and faces he repeatedly illuminated. Even though their status ranges from historical to poetical and mythical, the sexual manoeuvres between them crystallise power-structures at work in Blake's interpretations of regal love – and versions thereof. All this can be seen to originate in Blake's adaptation of Genesis: primal separation leads invariably to love and lust.

Blake's first encounter with Edward and Eleanor dates back to his apprenticeship to the official engraver to the London Society of Antiquaries, James Basire. Blake was sent to Westminster Abbey to do preparatory drawings for Richard Gough's *Sepulchral Monuments of Great Britain* and Sir Joseph Ayloffe's *Account of Some Ancient Monuments in Westminster Abbey*. During this stint he was fortunate enough to witness an exceedingly rare event, the opening of a royal tomb – the exhumation of Edward I, on 2 May 1774.[4] He made two sketches of the body, which he later worked into drawings. Their companion piece is a crowned, youthfully idealised Queen Eleanor, drawn from her medieval tomb.[5] Edward I and Queen Eleanor have a continual resonance in Blake's work. In 1779 he painted a watercolour *Edward & Elenor*, surviving only as an engraving from 1793.[6] Another lost watercolour, *The Bard, from Gray* was exhibited at the Royal Academy in 1785. There are also 14 watercolour illustrations to Thomas Gray's *The Bard* (*c.* 1797–98), made for Ann Flaxman, as well as a tempera painting of 1809 with the same title. And finally, the sketches done for William Hayley in 1805,[7] and for John Varley in 1819.

While Blake delivered a solid statement about female virtue in the *Edward & Elenor* picture (1779, 1793), he was able to delve into a more complex interpretation of their relationship once he was commissioned to illustrate Gray's poems in watercolour. In Design 4, illustrating Gray's 'On a rock, whose haughty brow', Edward is looking up to the last bard prophesying the end of his dynasty. Blake's choice of title – *Edward & his Queen & Nobles astonishd at the Bards Song* – further underlines his painterly preference for Edward's response rather than the curse itself (BA. Gray's 'Poems', 56). This set-up is restated in the description to the 1809 tempera: 'King Edward and his Queen Eleanor are prostrated . . . by the terrors of his harp on the margin of the river Conway' (E 542). Another watercolour, Design 10 – *The Death of Edwards Queen Eleanor from this line 'Half of thy heart we consecrate.'* – depicts Edward as a bereaved husband (BA. Gray's 'Poems', 62). Here we see how the curse acted on Eleanor. In other words, her death is a direct consequence of Edward's military campaigns.[8]

Edward was besieged at Conway in the 1290s. Eleanor, however, died a few years earlier of natural causes. The Conway scene is no window to Eleanor's death. Blake has transformed the Edward story by means of a flashback: his comment could be that the Conway situation came about *because* of Eleanor's death. Edward's massacre of the Welsh Bards is an eighteenth-century myth and originated with Gray. In the wake of the

Welsh cultural revival the absence of manuscripts tended to be explained with Edward's devastating conquest. The main popularisers were William Owen Pughe and Edward Williams, or Iolo Morganwg, who published two volumes of poetry with Joseph Johnson, Blake's sometime employer.[9] Blake owned Thomas Percy's *Reliques of Ancient English Poetry* (1765) and it is likely that either through Johnson or his own reading he became aware of the argumentative strategies of those trying to propel the Welsh national movement.[10] The point is that Blake broke with contemporary interpretations by adding to the Bard-massacre myth a moment of private mourning, something which is not developed or even suggested in Gray. Could it be that Blake used the combination of sad husband and dead wife to signify to Ann Flaxman, the first intended viewer of this picture, the deep feelings of her husband John Flaxman who had commissioned the Gray watercolours as a gift for her? Given that Edward's grief and the eleven Eleanor crosses, erected wherever the funeral procession stopped, were legendary, Blake could easily focus on love. Design 10 is a moment from memory. Eleanor is long gone. The family is no longer intact. In this treatment of the couple, Blake emphasises that their love is based on loss, death and absence.[11]

Another series of Edward and Eleanor drawings, part of the so-called 'Visionary Heads', are the drawings done for the water-colourist and astrologer John Varley in the late 1810s. Varley proposed that human beings could be categorised not only according to race, social rank or moral status, but also according to their horoscopes. Each zodiac, so argued Varley in *Zodiacal Physiognomy* (1828), could be associated with certain physical characteristics.[12] Interpretations of Blake's Visionary Heads are few and far between. While Martin Butlin suggested that Blake 'humoured the credulous Varley's beliefs', David Bindman argued that the Visionary Heads are the result of a 'parlour game'.[13] Jason Whittaker, however, rightly noted that the Visionary Heads include some of Blake's old favourites.[14] Ever since Anne Mellor's seminal article Blake's Visionary Heads have been associated with the pseudo-sciences.[15] It is, indeed, easy to divide these heads into villains, heroes and deliberately constructed personalities. What has so far been overlooked is how these spirits interacted. The most famous episode of the kind of spiritual encounters recorded by Blake was a meeting of Edward I and William Wallace.[16]

There are only a few of Blake's drawings in Varley's *Zodiacal Physiognomy*. They were each influenced by Lavater in different ways, yet in their collaboration they pushed physiognomy in wholly new directions. Varley wanted to achieve what Lavater had never been able to accomplish, namely to penetrate the body and take a look at man's spiritual situation. Blake, on the other hand, conceived his Visionary Heads as disentangled from definable bodies. Their shapes were unstable. The Edward–Wallace episode can, of course, be interpreted as continued conflict, but their confrontation is evidently just a struggle for attention: without much effort one spirit is dispersed by another more persistent one. I believe that the Visionary Heads can be linked to the flexible soul-body Blake envisaged in *Jerusalem* (1804–27):

> And they conversed together in Visionary forms dramatic which bright
> Redounded from their Tongues in thunderous majesty, in Visions
> In new Expanses, creating exemplars of Memory and of Intellect
> Creating Space, Creating Time according to the wonders Divine
>
> (E 257f., 98: 28–31)

Lavater, moreover, contended that through the Fall words came to replace naturally motivated gestures. In due course, the human face was turned into a mask, and therefore divided into types of character. In *Aussichten in die Ewigkeit* (1768–73) Lavater deliberated about how after resurrection man would gain a new form of existence, in a new body which superseded all uttered expression. In the disembodied soul nothing would be accidental or arbitrary.[17] A Lavaterian approach offers new insights into Blake's aesthetic treatment of faces.

One of Blake's Edward drawings is inscribed 'King Edward the first as he now exists in the other world. According to his appearance to Mr Blake. He here has his skull enlarged like a crown'.[18] The description can be traced back to what Blake told Varley, while working on this particular portrait:

> Stern, calm and implacable, yet still happy. I have hitherto seen his profile only, he now turns his pale face towards me. What rude grandeur in those lineaments! . . . He bends the battlements of his brow upon you; and if you say another word, will vanish. Be quiet, while I take a sketch of him.[19]

We can infer from the verbal portrait that Edward's spirit appeared and disappeared at will. Judging from the drawing, the spirit did not just turn its head. The 'bending of the battlements' translates as swollen forehead.[20] That a spiritual body regained its potential for flexible expression is a key notion of Lavater's physiognomic doctrines.[21]

Another curious element of this Edward story is that he promised Blake to return with his family.[22] Is the sadness in his eyes a reminder of his loss? We can assume that Blake was sympathetic towards Edward. Many years before he had lost his favourite brother, Robert. This loss affected Blake professionally. He claimed that Robert's spirit revealed to him the 'wished-for secret' of relief etching, used to create the illuminated books. Eleanor and Robert have quite literally a lingering presence. Robert, for example, reappeared as Blake's mirror-image in *Milton* (1804–18).[23]

Eleanor's continuance in Edward's rule and actions, by comparison, works as a reminder of Eleanor's sacrifice, a notion which accords well with Lavater's view of gender relations in terms of oil and vinegar. Back to the *Edward & Elenor* picture (1779, 1793). Its subject matter is female virtue and mixing body fluids. Eleanor is sucking poison from a wound inflicted by an assassin during the Crusades. Saving Edward is a lengthy process. While sucking the poison out of his body, she allows it to enter her own. Nursing Edward back to life, she puts her own life at risk. Blake uses Gray's *Bard* as a springboard for regret. Eleanor's appearance in the Gray illustrations is justified: she laid the foundation for what was going to happen at Conway. Design 10 may therefore be a cruel inversion. Despite her visceral sacrifice her family is doomed. She haunts Edward.

Another royal and seldom discussed couple appears in the large Blake-Varley Sketchbook: Rowena, a beautiful Saxon, and Vortigern, a fifth-century British king. Blake's Vortigern is a middle-aged, virtuous-looking king. But since Rowena exists in two versions, there is no simple narrative. According to the first sketch she is a naked, voluptuous, heavily bejewelled woman. In the second her face is sculpted with slanted eyes. Both figures wear crowns.[24]

Vortigern is a minor figure in the Arthurian cycle and it is difficult to estimate to what extent the contemporary sources influenced Blake's representation. His story exists in many versions but it is usually associated with Saxon colonisation,[25] Rowena's beauty and Vortigern's foolish love.[26] It is also a tragic and highly dramatic story. Charles Alfred Ashburton wrote that, once married, Rowena poisoned Vortimer, Vortigern's rebellious son from a previous marriage.[27] Since the publication of James Granger's *Biographical History of England* (1769–74) illustrating English history had become extremely popular and potentially lucrative. With the ever-increasing number of illustrations, minor historical figures – such as Vortigern and Rowena – began to receive more attention. Robert Bowyer, a miniaturist and print dealer, exhibited paintings to be engraved for an illustrated edition of Hume's *History of England* (1793–1801).[28] He based his Historic Gallery (1792–1806) in Pall Mall, where the published parts of the *History* could be inspected. One of these commissioned paintings was William Hamilton's *Vortigern and Rovena*.

What makes Blake's depiction of Vortigern unique is that the image is accompanied by two Rowenas. By the end of the eighteenth century the story of Vortigern and Rowena had become a popular subject. It was engraved for *English History Delineated*, in the early 1750s,[29] Smollett's *History of England* (1758–60), sketched by Henry Fuseli,[30] and painted by Nicolas Blakey, Francis Hayman, Angelica Kauffmann, John Hamilton Mortimer and John Francis Rigaud.[31] The story of Vortigern and Rowena was revised in John Harrison's new edition of Paul de Rapin-Thoyras's *History of England* (1784–89),[32] with Harrison claiming that Vortigern was not a gallant knight, but an ambitious, weak, and cruel opportunist. He also questioned the role attributed to Rowena. His new emphasis on a young, virginal Rowena fitted in nicely with the overall conception of Bowyer's Historic Gallery.[33] Another marked event or rather scandal was *Vortigern*, the alleged Shakespeare play, written by W.H. Ireland and performed only once in 1796. Ireland later admitted that he had been inspired by Mortimer's new angle on the Rowena story.[34] In *Vortigern* Rowena is a tragic figure, an obedient daughter, a queen, and finally a suicide. In a satire of that play, written in the same year, the love story is torn to pieces.[35] Next, Vortigern features as a cowardly traitor in Joseph Cottle's *The Fall of Cambria* (1809) as well as a victim of a magic revenge plot against Christian Britain, instigated by a sorcerer but spoilt by Merlin, in Thomas Curnick's poem *Vortigern and Rowena* (1814).

Since Blake's Rowena has the same dynamic physiognomy as identified for Edward, I propose to read her according to Lavater's character-codes, which associated moral with physical beauty.[36] Blake's representation of Rowena is deeply moralistic and his stance implies censure. Rowena is double-faced or at least part of her is reptile-like. She is a temptress who causes Vortigern's downfall. Both Eleanor and Rowena are crucial to the careers of their partners. They affect them in different ways. While Edward rises to fame, Vortigern loses everything. But why does Blake furnish a male and a female with such power-physiognomies? My answer is that Edward and Rowena have similar roles in their respective relationships. Throughout, Blake's rendering of female virtue is unmistakably paired with self-sacrificing love. Blake probably saw Vortigern as a victim, who could not be saved, since he was with the wrong kind of woman. While Blake associated Edward and Eleanor with an interdependent power-sacrifice relationship, the distribution of good and evil between Vortigern and Rowena is dynamic and, likewise, initiated by the female.

The figure which links love (Eleanor) and lust (Rowena) is Ahania. Her identity is shaped through Urizen's wound and her sacrifices for him. Like Rowena, her identity is difficult to pin down. There are several levels which describe the primal separation.

Blake's trio of books, *The Book of Urizen* (1794), *The Book of Ahania* (1795), and *The Book of Los* (1795) were produced after the arrival of Lavater's *Essays on Physiognomy*. In the Urizen books the link between Blake and Lavater is especially strong. Each of these books extrapolates on the fall of man. The narrative flow is hesitant and has a tendency to go back on itself. On the final plate of *The Book of Urizen* we see a fully-clothed Urizen sitting down, and entrapped in a net. On the frontispiece to *Ahania* this scene seems to continue. The net has been replaced by a human figure, a process not uncommon in the Urizen books: Ahania appears. Reading this with Lavater in mind, it becomes clear that the net-device may be an analogy to Lavater's superimposed net-diagrams, conceived to attribute facial angles to types of character. So, what Ahania *is* is more or less projected.

Ahania begins with a Star-Wars scenario. Urizen's oldest son Fuzon attacks his father with a 'howling Globe' (E 84; 2: 18) and causes Ahania, emanation, 'parted soul' and 'Sin' (E 84; 2: 32, 34) to come out of Urizen's body. She shrieks for pain. Urizen's body seems castrated, and yet it might as well have given birth. Urizen's creative powers are not diminished: he excretes 'Eggs of unnatural production' (E 85; 3: 10) his tears are 'Many sparks of Vegetation' (E 86; 3: 60) and his 'white Lake' conglobes into 'the bones of man' (E 87; 4: 14–21). Ahania is also Urizen's 'invisible Lust', jealously hidden 'in darkness in silence' (E 84; 2: 30, 36). She cries out from the 'verge / Of Non-entity', longing for his body: 'I cannot touch his hand: / Nor weep on his knees' (E 88; 4: 53–4, 65–6). Ahania wants to return to the 'golden palace' where sexual union continually affirms eternity (E 89; 5: 3).

On the frontispiece Ahania is naked, almost child-like, wringing her hands while crouching between Urizen's legs. She is a beautiful, voluptuous female, with long wavy hair. In the second portrait of Ahania, the work's title-page, her face has a similar worried look, but her body and hair have changed for the worse. Ahania has turned into the ghost of her former self. Is this an illustration of her post-separation existence as a split-off satellite? 'As the moon anguishd circles the earth; / . . . a death-shadow, / Unseen, unbodied, unknown' (E 85; 2: 40–3). Just like Eleanor and Rowena, Ahania is an amorphous figure; and yet her hybrid state, being materially attracted but without fixed form, makes clear how what is defined as female by Lavater influences male behaviour. By getting rid of her Urizen intends to make his creation unambiguous, measurable and thus identifiable. Indeed, in *The Four Zoas* (1795–1804), where Ahania's story is revised, Urizen accuses her of shape-changing:

> . . . Wherefore hast thou taken that fair form
> Whence is this power given to thee! once thou wast in my breast
> A sluggish current of dim waters . . .
> And thou hast risen with thy moist locks into a watry image
> Reflecting all my indolence and my weakness & my death
>
> (E 329; 43: 11–18)

Urizen compares Ahania to Vala, the temptress of Albion, shrinks back in horror and rejects her power, too insignificant to function on its own. Towards the end when Urizen resolves to redeem himself and become human again, he duly changes back into a young man. Back flies Ahania to die of joy (E 391; 121: 36–7). Blake's eternity is a place of naked youthfulness founded on female subordination.

The story of genderfication in Blake has gone full circle: Ahania's existence ceases where it started. Her birth and death are all part of an eternal cycle, created through the physical prowess of male authority. The female is a secondary symptom of a change within the mind of the male. At the centre of Blake's creation myth is a male monolith who has to learn to console his inner troubles, withstand the female or integrate it into his psychic life. The same is suggested to us, Blake's readers, in Ahania's funeral oration: 'Regenerate She & all the lovely Sex / From her shall learn obedience & prepare for a wintry grave / That spring may see them rise in tenfold joy & sweet delight / Thus shall the male & female live the life of Eternity' (E 391; 122: 12–15). What is female is compared with winter, and thus a cyclical experience. It is the foundation for all that is male but it still does not create on its own account. The female plays a minor but crucial role in Blake's imagined world. After her sacrifice Ahania evinces the dangerous appeal of Rowena. Urizen, like Vortigern, does not seem to be aware of it.

Notes

1. Mary Lynn Johnson, 'Blake's Engravings for Lavater's *Physiognomy*: Overdue Credit to Chodowiecki, Schellenberg, and Lips', *BQ* (2004), 38:2, 52–74.
2. Johann Caspar Lavater, *Physiognomische Fragmente*, 4 vols, 1774–78, III, 297.
3. Tristanne Connolly, *Blake and the Body* (Basingstoke: Palgrave, 2002), 189.
4. Joseph Ayloffe. *Account of the Body of King Edward the first . . .* , 3.
5. Martin Butlin, *Paintings and Drawings of William Blake, Plates and Text*, 2 vols (New Haven and London: Yale University Press, 1981), Text, nos 1, 2, 3–11.
6. Butlin, Text, no. 16.
7. G.E. Bentley Jr, *Blake Records* (Oxford: Clarendon, 1969), 165.
8. Irene Tayler, *Blake's Illustrations to the Poems of Gray* (Princeton, NJ: Princeton University Press, 1971), 157.
9. Evan Evans, *Some Specimens of the Poetry of the Antient Welsh Bards*, 1764, iii; Edward Williams, *Poems, Lyric and Pastoral*, 2 vols, 1794, I, xviii–xix.
10. Thomas Percy, *Reliques of Ancient English Poetry*, 4th edition, 1794, xl–xli; Nick Groom, *The Making of Percy's Reliques* (Oxford: Clarendon, 1999), 94.
11. Appendix to Paul de Rapin-Thoyras, *Rapin's impartial history of England*, 5 vols, printed by and for J. Harrison, 1784–89, I, viii–ix, viii; Richard Gough, *Sepulchral Monuments of Great Britain*, 2 vols (1786), I: 1, 64, 65.
12. John Varley, *A Treatise on Zodiacal Physiognomy* (1828), iii.
13. Butlin, *Paintings and Drawings* (1981), Text, no. 495; David Bindman, *Blake as an Artist* (Oxford: Phaidon Press, 1977), 202; G.E. Bentley Jr, 'Blake's Visionary Heads: Lost Drawings and a Lost Book', in *Romanticism and Millenarianism*, ed. Tim Fulford (New York: Palgrave, 2002), pp. 183–205, 184.
14. Jason Whittaker, *William Blake and the Myths of Britain* (New York: St Martin's Press, 1999), 180.
15. Anne Mellor, 'Physiognomy, Phrenology, and Blake's Visionary Heads', in *Blake in his Time*, eds Robert Essick and Donald Ross Pearce (Bloomington and London: Indiana University Press, 1978), pp. 53–74.
16. Alan Cunningham, *The Lives of the Most Eminent British Painters, Sculptors and Architects*, 6 vols, 1829–33, II, 168; Walter Copper Dendy, *The Philosophy of Mystery* (1841), 90; Jane Porter, *The Scottish Chiefs*, revised edition, 2 vols, 1804; Dublin, 1841, II, 468.

17. Johann Caspar Lavater, *Aussichten in die Ewigkeit*, 3 vols, Hamburg, 1768–73, II, 66.
18. Butlin, *Paintings and Drawings* (1981), Text, no. 735.
19. Butlin, *Paintings and Drawings* (1981), Text, no. 735.
20. James G. Ingli, 'Some Not-So-Familiar Visionary Heads', *BQ* (1979), 12:4, 244–49.
21. Lavater, *Aussichten*, 1768–73, III, 50–1.
22. Bentley, *Blake Records*, 260–1.
23. Alexander Gilchrist, *The Life of William Blake* (1863; Mineola, NY: Dover Publications, 1998), 70–1.
24. Christie's catalogue of *The Larger Blake-Varley Sketchbook*, 21 March 1989 (London: Christie, Manson & Woods, 1989), 40–2.
25. Christopher A. Snyder, *An Age of Tyrants: Britain and the Britons A.D. 400–600* (Stroud: Sutton Publishing, 1998), 102.
26. David Hume, *The History of England*, 2 vols, 1762, I, 14–15.
27. Charles Alfred Ashburton, *A new and complete History of England*, 1791, 35–6.
28. Robert Bowyer, *Proposals for a most splendid national work of The history of England* (1793); T.S.R. Boase, 'Maklin and Bowyer', *Journal of the Warburg and Courtauld Institutes*, 26 (1963), 148–77, 169.
29. Timothy Clayton, *The English Print* (New Haven and London: Yale University Press, 1997), 93, 97.
30. Christian Klemm (ed.), *Johann Heinrich Füssli: Zeichnungen* (Zürich: Kunsthaus, 1986), 27.
31. Simon Keynes, 'The cult of King Alfred the Great', *Anglo-Saxon England*, 28 (1999), 225–356, 299, 314–16.
32. De Rapin-Thoyras, *Impartial history* (1784–89) I, 17–25.
33. Juliet Feibel, 'Vortigern, Rowena, and the Ancient Britons: Historical Art and the Anglicization of National Origin', *Eighteenth Century Life*, 24:1 (Winter 2000), 1–21; Cynthia E. Brown, 'Robert Bowyer's Historic Gallery and the Feminization of the "Nation"', in *Cultural Identities and the Aesthetics of Britishness*, ed. Dana Arnold (Manchester: Manchester University Press, 2004), pp. 15–34.
34. W.H. Ireland, *An Authentic Account of the Shakesperian Manuscripts* (1796), 20–1.
35. Wally Chamberlain Oulton, *Precious Relics; or the Tragedy of Vortigern Rehearsed* (1796), 41–4.
36. Johann Caspar Lavater, *Essays on Physiognomy*, 3 vols (1789–98), I, 128–65.

7

Blake's Golden Chapel: the Serpent Within and Those Who Stood Without

Eugenie R. Freed

In the 1970s and 1980s, the final twenty years of apartheid in South Africa, teaching Blake (or anything else) at the University of the Witwatersrand in Johannesburg was a challenging experience.

My colleague Dr David Webster, a lecturer in anthropology at Wits (pronounced 'Vitz'), involved himself in a support group for the families of detainees after one of his own graduate students was detained by the South African Police in 1981. Ignoring police harassment, he helped to track down those who had been banished or detained, investigating and publicising the conditions of detention. On 1 May 1989 David was killed outside his home in a drive-by shooting. The entire university community united in outraged protest at his death, but the official 'investigation' into the incident drew a blank. Nine years were to pass before a former police employee, by then behind bars for other apartheid-era crimes, was convicted of David Webster's murder as well. He had been paid a large bonus on completion of the assignment.

On the Wits campus we learned to live with demonstrations, frequent and militant, against the blatant unfairness of the apartheid system, whose discriminatory laws imposed multiple disabilities on all black people from birth.

I remember being scared witless by the anger and aggression of student protesters and their supporters, advancing in traditional African warrior formations, stamping, roaring, ululating. The police opposing them, kitted out in riot-gear that made them look like aliens from outer space, used batons, 'sjamboks' (long lacerating cattle-whips), tear-gas, dogs, rubber bullets and real bullets, in various combinations. Our campus became a battlefield. Scores of protesters at a time were dragged away and locked up. Student leaders were detained without trial, and kept in detention so that they would miss their exams. Staff members intervening on their behalf were harassed by the police; David Webster, who defied them, was assassinated. Standing amongst colleagues and students at a mass outdoor assembly in tribute to David, I remember noting the line of riot-helmets bobbing incongruously above the wall behind the speakers. The police were taking no chances.

Often these disturbances blocked entrances and exits, preventing movement around the campus. Clouds of tear-gas filled classrooms and offices with searing, choking fumes. Frustrated protesters vandalised university buildings. A colleague in the Department of Political Science was researching and writing a history of black resistance movements in South Africa. One night his study – just below mine – was set on fire and its contents destroyed. The police never found the perpetrators.

A British colleague, a medievalist who taught in the Wits English Department during the mid-eighties, wrote later of the experience that 'we were all in a position to feel something of what it was like to be inside [Langland's] beleaguered Unity Holy Church'. Those of us who remained 'inside' struggled on, trying to continue giving classes in an environment so violent and unstable that our disciplines seemed all but irrelevant.

The gross injustices of the apartheid system under which we all lived, and the means by which it was enforced, were a constant source of bitterness, pain, anger, despair. Torture in detention was common; some activists paid with their lives for opposing the system. Many, black and white, students, teachers, and others, lost hope, and either left South Africa, or fell into despair. Those of us who didn't give up were no 'heroes of the Struggle', but ordinary people, who dared not allow the evils of apartheid to overwhelm the continual endeavour we were all engaged in: to make something of our lives in spite of it. Studying and teaching in those beleaguered classrooms – whatever the discipline – was only one element of that endeavour, but it was vital. It helped us to survive, in a meaningful sense, while South Africa lurched towards that astonishing day in February 1990, when State President F.W. De Klerk stood up in the Houses of Parliament in Cape Town to legitimise the various resistance movements, paving the way for the release from prison of Nelson Mandela and for South Africa's first democratic election in 1994.

Teaching Blake in that apartheid environment necessarily had special significance. Working at Wits during the week, I met other groups of students every weekend, at off-campus venues, through an anti-apartheid organization offering live teaching support to black students registered for degrees by correspondence. The government's policies of 'segregated education' threw so many obstacles in their path that it virtually excluded most of these people from higher education in any other form. The *Songs of Experience*, set against a historical background of political, social and religious repression, seemed poignantly relevant to men and women whose 'Divine Humanity' apartheid denied. For such students, the theme of *exclusion* as Blake takes it up in the *Songs* had a painfully personal resonance.

The untitled poem in Blake's *Notebook* beginning 'I saw a chapel all of gold' is surrounded by drafts of poems that became *Songs of Experience*

(1794). David Erdman suggests 'a beginning date of 1791 or later' (*N* 7, n.2), and a terminal date of late October 1792 for the whole series of poems written into the reversed *Notebook* between pages 115 and 99 (*N* 7). Its positioning on p. 115 places 'I saw a chapel . . .' near the beginning of this period. 'My Pretty Rose Tree', 'The Clod and the Pebble' and 'The Garden of Love' appear on the same page.

Blake wrote this disturbing lyric immediately below his draft of 'The Garden of Love'. In both poems the central image is a chapel whose gates are 'shut', excluding those who wish to enter and worship:

I saw a chapel all of gold	1
That none did dare to enter in	2
And many weeping stood without	3
Weeping mourning worshipping	4
I saw a serpent rise between	5
The white pillars of the door	6
And he forcd & forcd & forcd	7
[Till he broke the pearly door *del.*]	7a
Down the golden hinges tore	8
And along the pavement sweet	9
Set with pearls & rubies bright	10
All his slimy length he drew	11
Till upon the altar white	12
Vomiting his poison out	13
On the bread & on the wine	14
So I turnd into a sty	15
And laid me down among the swine	16

(From the Erdman facsimile of Blake's *Notebook*; *N* 115)

Early critical readings of this poem focused almost exclusively on the sexual significance of the serpent. Hazard Adams (240–2) and Leopold Damrosch Jr (205–9) offered sexual interpretations; David Wagenknecht (188) identified the serpent with the 'Spectre' in *America* 5.6–7, 'staining the temple long / With beams of blood . . .' (E 53). Kathleen Raine (1968) linked the poem to the sketch of a woman with a Gothic shrine between her thighs on p. 22 of the MS of *The Four Zoas*, finding in it '. . . the defilement of the bodily house by the serpent of sexuality' (i.195–9). E.P. Thompson (1968), ignoring the phallic bias of mainstream literary criticism, originally associated the chapel with the rise of Methodism (44).

W.H. Stevenson's note fairly sums up the majority view: 'The imagery of ["The Garden of Love"] makes it clear that the "chapel of gold" is the temple of innocent love, defiled by repression' (146).

The assumption is that both 'chapels' are metaphoric. Yet in the late eighteenth century the doors of many chapels were literally 'shut' to those who could not afford to pay rent for a pew (Gardner, 139). Mrs Sarah Trimmer, an energetic social reformer, complained in 1787 of 'doors shut against [the] entrance' of poor people, since 'very few parish churches in the metropolis . . . furnish seats for the poor' (cited by Gardner, 114). The situation was commonplace around the time when Blake composed both 'The Garden of Love' and 'I saw a chapel . . .'

But, as Heather Glen points out, 'the breaking open of the excluding chapel is an image which the Swedenborgians used of their New (as opposed to the old) Church' (167). Blake had sampled Swedenborg's writings before associating himself, in 1789, with the Swedenborgian community of the New Jerusalem Church (Paley, 65; Erdman, 139–46, 176–7; Bentley, 696). By the time he wrote these two poems, he had withdrawn from that community. But he continued for a while to receive and read their publications (Erdman, 176–7n.3), and his interest in Swedenborg's writings, doctrines and visions persisted lifelong (Raine, 1985: 101).

Blake had evidently read Swedenborg's *The True Christian Religion* (*TCR*), which compares the sacrament of Holy Communion 'without the spiritual sense' to a buried church, inaccessible, but 'containing altars of gold . . . [and] ornaments made of precious stones . . .' (*TCR* 669, 701). Was this why the 'many' who 'stood without' the splendid chapel in Blake's poem did not 'dare to enter in'?

Perhaps. But whether or not Blake had Swedenborg's passage in mind, the two visionaries shared a common, obvious, source of inspiration: the biblical Book of Revelation. Blake's 'chapel all of gold', its 'pearly door' hung upon 'golden hinges' between 'white pillars', its pavement 'set with pearls and rubies bright', suggests St John's New Jerusalem rather than Swedenborg's.

It was this 'holy city' of 'pure gold' (Revelation 21:18) 'coming down from God out of heaven, prepared as a bride adorned for her husband' (21:2), that inspired Blake's treatment of his chapel. The biblical city has no temple, and therefore no priests, 'for the Lord God Almighty and the Lamb are the temple of it' (21:22). The city's gates, each 'of one pearl' (21:21), 'shall not be shut at all' (21:25), for through them 'there shall in no wise enter . . . any thing that defileth . . . or maketh a lie' (21:27). Blake's golden chapel, its 'pearly door' tightly shut until a slimy serpent forces it open to defile the jewelled interior and 'altar white', is clearly an ironic 'negation' of the New Jerusalem St John imaged as a virginal bride.

If, as Heather Glen suggested, the lyric was inspired by Blake's brief encounter with the Swedenborgian New Jerusalem Church, it may refer to one in particular of several disputes raging in that community in the late 1780s and early 1790s concerning the introduction of an ordained priesthood (Erdman, 141–3; Glen, 167, 375n.6; Thompson, 1993: 143–5, 169–71). Robert Hindmarsh, a printer and publisher, held a powerful position in the Swedenborgian community in London during this period. Hindmarsh advocated 'an Episcopal (indeed papal) form of government, with the power to ordain priests derivative from his own supposed authority' (Thompson, 1993: 143).

By 1792 Hindmarsh was proposing 'an elaborately priestly form of government with "one visible Official Head"' (himself or his father, a former Methodist minister) rather than '"the Votes of the People at large"' (ibid.). Increasingly, the tendency was 'to establish ceremonial, to ordain a priesthood, to expel democracy and to establish ritual forms' (170).

Blake would certainly have found this development repugnant. Thompson attributes 'The Garden of Love' to Blake's response to this aspect of Hindmarsh's influence (144), and conjectures that Blake wrote 'I saw a chapel . . .' after walking past – and *not* entering – the chapel in Great Eastcheap where the London New Jerusalem community regularly met (170). Paley suggests that the inscription 'Thou shalt not' over the door of the chapel in 'The Garden of Love', is a negation of Swedenborg's words *Nunc Licet* ('Now it is allowable . . .'), inscribed over the door of the Great Eastcheap church.

The words *Nunc Licet* derive from Swedenborg's assertion in *TCR* 508: '. . . that now it is permitted to enter *with the understanding* into the mysteries of faith . . . in the new church . . . it is permitted *with the understanding* to approach and penetrate all its secrets, and also to support them from the Word' (my emphasis). At the founding conference of the New Jerusalem Church, attended by Blake and his wife in 1789, this principle was adopted as article XXXIII (Hindmarsh, 124; Erdman, 141–3). It deliberately *counters* an earlier vision in which Swedenborg hears a priest declaiming from the pulpit that the mysteries of the faith are impenetrable to the human intellect (*TCR* 185). Challenging the priest, he asserts that 'mysteries' never openly displayed or examined, may be worthless or dangerous, and quotes Isaiah 59:4–5, 'they trust in vanity, and speak lies . . . They hatch cockatrice's eggs, and weave the spider's web: he that eateth of their eggs dieth, and that which is crushed breaketh out into a viper.'

Blake too utterly rejected 'mystery' in religious worship, and with it the implication that it is the exclusive right of the ordained priest to expound the 'mysterious' meaning of the elements of faith. In 1790, against a prefatory passage to Swedenborg's *Divine Providence* reading 'all the grandest & purest Truths of Heaven must needs seem obscure and perplexing to the natural Man at first View' (translator's preface, xviii; E 609), Blake wrote angrily 'Lies & Priestcraft'. He demands, in a poem drafted a few pages away from 'I saw a chapel . . .':

> Why darkness & obscurity
> In all thy words & laws
> That none dare eat the fruit but from
> The wily serpents jaws . . .

> ('To Nobodaddy', *N* 109)

The 'wily serpent', the priest, is supposedly the only *authorized* interpreter of the 'words & laws' promulgated in 'darkness & obscurity' by this 'Father of Jealousy'.

Milton's prose treatise of 1642, *The Reason of Church Government* (*RCG*) is a readily identifiable source for Blake's image of this insidiously invasive serpent-priest. Blake had evidently read this work with careful attention (Wittreich, 147–219).[1]

Milton's sentiments were strongly anti-clerical. Milton accused the 'Prelat Bishops' of his time of '[proclaiming] the best of creatures, mankind . . . unpurifi'd and contagious . . . [making] profane that nature which God not only cleans'd, but Christ also hath assum'd' (*RCG* 845).

Every true Christian, Milton wrote, is 'sanctified' – made holy through divine grace – and 'adopted', being, in a special sense, a child of God (*RCG* 844; Hebrews 10:10; Ephesians 1:4–5). The possession of such 'glorious privileges' confers upon each individual Christian a holiness exceeding that of 'any dedicated altar or element' (844; 'element' being the bread and wine of the Eucharist). Milton rejected as specious the distinction between laity and clergy. If every faithful Christian would 'open his eyes to a wise and true valuation of himselfe', Milton asserted, he would recognise *within himself* 'that Priestly unction and Clergy-right whereto Christ hath entitled him', for he is of 'a royall Priesthood, a Saintly communion, the household and City of God' (*RCG* 844).

Like Milton, Blake found no justification for the ordaining of priests. The very suggestion that an ordained priest is a 'holy man' denies the intrinsic holiness of *every* being created in the 'Divine Image'. Blake would have recognised in Milton's exposition a principle close to his own concept of 'Divine Humanity'.

At the climax of his lengthy diatribe Milton urged his reader to:

> consider well from what a masse of slime and mud, the sloathful, the covetous and ambitious hopes of Church-promotions and fat Bishopricks, [Prelaty] is bred up and nuzzl'd in, like a great Python from her youth, to prove the general poison both of doctrine and good discipline in the Land. . . .

> (*RCG* 858)

The 'great Python' of Prelaty is female in gender – as in Milton's source (also a major source for Blake), the serpent 'Errour' in Spenser's *The Faerie*

Queene. Spenser's monstrous creature drags a tail like a 'huge train', and '[spews] out of her filthy maw / A floud of poison' that 'all the place defiled' (*The Faerie Queene* I.i.18, 20). Though female, Spenser's serpent is a 'type' of Satan. Her act of vomiting when attacked by the Red Crosse Knight was partly inspired by a verse from Revelation, in which 'unclean spirits . . . come out of the mouth of the dragon, and . . . out of the mouth of the false prophet' (Revelation 16:13). Milton, denouncing the degeneracy of the clergy in *Of Reformation* (1641), had there described the Church in its *'Depravities'* darkened by 'the huge overshadowing train of *Error*' (524), defiling the very concept of the Holy Communion: 'That feast of free grace . . . to which *Christ* invited his Disciples . . . became the Subject of horror' (523).

Milton's Python, spreading a 'general poison . . . pestilent alike to all' (*RCG* 844) is a 'sport' (in the genetic sense) of Spenser's spewing 'Errour', and both are descended from the dragon of Revelation. Blake's vomiting serpent is of this family, a vivid and repulsive metaphor for the 'false prophet', the self-serving and hypocritical priest taking possession of the rite of the Lord's Supper. What Blake describes in 'I saw a chapel all of gold . . .' is the forcible intrusion into 'the household and City of God' of this slime-born monster.

Priestly serpents – Satanically serpentine priests – abound in Blake's poetry and art of this period. They include the reactionary Archbishop of Paris, rising 'in the rushing of scales and hissing of flames . . .' to pour his contempt upon the common people in *The French Revolution* (1790; 127; E 291); the writhing worms refracting the image of the priest at the graveside in the plate of 'The Garden of Love' (1794; Plate 40); the serpentine priests who deceive the protagonist of 'Infant Sorrow' in its draft form (*N* 113, poem 17: f,g). At the end of one of the two versions of 'Night the Seventh' of *The Four Zoas* a snaky priest-charlatan appears: the despicable 'Prester Serpent', a hooded cobra cowled like a monk. He runs along the ranks of soldiers, whipping up the psychosis of war as he sends them into battle (90 [98], 22–30; Magno and Erdman, 204; E 363).[2]

To claim, as Damrosch did, that 'I saw a chapel . . .' presents 'the sexual initiation [as] an epiphany of disgust' (209), is partly to miss the point. What the poem does present, in a development of the imagery of Revelation 21, is Blake's own vehement rejection of 'Priestcraft'. The deliberate alteration of the sex of Milton's serpent in *RCG* intensifies the metaphor. Milton himself eventually changed the gender of his she-python of Prelaty, transmuting it into the ultimate form assumed by Satan (*Paradise Lost* X.514, 529–31). Violating the sanctity of 'the household and City of God', Blake's serpentine priest arrogates to himself the right to exclude the hapless multitude from the 'mysteries' of faith, while committing a vile rape upon the virginal bride of Revelation 21:2.

The final two lines of 'I saw a chapel . . .' become more comprehensible in the light of this reading. Heather Glen (86) relates them to the radical reaction against Edmund Burke's notorious prediction that: 'Along with its natural protectors and guardians, learning will be cast into the mire, and trodden down under the hoofs of a swinish multitude.'

Glen cites the ironic titles, inspired by this phrase, of a few of the many contemporary radical pamphlets directed against Burke: *Pig's Meat, Rights of Swine, Hog's Wash* (172). Blake's protagonist turns with revulsion *away* from what he sees before him: a self-appointed caste of corrupt, self-serving priestly intermediaries who interpose themselves between the laity and the Word of God, defiling St John's vision of the pure, unmediated communion of the Christian soul with 'the Lord God Almighty and the Lamb'. In a gesture expressive of disgust at what Blake later termed 'a pretence of Religion to destroy Religion' (*J*, 38 [43].36, E 185), the speaker of the poem joins the despised and outcast multitude, preferring to share the mud of their sty.

Recently (April 2004) I received a letter from a former student, then submitting his PhD at a British university. I had taught him at Wits in the later 1980s, when he was an exceedingly angry young man – justifiably so. I end this piece with an extract from his letter:

> One day, you will perhaps understand ... that a young boy from the townships, typically handicapped by the environment that was at best mired in cynical oppositional politics, and at worst shaped on the anvil of apartheid-induced diffidence, was moved by ... Blake and Milton ... Those images of London competed with my childhood memories for a place in my psyche. And they both stayed, sitting uncomfortably as they did next to each other as I embraced Blake's Vision – no less palpable than Milton's *'profundem lumen'*. Light into Darkness. That happened to me ...

Notes

1. Milton's prose works could have been available to Blake in Thomas Birch's edition published in 1738, if not in John Toland's earlier, more accurate, edition of 1699. William Hayley (later Blake's patron) quotes repeatedly from a specific collection of Milton's *Prose Works* in two editions of his biography of Milton published in 1796. Frustratingly, Hayley never reveals whose edition he used.
2. Peter Otto perceptively analyses Blake's sketch of the Prester Serpent in terms of 'Urizen's phallic religion' (15–17).

References

Adams, Hazard, *William Blake: a Reading of the Shorter Poems* (Seattle, WA: University of Washington Press, 1963).

Bentley, G.E., Jr, *Blake Books* (Oxford: Clarendon, 1977).

Blake, William, *The Notebook of William Blake: a Photographic and Typographic Facsimile*, ed. David V. Erdman (Oxford: Clarendon, 1973; revised edition 1977) (*N* in text).

Blake, William, *The Four Zoas. A Photographic Facsimile*, ed. Cettina Tramontano Magno and David V. Erdman (Lewisburg, PA: Bucknell University Press, 1987).

Blake, William, *The Complete Poems*, ed. W.H. Stevenson (London: Longman, 1971; second edition 1989).

Blake, William, *Songs Of Innocence and Of Experience*, ed., with introduction and notes, Andrew Lincoln (London: The Tate Gallery/The William Blake Trust, 1991).

Burke, Edmund, *Reflections on the Revolution in France*, ed. Conor Cruise O'Brien (London: Penguin, 1968).

Damrosch, Leopold Jr, *Symbol and Truth in Blake's Myth* (Princeton, NJ: Princeton University Press, 1977).

Erdman, David V., *Blake: Prophet against Empire* (Princeton NJ: Princeton University Press, 1977).

Gardner, Stanley, *Blake's Innocence & Experience Retraced* (London: The Athlone Press, 1986).

Glen, Heather, *Vision and Disenchantment: Blake's* Songs *and Wordsworth's* Lyrical Ballads (Cambridge: Cambridge University Press, 1983).

Hayley, William, *The Life of Milton, in Three Parts* (London: Cadell and Davies, 1796). A facsimile, with introduction by J.A. Wittreich Jr (Gainesville, FLA: Scholars' Facsimiles and Reprints, 1970).

Hindmarsh, Robert, 'An Account of the First General Conference of the Members of the New Jerusalem Church, London, April 13–17, 1789' (1790), in Harvey F. Bellin and Darrell Ruhl (eds), *Blake and Swedenborg: Opposition is True Friendship* (West Chester, PA: Swedenborg Foundation, 1985), pp. 121–31.

Milton, John, *Complete Prose Works of John Milton*, vol. I (1624–1642) (New Haven: Yale University Press, 1953).

Milton, John, *The Poems of John Milton*, eds Alistair Fowler and John Carey (London: Longman, 1968).

Otto, Peter, 'A Pompous High Priest: Urizen's Ancient Phallic Religion in *The Four Zoas*', *BQ*, 35 (2001): 4–22.

Paley, Morton D., ' "A New Heaven is Begun": William Blake and Swedenborgianism', *BQ*, 13 (1979): 64–90.

Raine, Kathleen, *Blake and Tradition*, 2 vols (Princeton, NJ: Princeton University Press, 1968).

Raine, Kathleen, 'The Human Face of God', in Harvey F. Bellin and Darrell Ruhl (eds), *Blake and Swedenborg: Opposition is True Friendship* (West Chester, PA: Swedenborg Foundation), pp. 87–101.

Spenser, Edmund, *The Faerie Queene*, ed. A.C. Hamilton (London: Longman, 1977).

Swedenborg, Emmanuel, *The True Christian Religion*, 2 vols, translated from the Latin by John Chadwick (London: The Swedenborg Society, 1988).

Thompson, E.P., *The Making of the English Working Class* (Harmondsworth: Penguin, 1968).

Thompson, E.P., *Witness against the Beast* (Cambridge: Cambridge University Press, 1993).

Wagenknecht, David, *Blake's Night* (Cambridge, MA: The Belknap Press of Harvard University Press, 1973).

Wittreich, Joseph Anthony Jr, *Angel of Apocalypse* (Madison: University of Wisconsin Press, 1975).

8
How to Nearly Wreck Your Life by Living Blake

Addie Stephen

Reading Blake was a classic born-again conversion for me. Apart from Blake, I have no way to understand spiritual eccentrics of any stripe, from fundamentalist Christians to Moonies. While this may seem a suspect boon, it's valuable for connecting with my rural neighbours – I can instantly translate their Christ into Blake's. Blake was my original conduit to a spiritual life richer than any offered me through the seventeenth-century metaphysicals. I could make mere metaphor my god-term with Donne or Herbert, but that didn't change the way I lived my life. Before Blake, I was in danger of becoming the kind of empiricist he loathed.

Now that I am a mental traveller thirty years down the road and well into the lamp-lit interior of my mind, I know that reading Blake guided many of my decisions and informed many of my core values. My understanding of deep structure – of the psyche or ideology or politics – arose from Blake. Influenced (anxiety intact) by psychoanalysts Freud and Jung and Dorothy Dinnerstein, anthropologist Mary Douglas, poets Adrienne Rich and Alicia Ostriker, and philosopher Denis deRougement, I sought some kind of transcendence through Blake. Later I sought it through Buddhist meditation. My feminism was surely shaped both with and against Blake. I probably owe even my choice of close friends to Blake, because the people I love tend to be visual artists as well as writers. And without Blake I wouldn't have done the things that made me look like a fool in my professional life, like giving up a big corner office in order to squash my spectrous ego which, unchecked, could have turned me viciously Urizenic.

Spectre-trouble also led me to actions that nearly wrecked my personal life. We don't live in Blake's Eternity most of the time; we live in Ulro, or Generation at best, where they don't understand these matters. I speak thus far only of trivialities such as career and money and health insurance, all but one of which I've kissed goodbye, blessing them upon their way. (Dumped the career and the money; kept the health insurance.) To explain my literalist reading of 'Visions of the Daughters of Albion', *The Four Zoas*, *Milton*, and *Jerusalem*, I'll need to establish credibility as a thoughtful person instead of a moral moron.

I first read Blake in the 1970s, so I was in the generation that saw him transformed from a precursor or transitional figure to the category of major author, mediated by those lovely paradigm shifts in the late 1960s and 1970s in Romanticism, feminism, art history, and psychoanalytic theory. Blake was a fixture of pop culture by that time, discovered by everyone from spiritualists to cookbook writers – in any alternative store in America or England, Blake adorned posters and calendars – but most Blake scholars still laboured in the vineyards of specialisation, fairly isolated from mainstream academe, except for Damon, Frye, Erdman, and pre-anxiety Bloom. The Erdman/Bloom *Complete Poetry and Prose* had been out for a decade, but no one I knew had read it. I was more likely to hear Emerson, Lake and Palmer's rendition of 'Jerusalem'.

That changed in graduate school, where I was headed for a dissertation on Donne. One day I walked into the wrong room – I thought it was a seminar on Freud – and found myself in a Blake seminar taught by a former Catholic nun, of whom it was said that Blake got her out of the convent. I knew him only through 'Songs of Innocence'. Little lamb, who made thee? I was not impressed. But I was also a commuting student and a single mother with a part-time waitressing job, a house full of boarders, and a carpool partner, so I had to take what was available. The charismatic teacher was a popular campus figure and I was lucky to get into her oversubscribed seminar at all.

I took notes on Berkeley, Bindman, Bacon, Butts, Bloom, on Frye, Swedenborg, Lavater, Dante, Damon, Flaxman, and Hayley, only half of whom I'd heard of. But every time she quoted Blake, I winced. Whatever this was, it wasn't poetry as I'd learned and then taught it. The stuff had no discernible rhythm, except when it (dreadfully and easily) rhymed.

And so did I begin my resistant reading of Blake. And so did I hurl my brick-thick *Poetry and Prose* across the room, I threw that damn book against walls for weeks while I tried to break its back or his code. But something was at work in me. I knew his was a brilliant mind intent upon creating a mental cosmos, but his words on the page seemed unintelligible. I used Freud's soothing rationalism as an antidote to Blake, until I realised that his hypotheses were as wild-minded as Blake's. When I arrived at *The Four Zoas*, I re-commenced flinging, but by this time, I possessed duct tape. As I write this, I'm admiring its three decades of staying power on the broken back of my first Blake.

My professor was the perfect guide to Blake. One day, around my fourth reading of *FZ*, all at once I got it, I simply got it. I do not remember where I was sitting, nor which passage fuelled my breakthrough, but I felt Blake's giants coursing through me. I remember the way the light was coming through a window. I remember breathing out deeply, backing up from his pages, leaning back down. I thought I might lose consciousness.

In a sense I did lose ordinary consciousness, then and thereafter. This man understood the plagues of the psyche, had also known its joys and delights. He'd surveyed human history and the interior of his own mind. There was no god but ourselves, and he and she were everywhere. The Human Form was Divine. A Last Judgement could pass upon me between breakfast and lunch. I could live in the present moment and in Eternity at once. Perception was all. Only contraries could lead to progression. I could drive my cart and my horse over the bones of the dead. And everything that lived was Holy.

When I re-read 'The Book of Thel', altered thus, I stood before my own grave. Now Los and Urizen wrestled in my own body. Now I lived in both heaven and hell all the time, except when operating a motor vehicle, serving hot dogs at the restaurant, or supervising fingerpainting. My friends could not understand what I said, but they were kind, most kind. God knows what they really thought. I did not care. I had found a song in my soul. I would learn this man's system rather than another man's, rather even than a woman's, until it gave me the courage to create my own, which I also knew I would one day do.

There followed year upon year of parsing his every word and image. My dissertation and my first book were the fruit of thinking that Blake knew everything that Freud knew, but a hundred years before him. Here was the explanation of why humans make war upon themselves and each other, why men and women tear out each other's vitals. The Human Imagination was the site of these wars, but there was no need to despair, for intellect and imagination would always keep the Divine Vision in time of trouble. There were ways into Eternity in ordinary life. We didn't have to destroy each other. We could love each other, and ourselves, through imagination and compassion. I believed all of it, and I wish I still did.

I travelled to the Rosenwald collection in Washington, where Lessing Rosenwald gave me a Trianon facsimile. I went to the Huntington in California, to the British Museum and the Tate in London, to Cambridge. I held in my hands the surviving fragment of his plates. I met with David Bindman to discuss my approach to Blake's art. At the Swedenborg Society in London I pored over books. Originals of Blake were delivered into my hands, hands I washed in a sacred rite that privileged me, along with my letters of introduction, to touch what he had created. I met Alicia Ostriker, who'd written one of the Blake books I most admired. She later became for me his living inheritor among poets, an American Blake worthy of Whitman. I stood for hours in front of the 1795 prints at the Tate. I went to the house, by then a pub, where he and Catherine lived during those lean London years, and then to the Felpham cottage with its stark hearth. I peered into the private garden where he read *Paradise Lost* to Catherine, both of them, so the story goes, nude as figs. He was not merely my scholarly subject, but my hero, and my journeys to Blake landmarks were ritual pilgrimages.

For the next two decades, in those waning years of author seminars, I taught Blake in courses such as Milton and Blake. (Outside of class, I called it Two Dead White Guys.) When we'd finish Milton and enter Blake, I'd watch the lights go out for some students – the smart but plodding ones who never made bibliographic errors. For others, there'd be sudden flashes of insight in 'The Marriage of Heaven and Hell' that held through 'The Book of Urizen'. When we reached the later prophecies, the flashes dimmed, but for one or two, perception was forever altered. It was difficult not to proselytise, but I guarded against it. They got it or they didn't. Most of the comprehension would have to occur in private. Eventually, I found an even better way to teach Blake. Reorganising our curriculum in the wake of cultural studies, we revised our period courses, and the Romantics became what I called The Visionary Imagination, in which Blake kept company not only with Milton, but with Keats, Heraclitis, Buddha, H.D., Adrienne Rich, Louise Erdrich, Thich Nhat Hanh.

My personal life paralleled my professional one. In my case, the correlation was high. I decided to live out his principles as much as I could, and that's how the trouble began. It was one thing to treat others with kindness and compassion, to speak of delight, to encourage mental fight in people's lives, to ally myself with the weak and weary when I could. Much of that I'd done anyway, as a feminist and a leftist. But without Blake, I wouldn't have tried to live out the visions of the Daughters of Albion. Which is a very, very bad idea.

I blame Oothoon. Her, and Enion, yes and even Enitharmon at her best, giant goddesses I thought of as personages, not characters, those Blakean babes who overcame possessiveness to welcome other women into their tents, and actually thought sharing their mate with another woman was a *good idea*. You can dismiss it as Blake's pornographic fantasy, but that's too easy. Oothoon's monologue on 'the moment of desire' is a worthy Ur-text on far larger matters. 'Father of Jealousy, be thou accursed from the earth!' is not merely sexual. I've felt jealousy. I think it's the second sickest human emotion, hatred being the first. 'Can that be Love, that drinks another as a sponge drinks water?' I've done that, and had it done to me. It's useless to 'cloud with jealousy his nights, with weepings all the day', or he mine. Oothoon named that instinct 'self-love that envies all! A creeping skeleton / With lamplike eyes watching around the frozen marriage bed.'

My time was the 1970s instead of Blake's 1790s, and many people who ought to have known better were experimenting with sexual freedom. My generation was supposedly swapping partners and tying each other to bedposts at alarming rates. But I don't think I got my ideas from the cultural climate as much as from the books I read. I never wore flowers in my hair, never had a one-night stand. I'm instinctively a monogamist (if serial qualifies) who could count the men or women I have slept with on one hand. Or two. So trying to live out Blake wasn't a rationale for hedonism; I was trying to alter my unconscious, and those of others. It may be a doomed enterprise, but it's sweet. No one who has internalized Blake can avoid thinking about how to live her sexual life. Acting on one's politics and teaching lovely poems is easy compared to contemplating this, especially in the face of fears of loss instilled in you before you could speak, entirely without your permission.

My observations of what jealousy did to others convinced me that people are eaten alive by it. Genuine and abiding affection for another person is not about ownership, exclusivity, or possession. Married as a teenager, I faced that monster when my husband cheated on me, and it made me literally sick. But by then I was reading Blake, and, face in the toilet, I swore I would never be so poisoned again. I left that marriage, and while I knew I was a pair-bonder, I also knew that next time around, I would conduct my primary relationship quite differently.

Oothoon's monologue is a sophisticated analysis of the etiology of war and prohibitive religion, and it locates their sources in the same hearts that feel individual pain. Although 'Visions . . .' is early, the later prophecies are all extensions of her thought – and Thel's at her graveside, and the Mental Traveller's when the child's shrieks are caught in cups of gold, 'and all is done as I have told'. I wanted not to feed that cycle of human history, I wanted to contribute to a parallel one that might undo the 'crafty slaves of selfish holiness'.

One person seldom fulfils lifelong all the needs or desires of another, in any way at all, to say nothing of sexually. Then should we all do everything we want? That's mere greed. But moderated by compromises with the hellish social and psychological realities we all know, I saw no reason to deny my own mate a girl of 'mild silver or furious gold', even if my mate could not, out of his own fear, truly offer me the same freedom. It took some wrestling with my feminism – was I accepting a mere double standard? – but my compensations were real. I had books to write, and a powerful need for independence and solitude. And none of my male partners had a problem with my being with a woman, which I occasionally was. With or without that, to become the Prohibitor 'till beauty fades from off my shoulders darken'd and cast out' would eventually make me 'a solitary shadow wailing on the margin of non-entity'. Bad place to be, that. And maybe this will seem superficial, but the biggest pay-off was seeing my partner so happy. Nothing in this world will make a straight man happier than permission to desire a woman other than his primary Beloved without guilt. Nothing in this world or the next. Trust me on this.

Of *course* there were other compensations. My primary erotic identity is a weirdly sublimated voyeurism. I didn't have to watch; I just needed to know. This has something to do with textuality, but I really don't feel like performing an Irigarayan analysis on it – I see eroticism in words as much as in images. Enough said. (Well, *you* try writing about *your* sexual kinks. It's not easy.)

Ethically, the Blake figure I most despised was Urizen and his minions, all forms of rulers, controllers, possessors. The god that prohibits desire has made shadows of us all. I vowed he would not ruin me. What I forgot, of course, is that the women with whom my serial mates and I entered into complex liaisons had not read Blake. Neither had my partners. All they knew, and not until well into the partnership (usually years) was that they felt like the luckiest men alive while it lasted, and never knew what hit them when it ended badly. As it always did.

Here's how it worked (and then didn't) with the first two mates of my post-early-marriage life. Years into monogamous householding, when they'd grown close to a female friend and there was mutual attraction, I said some variant of *If your relationship deepens, that's all right with me. I don't want to be deceived or betrayed, and I don't want you to lie, because lying hurts the liar most. And I have a few boundaries.* (You mean there were terms? Of course, I'm not *that* stupid.)

The terms: She can't wish me harm. I want her to wish me well, so it would have to be a friend. Whether she is partnered or not is her business, for whatever agreement exists between that person and another is not mine to legislate. Since we are creatures of infinite fantasy, she might do things with my partner that I would not do – but if she leaves the relationship, he cannot ask me to be her stand-in. I am me, not her. (When *that* one got violated? That was the worst.) Above all, I ask discretion, that I not be caused to look a fool by the dim lights of the public worlds I live and work in, because I am a private person. And I never, ever want to do damage control. This last is important, because people falling in love are temporarily insane. I do not exaggerate; clinical definitions briefly apply. New lovers are completely altered, so they think they're being subtle when they're not, or else they just can't bring themselves to care. People falling in love are fun to watch, but you wouldn't want to have to *explain* them.

Every time, my partner thought at first there must be a hitch – was it a twisted loyalty test? When he got home, would there be hell to pay? When there wasn't, he began to believe it. He did not ever love me less. Often he loved me more. For a while, this made for the best of all possible worlds. But every single time, every single one of my (reasonable? I still think so) boundaries was eventually broken, by her or by him or by both, almost as if it had to happen eventually.

After one month, or one year, or ten long years, someone in the emotional (and occasionally, but not necessarily, physical) triangle couldn't take it. Someone lost his/her mind, felt that old possessiveness, behaved badly, got hurt. And that someone was not ever me, in the short run. In the longest of these relationships, when she fell into that possessive form of love with my partner and wanted him for herself, she found herself wishing I were dead. She had no one in whom to confide this fantasy of doing away with me – except her closest friend and sometime-lover, me. That one tested my Blakean principles hard. In another case, the woman got far too involved with me. Nor did that turn out well.

After fifteen years of living this way on and off, I was dead tired of it, lifetime wearied. There had been three relationships, all intricate. Now I was too old for this stuff. The situations not only fell apart, but were as ruinous as divorce, and why not? Consider what happens when the egos and hearts of just two people entangle. When there's a third party, what you get is not one-third more pain, it's exponential; not just multiplied, but squared; not just squared, but cubed. The term 'clusterfuck' must have been invented for such situations. If Mormon marriages of the nineteenth century didn't end in clusterfucks, it must be because they were patriarchal. I'll bet not many Mormon women said, 'Wait just a minute here.'

For fifteen *more* years I practised straight and straightforward monogamy. And then a friend grew very close to me and my partner of a decade. She knew nothing of my colourful past, which had taken place in a different state of the American union, as well as a different state of mind. He did know, but regarded himself as the one who came along after I'd discovered how crazy it was, alas. He sometimes sulked. 'Tell me that story again.' I'd say, 'No, it ended in a big mess.' He'd say, 'But that part before the mess?'

An unconventional thinker in every way, Julia seemed entirely secure in herself. At this time of her life, she longed for affection she would never quite get inside her primary relationship, one she will not leave, for good reason: she loves her mate. When she and my partner worked on a project together, their mutual attraction became obvious, but her faithfulness to me as friend was equally clear. I was impressed. I told my mate he must never pressure her, but that if anything eventually happened between them, it was okay. She was so ethical that I thought it likely she'd still decide against it. And for a long time, she did.

But then she didn't. She thought what they did was merely playful. But it was also sexual. At first, her references when she and I were alone acknowledged that I knew. Then something shifted. She did not know her own mind about what she wanted, nor how to include or exclude me, one of her closest friends – and while I didn't want to be included sexually, I wanted our emotional bond intact or deepened. But despite her being one of the most creative souls I know, Julia could not figure it out. Perhaps she had no model for how such an arrangement would work, and she wanted to keep such high boundaries between her relationship with me and her relationship with him that all sense of our previous closeness began to dissolve. Sometimes she flirted with me, but I did not take that seriously – a bisexual woman knows when a straight woman is playing with her own boundaries just to scare herself. Boo.

In the end, she broke my biggest taboo, probably without quite realising it, and certainly without intending me any harm, I know that. In public she was indiscreet about their relationship, violating my request that this remain private, and in the end I had to do damage control in painful ways that humiliated me. Then she included me in the 'enemy' category for a while, much to her own later sorrow. In record time, she seemed to want my mate to mislead me to some degree. Bless him, he would not. All of this made me unspeakably sad – and then quite speakably mad. After a lifetime of pride that I could deal with anything, I couldn't take my friend shutting me out. I screamed at her. To an outside observer who did not know my sexual history, I probably looked and sounded just like any other jealous wife. That in itself was mortifying. Enough is enough. (You don't know what's enough until you know what's too much. That, too, is Blake; but one should not have to learn it again and again.)

We don't live in Eden, or in an Eternity where jealousy and betrayal and deceit do not dwell. Most of us are too afraid for that. If I have something to be glad of here, it's that through this experience I discovered that my mate shares my vision of fidelity and integrity. It has cost him dearly, because I know that his affection for Julia meant a great deal to him. My other mates got the fruits of my Blakean sexual principles, but this most worthy one barely felt that 'moment of desire' before he had to forgo it, if he wanted a life with me. For a while, Julia and I needed distance. But I'm as lucky in my ultimate friendship with her as I am in my choice of mate. When she and I realised we could lose each other over this, we rescued ourselves and each other. We are once again close, and we are careful of each other's hearts, too.

I've switched Blakes in my deep middle age. We've all heard the story of how, early on in their marriage, Blake asked Catherine if he could bring other women into their relationship, and she said no. She became the dread prohibitor. I have finally become Catherine, the realist. How predictable it now seems. Given such a gift from the heart of me – *you can borrow my man* – I did not understand how a friend could do anything that was not kind toward me. Well, that's so myopic that I'm now embarrassed by it. Such largesse from wonderful me! No wonder the friends I lured, yes probably lured, to my tent ended up feeling I could go screw myself. Or die. All the time I thought I was being Oothoon, maybe I was a prime manipulator. Maybe I was Enitharmon disguised as Enion. I wouldn't put it past me.

I wish the Blakean ideal were possible, and I still think it's right-minded. I didn't ever make it work, but I believe in the ethic at its heart. Still, there will be no more girls of mild silver or furious gold around this house.

9

Aesthetic Agency? Enitharmon in Blake's *Europe*

Nancy Moore Goslee

Although Blake refers briefly to Enitharmon in his 1793 *America* (E 53; 7:4), she emerges in *Europe* the next year as a dominant – and dominating – character. While most feminists see reason for optimism in Blake's sympathetic portrayals of women through 1793, Enitharmon's role in *Europe* has seemed to announce Blake's fall into misogyny, for she not only dominates the poem but in her practices of bondage becomes a dominatrix out to spoil everyone's fun. Several recent readings, however, point the way to a more sympathetic view of her character, or at least of Blake's purposes in developing such a character. In this chapter, I will build upon these readings by focusing upon Blake's thematic testing of his visual and verbal arts. Enitharmon, I propose, is not simply a forerunner of the hostile, torturing, and yet dependent female figures that appear so frequently in Blake's later poetry, but an experiment in aesthetic agency that precedes – though it may lead to – Blake's refiguring of her as a subordinate emanation in the almost-contemporary *Book of Urizen* (see Viscomi, 279). Nor is Enitharmon yet relegated, in *Europe*, to her later role as custodian of material space, subordinate to Los's prophetic power over time. This figuration does not appear until Night One of *The Four Zoas* (E 305; page 9, lines 19–27). Yet as this final characterization of her role develops there and continues through *Milton* and *Jerusalem*, it draws, as W.J.T. Mitchell has shown, upon traditional, gendered hierarchies of the verbal and visual arts and is thus profoundly integrated into Blake's development of his own primary arts as prophetic modes of redemption (129–30). Thus, critics have tended to read it back into *Europe* as well.

Instead, I read Enitharmon's actions in *Europe* as Blake's response to Orc's role in *America*: with Enitharmon, Blake tests the resources of his own visual and verbal arts to propose a gendered analysis of revolutionary desire – desire both political and erotic – and its restraints. That testing develops both as Enitharmon seems to experiment with temporal and spatial modes of prophecy and as Blake represents her interventions through his at times conflicting visual and verbal modes. She becomes one of those transgressive women prophets of the early 1790s that the *Critical Review* so disarmingly refused to discuss (Mee, 47). If she also transgresses Blake's earlier prophetic revolutionary ethos, she explores both the necessity for some binding or swaddling of revolutionary excess and the dangers of an over-reactionary attempt to civilise those impulses. In this reading, I will not exonerate Enitharmon from responsibility for a binding of sexual energies, as Julia Wright has recently proposed – though my thinking owes much to her reading. Nor will I exonerate her fully as a dominatrix constructed, in spite of her belief in her own agency, by patriarchal visions of women as either too powerful or too victimised – though I will draw on the specifics of Helen Bruder's contextualising of her role with visual and verbal satire of the Revolutionary era (133–78). In this necessarily brief analysis of Enitharmon's interventions, I will focus primarily upon the text and illumination of a single plate early in the body of the main 'prophecy'. I will then look, even more briefly, at a later ekphrastic image in the narrative of Enitharmon's prophetic 'dream' of European history.

One of the most beautiful but also one of the most puzzling plates in this visually magnificent but extremely enigmatic poem is plate 6 [7], to use Dorrbecker's numbering from his facsimile of Copy B (in BA [B], plate 6; in E, 62; plate 4).[1] This plate is puzzling for a number of reasons. First, visual and verbal accounts of the same 'event' do not quite coincide. Second, the visual illumination itself offers at least two possible representations of a temporal narrative. Third, Blake's visual illumination represents Enitharmon to our gaze in a way that opposes, even undermines, the speech that she begins just above the illumination and continues below the half-page illumination on the next plate. Finally, the plate questions more radically our epistemologies of space and time as it participates in prophetic, millennial, and apocalyptic discourses.

In the Preludium to *Europe* (BA [B]: 3–4; E 60–1: 1–2), the Shadowy Female has already raised the theme of binding in a call to her 'mother Enitharmon'. Whether her call for help historically precedes and prompts Enitharmon's actions as response in the main 'Prophecy', or whether the 'response' is an explanatory narrative history of her plight is not at all clear. This obscurity and indeterminacy, more than clear prediction of future events, characterises prophecy (Mee, 25; Balfour, 1) and especially this one (Rajan, *Supplement*, 253–62; *Vision*, 394–6). Lamenting her physical and psychological burden in giving birth to a succession of 'howling terrors, all devouring fiery kings' (see Swearingen, 112 and Wright, 94–6), the Shadowy Female is ambivalent toward Enitharmon's responsibilities in this female economy. Asking her to 'Stamp not with solid form this vig'rous progeny of fires' (BA[B]: 4:8; E 61; 2:8), she pleads that her progeny be left unbound. Asking in line 13, 'who shall bind the infinite with an eternal band? / To compass it with swaddling bands? And who shall cherish it / With milk and honey?' she may suggest that such binding is a nurturing and not

wholly counter-revolutionary civilising. If we relate this binding or stamping not only to the enslaving shown in the *Visions of the Daughters of Albion*,
but also to the 'bounding line' that defines Blake's own graphic art, then
Enitharmon's aesthetic and cultural work is indeed linked to spatiality as
the later Enitharmon's will be, but in a dominant instead of a subordinate
role.

With the opening of the main 'Prophecy', the descent of a 'secret child'
resembling the infant Christ in Milton's ode 'On the Morning of Christ's
Nativity' may be either one more example of the problem the Shadowy
Female complains about, or a special case that will meet and address her
call for help – for a prophetic response, as Balfour suggests (137). This mysterious child may be a Christ-child full of revolutionary potential that will
be distorted in the following 1800 years by his organized church, an infant
Orc with similar potential, or even an adolescent Orc mysteriously descending in the 1780s (Tannenbaum, 168; Lawson, 46; Ferber, 215–19). Though
his arrival makes war cease, the maintaining of that peace is quickly linked,
on the next plate, to the ambiguities of binding and unbinding.

On the next plate, which will be the major focus of my analysis, responsibility for binding and unbinding loosens further, as verbal text and visual
illumination represent this responsibility with different presumptions of
narrative action. When Los, another character developed in this poem,
opens the festivities to celebrate the 'secret child's' descent, he extends the
range of significance for 'binding' from the ambiguous constraints upon
the 'fiery kings' to a festival of the arts: 'Seize all the spirits of life and bind
/ Their warbling joys to our loud strings / Bind all the nourishing sweets
of earth / To give us bliss. . . .' (lines 6–9; see Swearingen, 114). He then
adds to this complexity by calling Orc as if he is one of those 'fiery kings'
already bound by Enitharmon: 'Arise O Orc from thy deep den, / First born
of Enitharmon, rise! And we will bind thy head with garlands of the ruddy
vine; / For now thou art bound; / And I may see thee in the hour of bliss,
my eldest son' (10–14). The primary binding civilises or imprisons, while
the second celebrates the ensuing peace. Los neither explains who has
bound their son, nor whether Orc will share their 'bliss' nor how the 'rising'
can take place within the framework of binding – unless he sees the incarnation of the secret child as Orc's binding into material form. Clearly,
however, he approves the process. As the verbal text continues, Orc responds
to Los's call as if challenging both levels of binding: 'The horrent Demon
rose, surrounded with red stars of fire, / Whirling about in furious circles
round the immortal fiend' (15–16). And then, responding to this display of
energy, 'Enitharmon down descended into his red light, / And . . . her voice
rose to her children . . .' These lines, enclosed in a cloud-like white space
with a sky-blue background in copy B, occupy the top half of the plate.[2]

Below the plate's verbal, 'heavenly' text, the illumination shows the gold
and 'red light' of Orc's earthly den, though Orc himself still sleeps, in a

cooler, twilight blue space. A sensuous female nude with flowing hair, almost as provocative as the writhing Oothoon in *Visions of the Daughters of Albion*, Enitharmon hovers on a cloud over the still-sleeping, face-down figure of Orc. Held in her hands is a cloak or blanket, creating for our view a diagonal line separating the two figures; she either covers or uncovers him. As Enitharmon rests upon gold clouds that cluster above that diagonal line, just above her, smaller figures dance on the right and left, collapsed on the left in the gold light that emanates from Orc's halo of flames or from Enitharmon's fiery cloud. Like any visual image, the illumination stops time and in a broad sense stops history; but this one also redirects the verbal narrative above it. It pivots between the narrator's report that the 'Horrent Demon rose' at Los's call and Enitharmon's own call on line 18 and on the following plate: 'thus her voice rose to her children. . . . who shall I call? Who shall I send? That Woman . . . may have dominion?' To illustrate the first, Enitharmon's act should be an uncovering, but an uncovering of a civilised Orc who need be bound only with the Dionysian 'garlands of the ruddy vine' (BA [B] 6:11); to illustrate the second, her act should be a covering, a reinforcement of woman's dominion and a damping of the 'red stars of fire / Whirling about in furious circles round' Orc (BA [B] 6:15–6).

Though critics have argued whether Enitharmon can see Orc beyond her veil or not, the point is almost an academic one, as Blake directs our gazes: we look at her, and only then follow the direction of her gaze. From her image alone, we might think that Enitharmon is an unbound, released Oothoon or Earth, celebrating her sexual freedom, and thus continuous with Blake's advocacy of sexual, political, and imaginative liberty in his earlier works. The figures look like lovers, resembling representations of Psyche gazing at the sleeping Eros (for the critical history, see Dorrbecker, 183; Okada, 41–5). Yet the verbal narrative in the cloud-frame at the top of the plate tells us that Enitharmon gazes at her son. In a carefully-historicised reading of verbal and visual propaganda during the 1780s and 1790s, Helen Bruder traces how almost all parties in the revolutionary era figure illegitimate power as unleashed female sexuality and thus call 'Womans love . . . Sin' (BA[B]: 7:5; E 62; 5:5; Bruder, 169). In this plate, she argues, the suggestion of incest reflects Blake's sympathetic rethinking of graphic and verbal attacks on Marie Antoinette for molesting her very young son. Thus Blake identifies Enitharmon both with the propaganda of a sexually-licentious Marie Antoinette and also, in the following plates, with her reconstructed image as a domestic, virtuous mother repressing sexuality. He does so, in Bruder's reading, to show a Wollstonecraft-like critical sympathy for both libertine and domestic versions of her constructedness. While I agree with much of this reading, I would interpret Enitharmon's gazing at Orc as developing a further mythic momentum that recognises, as *America* only begins to, the dangers of anarchic, liberated desire. Thus the illumination represents not so much a queen's patriarchal construction by false propaganda as a

Phaedra-complex, in which she confronts the consciousness of her own desire and – unlike Phaedra – overreacts in covering it again.

For at this point, I see Enitharmon as a prophet who attempts, as Blake himself does, to confront and give some form or limit to the violence of revolutionary desire but who intervenes and overreacts in her aesthetic agency. Because the last phrase in the verbal text above Enitharmon on plate 6 [7] is 'the distant heavens reply' (to her voice rising to her children), Wright argues that the speech on the next page is spoken by a Urizenic voice from the 'heavens' that opposes Enitharmon's joyous, lyrical account of communal existence in her 'crystal house' – and thus that the speech's agenda of sexual repression, secrecy, and manipulative entrapping 'nets' is not hers. Though there is indeed ambiguity about who utters this prophetic speech, as about several other speeches in the poem (Wright, 72–4; Dorrbecker, 154–5; Bruder, 160–2), the indirect discourse of Enitharmon's later dream-thoughts and speeches on plates 14:25–31 and 16:22 (BA[B]; E 64:12, 66; 14), *pace* Wright (xx), support its views. Here, as later, the 'night of Enitharmon's joy' is a prophetic vision of desire evoked and then exploited, bound by woman's power: 'Who shall I call? Who shall I send? / That Woman, lovely Woman, may have dominion / Arise, O Rintrah thee I call! & Palamabron, thee! / Go, tell the human race that Womans love is Sin.'

Enitharmon's verbal message to her sons recalls in a complex way Blake's visual image of her on the preceding plate, for it is '*lovely* Woman', the object of a male gaze (or any reader's gaze, for that matter) who will dominate in Enitharmon's envisioned regime through her desirability (see Bruder, 169). The last line of this passage also exploits the ambiguities of the preceding illumination: 'Womans love is Sin!' Her syntax suggests that women are both objects and subjects of desire. As subject, however, Enitharmon re-directs the male gaze that exploits and dominates women to a female gaze of surveillance that sublimates her own desire into a power to regulate the current chaos of revolutionary desire. As Wright argues, then, Enitharmon indeed thinks that the songs, dances, and communal revelry in her moonlit crystal house should be normative – but she herself replaces Orc as a messiah-figure and as her own evangelist, seeking to colonise Orc's earthly terrain of human existence – hence her call for prophets. This interpretation converts the undecidability of Enitharmon's visual gesture on plate 6 (7) – either a covering or an uncovering – into a decided narrative sequence: she uncovers and then re-covers Orc.

This temporal narrative pressure, however, does not fully account for the visual ambiguity or power of interruption in the design. For the mode of prophecy, as Ian Balfour has shown, interrupts linear time with spatial, visual pauses to point toward a redefining of that linear time (95–105). And as Morton Paley has pointed out, if Enitharmon uncovers Orc in the illumination, she enacts the root meaning of the word 'apocalypse' and thus anticipates the confusingly-motivated beginning of apocalypse at the end

of the poem (64). Both her visual gesture and her ensuing verbal pro-
nouncements enter the discourse of prophecy, millenarianism, and apocalypse described by Paley, Behrendt, Mee, and others, a discourse both visual
and verbal that develops in the 1790s to frame and interpret the enormous upheaval of the French Revolution. Enitharmon participates in
that discourse as prophet, intervening in history's temporal sequence. We
might see Los as an accidental apocalypticist and Enitharmon as a post-
millenialist, delaying the second coming of this ambiguously messianic Orc
until her prophetic injunctions to her other sons have created a decorous,
dualist culture dominated by women (for this terminology, see Behrendt,
381 and Mee, 36–7).

Though she falls asleep in the middle of this call to her more docile sons
to promulgate her doctrine, she dreams prophetically of its fulfilment.
Because her dream seems to be our linear history, an envisioned salvation-
narrative for Enitharmon but almost a damnation-narrative for us, and
because it brings us – Blake's audience – up to the present time of 1794,
focusing more on the recent past of the 1780s, we see it as determined. Yet
because for Enitharmon her dream is a prophetic vision of how the future
might be, it is ironically open to her – or even our – acting otherwise, as
the people of Nineveh chose to do after Jonah's warning. Thus, though
narrated in a past tense, it offers opportunities for re-visioning, either for
alternate futures from 1794 or for alternative understanding of the time
before that.

The latter possibility is demonstrated within her prophecy of history to
come, as the narrator's voice explains her dream with an ancient history
apparently preceding any of the poem's events thus far. Equally negative
in its account of binding, this ur-history questions Enitharmon's agency
and her erotic economy. Further, it develops through an iconic emblem, an
architectural monument that employs fixity in space as a negating limit
linked to male repressive power. This emblem is the serpent-temple, the
pre-Christian locus of natural religion (Smiles, 84–96; Mee, 81–6), to which
Albion's angels retreat to plan further repressive measures after the barely-
mentioned success of Orc's American revolution. No illumination in *Europe*
illustrates this verbally described temple, though its history recontextu-
alises three of the work's most magnificent illuminations: the serpent
coiling up the left margin of this plate (BA[B]11), the one on the title page,
and the frontispiece deity with his compasses: 'Thought chang'd the infinite into a serpent', the universe takes on its Newtonian shape of 'earths
rolling in circles of space', and humans are bound into 'this finite wall of
flesh. / Then was the serpent temple form'd, image of infinite / Shut up in
finite revolutions, and man become an Angel; / Heaven a Mighty circle
turning; God a tyrant crown'd' (BA [B] 11: 16–23).

If this mythic fall precedes the birth of the secret child and Enitharmon's
prophecies of a millennium in which all are bound primarily by women's

repression of sexuality, then she would seem to speak for that Urizenic 'tyrant crown'd', even if she believes her mission and her imagination are independent. If the myth is also an account of the much more recent Enlightenment with its Lockean binding of the five senses and a Newtonian regulation of the cosmos (see Mulvahill, 393), then her binding of sexuality and imagination has led to that later binding and determined our 'finite' perceptions of self, community, and universe. In the first case, we might see her more easily as a victim or puppet of patriarchy. In the second case, she becomes a more autonomous, more powerful figure, prophetically imagining an Enlightenment space and time, and prompting with her binding and swaddling the dubious creative acts of the father deity.

With this prophetic dream of alternate yet interlocking myths of binding, an even more ambiguous uncovering or unbinding completes the process marked by Enitharmon's hesitating cloak on plate 6 [7]. If her efforts to manage revolutionary desire in a peaceful millennium have failed, Blake's allowing her the agency to test these efforts has revealed to his audience, if not at first to her, the intricate networks of dependency and complicity in our fallen constructions of a European culture. At a moment in our history when we debate how to respond to terror and yet preserve a glimpse of human capabilities for cooperative liberty, perhaps Blake's own ambivalence in 1794 offers consolation.

Notes

1. See Viscomi (275–9) for a description of copies and the Blake Archive for colour facsimiles of Copies B, E, H, and K.
2. By hypothesising that her claim to prophetic autonomy is in some sense positive, I would modify Saree Makdisi's argument (11, 38ff.) that Blake already challenges an individuating imagination – precisely because Enitharmon's dream-vision does indeed lead to a critique of the Lockean senses.

References

Balfour, Ian, *The Rhetoric of Romantic Prophecy* (Stanford, CA: Stanford University Press, 2002).

Behrendt, Stephen, 'History When Time Stops: Blake's *America, Europe,* and *The Song of Los*', *Papers on Language and Literature*, 28: 4 (Fall 1992), 379–92.

Blake, William, *Europe*, The William Blake Archive, eds Morris Eaves Robert N. Essick and Joseph Viscomi, 5 September 2005, http://www.blakearchive.org.

Bruder, Helen P., *William Blake and the Daughters of Albion* (New York: St Martin's Press, 1997).

Dorrbecker, D.W. (ed.), 'Introduction', in *William Blake: the Continental Prophecies* (The William Blake Trust: Princeton, NJ: Princeton University Press, 1995).

Ferber, Michael, 'The Finite Revolutions of *Europe*', in Jackie Di Salvo et al. (eds), *Blake, Politics, History* (New York: Garland, 1998), pp. 212–34.

Lawson, Bruce, 'Blake's *Europe* and his "Corrective" Illustrations to Milton's *Nativity Ode*', *Mosaic*, 25: 1 (1992), 45–61.

Makdisi, Saree, *William Blake and the Impossibility of the 1790s* (Chicago: University of Chicago Press, 2003).

Mee, Jon, *Dangerous Enthusiasm: William Blake and the Culture of Radicalism in the 1790s* (1992; reprinted Oxford: Clarendon Paperback, 1994).

Mitchell, W.J.T., *Iconology: Image, Text, Ideology* (Chicago: University of Chicago Press, 1986).

Mulvahill, James, ' "The History of All Times and Places": William Blake and Historical Representation in *America* and *Europe*', *CLIO*, 29: 4 (2000), 373–94.

Okada, Kazuda, 'Orc Under a Veil Revealed: Family Relationships and their Symbols in *Europe* and *The Book of Urizen*', *BQ*, 34 (Fall 2000), 36–45.

Paley, Morton, *Apocalypse and Millennium in English Romantic Poetry* (Oxford: Clarendon, 1999).

Rajan, Tillotama, *The Supplement of Reading: Figures of Understanding in Romantic Theory and Practice* (Ithaca: Cornell University Press, 1990).

Rajan, Tillotama, 'Disfiguring the System: Vision, History, and Trauma in Blake's Lambeth Books', *Huntington Library Quarterly*, 58: 3–4 (1996), 383–411.

Smiles, Sam, *The Image of Antiquity: Ancient Britons and the Romantic Imagination* (New Haven: Yale University Press, 1994).

Swearingen, James E., 'Time and History in Blake's *Europe*' *CLIO*, 20: 2 (1991), 109–21.

Tannenbaum, Leslie, *Biblical Tradition in Blake's Early Prophecies* (Princeton, NJ: Princeton University Press, 1982).

Viscomi, Joseph, *Blake and the Idea of the Book* (Princeton, NJ: Princeton University Press, 1993).

Wright, Julia, *Blake, Nationalism, and the Politics of Alienation* (Athens, Ohio: Ohio University Press, 2004).

10

'No Earthly Parents I confess': the Clod, the Pebble and Catherine Blake

Germaine Greer

Catherine Blake is agreed to have been 'one of the best wives that ever fell to the lot of a man of genius'.[1] She was William Blake's pupil and disciple, his domestic servant, his technical assistant and the silent companion of his sleepless nights. She existed to satisfy his wants, having apparently no wants of her own. There are those who say that she was happy to sit naked outdoors with her husband, and those who say that this is a vile libel on both of them.[2] Best of all, for the wife of a man of genius, she was childless. If there had been hungry children in the house, Catherine could hardly have spent one shilling and ten pence out of the family's last half-crown on the materials that would go into the printing of *The Songs of Innocence and of Experience*.[3]

How the Blakes' childlessness was achieved is a matter seldom discussed by Blake scholars. When William and Catherine were married in August 1782, she was just twenty and he was five years older. In the normal course of events their first child would have been christened within two years of the wedding, but no child was ever to arrive. This may have been because one or other partner was infertile, though primary infertility in young people is very rare. Still, as none of William's siblings was to produce offspring either, we might suspect the existence of a congenital or genetic factor in William's case. The chemicals that were used in engraving might also have played some part in reducing the Blakes' fertility. No sign of hope for children or of disappointment in having none is to be found in Blake's personal writings. The apparent lack of regret on either side suggests that the Blakes' childlessness might have been deliberately contrived. Their reproductive career was certainly very different from that of their parents.

Willliam's father James Blake was a year younger than his wife Catherine, who was about thirty when he married her in 1752; her relatively advanced age would prove a limiting factor on their fertility. Their first child was born nine months later on 10 July 1853, their second on 12 May 1755, their third, William, on 28 November 1757, their fourth on 20 March 1760, their fifth on 19 June 1762, their sixth on 7 January 1764, and their seventh on 4 August 1767. There the elder Blakes' reproductive career came to an end. The spacing of the births, such as it was, was probably the effect of breast-feeding, and later of the elder Catherine Blake's reduced fertility as she approached menopause. The second and fourth of the babies died young. The seventh was Robert, who became William's soulmate, only to die in William's house in 1787 when he was nineteen.

The elder Blakes with their five surviving offspring achieved a fairly respectable family size for people of their class. The Boucher family may be considered typical of families of a lower class, with thirteen children, eleven surviving, none of whom received any formal education. Catherine was the last-born of the Boucher children. The concern shown by the elder Blakes when 25-year-old William decided to marry her probably had as much to do with a perception that the couple would follow the family-building pattern of the feckless poor as with plain class prejudice. This prejudice was to follow Catherine all her life. Few of her words are ever reported but, when they are, her lower-class speech patterns are usually, and unkindly, repli-cated. Crabb Robinson reports her reminding her husband of the first time he had a vision of God: 'You know, dear, the first time you saw God was when you were four years old and He put his head to the window and set you a-screaming.'[4] When the couple were living in neglect and poverty, Catherine is said to have explained their evident failure to wash as being because 'Mr Blake's skin don't dirt.'[5]

The story of how Blake came to marry Catherine is often told. In the summer of 1781 he was rooming in the house of her father, a market gardener at Battersea, by way of enjoying a restorative holiday.

> He was relating to the daughter, a Girl named Catherine, the lamentable story of Polly Wood, his implacable Lass, upon which Catherine expressed her deep sympathy, it is supposed, in such a tender and affectionate manner, that it quite won on him, he immediately said, with the sud-denness peculiar to him, 'Do you pity me?' 'Yes indeed, I do,' answered she. 'Then I love you,' said he again. Such was their courtship.[6]

According to Fuseli, Blake married 'a maidservant';[7] as the youngest child of an already over-burdened labouring man, Catherine is almost certain to have been placed in service by the age of eleven or even before. William may have been truly blind to class difference but, by marrying Catherine, he secured for himself for life an unpaid assistant and maid-of-all-work. 'She prepared his colours, and was as good as a servant. He had no other.'[8] In a letter of 1802, William Hayley sang her praises to Lady Hesketh:

> the good woman not only does all the work of the House, but she even makes the greatest part of her Husbands dress, & assists him in *his art* –

she draws, she engraves, & sings delightfully & is so fully the Half of her good Man, that they seem animated by one Soul . . .'[9]

Without Catherine beside him William could not have moved out of his elder brother's house and set up an independent household. Though she was no more likely than any other servant to accompany him to Mrs Mathews's salons where he recited and sang his poems, as he was incapable of making himself comfortable anywhere without her assistance, whenever he travelled she had to go with him. He taught her to read and write, and to draw and colour his engravings.

Catherine was a pretty dark-eyed thing when William married her in 1782.

She lost her beauty as the seasons sped – 'never saw a woman so much altered' was the impression of one on meeting her after a lapse of but seven years . . .'[10]

Others remarked on her 'dirty' and 'poor' clothing. As Blake was to write in his copy of Lavater:

Let men do their duty & the women will be such wonders; the female life lives from the light of the male: see a man's female dependents, you know the man.[11]

Catherine mirrored her man in everything. She believed literally in his visions, and she espoused all of his beliefs. She echoed what he said and expressed herself in the same terms.[12] Her fervour in voicing her husband's convictions regardless of the circumstances twice placed her husband in jeopardy.[13] In Catherine's clamouring there is an element of unconscious parody that derives from her inability to criticise William on any ground. So far over the top did she go that some believed she was by far the madder of the two.[14] When William could not sleep, Catherine rose with him and sat by him for hours on end without moving or speaking as he drew and wrote. When their income dwindled, instead of going out to work (as she would do after his death) she sat and starved with him.[15] Contemporaries visiting them found this togetherness quaint; according to Yeats it was ideal, but according to others Blake chafed at the aridity of their intercourse, and longed for female company of a different kind, even suggesting to Catherine that he bring another woman into the house.

Blake had married a woman whom he could dominate unconsciously and absolutely, and for this there was a price. Because of his absolute dependence on her, Catherine could confine and limit him. Blake was no more likely to have had a liaison with Mary Wollstonecraft than he was with Polly Wood; if he entered into a relationship with Wollstonecraft it would have been stormy, but ultimately liberating. Catherine's self-abnegating devotion nailed his feet to the floor. In later life she drew him as Apollo/ Alexander, huge-eyed, browless, with hair like flame, in god-like profile.[16] The Blakes' does indeed seem to have been a marriage of heaven and hell, of deep communion otherwise known as stifling possessiveness.

After Blake's death, Catherine worked for the family of the painter John Linnell as a housekeeper, and apparently an efficient one, though she claimed that she was obliged to sit in communion with her dead husband for two or three hours each day.[17] When it came to selling his works she would do nothing without consulting her own projection of him. All his life he had been dual-voiced, both male and female; now, with all that she had absorbed from him, she was able to be him and for the first time to be herself, a transformation that Blake would have been the first to understand. People who knew her as a widow did not recognise her in J.T. Smith's account of her as Blake's submissive wife.[18]

No aspect of a marriage is more mysterious than the sexual relationship of the spouses. The Blakes' failure to have children is usually assumed to be Catherine's failure. Some commentators have suggested that Catherine did indeed conceive only to miscarry. Edwin J. Ellis believes that Catherine and William quarrelled so violently over the suggestion that William should take a concubine, that Catherine fell and lost her baby.[19] Kerrison Preston accepts the far-fetched hypothesis as consensus.[20] Wicksteed takes a contrary view, that Blake suggested taking a second sexual partner because his 'reading of the Old Testament and his own reasoning convinced him that a childless wife should delight "to give her maiden to her husband"'.[21] Foster Damon interprets *The Book of Thel* 'with its strange ending [as] an elegy to the Blakes' dead daughter, their only offspring'.[22] A still-born child of the Blakes would have had to be buried. Parish records and lying-in books have been searched and yield nothing.[23]

Secondary infertility, that is, female infertility resulting from infection after childbirth, miscarriage or stillbirth is much commoner than primary infertility. If Catherine did indeed conceive only to miscarry, it is likely to have been in the first years of her married life. If she conceived for the first time just prior to the writing of *The Book of Thel*, which was etched in 1789, six or seven years into the marriage, the relationship is already markedly subfertile. Contraception was certainly possible in the 1780s; Francis Place, an early pioneer of birth control, lived only a few doors away from the Blakes. Though Malthus had not yet published, Malthusian ideas were in the air. The progressives and radicals whose company Blake frequented had begun to discuss the possibility of sex without pregnancy or the fear of pregnancy. If the Blakes had deliberately avoided conception by any of the means then available, the result is more likely to have been fewer children than no children at all. The methods available to them were: complete abstinence from sexual relations, periodic abstinence from sexual relations, abstinence periodic or complete from vaginal penetration, avoidance of ejaculation within the vagina, or various barrier methods, pessaries and condoms. Many wives were spared pregnancy by their husbands' resort to anal and oral intercourse, or to coitus interruptus, all of which were condemned by organised religion as perversions.

It is more difficult to imagine a character as rhapsodic as Blake consenting to employ the kinds of self-discipline that were becoming commoner as middle-class birth rates begin to fall, than it is to imagine him refraining from intravaginal intercourse altogether. The notion of the Blakes being in the habit of sitting together outdoors stark naked reinforces the idea of abstinence rather than indulgence. (One is reminded of Gandhi sleeping with his grand-daughters to prove that he had conquered the desires of the flesh.) Blake is usually thought of as a champion of sexual love, but it may have been, like the rest of Blake's universe, in his head. One thing is certain; the birthing mother gives birth to a creature that must die. Blake had lost two siblings, that we know of, before his beloved brother Robert died slowly and painfully in his arms. One way to construe Thel's journey in *The Book of Thel* is to interpret it as a baffled quest for pregnancy.

> Then Thel astonish'd view'd the Worm upon its dewy bed.
>
> Art thou a Worm? Image of weakness, art thou but a Worm?
> I see thee like an infant wrapped in the Lilly's leaf:
> Ah! weep not, little voice, thou canst not speak, but thou canst
>   weep.
> Is this a Worm? I see thee lay helpless & naked: weeping,
> And none to answer, none to cherish thee with mother's smiles'
>
> (E 5)

The salient fact about Thel is that, though she is within a hollow vale, the traditional setting for the complaint of the seduced and abandoned woman, she is a milk-white virgin looking for a meaning in her life. The lily and the cloud both advise her in their different ways to preserve her virginity and its promise of immortality. She is unswayed.

> But Thel delights in these no more because I fade away
> And all shall say, without a use this shining woman liv'd,
> Or did she only live to be at death the food of worms.
>
> (E 5)

Enter the weeping worm, of the same tribe as those that would consume the virgin, who would pass through their guts in death as in life mother's milk becomes infant excrement. Those in search of Freudian symbols have here a plethora, the worm within the leaf as infant within the womb, the mother as eaten and defecated by the infant.

> The Clod of Clay heard the Worms voice & rais'd her pitying head;
> She bow'd over the weeping infant, and her life exhal'd
> In milky fondness, then on Thel she fix'd her humble eyes.
>
> (E 6)

This Clod of Clay is the same Clod of Clay that sings the song of altruism in 'The Clod and the Pebble'. Here too she sings the song of mother love; clods live not for themselves, but are trodden into cold obscurity, understanding nothing of their own function.

> I ponder, and I cannot ponder; yet I live and love.
>
> (E 6)

Seduced into self-sacrifice the virgin enters the Clod's realm of death, where nothing is to be heard but the sound of mourning, breathing out from (the same) hollow pit, a series of questions about human destiny.

> Why a tender curb on the youthful burning boy!
> Why a little curtain of flesh on the bed of our desire?
>
> (E 6)

The conclusion, that desire is thwarted by carnality, cannot sensibly be interpreted as a defence of carnality. The terrified virgin shrieks and escapes from the Clod's realm of base embodiment towards eternal life. The same linking of childbirth with the imposition of mortality can be found in 'To Tirzah':

> Thou Mother of my Mortal part.
> With cruelty didst mould my Heart.
> And with false self-deceiving tears,
> Didst bind my Nostril, Eyes & Ears.
>
> Didst close my Tongue in senseless clay
> And me to Mortal Life betray:
>
> (E 30)

Citing another passage from *Jerusalem*, James King remarks, 'Consistently, Blake looked at the phenomena of birth and creation with a jaundiced eye, as in Jerusalem where a foetus is compared to a malignant tumour.'[24]

In view of the fact that Blake regarded death as a minor transmutation, which could easily be negated by returning in visions, human offpsring were surplus to requirements. Instead of living children, Catherine would have William's spiritual presence after his death. As an allegorical dissuasive from pregnancy *The Book of Thel* would, one imagines, be pretty effective, and not all that far-fetched. Factually, to be pregnant is to be closer to death, to be an object of terror and suspicion as well as veneration.

Catherine might well have accepted William's refusal to make her pregnant in the earlier years of their marriage quite readily, but after five years or so she might well have begun to grieve and complain. Dissension between them is recorded; we know that it was not about money, or religion or politics. In all these Catherine followed William's lead without demur; we would be surprised if her desire for children was so easily banished. This can be no more than hypothesis, but as a hypothesis it should be borne in mind.

In all Blake's work we may trace the same flight from carnality, nowhere more than in his graphic art. Blake's bodies are not bodies but emanations: they have no navels and small, veiled or (in the case of women) non-existent genitals. The male figures have nipples sometimes, the females never. All are blonde, free of body hair. None is studied from life. All are reworked, and often anatomically impossible, types. Yet in the popular imagination Blake is considered a hero of sexual liberation, perhaps because his ideal of gratification is dissociated from reproduction, and possibly also because it is free of any identification with any particular way of sex. As Blake contests the idea of guilt, he is also taken to assert the values of libertarianism, including those of sexual freedom. Yet he had no partner but Catherine; he said that he would have shared her with another man with perfect equanimity, and perhaps he would have. This would be more likely if he had no interest in her issue. Sharing Catherine with another man might have been as easy for William as sharing her with a baby might have been difficult.

The Clod of Clay resurfaces in 1794, when Catherine and William collaborated on the 'Songs of Experience' and began to issue the whole sequence as *Songs of Innocence and of Experience: Shewing the Two Contrary States of the Human Soul.*

The CLOD & the PEBBLE.

Love seeketh not Itself to please,
Nor for itself hath any care;
But for another gives its ease,
And builds a Heaven in Hells despair.

So sung a little Clod of Clay,
Trodden with the cattles feet:

But a Pebble of the brook,
Warbled out these metres meet.

Love seeketh only Self to please,
To bind another to Its delight:
Joys in anothers loss of ease,
And builds a Hell in Heavens despite.

(E 19)

In this tiny fable, here transcribed exactly as Blake wrote it onto the copper plate, the song of the clod can be seen to be a song of innocence, and the song of the pebble a song of experience, the ideal contradicted by the real, encapsulating and compressing the whole schema of *Songs of Innocence and of Experience* into a single poem no longer than a nursery rhyme. Blake's publishing practice, however, gives little justification for seeing the poem as a summary of the whole series. In most of Catherine Blake's printings 'The Clod and the Pebble' appears as the second of the *Songs of Experience* proper,[25] and this is the practice followed in most modern editions. In three of the surviving copies 'The Clod and the Pebble' is bound as the last of the poems in the combined sequence, immediately before a full page engraving of a naked young man borne up by winged putti, which is not known from any other source.[26] He stands in the striding posture of the young Apollo Belvedere, looking, as the Apollo does, over his left shoulder, but his hands are joined as if in prayer. The figure is beardless, his long hair loosely bound on the nape of his neck. Unusually for Blake, the figure's genitals are not only exposed to view but emphasised by strong shadow. The figure is not identical with Eros, because Eros is usually depicted with his own wings rather than supported by *amorini*. The piety of the posture recalls Guido Reni's *Amor Divino*, also known as *L'Anima Beata*, which in its original form was equally naked.[27]

The stereotyping technique used for printing the *Songs* was crude and laborious. First William dipped his pen into a compound which would resist acid, and wrote the poems and drew the designs on the plate; the rest of the plate was then eaten away with aquafortis, leaving the pen-marks standing proud and ready to take the coloured inks. William had taught Catherine how to ink the plates and how to print them off, and how to embellish them in watercolour. It was Catherine's job to sew the sheets together and attach the endpapers and boards. We have no idea how much initiative she was allowed to show, or whether she and William discussed the order of the poems. Certainly William himself had difficulty deciding on a final order, even switching some poems back and forth between innocence and experience.

Blake's engraving of the poem is a full page image of the brook, dominated by the figures of four sheep and two bullocks, all head down drinking at the water's edge in the upper not-quite half. The poem, divided into three quatrains by fluttering streamers like trailing aquatic plants, is written as it were in or on the brook, while the lower border of the plate is the near edge of the brook, where a female mallard floats, and one frog sits while another leaps into the water, and a fat worm lies at length. Neither the clod nor the pebble can be seen. None of the poems in the sequence is more various in its printed appearance than 'The Clod and the Pebble': the text was printed at different times in green, in gold and in red; the surrounding landscape is sometimes dark and harsh, sometimes ruddy as with sunset, and sometimes mellow and golden. Sometimes the tree in the top right-hand corner is embellished with leaves. The stream may be anything from dark and muddy to sunlit pale blue.

The text as engraved is embedded in the natural world which, as is usual with Blake, is conceptually rather than accurately depicted. Just as we must seek the models for Blake's illustrated types in art rather than nature, his text too is conscientiously literary. His models were not those of his classically educated contemporaries but, though he read neither Latin or Greek, his songs, and in particular, 'The Clod and the Pebble', are examples of truly ancient forms. The extravagance of Blake's enthusiasm for classicism is itself romantic; the political and cultural models followed by the French Revolution were all constructed on a version of classical republicanism. Blake's kind of artistic fundamentalism was, like all fundamentalism, an imaginary return to imaginary beginnings.

Blake wrote the title of his poem in larger characters than the text proper, capitalising the two nouns. He knew that the title, 'The Clod and the Pebble' was enough to apprise his readers that what followed, though mightily compressed, would be a fable. Generally speaking the fable is a fairly wordy construction often beginning with a statement of the moral, then setting the scene, then narrating the events and statements of the proponents, and then restating the moral. The collection known as Aesop's Fables was one of the first books printed in English, which makes it one of the first literary texts to be made available to a public more general than had access to manuscripts, a public that included women and children. The life of Aesop the Phrygian is mostly legend; the fables themselves are both older and younger than Aesop, being gathered from sources as ancient as Hesiod and Aeschylus, as well as from moralists of the middle ages. Caxton's printing of 1484 was the first of hundreds of versions of Aesop in the vernacular. Like the Bible, Aesop was never out of print. Cheap versions, expensive versions, illustrated, versified, even variorum editions of Aesop were to be produced for every generation. The putative readers were children of all ages and, therefore, women.

Aphra Behn provided verse paraphrases of the fables for Francis Barlow's new ployglot edition of 1687, an exercise that forced her to compress the whole action of each prose fable into a single quatrain.

> The wanton Grasshopper implores the Ant
> In winter season to relieve her want,
> But she replyd – thou all the plentious spring
> Tookst care for nought but how to dance and sing.[28]

In the eighteenth century Aesop fed back into English literature via the verse fables of Jean de la Fontaine. The English verse fable is usually written in a narrative metre, in heroic couplets or hudibrastics, and adopts a rallying tone, often rendered burlesque by the use of elaborate rhyme. One of Fontaine's earliest translators who was also to become an imitator and ultimately to write original Jacobite fables of her own was Anne Finch, Countess of Winchilsea.

When Blake was beginning to think about the *Songs of Innocence and of Experience* the bookstalls were loaded with fables ancient and modern, many of them intended for the instruction of the young. One of the most successful publications was Edward Moore's *Fables for the Female Sex*, first published in the 1740s and regularly republished, with three new editions in the 1780s. *Visions in Verse for the Entertainment of Younger Minds* by Nathaniel Cotton the elder, was hugely popular, being regularly republished over more than fifty years. Of particular interest to Blake as he was beginning to think about issuing his own small book may have been the 24-page chapbook selection of Aesop's fables that appeared in 1780.[29] There were also Aesop imitators like 'Abraham Aesop' whose *Fables in Verse for the Improvement of the Young and Old*, first published in 1758, was reprinted in 1765 and 1783. A translation by Robert Lloyd and Charles Dennis of the *Contes Moraux* of Marmontel appeared four times between 1764 and 1790.

In the fable truths of human behaviour are demonstrated by non-human actors, by animals, trees and even insects. Every child of Blake's generation would have known the fables of the hare and the tortoise, with its moral (slow and steady wins the race) and the ant and the grasshopper (*carpe diem*). Blake descends to an even lower order and animates the completely inanimate to give us an assertion made by a lump of clay and a counter-statement made by a pebble. He sets no scene, and supplies no narrative of events, and he draws no moral. Instead both speakers utter their own equally confident generalisations. Normally in a fable the last speaker is in the right; the clod's naivety must be eclipsed by the cynicism of the pebble, but Blake's readers do not get off so lightly.

When the song begins we do not know who is speaking, or, given Blake's orthography, that anyone is speaking. So the clod's view of love is presented to us without context, as a generalisation, a hymnic statement of belief expressed with utter certainty.

> Love seeketh not Itself to please,
> Nor for itself hath any care;
> But for another gives its ease,
> And builds a Heaven in Hells despair.

This version of love is absolutely disinterested, *agape* not *eros*, *caritas* not *amor*. The Clod can be seen to have absorbed the lesson of St Paul's first epistle to the Corinthians:

> Charity suffereth long, and is kind. Charity envieth not. Charity vaunteth not itself, is not puffed up, doth not behave itself unseemly, seeketh not her own, is not easily provoked, thinketh no evil, rejoiceth not in iniquity, but rejoiceth in the truth; beareth all things, believeth all things, hopeth all things, endureth all things. Charity never faileth . . .

Even as we recognise scriptural authority for the Clod's assertion we begin to suspect an element of overstatement. We might agree that love 'seeketh not Itself to please', but doubt whether having no care of oneself at all was entirely a good thing. The quatrain seems to right itself with the idea of building 'a Heaven in Hell's despair' only to wobble, because the idea of a heaven in hell is disturbing. The syntax doesn't allow us to know if it is hell that is driven to despair or if despair is just part of hell. Love that pitches its dwelling in the mansion of perdition could be thought to be looking for comfort in the wrong place. In the teasing ambiguity of these apparently simple lines there is more than a prickle of suggestion that self-sacrificing altruism makes life hell for everyone. It is only when we find out that it is a clod who is speaking, at the beginning of the second quatrain, that we must entertain the suspicion that such orthodoxy serves merely to justify servile inertia.

The convention of speaker A being routed by speaker B was typical of comic verse, as practised by Blake in *An Island in the Moon*:

> *Quid* – O ho, Said Doctor Johnson
> 　To Scipio Africanus
> 　If you don't own me a Philosopher
> 　Ill kick your Roman Anus
> *Suction* – A ha' To Doctor Johnson
> 　Said Scipio Africanus
> 　Lift up my Roman Petticoatt
> 　And kiss my Roman Anus

(E 458)

The joke turns on the substitution of so few words in the second stanza in order completely to contradict the first, a trick that Blake repeats in 'The Clod and the Pebble'.

The apparent simplicity that 'The Clod and the Pebble' shares with the rest of the *Songs of Innocence and of Experience* owes less to comic verse however than to Blake's experience of two kinds of popular verse, the hymn and the ballad. His recourse to common metre, the four-stressed quatrain rhyming alternately, is tantamount to a confession of didactic intent. The chime creates an instant mnemonic, but ultimately the suggestion of certainty is undermined by a suggestion of facetiousness.

> So sung a little Clod of Clay,
> Trodden with the cattles feet:
> But a Pebble of the brook,
> Warbled out these metres meet.

The barbarism 'sung' for 'sang' is the first indication of instability in the poem's argument. 'Trodden with' instead of 'trodden by' is also oddly vernacular, not to mention the unsyntactic colon followed by a 'But' that does not contradict or modify what goes before. Syntactically no conjunction is needed; the 'but' serves only to strengthen the impression of refutation, which is then belied by the tinge of vulgarity in 'warbled out' and the patness of 'metres meet', as it were, 'tra-la-la'. What the Pebble then warbles is anything but melodic:

> Love seeketh only Self to please,
> To bind another to Its delight:
> Joys in anothers loss of ease,
> And builds a Hell in Heavens despite.

The staccato succession of strenuous glottals, alternating with plosives and continuants, strung on snaking long vowels, strikes the ear like an assault, the words having to be hissed out as if through clenched teeth. The flat contradiction of the famous Pauline definition is shocking enough without the suggestion of bitter rage that peaks in the word 'Hell', balanced on the caesura in the final line. The poem remains gnomic; as its simple cadences reverberate we are left to wonder whether perfect love is impossible for fallen human nature, whether self-sacrifice is not always disguised self-interest, whether Blake did not have to pay a high price in loss of freedom for Catherine's devotion, or whether Catherine did not have to pay an even higher one. One way to interpret the belief that Catherine and William Blake were animated by 'a single soul' is to conclude that one soul cannibalised the other. We shall never know which cannibalised which.

Notes

1. *DNB*, 'William Blake'.
2. The anecdote is attributed to Thomas Butts by Alexander Gilchrist, but later denied by Samuel Palmer and John Linnell; see G.E. Bentley Jr, *Blake Records* (Oxford: Clarendon, 1969), 53–4, and *Blake Records Supplement* (Oxford: Clarendon, 1988), 11–12.
3. J.T. Smith, *Blake Records*, 32.
4. Crabb Robinson, *Blake Records*, 542–3.
5. George Richmond, *Blake Records*, 294.
6. Frederick Tatham, *Blake Records*, 517–18.
7. Reported by Joseph Faringdon in his diary, *Blake Records*, 52.
8. Seymour Stocker Kirkup, writing to Swinburne, *Blake Records*, 221–2.
9. *Blake Records*, 106.
10. *Blake Records*, 24. Bentley, quoting Gilchrist, appears to think that the observer was John Flaxman, who had been in Italy from 1787 to 1794.
11. Quoted by Alicia Ostriker, 'Desire Gratified and Ungratified: William Blake and Sexuality', in Hazard Adams (ed.), *Critical Essays on William Blake* (Boston, MA: H.K. Hall and Co., 1991), 104.
12. Gilchrist, *Blake Records*, 237, 245, 399.
13. *Blake Records*, 124–5, 236–7.
14. George Cumberland to his son, *Blake Records*, 236.
15. Samuel Palmer, *Blake Records*, 276.
16. Now in the Fitzwilliam Museum, Cambridge.
17. *Blake Records*, 373–4.
18. Joseph Hogarth, *Blake Records*, 374.
19. Edwin J. Ellis, *The Real Blake* (London, 1907), 90–1.
20. Kerrison Preston, *Blake and Rossetti* (London: Alexander Moring Ltd, 1944), 29.
21. Joseph Wicksteed, *William Blake's 'Jerusalem'* (London: Trianon, 1954), 215.
22. S. Foster Damon, *A Blake Dictionary: the Ideas and Symbols of William Blake* (Providence, RI: Brown University Press, 1988), 401.
23. Tristanne J. Connolly, *William Blake and the Body* (Basingstoke: Palgrave, 2002), 107–8.
24. James King, *William Blake: His Life* (London: Weidenfeld and Nicolson, 1991), 11.
25. Newhaven, Yale Center for British Art, B1978.43.1546–1579; Cambridge, Fitzwilliam Museum, Department of Paintings, Drawings and Prints, P124–1950 (two copies); Washington DC, Library of Congress, Lessing J. Rosenwald Collection, PR4144.S6 1826.
26. Washington DC, Library of Congress, Lessing J. Rosenwald Collection, PR4144.S6 1794 (1789, 1794).
27. Reproduced in G. Greer, *The Boy* (London: Thames and Hudson, 2003), 90–1.
28. G. Greer (ed.), *The Uncollected Verse of Aphra Behn* (Stump Cross: Stump Cross Books, 1989), 75, 192.
29. BL chapbook 1780 12315.aaa.6 (8).

11
The Impact of Feminism on Blake Studies in Japan

Yoko Ima-Izumi

'How would you describe the state of feminist Blake criticism in Japan? Is it prosperous?' That was the last question addressed to me when I was about to close my presentation at the International Conference on 'Blake in the Orient', which was held in Kyoto, Japan, in 2003. My answer was 'No, it is not. The paucity of women who are involved in studying Blake from the feminist point of view is startling.' I expected a follow-up question, such as: 'About how many women are involved in feminist Blake criticism in your country?' But time was up, and I did not have a chance to elaborate on the state of feminist Blake scholarship in Japan. This chapter will serve as a full answer to this question.

The history of Japanese Blake studies from a feminist perspective can be divided into five distinctive periods, each lasting about twenty years and each including important developments – except for the first period, where feminism had no public visibility:

I	1893–1909
II	1910–32
III	1933–59
IV	1960–83
V	1984–present

The first period started with the 1893 *Dictionary of Famous Names from around the World*, which introduced Blake to the Japanese public, and which was soon followed by publications of translations of Blake's early poems. It was no coincidence that a fairly large number of the greats of Japanese literature and philosophy started reading Blake all at once, for Japan in the late nineteenth through the early twentieth century was eager to assimilate western ideas into its own way of thinking. Blake came to be seen as a western great, and his work rapidly became known to would-be scholars.

The wave of westernisation served as a momentum toward the launch of women's higher education in the 1870s and after. In 1874, the Japanese

government established the Women's Normal School (currently Ochano-
mizu Women's College) to train women teachers. It was followed in 1890
by the foundation of the first private institution to teach English to women,
the English School for Women (currently Tsuda Women's College). This
English School was meant to nurture the new generation of women who
could acquire a global view through an excellent command of English.
Despite these efforts to improve women's education, there is no evidence
that Blake was taught to or read by women. The desire to understand Blake
seems to have been confined to male readers. But the first period certainly
prepared for the larger-scale encounter with Blake that was to follow.

The perspective of Blake scholarship was broadened in the second period,
1910–32, when his major works became available, and the following editions could be purchased in Japan: the Oxford edition of *The Poetical Works
of William Blake* edited by John Sampson (1905, 1913, 1914), the Muses'
Library edition of *Poems of William Blake* edited by W.B. Yeats (1905), and
the Aldine edition of *The Poetical Works of William Blake* edited by William
Michael Rossetti (1890 1909, 1914). Muneyoshi Yanagi, on whom I am
going to focus shortly, placed an order for 110 copies of the Oxford edition
with the Maruzen Bookstore in 1921 for a series of lectures on Blake, which
he was giving to schoolteachers in Nagano (Imai, 71).

It was also the time of the first feminist movement in Japan, and Blake
studies and feminism went hand in hand. Notable Blake scholars in the
1910s, especially Yanagi and Bunsho Jugaku, were among the members of a
newly established artistic group called 'Shirakaba' or 'White Birch', while
'New Women' established a group for women artists, which they named
'Seito' or 'Bluestocking' after their eighteenth-century British precursors.
The two artistic groups inaugurated their journals – landmarks in the history
of modern Japan – at about the same time, *Shirakaba* in 1910 and *Seito* in 1911.
Shirakaba men and *Seito* women characteristically glorified free love, intending to liberate the individual from moral and institutional restrictions, and
provided scurrilous journals with gossip topics (Matsuhashi, 60).

The contributors to *Seito* were all women, and endeavoured to enhance
their status in society and to defy the long-established convention of 'good
wife, wise mother' (Haga, 3–68), confined in a highly cloistered society. *Seito*
was soon followed by the establishment of two other well-known women's
magazines: *Fujin Koron* or *Woman's Review* (1916) and *Shufu no Tomo* or
Housewife's Companion (1917). The manifesto of the 'New Women', which
has often been quoted as the first sign of Japanese feminism, was vigorously
presented by Raicho Hiratsuka (1886–1971) in the inaugural issue of *Seito*:

> In the beginning, woman was the sun, an authentic person. Today, she
> is the moon, a pale-faced sick moon, living through others, and reflect-
> ing the brilliance of others.

> (Hiratsuka, 328)

These self-assertive words by women were familiar to the *Shirakaba* members, among whom Yanagi established himself as the first substantial Blake scholar in Japan. He showed himself supportive of the empowerment of woman, especially in his love letters to his future wife, Kaneko Nakajima. Kaneko was a promising student when she met Yanagi, showing signs of becoming an international singer; she would eventually be received with admiration in Germany. Yanagi revealed his deep understanding of the effect of social pressure on professional women, as he pointed out in his letter to Kaneko in 1911: 'It is difficult for a woman to become an artist in Japan . . . Most women give up art and become housewives' (22 December 1911; Matsuhashi, 34). He assured her in the same letter that she 'was sent into this world to be a woman and, at the same time, an artist', and he was convinced that 'it is my mission to help you achieve your calling as an artist' (34–5). He continued to encourage her the following year: 'You should get opportunities to listen to a great number of the geniuses playing, and I believe you should go abroad as soon as possible' (12 September 1912; Matsuhashi, 50). His desire to make Kaneko a world-class professional singer peaked in 1913: 'If you could not become an excellent singer', he wrote, 'it would be as painful to me as if I were stabbed in the chest . . . If you ended up being a singer established only in Japan, I would have to question my fate of being your lover' (30 March 1913; 61–2). I have been quoting Yanagi's love letters to Kaneko, because they show that he proved himself an advocate of the kind of feminist movement promoted by *Seito*, and because these letter-writing years overlapped with the time in which he was engaged on his nearly 800-page *William Blake: His Life, Works and Thought*, which was published in 1914.

Yanagi's book on Blake was read both inside and outside the *Shirakaba* circle, and was favourably reviewed by Takeshi Saito, who would be remembered as an author of a variety of works contributing to the promotion of English literary studies in Japan. It may be expected that Yanagi's book would show some signs of feminist impact, for it was written during his immersion in the flow of the feminist ideas of the 1910s, as we have observed in his letter writing to Kaneko. And it does indeed reveal his genuine fascination with the joy and triumph of a glorious life praised by Blake's female characters such as Vala and Enitharmon – that is, women characterised by their 'female will' and by their independence from men. Yanagi commented, for example, on the banquet scene of Los and Enitharmon on the second Night in *The Four Zoas* (FZ 2 34:1–36; E 322): 'The most beautiful lines of *The Four Zoas* are these words blessing the sexual union [of Los and Enitharmon]' (Yanagi, *Writings*, vol. 4: 154). His fascination even increased when he referred to Vala's song toward the Sun in the ninth Night in *The Four Zoas*: 'The lines that show Blake's grand love most clearly are the following lines that he sang toward the Sun. No lines have ever been equal to these lines in depth of thought in the history of

English Literature' (Yanagi, *Blake*: 160). From our vantage point almost a hundred years later, we can see that these lines about female glory and triumph are almost always expressive of female domination over the male. But Yanagi did not examine what the lines he singled out should mean or how problematic they could be in terms of gender, however progressive he may have been at the time.

It is in the second period that the first scholarly article on Blake was published by a woman scholar, Suzuko Yoshida. This article, 'On Blake's "Auguries of Innocence"', was included in an alumni bulletin of a women's college in 1931 (Yoshida, 95–9). We should note that this piece took shape in a women's college. As is the case today, places such as women's colleges or women's centres often encourage their members to develop an independent attitude and feminist consciousness.

There was another piece of writing by a woman in the second period. This appeared in an epochal monthly hand-made journal *Blake and Whitman* (1932–33), which was edited by Yanagi and his scholar-friend, Bunsho Jugaku. Shizu Jugaku, his wife, composed a short essay with a brief history of the journal in its final issue. She was well qualified to write it, for she (and her husband) had been responsible for binding five hundred copies each month with thread and needle. The figure of 500 was surprisingly large at the time for a circulation of this kind of journal, especially one dealing with two foreign artists, whose names had not even been heard by most lay people in Japan. I.A. Richards, a friend of Yanagi's, stopped in Japan on his way back to England from the USA and did not conceal his surprise when he learned about the journal from Yanagi in 1931. He said, as Yanagi recollected: 'It is absolutely improbable that such a journal should exist in England . . . even if it did, it would never attract that huge number of subscribers' (Yanagi, 'Miscellaneous Notes': 429). It was not surprising to Shizu that 500 copies of the journal should circulate each month. It was more incomprehensible to her that there was much less demand for it at the end of 1932 than before, as she complained: 'On what did they spend the fifty sen [0.5 yen] that they used to pay for our journal?' It is clear that she dedicated her life to the making of the journal at this time, as she herself made clear: 'I decided to help it [making the journal from editing to binding] as far as my strength would take me, because I understood the significance of such a work' (Shizu Jugaku, 'Postscript', 567). Very few women could speak of the value of an academic journal the way Shizu did in the early 1930s.

Her husband Jugaku was the major writer and editor of the Blake section in *Blake and Whitman* and he was able, in the early 1930s, to tackle the issue of gender, which Yanagi only glimpsed into in the 1910s. Jugaku explained his view of women to the readers of *Blake and Whitman* when he wrote that it is 'optimistically blind' to think 'women were merely the means by which to please men, to bear children for men, and to take care of the household'

(Jugaku, 1931: 262). He condemned the lack of women's personal and social rights and welcomed their independence and aggressiveness. It is noteworthy that Jugaku repeatedly referred to Catherine Blake, making her unusually prominent in his criticism. The role of Catherine Blake is often a neglected area, even today. Jugaku gave much credit to Catherine for Blake's accomplishment, explaining that she was strongly determined to learn writing and painting from her husband and to help him to carry out his work. He called Catherine 'a wonderful woman' and even said: 'Everyone should know that Blake owed his happy married life to Catherine's virtue' (Jugaku, 1934: 27).

Jugaku briefly introduced a gender-based reading of Thel's motto, with particular attention to the following lines: 'Can wisdom be put in a silver rod? / Or Love in a golden bowl?' (*The Book of Thel*, 'Thel's Motto', E 3). With a reference to the socio-psychological symbolism in 1930s' Japan, he regarded wisdom as 'typical of the male' and 'Love' as 'representative of the female' (Jugaku, 1934: 59–60), and emphasised that what belonged to the male should not be put into the female sphere, and vice versa. He remained the only writer in Japan until the mid-1980s who ever developed a gender-conscious analysis of Blake's work. This distressing situation contrasts with the appearance of the pivotal work by Susan Fox in the English-speaking sphere, 'The Female as Metaphor in William Blake's Poetry' in 1977, which was followed by Anne K. Mellor's 'Blake's Portrayal of Women' and Alicia Ostriker's 'Desire Gratified and Ungratified: William Blake and Sexuality' in 1982–83.

It should be noted here that Jugaku's 1931 list of significant eighteenth-century women involved in raising the consciousness of their gender anticipated scholarly attention more than seventy years later: 'Sara Jennings, Mrs. Howard, Mrs. Siddons, Fanny Burney, Mrs. Thrale, Mrs. Mary Wortley Montagu, Mrs. Elizabeth Montagu, Mrs. Vesey, Mrs. Delany, Mrs. Chapone, Hannah More . . . and Mary Wollestonecraft' (Jugaku, 'Blake in *Poetical Sketches*', 262). Japanese scholars of Romanticism have recently started seriously exploring these re-emerged women writers. This also shows how far ahead of the times his ideas were.

Blake scholarship in the third period in Japan, 1933–57, was inevitably affected by the Second World War, but with the end of the war, Blake scholars resumed writing, and during this time five women, including Yoshida, who had published one essay in the previous period, published seven essays on Blake. In these publications no trace of feminist influence is seen, though western feminist ideas began to be introduced to the Japanese through translations of such works as Virginia Woolf's *A Room of One's Own* (translated in 1952) and Simone de Beauvoir's *The Second Sex* (translated in 1955).

Twenty-one women joined Blake scholarship in the fourth period, 1958–83, and they produced forty-nine publications on Blake. Two women were invited to contribute to a journal, *Bokushin* or *Faun*, which was published in two small volumes in 1976. One of them, Shigeko Tsuchiya, started her productive career in the early 1960s and would continue to publish for forty years. She presented a model of a lifetime woman scholar of Blake through her writings, which amounted to as many as fourteen publications during the fourth period alone. Other women were also energetically writing on Blake, and it was fairly unusual for them to produce only one publication; whereas during the previous period it was quite usual for women to publish only single articles. This indicates that women had finally attained what the New Women at the time of *Seito* had endeavoured to acquire, that is, a stable position in society as professionals. But in terms of feminism, things remained bleak. None of the women scholars of Blake adopted a feminist approach, although they had easy access to the classic articles by Fox, Mellor, and Ostriker. It is obvious from G.E. Bentley Jr's *Blake Studies in Japan: a Bibliography of Works on William Blake Published in Japan 1893–1993* that the most frequently-discussed topics until the mid-1980s were God, Christianity, revolution, Urizen, vision, innocence and experience, and composite art.

The fourth period was crowned by the arrival of Kenzaburo Oe's *Rouse Up, O Young Men of the New Age* (1983) with its title quotation taken from Blake's *Milton*. This novel and the others which followed, which would eventually bring him the Nobel Prize for Literature (1994), belong to a peculiarly Japanese fictive tradition called the 'I' novel, where the first person singular narrator is expected to reveal what can be regarded as the novelist's own private life. The narrator of *Rouse Up*, as is expected, discloses his relationship with his retarded son, Iyo, and even confesses his earlier desire to murder him. Transplanting Blake's poems into his own fictive space, Oe provides new meanings for them until they become a part of his own creations. He deconstructs Blakean visions through the eyes of a Japanese living in the late twentieth century. His primary fascination with the male-oriented vision – his son's, his own, and Blake's – was powerful enough to make scholars retreat from whatever feminist interests they might previously have had.

Oe's popularity among Blake scholars in Japan seems to have continued to encourage them to explore a male-centred visionary world in Blake's work in the fifth period, 1984–present. This stage, however, has also been characterised by a clear trend toward feminism, which became a focal point in academic and social debates in the late 1980s in Japan, in response to the second wave of the American feminist movement. Japan became an economic superpower and, abandoning the American-European modernisation model, began to draw attention to its own national identity and tradition. Japan ratified the Convention on the Elimination of All Forms of Discrimination Against Women (CEDAW) and The Equal Employment Opportunity Law (EEOL) in 1985. Even though Japanese feminism in 1980s was called 'housewife feminism' because the government revised the tax and pension scheme 'in favor of housewives' (Kanai, 7), the academic world demonstrated a more positive approach, for four women determinedly began a feminist exploration of Blake by paying particular attentions to gender difference. The author of the present essay, having come across American feminist writings in the late 1970s and the early 1980s, presented to Yale University a dissertation on Blake (paradoxically entitled *Brotherhood in Blake*; 1985), the last chapter of which was written with the encouragement of the feminist critic Margaret Homans. In 1986, the oldest and the most conservative Japanese non-commercial journal, *Studies in English Literature* published by the English Literary Society of Japan (founded in 1924), included for the first time an article on Blake with particular focus on the issue of representation and gender: 'Psychic Operations Symbolized by the Female in Blake's *Jerusalem*' (the author being myself). The publication of this article in the canonical journal exemplified a breakthrough in the long silence of feminist Blake scholarship in Japan, and it was followed by three other essays, Keiko Hori's 'The "Nameless Shadowy Female", in *America* and *Europe*' (1986), Hatsuko Niimi's 'The Sorrows of Daughters of Albion: Oithona, Oothoon, and Mary Wollstonecraft' (1988), and Masae Kawatsu's 'A Speaking Woman in Blake's *Visions of the Daughters of Albion*' (1989).

It is ironic that a growing interest among Blake scholars in feminism turned their attention to un-canonised Romantic women writers, who were highlighted, and their work increasingly available, as the result of a surge of feminist theories. In the most recent peer-reviewed collection of essays by the members of the Association of English Romanticism, *Voyages of Conception: Essays in English Romanticism* (2005), there are four feminist-minded scholars (three women and one man) writing on Romantic women writers. By contrast, there is only one feminist essay on Blake (my own 'Blood in Blake') which examined the transformation of the highly sexualised metaphor of blood into sperm and milk in relation to the male/female struggle. It may be true that feminist Blakeans have started reading and/or writing on Romantic women writers, but there are still feminist achievements on Blake. Besides the above-mentioned essay in *Voyages of Conception* there are Hatsuko Niimi's '*The Book of Ahania*: a Metatext' (2000) and my own *Blake's Re-Vision of the Female in his Composite Art* (2001). Japanese feminist scholarship on Blake is thus maintained at a minimum level, and this situation is reflected in that of other canonical greats of Romanticism. Kazuko Iki, one of a few women scholars who started their academic careers right after the Second World War, pronounced, 'there has not been a single feminist essay on Keats in Japan', on the occasion of her keynote lecture at the 31st Conference of the Association of English Romanticism in Japan in 2005. Speculating about a complete lack of feminist scholarship on Keats, she stated that: 'A woman scholar would be disadvantaged by taking a feminist approach in this male-dominated society.' This probably represents the sentiments of most potential feminist women scholars in Japan. As one of the other possible answers to the paucity of feminist women scholars on Blake, I could point out an unspoken tenet in Japan: 'Women should work on women writers' (as was once said to me). Women would not be penalised for adopting a feminist approach to writers of the same sex.

The conference on 'Blake in the Orient' (2003) gave me an opportunity to interpret the early reception of Blake in Japan against a feminist socio-cultural background. And the question about feminist scholarship on Blake, with which I began the present chapter, was raised. What I would have said, if I had had the time, is: 'There are less than half a dozen, including myself, who are adopting feminist approaches to Blake in Japan. But I am planning to persuade more people, especially women, to engage in it, for it certainly enables us to dis-cover what used to be covered.'

References

Bentley, G.E. Jr, *Blake Studies in Japan: a Bibliography of Works on William Blake Published in Japan 1893–1993* (Tokyo: Tsurumi Shoten, 1994).

Fox, Susan, 'The Female as Metaphor in William Blake's Poetry', *Critical Inquiry*, 3 (1977), 507–19.

Haga, Noboru, *Good Wife, Wise Mother* (Tokyo: Oyamakaku Publishing Co., 1990).

Hiratsuka, Raicho, *In the Beginning Woman Was the Sun: the Autobiography of Raicho Hiratsuka's Life* (Tokyo: Otsuki-Shoten, 1971).

Hori, Keiko, 'The "Nameless Shadowy Female" in *America* and *Europe*', *Memoirs of Osaka Educational University*, 1:35:1 (1986), 15–24.

Imai, Nobuo, *The Periphery of the White Birch Journal: the Intersection of the White Birch Movement and School Education in Nagano* (Nagano: Shinano Educational Committee, 1986).

Ima-Izumi, Yoko, 'Blood in Blake', in *Voyages of Conception: Essays in English Romanticism* (Tokyo: Kirihara-Shoten, 2005), pp. 56–72.

Ima-Izumi, Yoko, *Brotherhood in Blake: Psychology and Poetics* (Dissertation Abstracts International 46: 3359A: Yale PhD; Ann Arbor, Michigan: University Microfilms International, 1985).

Ima-Izumi, Yoko, 'Psychic Operations Symbolized by the Female in Blake's *Jerusalem*', *Studies in English Literature*, 53: 2 (1986), 241–56.

Ima-Izumi, Yoko, *Blake's Re-Vision of the Female in His Composite Art* (Tokyo: Sairyu-Sha, 2001).

Jugaku, Bunsho, 'Blake in *Poetical Sketches*', *Blake and Whitman*, 1:6 (1931), 262–7.

Jugaku, Bunsho, *William Blake* (Tokyo: Kenkyu-Sha, 1934).

Jugaku, Shizu, 'Postscript', *Blake and Whitman*, 2:12 (1932), 567–8.

Kanai, Yoshiko, 'Issues for Japanese Feminism', in *Voices from the Japanese Women's Movement*, ed. AMPO-Japan Asia Quarterly Review (New York: M.E. Sharpe, 1996), pp. 3–22.

Kawatsu, Masae, 'A Speaking Woman in Blake's *Visions of the Daughters of Albion*', *IVY: The Nagoya Review of English Studies*, 22 (1989), 35–51.

Matsuhashi, Keiko, *An Eternal Alto Singer: the Biography of Kaneko Yanagi* (Tokyo: Suiyo-Sha, 1999).

Mellor, Anne K., 'Blake's Portrayal of Women', *BQ*, 16:3 (1982–3), 148–55.

Niimi, Hatsuko, 'The Sorrows of Daughters of Albion: Oithona, Oothoon, and Mary Wollstonecraft', *Tohogakuen School of Music Faculty Bulletin*, 14 (1988), 99–120.

Niimi, Hatsuko, '*The Book of Ahania*: a Metatext', *BQ*, 34:2 (2000), 46–52.

Ostriker, Alicia, 'Desire Gratified and Ungratified: William Blake and Sexuality', *BQ*, 16:3 (1982–3), 156–65.

Yanagi, Muneyoshi, *William Blake: His Life, Works and Thought* (Tokyo: Rakuyo-Do, 1914; reprinted in *The Complete Writings of Muneyoshi Yanagi* [vol. 4, Tokyo: Chikuma-Shobo, 1981]).

Yanagi, Muneyoshi, 'Miscellaneous Notes', *Blake and Whitman*, 1:9 (1931), 428–31.

Yanagi, Muneyoshi, 'Postscript', *Blake and Whitman*, 1:10 (1931), 475–9.

Yoshida, Suzuko, 'On Blake's "Auguries of Innocence"', *Alumni Bulletin of Doshisha Girls' College*, 57 (1931), 95–9.

12
Blake's Mary and Martha on the Mount of Olives: Questions on the Watercolour Illustrations of the Gospels

Mary Lynn Johnson

Is the Jesus of Blake's biblical watercolour series a misogynist, a feminist, or something else entirely? Do 'dozens' of these designs 'call for no further comment' (Frye, 408), and is the segment on the life of Christ, lacking the 'vigorous characterization' of 'The Everlasting Gospel', pictorially the 'least interesting' of the lot (Bindman, 143)? Among Blake's 80-odd biblical water-colours for his patron Thomas Butts (Butlin 433–526, *c.* 1800–05), do only the sub-series on Genesis, the Crucifixion/Resurrection, and the Apocalypse approach the brilliance of the large colour prints and the most striking of the series on Milton and Young? Or might subtle novelties in illustrations of Jesus' encounters with women unobtrusively render these designs less conventional than they appear? By choosing subjects or empha-sising details passed over by earlier artists, or by attending to, and mending, jarring textual discrepancies, does Blake unsettle viewers' expectations, defamiliarise well-known (perhaps too well-known) Gospel stories of women, and open both texts and their associated iconographic traditions to interpretative possibilities that engage feminist biblical scholars of our time?

A proper expository commentary might investigate an unassuming, pale-hued, linearly-arranged watercolour that illustrates a subject utterly without precedent in Christian art: 'And when they had sung a hymn, they went out into the mount of Olives' (Mark 14:26; compare Matthew 26:30). There is no question about the reference, for Blake inscribed 'Mark XIV c 26 v' directly under his monogram in the bottom right of the picture now known as *The Hymn of Christ and the Apostles* (Figure 12.1; Butlin, 490, private collection) or – to cite Bindman's title – *Christ accompanied by figures with musical instruments* (143). What is truly astonishing, apart from the uncon-ventional choice of text, is that the figures closest to Jesus, on his immediate right and left, are women – so unlikely here that Robertson guardedly describes them as '(apparently) female' (51). Even Butlin does not fully

Figure 12.1 William Blake, *The Hymn of Christ and the Apostles* (private collection)

acknowledge their presence: he attributes an alternate title, *Christ and a Heavenly Choir* (from a sales catalogue quoted by Rossetti) to the 'fact that there are only six figures besides Christ, that some of these play musical instruments and that two look very feminine' (Butlin 358). Don't their bustlines clearly differentiate them from the beardless, long-haired, but flat-chested John (at the far left), traditionally the softest-featured of the twelve disciples? Who are these women, and how did they get into the picture? What has led up to this scene, and what is to follow? How is this design related to others in the series?

According to the text cited in the inscription, the hymn – which biblical scholars identify as the Hallel or song of praise (Psalms 113–18) after the Passover meal – is sung *before* the disciples move outdoors. The preceding verses allow for no interval between the Last Supper, or Institution of the Eucharist (traditional subjects in the visual arts), and the hymn: 'And he said unto them, This is my blood of the new testament, which is shed for many. Verily I say unto you, I will drink no more of the fruit of the vine, until that day that I drink it new in the kingdom of God. And when they had sung a hymn, they went out into the mount of Olives' (Mark 14:24–6). In a glaring break with tradition, Blake omits the Last Supper from the watercolour series; but in resetting this hymn-singing scene from the Upper Room to the Mount of Olives (as indicated by the fruit-bearing olive trees in the background), he leaves open a possibility not permitted by Mark's words: did women partake of the Last Supper? Even if that impertinence is peremptorily dismissed, the fact remains that in *The Hymn of Christ and the Apostles* Blake has placed, without textual authority, not one but two women in Jesus' innermost circle between the Last Supper and the approach to Gethsemane. Peter, James, and John are named in this select group (Mark 14:33); the fourth male disciple is probably Peter's brother Andrew, else-where mentioned second or fourth among the disciples (Matthew 10:2; Mark 3:6; Luke 6:14). Since the two women are posed as a contrasting pair, they are probably Mary and Martha, the only female followers of Jesus who always appear together, as instructive contraries. Which sister is which? The distinction between the two, evident in *Christ in the House of Martha and Mary: 'And Martha Was Cumbered With Much Serving'* (Butlin 489) and in *The Raising of Lazarus* (Butlin 487), may (or may not) be part of a visual storyline that also includes *Mary Magdalene Washing Christ's Feet* (Butlin 488), *The Entombment* (Butlin 498), and *The Magdalene at the Sepulchre* (Butlin 504).

As Butlin notes, *Mary Magdalene Washing Christ's Feet* is 'a pendant, in reverse' (358) to *Christ in the House of Martha and Mary*; the two works are designed to be viewed together. In each picture attention centres on a woman at Jesus' feet; also, at each table, a woman dines alongside the male guests. By contrast, in Blake's only *Last Supper* painting (Butlin 424), a tempera of 1799 in an earlier and quite distinct set of biblical illustrations for Butts, John the 'beloved disciple' is next to Jesus, as required by the text and iconographic tradition. With his long, curly reddish hair, delicate hands crossed over his chest, and flowing blue gown, John looks at least as womanish as his famous counterpart in Leonardo's painting of the same subject – whom enthusiasts of Dan Brown's *The Da Vinci Code* take to be Mary Magdalene. His languid pose, and that of the two semi-nude beardless males in the foreground who lean toward each other and lock eyes expres-sively, results from Blake's decision to represent the diners as reclining rather than sitting – 'the posture used in eating at table by the latter Jews, Greeks, and Romans' (Parkhurst, *Lexicon*, 33), as Blake may have learned from his study of New Testament Greek or from Poussin's two *Seven Sacraments* series (Butlin 332); also anticipated in sixth-century mosaics at Ravenna (Schiller II, 30–1). Jesus also reclines in the watercolour banquet scenes, but if John appears at all, it is as a more masculinised youth sitting upright across the table, witnessing the foreground drama of the conversation with Mary and Martha.

In pairing *Christ in the House of Martha and Mary* with what Butlin calls the 'associated subject' (358) of *Mary Magdalene Washing Christ's Feet*, is Blake making artistic and theological use of the confusion, since the time of the Church Fathers, between Mary of Bethany, Mary of Magdala, and an unnamed sinner who washes and anoints Jesus' feet and dries them with her hair? Even in Blake's time, biblical commentators (see bibliography for a sampling) disputed the conflation of Mary Magdalene and the sinner, as proclaimed by Pope Gregory the Great in 591 AD and universally adopted in western art. The commentator Thomas Brown, for example, calls upon all Protestants to recognise Mary Magdalene as 'a lady of distinction; of a great and noble mind, and of chaste life and conversation' and to resist an attack on her character he attributed to Catholics:

> The *Talmud* speaks of a lewd woman, called *Mary Magadella*, or *the plaiter* [of hair]: An epithet given to all prostitutes in those times ... but this has no relation to the name of *Magdalene*: yet this is the *great* authority of the Church of Rome for prostituting so exalted a character in the Gospels ... From that corrupt fountain, then, sprang up this gross error, and obtained credit in the darkest ages of Popery, almost universally, and hath continued a popular opinion, to this day ...
>
> (note to Luke 8:3; 202)

Did such a close reader of the Bible as Blake blindly fall into this error? Or did he choose to blend the sinner with two different Marys for reasons of his own?

Feminist theologians and art historians have persuasively argued that patriarchal opposition to women's leadership in the early church led to the denigration of Mary of Magdala. But the fusion, despite inconsistencies, of the evangelists' accounts of this Mary's involvement in an anointing (Matthew 26:6ff.; Mark 14:3:ff.; Luke 7:36ff.; John 12:3ff.) – which fulfils the identification of Jesus as the Christ (the 'anointed one') – also results from the effort, over centuries, to 'harmonise' the Gospels by interweaving them into a single composite narrative. Similarities among the texts, almost as striking as their differences, seem to point uncertainly toward an underlying event encapsulated in the compelling image of the penitent sinner who 'loved much' (Luke 7:47) and expressed her love in a gesture of astounding, almost dangerous extravagance and intimacy. In all four Gospels a woman – nowhere called Mary Magdalene – brings precious ointment (of spikenard, in Mark and John; compare Song of Solomon 1:12) in an alabaster box (Matthew, Mark, Luke) to a feast in Bethany (Matthew, Mark, and John) in the home of Simon the leper (Matthew and Mark) or Simon the Pharisee (Luke), where Lazarus dines (John); she pours it on Jesus' head (Matthew, Mark) or feet (Luke, John); the odour fills the room (John); the woman weeps (Luke) and dries Jesus' feet with her hair (Luke, John); the disciples (Matthew, Mark) or Judas alone (John) protest her wasting money better spent on the poor; Jesus replies that she has anointed him for burial (Matthew, Mark, John). In Luke, the event falls in the middle of Jesus' ministry; in the other Gospels it is the first episode in the Passion narrative, occurring either two days (Matthew, Mark) or six days (John) before the Passover. In Matthew, Mark, and Luke the woman is unnamed (a notorious 'sinner' in Luke, Mary Magdalene in the Authorized Version's chapter heading); in John, she is Mary the sister of Martha (who serves the meal) and Lazarus.

Neither *Christ in the House of Martha and Mary* nor *Mary Magdalene Washing Christ's Feet* bears a textual citation in Blake's hand. But the episode with Mary and Martha, which occurs in only one Gospel, is cited among inscriptions (probably by someone in the Butts family; Butlin 335–6) on old mats or mounts for the series: 'Luke 10 ch: v. 41st & 42' and 'But Martha was cumbered about much serving' (Luke 10:40). Although no such reference exists for *Mary Magdalene Washing Christ's Feet*, Butlin proposes (358), without comment, John 12:1–8 – in which Mary of Bethany is the anointer, Lazarus the (implied) host, and Martha the server. Other details point to Luke 7:6–48: the kissing of Jesus' feet and the conversation with an old bearded man who appears to be the reproachful Simon the Pharisee, rather than Lazarus.

If Blake purposefully fused Luke's and John's stories and conflated the two Marys with Luke's 'sinner', shouldn't the two banquet scenes be viewed in the chronological order required by the harmonisation of the Gospels, rather than in the order indicated by Butlin's catalogue numbers (the order of Luke's Gospel)? Placed side by side, with the two figures of Jesus framing contrasting images of a woman at his feet, the pair form a before-and-after sequence. In scene one, *Christ in the House of Martha and Mary* (Butlin 489), the busy older sister, hair in a chignon, sandals on her feet and tray in hand, complains that her pensive, barefoot younger sister is oblivious to everything except Jesus' words. Jesus responds by informing Martha that she is 'troubled about many things' rather than the 'one thing . . . needful' (Luke 10:41) and commends Mary, sitting at his feet (as his pupil, in the way Paul was brought up 'at the feet of Gamaliel', Acts 22:3), for having chosen 'that good part, which shall not be taken away from her' (Luke 10:42). Across the table, at the far left, a figure in a sleeveless gown, like Martha's, apparently a woman, takes in the difference between the two sisters that Jesus is pointing out. If this picture is viewed as preceding, rather than following, *Mary Magdalene Washing Christ's Feet* (Butlin 488), then Mary the sister of Martha, her hair loose, her hand at her forehead, is not only pensive but penitent: in scene two, in the person of the sinner traditionally called Mary Magdalene, she bathes Jesus' feet with her tears, kisses and anoints them with costly spikenard, and grasps the end of her longest tress in preparation for drying his feet with her hair. Although in this pair of pictures the foot-washing woman, seen in profile, does not especially resemble Mary of Bethany, seen seven-eighths of full face, the women's long hair implies at least a thematic identity, as supported by John 12:1ff. and by other pictures in the series.

Does Martha, too, have a part in the before-and-after sequence? Is she the demurely veiled seated woman, seen in profile, in the left foreground of *Mary Magdalene Washing Christ's Feet*? If she has been serving the meal (some harmonisers of the Gospels surmised that John's Lazarus was a guest in the home of Luke's Simon the Pharisee), has she taken the Master's teachings to heart and turned her back on her former overwrought, hyper-domestic self? Now barefoot like others whose feet have been washed by the host's servants, has she found a way both to set *and claim* a place for herself at the table?

A full-length essay on Blake's pictorial identification of Mary of Bethany with Mary of Magdala should also consider another pair of pictures: *The Raising of Lazarus* (Butlin 487), a subject traditionally interpreted as a foreshadowing of Jesus' resurrection, and *The Magdalene at the Sepulchre* (Butlin 504). In *Lazarus*, both Martha (on the viewer's left) and Mary (on the right) throw up their hands in surprise, but while Martha looks down at her brother, rising from the grave at Jesus' summons, Mary turns back to look up at Jesus himself. Isn't this the same Mary who, in *The Magdalene*, in the same pose, holds her head, in profile, at exactly this angle as she twists to look up at the risen Jesus behind her? Can she also be the long-haired central woman who muffles her face while holding the torch for Jesus' burial (*The Entombment*, Butlin 498)? And does this watercolour narrative, foreshadowed by the tempera *'Christ the Mediator': Christ Pleading Before the Father for St. Mary Magdalene* (Butlin 429), anticipate Blake's more elaborate interweaving of 'Mary/sinner' stories in 'The Everlasting Gospel' (*c.* 1818), encompassing Jesus' casting out of Mary Magdalene's seven devils (Luke 8:2) and his protection of the woman taken in adultery (John 8:3ff.)? When Blake's Jesus asks this later, still more complex Mary whether her sin, or sickness, was love or deceit, she replies:

> Love too long from Me has fled.
> Twas dark deceit to Earn my bread
> Twas Covet or twas Custom or
> Some trifle not worth caring for

That they may call a shame & Sin
Loves Temple that God dwelleth in
And hide in secret hidden Shrine
The Naked Human form divine
And render that a Lawless thing
On which the Soul Expands its wing
But this O Lord this was my Sin
When first I let these Devils in
In dark pretence to Chastity
Blaspheming Love blaspheming thee.

(E [f] 59–72, 522)

As Heppner notes in relation to other New Testament designs, Blake –
given free rein by Butts – sometimes constructed 'an implicit text of his
own' from 'disparate fragments' left by the evangelists, to produce 'not the
common denominator of the harmonizers but a new invention' (*Reading
Blake's Designs*, 174, 201–3; compare Pippen's latter-day 'diatesseron' of the
anointing narratives; 145ff.). Could *The Hymn of Christ and the Apostles* be
a stand-in for the 'One of you will betray me' announcement at the (omitted)
Last Supper? Aren't the hymn-singers sombre and subdued, as if their music
has died on their lips? Can Jesus, his left arm raised, his lips slightly parted,
be warning that his followers will be scattered (Mark 14:27) and that Peter
will deny him (Mark 14:30)? At the far left stands John, looking toward
Jesus, his troubled or bemused face in profile, a disregarded hymn-scroll in
his hands. Next to him is a middle-aged bearded disciple, probably John's
older brother James, his body concealing most of his harp, looking up
toward the trees. Third from left, behind the others, is an older bearded
man looking toward Jesus with a furrowed brow, probably Peter's brother
Andrew; if he also holds an instrument, it is concealed by the figures in the
foreground. Still another bearded man at the far right, presumably Peter,
resting his right fingers on his harp strings, directs his contemplative down-
ward gaze toward Jesus' upraised hand. Next to Peter is Martha, looking
toward Jesus, her mouth open in alarm, her outspread right fingers resting
on the strings of her lyre, at the same angle as Peter's on his harp. But on
Jesus' right, looking slightly upward along Jesus' line of sight, the female
lute-player remains calm, her mouth closed; exposing a bare right foot, she
keeps pace with Jesus. Surely she is Martha's sister Mary – but is anything
more implied?

Of the four musicians, this lute-player is the only one whose curved
fingers can be seen to touch the strings. Her loose hair rises into a curling
peak at the top of her head, something like a tongue of flame in traditional
paintings of Pentecost. In the Old Testament antitype for this design, *By
the Waters of Babylon* (Butlin 466, illustrating Psalms 137:1–4), male and

female Hebrew captives have hung their instruments (harp, lyre, serpent trumpet) in the willows because they refuse to sing the Lord's song in a strange land (compare the first and last designs of the Job series for Butts; Butlin 550:1, 21). Here, although other disciples have paused, one woman plays on alone. Is she both Mary of Magdala and Mary of Bethany, and does she keep on playing the Lord's song, in the face of Jesus' warning, to show that she and the other female disciples will not be scattered, nor will they deny their Lord?

Select bibliography

Apostolos-Cappadona, Diana, *In Search of Mary Magdalene: Images and Traditions* (New York: American Bible Society, 2002).

Apostolos-Cappadona, Diana, *Dictionary of Women in Religious Art* (New York: Oxford University Press, 1998).

Bindman, David, *Blake as an Artist* (Oxford: Phaidon, 1977).

Butlin, Martin, *The Paintings and Drawings of William Blake*, 2 vols (New Haven: Yale University Press for the Paul Mellon Centre for Studies in British Art, 1981). Catalogue-number citations refer to vol. 1.

Brock, Ann Graham, *Mary Magdalene, the First Apostle: the Struggle for Authority*, Harvard Theological Studies 51 (Cambridge, MA: Harvard University Press, 2003).

Brown, Thomas, *The Evangelical History of our Lord and Saviour Jesus Christ: Containing, in Order of Time, All the Events and Discourses Recorded in the Four Evangelists* (Rev. edn London: J. Buckland and J. Johnson, 1787).

Calmet, Augustin, *Calmet's Great Dictionary of the Holy Bible . . .* , 2 vols (London: Charles Taylor, 1797–1801).

Chilton, Bruce, *Mary Magdalene: a Biography* (New York: Doubleday, 2005).

Coakley, J.F., 'The Anointing at Bethany and the Priority of John', *Journal of Biblical Literature*, 107:2 (1988), 241–56.

De Boer, Esther, *Mary Magdalene: Beyond the Myth* (London: Trinity Press International, 1997).

Doddridge, P., *The Family Expositor: or, a Paraphrase and Version of the New Testament, with Critical Notes . . . Disposed in the Order of an Harmony*, 6 vols (London, 1739–56. I, sect. LX) 363n.

Frye, Northrop, 'Blake's Biblical Illustrations' [previously unpublished lecture], *Collected Works of Northrop Frye*, Vol. 16, *Northrop Frye on Milton and Blake*, ed. Angela Esterhammer (Toronto: University of Toronto Press, 2005).

Harper's Bible Dictionary, ed. Paul J. Achtemeier (San Francisco: Harper & Row, 1985).

Haskins, Susan, *Mary Magdalen, Myth and Metaphor* (NY: Harcourt-Brace, 1993).

Henry, Matthew, *Matthew Henry's Commentary on the Whole Bible*, 6 vols (1721; Peabody, MA: Hendrickson, 1991), Vol. 5, Matthew to John.

Heppner, Christopher, *Reading Blake's Designs* (Cambridge: Cambridge University Press, 1995).

Heppner, Christopher, 'The Woman Taken in Adultery: an Essay on Blake's "Style of Designing"', *BQ*, 17:2 (1983), 44–60.

Kitzberger, Ingrid Rosa, 'Mary of Bethany and Mary of Magdala: Two Female Characters in the Johannine Passion Narrative', *New Testament Studies*, 41:4 (1995), 564–86.

Maisch, Ingrid, *Mary Magdalen: the Image of a Woman through the Centuries*, trans. Linda M. Maloney (Collegeville, Minn.: Liturgical Press, 1998).

Macknight, James, *A Harmony of the Four Gospels . . .* , 2 vols (London, 1756).

Parkhurst, John, *A Greek and English Lexicon to the New Testament* (London, 1769).

Pippen, Tina, 'Wisdom's Deviant Ways', in Jane Schaberg et al. (eds), *On the Cutting Edge* (New York and London: Continuum, 2004), pp. 143–53.

Réau, Louis, *Iconographie de l'Art Chrétien* (Paris: Presses Universitaires, 1957).

Ricci, Carla, *Mary Magdalene and Many Others: Women Who Followed Jesus*, trans. Paul Burns (Minneapolis: Fortress Press, 1994).

[Robertson, W. Graham] *The Blake Collection of W. Graham Robertson, Described by the Collector*, ed. Kerrison Preston (London: Faber and Faber, 1952).

Schiller, Gertrud, *Iconography of Christian Art*, trans. Janet Seligman, 2 vols (London and Greenwich, CT: Lund Humphries / New York Graphic Society, 1971–2).

Shaberg, Jane, *The Resurrection of Mary Magdalene* (New York and London: Continuum, 2002).

Williams, William [Bell], *Mary Magdalene. A Sermon* (London, 1794).

13
The Trimurti Meet the Zoas: 'Hindoo' Strategies in the Poetry of William Blake

Kathryn Sullivan Kruger

In 1780 William Blake engraved *Glad Day*, which depicts a radiant youth, arms outstretched in the sun's aura. At a later date Blake wrote beneath the drawing: 'Albion arose from where he labour'd at the Mill with Slaves: Giving himself for the Nations *he danc'd the dance of Eternal Death*.'[1] This engraving, coupled with the inscription, is reminiscent of the Hindu god, Shiva, whose dance of death and rebirth is captured in Hindu art; the most famous portrayal of the god positions him in a ring of fire, his raised foot indicating liberation in his worship. In Blake's engraving, the youth he calls Albion represents the archetypal figure of humankind; his joyous and unfettered 'dance of Eternal Death' suggests a passage from *The Marriage of Heaven and Hell*, where we may understand the epigram as meaning 'the dance of Eternal Life'.[2] This famous representation of Shiva may have suggested to Blake the idea of rebirth and salvation embodied in *Glad Day*.

That Blake studied Hinduism has been saluted by Blake scholars since 1924 when S. Foster Damon stated that the poet was 'in accord with Eastern mysticism'.[3] The facts, however, were not fully established until David Weir's book, *Brahma in the West: William Blake and the Oriental Renaissance*, which provides persuasive evidence demonstrating Blake's access to a large body of material 'in the form of various mythographic representations of Hinduism'.[4] Weir proves beyond a doubt that Hinduism was not merely incidental to Blake's vision but one of its defining attributes, and that its influence on Blake dates from *The Marriage of Heaven and Hell* onward.

Prior to Weir, proof rested solely on Blake's acquaintance with two major Orientalists of the day, Sir Charles Wilkins, translator of the *Bhagavat-Geeta* (1785), and Sir William Jones, founder of the Asiatic Society (1784) and editor of the society's journal, *Asiatick Researches*. Notwithstanding these connections, Hinduism was a hot topic at the late eighteenth-century salon of the Flaxmans' good friend, Mrs Mathew. Ann Flaxman, who took notes on Jones's works, was, like Blake, interested in the Hindu pantheon, particularly the female deities.[5] Weir extends this circle to include, among other material, two significant books: Edward Moor's *The Hindu Pantheon* (published by Joseph Johnson in 1810) and Comte de Volney's *The Ruins, or, a Survey of the Revolutions of Empire* which sold out three editions in 1792, 1794 and 1796.

Study of the impact of Hinduism on Blake's prophetic vision reveals that whereas Blake was not concerned with Hinduism as a religion in competition with Christianity, he was interested in the strategies that Hinduism provided for presenting his own poetic vision. He respected Hinduism in part because it was ancient; he could separate the literature of Hinduism from the religion in the same way that he distinguished the poet and denounced the priest. In *The Marriage of Heaven and Hell*, Blake gives his prophet Ezekiel these words: 'The philosophy of the east taught the first principles of human perception' (Pl 12; E 39). More importantly, Hinduism intrigued Blake because it suggested a way for him to present the temporal and eternal worlds as interdependent. From his encounter with Hinduism, Blake adopted many of its devices and used these toward different purposes: to create the unique facets of the Zoas, to portray the universal character of Albion, and to describe a new Christian notion of time. This chapter focuses on these three strategies, suggesting how Blake fused eastern and western elements into a distinctive visionary world.

The Trimurti

The Zoas and their Emanations are, perhaps, the most peculiar invention in Blake's visionary poems. Nothing in western literary or biblical tradition can explain their existence. Should we take a closer look at Hinduism, however, we can see how Blake's rudimentary understanding of the Trimurti may have offered the poet the seminal idea for their creation.

Blake would have encountered an explanation of the Trimurti in both Volney's *Ruins* and in Jones's essay 'On the Gods of Greece, Italy, and India'.[6] The Trimurti constitutes the trinity of the godhead *Brahm* (Brahm is different from his incarnation Brahma), and illustrates how the primal god-power Brahm manifests in the world of time. Split into three aspects, Brahm is represented by the trinity of *Brahma*, the god of creation, *Vishnu*, the god who sustains creation, and *Shiva*, the god who destroys and renews creation. Once the creation is brought forth, Brahma's work, for the most part, is finished. Vishnu and Shiva, however, have a vast realm over which to rule. All pervasive, Vishnu's job is to preserve the universe. The great religious treatises, *Ramayana* and *Bhagavad Gita*, illustrate Vishnu entering the realm of time as a perfect human being to establish justice. He does this by incarnating as an *avatar*, such as Rama and Krishna. Vishnu has supposedly incarnated ten times to restore balance to the universe. Shiva, as well, is the object of fervent devotion throughout India, the destruction he causes considered necessary for renewal. His work completes the cycle of birth, life, death, and rebirth. Notice how a Shiva-like energy flows through much of Blake's poetry. In the poem 'The Tyger', from *Songs of Experience*, the questions asked with such rhythmic insistence – 'Did he smile his work to see? / Did he who made the Lamb make thee?' (19–20; E 25) – epitomise the Hindu belief that the god who creates also destroys, the power of destruction simultaneously the power of renewal. 'The Tyger' embodies the creative and destructive energy of the Trimurti while suggesting that violence is a form of benevolence when preparing for regeneration. If we were to consider the positive aspect of Shiva's nature, as Blake seems to do, we would then embrace the concept of renewal (and redemption) implicit in *The Songs*.

The Eastern notion of the macrocosm-in-the-microcosm represents a hallmark of Blake's poetry, and to a western consciousness is one of its most confusing aspects. In Blake's prophetic poems it works like this: Albion, the protagonist of *Milton, Jerusalem*, and *The Four Zoas*, is one being as well as the accumulative expression of all Englishmen and women. His body constitutes all of England as well as a single human form. He is best understood as embodying the macrocosm in the human form. Even more intriguing, the Zoas (like the Trimurti) represent Albion's different cognitive and sensory powers. Together, they represent the single creation, Albion. Each of the Zoas (Urizen, Urthona, Tharmas and Luvah) has its own defining attributes and reigns sovereign over its assigned realm. Only when the Zoas are united do they constitute the one expression of Albion. Such is the case with the Trimurti. In this analogy, Brahm is like Albion whose expression manifests in the characters of the gods Brahma, Vishnu and Shiva rather than the Zoas. Likewise, Brahma, Vishnu and Shiva each rule over a designated kingdom in the division of time. In his essay, 'On the Gods of Greece, Italy, and India', Jones explains that 'the Indian Triad, BRAHMA, VISHNU, AND MAHA'DEVA OR SIVA, are three *forms* of one of the same Godhead' (241). He continues,

> . . . the learned *Indians* . . . acknowledge only One Supreme Being, whom they call BRAHME, or THE GREAT ONE . . . and they suppose him to manifest his power by the operation of his divine spirit, whom they name VISHNU, the *Pervader* . . . When they consider the divine power exerted in *creating*, or in giving existence to that which existed not before, they call the Deity BRAHMA . . . and, when they view him in the light of *Destroyer*, or rather *Changer* of forms, they give him a thousand names, of which SIVA [is] . . . the most common.
>
> (242–3)

Just as the Trimurti are different expressions of One Being, Blake gives the Zoas god-like powers that together represent Albion. An interesting portrayal of this occurs in Blake's engraving 'The Vision of Ezekiel – the eyes of God and four-headed human figure: water colour (engraved 1794)' which offers a stunning depiction of four aspects of a single human consciousness. Here, Ezekiel strides out of a wind, winged, with arms outstretched. His face glares forward, whereas on each side of his head another face stares in opposite directions so that four aspects of Ezekiel are embodied in one human form. Likewise, in Hindu statuary, the god Brahma is depicted with four faces turned in each direction, portraying his omnipresence. Jones's essay includes an engraving of Brahma with four heads which the poet would have seen, possibly providing him with the idea for engraving Ezekiel in this unusual manner.[7]

Another connection between the Trimurti and the Zoas occurs with their female counterparts. Where each of the Trimurti has a female consort, so, too, the Zoas have their female Emanations. Each Hindu goddess manifests the feminine face of the god's unique qualities in the world. Jones writes, 'the *Hindu* goddesses are believed to be the *powers* of their respective lords' (1: 247). Just as the Trimurti represent the three aspects of the primal power and ultimately cannot be thought of as separate from this power, the female consorts are indistinct from their male counterparts. It is only in the realm of time that such distinctions of male and female can be made. Thus, Brahma, the Creator, manifests with his consort, Sarasvati (goddess of poetry, music and all intellectual pursuits). Vishnu, the Sustainer, has a consort named Lakshmi (goddess of good fortune), and whenever he incarnates as an *avatar*, Lakshmi incarnates with him. When Vishnu entered time as Rama, she married him as Sita; when he incarnated as Krishna, she married him as Radha. Shiva, the Destroyer, has three consorts; one can consider them as expressing three different aspects of Shiva's multifaceted nature. They are Parvati, Durga and Kali. (Shiva's consorts are given different names according to a region's dialect, but these names are most common today.) His first consort, Parvati, is renowned as a benign form of the mother goddess. Durga, his second consort, was created from the combined anger of several gods and manifests a righteous female energy. Of her Jones writes, 'The attributes of DURGA, or *Difficult of access*, are also conspicuous ... in this character she resembles MINERVA, not the peaceful inventress of the fine and useful arts, but PALLAS, armed with a helmet and spear: both represent heroick *Virtue*, or Valour united with Wisdom' (1: 252). Kali is Shiva's third and most renowned companion. Embodying the terror of annihilation, her tongue drips with the blood of victims; she wears a skirt of severed arms and a necklace of skulls. In the *Hitopadesa*, which Blake would have had access to, Sir Charles Wilkins also mentions the consorts of Shiva. He writes: 'In her destructive quality she is called Kalee (a name derived from Kala, time)' and 'Gowree is one of the names of the consorts of Seeva' which 'means a young woman (literally, a fair one)'.[8] Wilkins's statements acknowledge that Shiva's consorts embody different aspects of Shiva's powers of destruction and renewal. Likewise, the Emanations embody the chameleon aspects of Shiva's consorts – particularly the ways in which they manifest from Eden to Ulro – with two differences: each Emanation is given the ability to incarnate different states as continuous aspects of one personality, and each Emanation devolves. The Hindu goddesses merely reflect the god's power, whereas the Emanations have free will and use theirs toward divisive and recuperative purposes.

Like the Trimurti, the Zoas represent four unique kinds of powers assigned to a particular realm. Whereas the Zoas are subject to Albion, the Trimurti are subject to Brahm. Urizen portrays the reasoning function or intellect; Tharmas represents the senses; Luvah personifies the emotions; and Urthona (who eventually is subsumed by the artistic function, Los) represents the imagination. In their unfallen state when they are operating at their highest potential, the Zoas are neither male nor female, but both. However, when a Zoa 'falls' from Eternity into Experience, the world of time and space, it then splits into a male and female counterpart. Blake addresses the male aspect by its original name, Zoa, whereas he terms the Zoas' female counterparts or companions Emanations. Urizen is paired with Ahania, Luvah with Vala, Urthona with Enitharmon, and Tharmas with Enion. The moment a Zoa splits into male and female, that Zoa has fallen into the realm of Experience (marked by duality). Blake implies that if we were to see them with the eyes of Eternity, the Zoas and their Emanations would be undifferentiated from each other.

Let us consider for a moment the Hindu analogue. Brahma, Vishnu and Shiva are 'emanations' from the one primal creator, Brahm. As Brahm enters the world of time, it splits into three governing powers, each with a female consort. Just as the male facet of the Zoa retains its original identity and name, and the female Zoa acquires a new or secondary identity as an Emanation, so, too, Brahma, Vishnu and Shiva retain their male identity whereas their female counterparts are addressed by other names. However, there is no difference between the Trimurti and their female consorts. Hindu art and architecture often address this underlying unity by depicting the gods (particularly Vishnu) with both male and female body parts to express their union and unity.

A major distinction between the Trimurti and the Zoas exists in that Hinduism, unlike Christianity, does not represent the world of time as a fallen world. Although evil certainly exists and must be countered, according to Hinduism evil is not the condition on which the world operates. There is no 'original sin'. One of the main duties of the Hindu gods (and human beings in relationship with the gods) is to maintain the balance between good and evil, to reward and to punish according to deeds. This is a huge philosophical difference between the two religious traditions, and yet Blake was unconcerned with these differences. Hinduism intrigued him mainly because it offered strategies for representing eternity in the world of time, and it suggested ways in which he could characterise the primal forces buried within each human psyche. These ideas had never before been represented in western literary tradition, which is primarily centred on the hero and heroic action as well as on the linearity of time where eternity is viewed as separate from time. The similarity between the Hindu gods and consorts and Blake's Zoas/Emanations offers a strong case for Hinduism's influence in Blake's prophetic works where Hinduism offered an excellent means for expressing his psychological, political and spiritual vision.

Albion

As has already been discussed, Albion represents Blake's ideal human being; his universal qualities are representative of all Englishmen. As Blake's poetry develops, so, too, the character of Albion matures. To begin with, *The Four Zoas* (predecessor and prototype to *Milton* and *Jerusalem*) enacts the fall of Albion, the universal man, when his four Zoas (the four faculties of the human soul) fall into disunity. The poem depicts the Zoas' struggle toward unity, culminating in a celebratory feast in which Albion, who has been sleeping for most of the poem, participates. Blake links the poem's interior action, which takes place at the level of dream, to a historical landscape, wherein Albion represents all of England as well as the Englishman or woman who needs to undergo a similar process of spiritual redemption. Blake's language and imagery imply that Albion's transformation fulfils biblical prophecy, and the heaven on earth that the Eternal Man achieves represents England's primary goal and destiny.

In *Milton* we find a greater coalescence in Blake's visionary world. A strong correlation between *Milton* and Hindu lore occurs when Albion is summed up in a passage reminiscent of Wilkins's *Bhagavat-Geeta* when Krishna (the incarnation of Vishnu) gives Arjuna (a human being and hero) 'a heavenly eye, with which [to] behold my divine connection' (Lecture XI).[9] In other words, Krishna bestows the warrior, Arjuna, with the ability to behold Krishna in his eternal form as Vishnu. A comparable scene occurs in *Milton* wherein Albion's true form is also revealed:

> Then Albion rose up in the Night of Beulah on his Couch
> Of dread repose *seen by the visionary eye*;
> . . .
> His right foot stretches to the sea on Dover cliffs, his heel
> On Canterbury's ruins; his right hand covers lofty Wales,
> His left Scotland; his bosom girt with gold involves
> York, Edinburgh, Durham & Carlisle & on the front
> Bath, Oxford, Cambridge, Norwich; his right elbow
> Leans on the Rocks of Erin's Land; Ireland, ancient nation.
> His head bends over London: he sees his embodied Spectre
> Trembling before him with exceeding great trembling & fear.

> (*M* 39: 32–3, 40–7; E 140–1; emphasis added)

There is no plot connection between this passage and the *Bhagavat-Geeta* except in its presentation of the divine vision to a mortal eye. Just as the vision of Albion causes 'his embodied Spectre / . . . great trembling & fear', so, too, Arjuna is described as terrified by the overwhelming vision of time and space conflated into one, co-eternal moment. He exclaims:

> I behold, O God! within thy breast, the *Devas* (gods) assembled, and every specific tribe of beings . . . I see thee without beginning, without middle, and without end; of valour infinite; of arms innumerable; the sun and moon thy eyes; thy mouth a flaming fire, and the whole world shining with thy reflected glory!
>
> (XI, 91)

This vision of eternity in the realm of time that occurs in the *Bhagavat-Geeta* constitutes a characteristic Blakean move.

Furthermore, just as Blake describes Albion's body as a manifestation of England, Vishnu's body is illustrated in Hindu art as an embodiment of the entire universe; in these depictions one of his eyes is light, representing the day, and the other eye is dark, representing the night. The sun emerges from his mouth, and lesser deities such as the gods of wind, water and fire, are shown residing inside his body.[10] Also like Albion, both Vishnu and Brahma are often represented as sleeping gods, and the life we are living as but a small part of their dream. Vishnu, like Albion, stands apart from the creation as well as appearing in the form of an *avatar* or a character within the creation; Albion, too, resides outside the action of the Zoas as well as appearing as a character within the drama of the poem.

Time

> Then Eno a daughter of Beulah took a Moment of Time
> And drew it out to Seven thousand Years . . .
> And . . . in Every year made windows into Eden
>
> (*FZ* I: 222–4; E 304–5)

This eloquent passage describes a very Hindu notion that time is shot through with the presence of eternity. Blake's view of time bears many features of Hinduism. Traditional Christianity proposes a linear view of time beginning with the first immoral act (constituting a fall out of eternity), and then runs its course of a few thousand years until time stops in an apocalyptic moment that can be described as the destruction of the consciousness of time. However, Blake's Christian view of time is more Hindu-like; rather than occurring merely sequentially, time is concurrent with eternity. In both views time acts as a moral agency, but in Blake's view, the permeability of time with eternity is redemptive in nature; in other words, one does not have to wait until the end of time to receive a vision of eternity. These ideas may owe much to Hinduism which views time as a recurring performance, an eternal cycle of life, death, and resurrection. Blake suggests in both the *Songs* and prophetic books that eternity can be experienced at any moment in time.

In 1788, Sir William Jones published a paper 'On the Chronology of the Hindus' (Volume II of *Asiatick Researches*) in which he describes this vast, circular notion of time from 'one of the most curious books in Sanskerit'. Blake would have had access to this paper:

> The sun causes the division of day and night, which are of two sorts, those of men and those of the Gods; . . . This aggregate of four ages, amounting to twelve thousand divine years, is called an age of the Gods; and a thousand such divine ages added together, must be considered as a day of *Brahma*: his night has also the same duration . . . There are *alternate* creations and destructions *of worlds* through innumerable *Manwantaras*: the Being supremely desirable, performs all this again and again. Such is the arrangement of infinite time . . .
>
> (II: 7: 112–13)

Just as time in Hinduism is inscribed with the notion of circularity as well as with the eternal vision (and participation) of the gods, so, too, in much of Blake's poetry, time and eternity occur as concurrent states of consciousness. The *Songs* offer a superb example of eternity available in time (or vice versa). To some extent innocence constitutes consciousness of eternity and the divine vision, whereas experience equates with consciousness of future and past and the separation between self and other which results in feelings of guilt and grief. Apparently, Blake reinterpreted the Christian model of innocence and experience through an eastern model of time and eternity-in-time, claiming that we can enter the Garden of Eden or Eternity at any moment.

The Oriental Renaissance flourished in late eighteenth and early nineteenth-century England due, in part, to copious essays, translations and comparative mythographies. Weir (126) points out that because of the politics in England at the time, when these materials were introduced, they 'were immediately politicized by a radical ideology that question[ed] the operations of empire in distant dominions'. Although the study of Hinduism was for some an intellectual pursuit and for others a political one, only a mind as subtle as Blake's could grasp Hinduism's unique characteristics and distil a formula that, once incorporated into his own art, would alter traditional western literary models of poetry and prophecy. Blake's poetry, infused with basic Hindu principles and strategies, has enriched western literature in ways that we are just beginning to understand. The Oriental

Renaissance provides one of many keys to unlocking the mystery of the poet's genius, and offers a way to grasp those curious, even extraordinary aspects of Blake's poetry that many find so confounding. In short, Hinduism should be given its due as a vital influence in understanding Blake's work and thought.

Notes

1. Bernard Blackstone, *English Blake* (Archon Books, 1966), 6; my emphasis. 'Albion rose' colour-printed impression in the British Museum.
2. Robert Essick agrees that the inscription beneath the engraving *Glad Day* was made after 1800: 'The idea of Albion as a person does not appear in Blake's poetry until some of the later revisions of *The Four Zoas* manuscript': *The Separate Plates of William Blake* (Princeton, NJ: Princeton University Press, 1983), 128.
3. S. Foster Damon, *William Blake: His Philosophy and Symbols* (Boston & New York: Houghton Mifflin, 1924), 145.
4. (Albany, NY: State University of New York Press, 2003), 45.
5. I am indebted to Dr Helen Bruder's research on this. Her note to me on 5 April 2005 states, 'Ann's transcription of the "Hymn to Sereswati" instantly made me think of Ahania's song to Urizen in "Ahania."'
6. *A New Translation of Volney's Ruins*, 2 vols, 1802 (New York & London: Garland Press, 1979); and Jones, *Asiatick Researches* (Calcutta Edition, London: 1784 / 1799) Vol. 1.
7. For the Ezekiel engraving, see Kathleen Raine's *Blake & Tradition* (Princeton, NJ: Princeton University Press, 1968), Vol. 2, fig. 192. For the Brahma engraving, see Jones, 245. Weir (76–7) points to the resemblance between Blake's engraving of Beulah (*J*, plate 53) and a drawing from Moor's *The Hindu Pantheon* of the goddess Pedma; both are seated on an open flower wearing a tiered crown. Blake absorbed many details from eastern religious art and incorporated them into his own designs.
8. *Hitopadesa: Fables and Proverbs from the Sanskrit* (Gainesville, FL: Scholar's Fascimiles & Reprints, 1968), 208, 192.
9. *The Bhagavat-Geeta (1785)*, translated with notes (Gainesville, FL: Scholar's Facsimiles & Reprints, 1959), 90.
10. See John Bowker, *World Religions* (New York, NY: DK Publishing, 1977), 26–7.

14
Towards an Ungendered Romanticism: Blake, Robinson and Smith in 1793

Jacqueline M. Labbe

In 1793, as events in France were taking a decisive turn towards violence and international war, three poets published work reflecting on the revolution in France in which the personal, to utilise a familiar slogan, becomes political. For these poets, elements of their experience as British subjects and as artists blend to produce work both of a piece with previous efforts, and pointing in new, fruitful directions. And, in ways that suggest the broad applicability of tropes rather than an eclectic or individualistic turn, all turn to the historical and historicised figure of Marie Antoinette as particularly representative of the human cost of the events of 1793. For these three poets, 1793 is as significant a year as 1789: it signifies their new engagement with history as it is being made, and it raises, for their readers, and especially their modern critics, questions of gender and expectation. Do these poets – Charlotte Smith, William Blake, and Mary Robinson – write as women and a man, as worldly and secluded, as quotidian and visionary? Do they abide by the rules, or write their own?

Blake, as the archetypal iconoclast, is rarely discussed in the company of his peers. Most of his readers want him to be exceptional, unique, and even marginal, an embodiment, really, of his own artistic style. But, as Tristanne Connolly's chapter in this volume demonstrates, neither Blake nor his contemporaries are diminished by association; rather, congruences and trends are illuminated, made visible.[1] As a London poet, Blake shares with Robinson a feel for, and a sympathy with, the urban; both her celebrity and his obscurity are contingent on metropolitan living. Then again, as protégées of William Hayley, Blake shares with Smith the obligations attendant on the patronage system, even though, in 1793, Smith was in the process of being ejected from Hayley's circle just as Blake was being welcomed in. Politically, the three poets span a spectrum: in 1793, Blake was wearing the red cap of the Jacobins; Smith was sheltering émigrés in her Brighton home but also writing the pro-Revolutionary poem *The Emigrants*; Robinson was identifying, in print at least, with the persecuted French royals. Rather than isolating Blake, this suggests his affinity with his times, his responsiveness to a political openness that still characterised the England of 1793, but which was just about to change following the declaration of war by France in February, and the commencement of active hostilities.

If Blake was not the whole-hearted creature of difference he has been assumed, is he yet a fully masculinised product of a patriarchal culture, a poet for whom the feminine is either virginal or whoreish, innocent or monstrous – Thel and Oothoon or Enitharmon and the Female Will? Does he write as a man, with vision, in marked contrast to the materiality of Smith and Robinson as women? Do they in turn pursue a poetical ethic of care and a devotion to all things corporeal and earthly? On the one hand, we have Blake's exploration of rape and sexuality in his major 1793 texts *Visions of the Daughters of Albion* and *America: a Prophecy.* On the other, we have Robinson's sympathetic portrayal of the French king and queen as victims in her 1793 *Poems,* and Smith's similar characterisation of Marie Antoinette as betrayed mother, linked to her own self-portrait as harassed and terrorised, in *The Emigrants.* Such a partial description, of course, hides more than it reveals; even at the level of plot, the poets' 1793 output complicates more than it conforms to expectations. Indeed, even as 1790 is the year of Burke, 1791 the year of Paine, and 1792 the year of Wollstonecraft (and Paine redux), so too 1793 marks the establishment of Blake, Smith and Robinson as politicians in poetry: despite differences of style, their poetry emanates from a shared involvement with history as it is both witnessed and lived.

Provocatively so, for the three poets' 'history' is encased in the female body, and recorded via images of sex and motherhood. In 1793, the most public female body was that of Marie Antoinette, widowed in February when Louis XVI was executed, and executed herself in October after a trial that portrayed her as a sexual monster lacking in all natural maternal and feminine graces. Despite the erotic chivalry of Burke's descriptive prose in his *Reflections,* for most Britons she represented the worst of French excess right up until her death by guillotine, at which point she was suddenly recast as a model of sensibility and a martyred mother.[2] The two are connected; as Helen Bruder notes, 'Burke's portrayal of Marie Antoinette as the perfect sexualized victim is precisely what we see replicated in many of the poems *written after her death.*'[3] But in the years between Burke's charged prose and the queen's death, she was more whore than angel, more monster than mother. In 1793, this had not yet changed, as Bruder's point makes clear. What does it mean, then, that Smith and Robinson plainly characterise her as a grieving and pitiable mother? And how do we slot in Blake, with his Oothoon and shadowy virgin? Marie Antoinette as such does not appear in his poetry until 1794, in *Europe,* but as I hope to show, his embodiments of female sexuality and desire from 1793 act as counterparts to the purified victims of Smith and Robinson. Even as *America* displaces the revolutionary energies of the French Revolution back a generation, so too

Oothoon and her unhappy cohort, the dark virgin, cover for the French queen.[4]

Visions concerns itself with the expression of female desire and the costs of openly declaring what Oothoon calls 'love' but which Bromion and Theotormon interpret as lust. When she plucks the flower of the golden nymph, she lays claim to a kind of verbal freedom; she vocalises her actions and thus authorises them: 'I pluck thee from thy bed/ Sweet flower and put thee here to glow between my breasts/ And thus I turn my face to where my whole soul seeks' (E 46). Oothoon enacts a desire that is not necessarily sexual but that is seen to be, emphasising that, in Blake's culture, as soon as a woman seeks rather than waiting to be sought, she is identified as fair game. Her openness is regarded as looseness; that is, she has rejected the social strictures that require her to be the grateful, and passive, recipient of love. The entire plot of the poem is pre-scripted from the moment Oothoon plucks the flower of self-determination, which ironically leads only to greater repression for the momentarily freed woman. Bromion, in other words, reacts in an accepted, if perhaps overly violent, manner, since as any reader of, say, Fanny Burney, knows, to stray from the openly lit path of respectability is to forsake the protection of respectability. Oothoon's experience mirrors that of the hapless heroine of sensibility, but Blake extends it to the conclusion that is inevitable if there is no hero to preserve her virtue.[5] For Blake, the hero, Theotormon, is as implicated as Bromion, since he is unable to see beyond the event. Trapped in his own certainty that female sexual activity is synonymous with female moral lassitude, he luxuriates in his sufferings, while Oothoon is bound to her rapist and Bromion continues to taunt Theotormon with his conquest.

So far so familiar. Although the plot perhaps edges closer to Gothic as the poem progresses, its basic outlines are a clearly recognisable part of 1790s' culture. Oothoon is held responsible for her own fall, and Bromion and Theotormon are more interested in each other than they are in her. Having violated the cultural imperative that she stay silent, Oothoon suffers the usual punishment, and indeed welcomes it: the eagles' beaks, the search for ever-stronger modes of debasement, until she subsumes herself entirely to what she understands to be Theotormon's preferred sexual mode: voyeurism. Given that Theotormon has done little *but* watch and smile throughout the poem, she may well be right. Although her story is more than a 'melodramatic romance', as Bruder notes (87), it nonetheless does not break free from genre, as the Daughters of Albion recognise when they 'hear her woes, and echo back her sighs'. They do this because they know the script; they *know* what happens to the 'unashamed' woman. Blake allows Oothoon to articulate the confused duality of a woman who is both innocent and experienced, pure and defiled. That she ends up ventriloquising masculine sexual fantasies only emphasises the strength of the plot in which she is caught up.

The shadowy daughter of Urthona in *America* fulfils a fate complementary to Oothoon's. Whereas Oothoon 'loved Theotormon/ And . . . was not ashamed' (*Visions*, 'The Argument', 1–2), the dark virgin is 'invulnerable tho' naked, save where clouds roll round her loins' (E 51), a marker of her modesty and severe purity. She is untouchable until she is touched, unimpressed by Orc's impressive embodiments (eagle, lion, whale and so on) until he forces her awareness of his physical attributes. This is a rape just as much as Bromion's rendings, as the repetition of 'rend'/'rent' shows; when Orc 'siez'd the panting struggling womb' the dark virgin is violated, despite her 'first-born smile':

> O what limb rending pains I feel. thy fire & my frost
> Mingle in howling pains, in furrows by thy lightnings rent;
> This is eternal death; and this is the torment long foretold.

> (E 52)

She smiles because she knows her role; the violence of Blake's language and imagery indicate not pleasure, but agony. Where Oothoon's consciousness of love allowed her to gloss over the violence of her rape, the shadowy female's experience is only about violence. Orc may well be the spirit of revolutionary fervour, but Blake's stark rendering of his use of his energies in the Preludium suggest the poet's recognition that, as Bruder notes, 'no woman could ever be liberated by [Orc] and no woman ever is' (130). The dark virgin's similar experience to Oothoon's, and the different direction it takes, suggests that *America*, in its Preludium at least, follows two scripts: the semi-pornographic line that women enjoy rape, and the historical line that can only see women as symbols. This in turn hints that *Visions* is also about history: that is, shadowing Oothoon's plot is a revolutionary one. The two poems offer versions of a female-centred historical plot, focused on a historicised understanding of the cultural valence of the sexualised woman. And this returns us to Marie Antoinette, whose public persona combines the sexual identities of Oothoon and the dark virgin.

Blake does not explicitly mention Marie Antoinette, and as Bruder remarks, her public image as 'a flirtatious tyrant' has occupied 'the few critics who have found some trace of her in *Europe*' (162). Bruder's scrupulous investigation yields the insight that 'the events of the queen's imprisonment and death, and British reactions to these, initiated in Blake's mind a process of revisionist thinking . . . [where] the queen begins to be seen more as a scapegoat and victim than a tyrant' (162–3). For Bruder, Blake forms his ideas after the queen's execution; but his 1793 work shows that he has already begun to think about versions of female identity strikingly similar to the queen's. Further, he anticipates the sympathy that the queen attracts only after her death; those Blake scholars who see Marie Antoinette as a 'royal whore' in *Europe* are missing the point that, by 1794, this was no longer the dominant characterisation.[6] And by glossing over Marie Antoinette's cultural transformation from whore to angel, they also misunderstand her relevance to Blake's earlier output. In turning now to Smith and Robinson, I want to show that, in 1793, the queen was an iconic presence, an emblem of history, and a public embodiment of an ideology that despised the sexual woman.

Robinson knew Marie Antoinette personally, having met her in 1781 in Paris; Judith Pascoe notes that Robinson 'attracted the attention' of the queen, 'who requested the loan of Robinson's miniature of the Prince of Wales'.[7] In return, Robinson admired the young queen's beauty, spirit, and style, and her sympathy persisted when, in 1793, she published 'Marie Antoinette's Lamentation, in her Prison in the Temple'.[8] This poem was widely circulated, appearing first in the 8 March 1793 issue of the *Oracle* newspaper, then in the *European Magazine* for May 1793, and finally as part of Robinson's 1793 *Poems*. This multiple publication suggests its resonance for Robinson; despite the prevalence of pictures of Marie Antoinette as corrupt and impure, Robinson creates a 'martyr figure' (Pascoe, 52), signalling the turn the queen's fortunes were taking. For Robinson, whose sympathies were not, in the main, anti-Jacobin, the queen's status as victimised female overwhelmed her position as representative of the *ancien régime*.[9] Robinson, whose own public persona emphasised her sexuality and availability, constructs a queen overwhelmed with wifely and maternal sorrow. The opening image of her 'bosom' (1) is swiftly rendered tragic rather than erotic, transformed by line 5 into a 'sad breast' on which 'appears / A dreadful record – WRITTEN WITH MY TEARS!' (5–6). Equally, Robinson counters the sexual associations of Marie Antoinette's bed by 'o'erspread[ing]' her couch with metaphorical 'thorn[s]' and portraying the queen as terrorised by visions of her children 'ON THEIR FUNERAL BED!' (12, 24). The queen names herself as mother five times in the poem, and as wife/widow twice, even combining the two in line 34: '. . . let a WIDOW'D MOTHER's darlings rest!'[10]

For Robinson, the queen's ultimate identity is that of the violated mother: 'all the MOTHER RUSHES TO MY HEART!' (66). Her sole reference to her past avoids all sexual scandal by returning to her youth: 'The jocund MORN OF LIFE, that once was mine . . ./. . ./ I ne'er shall see THAT BLISSFUL MORN RETURN!' (16, 18). The poem engages with history only to renounce it; the queen suffers a generalised female woe that is in its own way as scripted as that in *Visions* or *America*. Imprisoned, powerless, mocked by her 'TYRANT JAILOR' (60), the queen has become a maternal romance heroine, her sexuality totally subsumed to her social role. While to present a woman as consumed by her maternal cares is not unusual, of course, what is remarkable about Robinson's poem is its prescience. Blake's poems are predicated on the social costs of and assumptions about expressions of female sexuality; when Robinson takes as her subject one of the most public of sexualised women she discounts this aspect of her persona entirely. More than that, she does so at a time when, for her readers, Marie Antoinette has not yet been rehabilitated by death, so that even as the imagery she uses and the emotions to which she appeals are unexceptionable, the overall thrust of the poem is itself revolutionary. By insisting that we see the queen as a mother – that is, as a woman rather than as a monster – Robinson forces a confrontation with the historic figure of the corrupt queen. Or rather, given that this is still history in progress, she challenges the myth of the powerfully sexualised queen on which both the revolutionaries and British culture as a whole relied. In this way, her depiction of the maternal martyr functions as a counterweight to Blake's violated virgins.

Charlotte Smith's long poem *The Emigrants*, published in May 1793, picks up on Robinson's re-evaluation of the queen. In Book 2, she too focuses on the queen as mother in a passage that was later reprinted in partial form in *The Universal Magazine* for August 1793 and *The Gentleman's and London Magazine* for September 1793.[11] What distinguishes Smith's maternal queen from that of Robinson is Smith's emphasis on the queen's faults, now atoned for through suffering but not forgotten. Robinson presents a pure heroine; there is no sense that she has a past or is at all culpable. For Smith, Marie Antoinette is *now* a 'hapless Queen', a 'wretched Mother, petrified with grief', but Smith does not shy away from her

> . . . fault[s], to which Prosperity
> Betray'd thee, when it plac'd thee on a throne
> Where boundless power was thine . . .
>
> . . . Whate'er thy errors were,
> Be they no more remember'd; tho' the rage
> Of Party swell'd them to such crimes, as bade
> Compassion stifle every sigh that rose
> For thy disastrous lot . . .[12]

Smith is not explicit, but her previous reference to 'Party rage' had linked it to 'base Venality' and 'private vice' which made 'even the wildest profligate recoil' (II: 118, 119, 120, 121). Clearly, she alludes to Marie Antoinette's sexualised past, and just as clearly pardons the queen. Robinson, because she does not admit any fault, cannot overtly cleanse a reputation; Smith, more openly revolutionary than Robinson, is also more nuanced in her depiction of a figure damned by historical events, rendered symbolic by a culture in need of a rationale for violence. Smith presents the queen as both a woman and a symbol, just as she presents France as both justified in its uprising, and 'unhappy' in its progress. Where for Robinson the queen is a representative of distressed womanhood, and for Blake the underlying image for sexualised female agency, for Smith she *is* France.

Smith does not mince words; although the political climate of spring 1793 is such that to write an openly pro-Revolutionary poem would be to invite prosecution under the Seditious Libel Act, she is adamant that there was a point to the original rebellion which had to do with exactly the corruption and 'venality' of which the queen had become the main representative. Further, she hints that such corruption is not confined to the French government of the late 1780s; her reference to 'a wretch, whose private vice/ Makes even the wildest profligate recoil' (II: 120–1)[13] very possibly alludes to the Prince of Wales, a home-grown, masculine version of the vicious queen of France, and elsewhere in the poem she reaches a height of rhetorical fervour in condemning the 'pamper'd Parasites! whom Britons pay / For forging fetters for them': 'learn, that if oppress'd too long, / The raging multitude, to madness stung, / Will turn on their oppressors; and . . ./ . . ./ . . . will redress themselves! / . . ./ As now in Gallia . . .' (I: 330–1, 333–5, 337, 343). Smith masks her sentiments with nods to the desirability of the British constitutional monarchy, among other safe subjects, but as with her turn to the queen, she does not shy away from controversy or prettify the ugly facts of war. The queen, then, is the culmination of Smith's parade of horrors: a victim, but not innocent.

Taken on its own, Blake's output in 1793 conforms to his increasingly detailed establishment of historicised myth; thus, Oothoon refers only to herself, and the dark virgin is a synonym for the new world impregnated with Orc's energy. But Blake, of course, did not live in an isolated bubble. As a radical inhabitant of London during a tense and oppressive historical period, he writes poems that respond to atmosphere and event. In 1793, the most visible female victim – of war, of revolution, of her own sexuality and its interpretation by others – is Marie Antoinette. As mother, wife, and lover, she fulfils for her peers the major female social roles, and her status as symbol means that these roles are mainly constructed by a voracious public. By extension, France takes on the aspect of its famous queen, a feminised location in both positive (mother) and negative (whore) terms. The French Revolution, in focusing social violence, fixed on Marie Antoinette as a symbol of the baseness of the *ancien régime*; British culture similarly used her as representative of French dissipation. By 1793 she has become all things to all people; Burke's romance heroine of 1790 leads to Robinson's peerless mother, Blake's sexual victim, Smith's repentant queen. Where Blake, ironically, most closely follows Burke in rewriting Marie Antoinette as sexual but violated, blamed for her own victimisation, both Smith and Robinson diffuse her sexuality through an emphasis on her motherhood. Is this, then, how the poets write as gendered beings? Do Smith and Robinson privilege the mother because they are mothers? Does Blake explore sexuality because of masculine drives?

Perhaps, but this seems both to simplify and trivialise what the poets do. 1793 is about politics and the making of history, and Blake, for all his sexual openness, at this point retreats from the contemporary moment to the past, a relevant past no doubt, but in political terms a safe bet. Robinson engages directly with the present with her move to rehabilitate a queen whose sexual reputation has overwhelmed her public persona. Smith, of the three, is at the height of her political intervention; her 1792 novel *Desmond* argued strongly in favour of the revolution, and *The Emigrants*, for all its strategic approval of British civilisation, is a radical call to her society to look to its own failings. Witnesses to and scribes of culture-shaking events, these poets locate history in the body of a historical female figure. And as a woman reading the Blake of 1793, I would argue that placing Blake in his literary context yields insights not visible to the purely gendered lens.

Notes

1. In *Historicizing Blake*, Steve Clark and David Worrall (eds) emphasise Blake's position as an artist among artists in the 1790s and later, but despite this valuable corrective he is still most often viewed as an anomaly rather than a member of a literary community (Basingstoke: Macmillan, 1994), 1–23.
2. See Judith Pascoe, *Romantic Theatricality: Gender, Poetry and Spectatorship* (Ithaca: Cornell University Press, 1997), ch. 4. Numerous prints from the period portray her as an idealised beauty, facing death with courage; examples include *The Martyrdom of Marie Antoinette* (28 October 1793) and *Death of Marie Antoinette* (23 October 1793).
3. See *William Blake and the Daughters of Albion* (Basingstoke: Macmillan, 1997), 167, my emphasis. Bruder's study is the first to recognise Blake's complex yet liberal approach to female sexuality, and my present argument is indebted to her discussions of *Visions of the Daughters of Albion* and *America: a Prophecy*.
4. Simultaneously, Smith was also using the American Revolution as a feint for her critique of current affairs in her 1793 novel *The Old Manor House*.
5. Another way to phrase this would be to note that Oothoon suffers as the conventional heroine might were she not saved. Smith's novels, however, frequently feature a secondary heroine whose open declarations of love are met with authorial sympathy.
6. Bruder cites David Erdman: 'Marie Antoinette was little more than Erdman's "royal whore" – prostituting herself for whatever power she could obtain' (162). Bruder, of course, usefully complicates this view. See Erdman, *Blake: Prophet Against Empire* (Princeton, NJ: Princeton University Press, 1969/1977), 227.
7. See *Mary Robinson, Selected Poems*, ed. Judith Pascoe (Peterborough: Broadview Press, 2000), 30.
8. Late in 1793 Robinson published a *Monody to the Memory of Marie Antoinette, Queen of France*, which first appeared in the *Oracle* of 18 December 1793, and was then published separately in 1794 as *Monody to the Memory of the Late Queen of France* (London: J. Evans, 1794).
9. Both Pascoe and Sharon Setzer argue that Robinson is 'more concerned with the gender politics that aligned Jacobins and anti-Jacobins than with the party politics that divided them' (Sharon Setzer, 'Romancing the Reign of Terror:

Sexual Politics in Mary Robinson's *Natural Daughter'*, *Criticism*, 39 (1997), 531–55, 532); Pascoe, *Selected Poems*, 52–3.

10. Terry Castle asserts that 'the queen's female acolytes tended on the whole to downplay the actual horror of her demise' but her concentration on the nineteenth and twentieth centuries means that she misses the relative grittiness of 1793 portrayals. (Terry Castle, 'Marie Antoinette Obsession', *Representations*, 38 (1992), 1–38, 34 n.46).

11. Betty Bennett's anthology *British War Poetry in the Age of Romanticism: 1793–1815* (New York: Garland Publishing, 1976) includes only one other poem about Marie Antoinette, 'Evening. An Elegy. Written on reading the melancholy Separation of the Dauphin from the Queen of France', by 'Eliza' (*The Gentleman's Magazine*, LXIII [November 1793], 1037–8). This poem strongly romanticises the queen as bereft mother, but was published a month after her execution.

12. *The Emigrants*, II: 156–64. *The Poems of Charlotte Smith*, ed. Stuart Curran (New York: Oxford University Press, 1993). Castle maintains that 'the charge of homosexuality was unquestionably the one that clung most damagingly' (18). However, for most British commentators, it was the accusation of incest with the Dauphin that seemed to prevail. Smith is politic in her vagueness.

13. These lines were omitted from the version published in the periodicals, which moves swiftly from an admiring mention of 'the brave Bernois [Henry IV], so justly called / The father of his people' to the 'innocent pris'ner, most unhappy heir / Of fatal greatness' (the Dauphin). In *The Emigrants*, Henry IV is called the 'darling of his people' (II: 116). While Stuart Curran speculates that the 'wretch' described in the omitted lines is Jean-Paul Marat, the description fits the Prince of Wales just as well, and such an association would provide a rationale for omitting the lines.

15
William Blake and Romantic Women Poets: 'Then what have I to do with thee?'

Harriet Kramer Linkin

If the first major change to the twentieth-century canon of British Romanticism was the inclusion of William Blake, the second major change was the inclusion of a fluctuating set of women poets, whose inclusion may have toppled the notion of a canon altogether. Although Blake surely would have appreciated being recognised, at last, 'among the greatest' (in John Keats's phrase), he might not have been quite so sanguine about that second development: all those Enitharmons finding rooms of their own, or at least spaces in our scholarship and teaching. This chapter explores Blake's intersection with Romantic-era women poets, subtitled with the line from 'To Tirzah' because I imagine Blake asking that very question in his belated (and bitter) addition to the *Songs*: 'Then what have I to do with thee?' (E 30). Until the mid-1990s, most of the scholarly work that took up Blake's intersection with the women writers of his day focused on his critical responses to them, especially Anna Barbauld and Mary Wollstonecraft. By the end of the twentieth century, critics began to position Blake's contributions to Romanticism within a larger spectrum of contemporary women writers, comparing his visionary work to Joanna Southcott's, for instance, or his lyrical work to Charlotte Smith's or Jane Taylor's (see Mellor, Zimmerman, Hampsey). Rather than compare or critique, I want to consider how contemporary women poets read and responded to Blake. That they read or responded to him at all may come as something of a surprise, but in fact quite a few did; indeed too many for this chapter to cover comprehensively, which queries what Blake had to do with Ann Batten Cristall, Smith, Mary Tighe, Felicia Hemans, and Lucy Hooper (the new daughters of Zelophehad).

I begin with Cristall, named by Stuart Curran as 'that rarest of Romantic poets, a follower of William Blake' (28). In 1795 Joseph Johnson published Cristall's single volume of verse under the same title as Blake's first book, *Poetical Sketches* (the only two volumes so titled until 1808). Many members of Johnson's circle subscribed to the project, including Wollstonecraft, who, with her sister Everina, furthered Cristall's efforts to support herself as a schoolteacher. Cristall's siblings both achieved success as artists, Joshua as a watercolourist and Elizabeth as an engraver, and thus likely knew Blake. But more than mere proximity invites readers to connect Cristall and Blake. Jerome McGann notes how lines 53–58 from Cristall's 'Before Twilight. Eyezion' evoke Blake's 'Song of Los' (198): 'A current of creative mind, / Wild as the wandering gusts of wind, / 'Mid fertile fancy's visions train'd, / Unzon'd I shot, and o'er each limit strain'd; / Around in airy circles whirl'd / By a genius infinite'. Duncan Wu observes that the unusual names Cristall devises for her visionary characters (Eyezion, Thelmon, Carmel) are a 'shade Blakean' (271) and that her original use of language 'is sometimes highly redolent of Blake, as when one of her characters is said to have "unzoned passions"' (272). Where McGann and Wu see affinity, Curran suggests deliberate citation: her title 'borrows the title of Blake's first collection', she 'makes a direct allusion to the last plate of *The Marriage of Heaven and Hell*, ending her "To a Lady, on the Rise of Morn" "Singing the heavenly song of liberty"', and her identification with nature 'reflects Blake's early view of natural processes as beneficent, countering restrictive human systems of law and morality' (28).

While Cristall's verse demonstrates capacious knowledge of many other poets, and resonates deeply with the work of Mary Robinson, Smith, and Ann Radcliffe, numerous poems clearly speak (back) to Blake, such as 'Song', which invokes several of Blake's *Songs*: 'Come, let us dance and sing, / While our spirits lightly wing; / Youth's gay fantastic spring / Wreathes the mystic bowrs!' (ll. 1–4). More than a song of innocence or experience, the lyric goes on to depict a moony bacchanal that concludes with an invitation to locate what critics used to call organised innocence: 'Round the sky, / The hours fly, / Launching to eternity! / Thus ever on the wing, / Come let us dance and sing, / Trampling on sorrow's sting, / Laughing at each sigh' (ll. 48–54). In this lyric and others, Cristall voices a sense of the female erotic or sexually active self in terms that may well invoke the Oothoon of *Visions*, as Curran proposes of 'To a Lady on the Rise of Morn', where a speaker exhorts a lady to 'Rise, blossom of the spring, / The dews of morn / Still linger on the barren thorn – / Arise and sing!' (ll. 1–4). Although Curran assumes the speaker to be male, Cristall never marks the speaker's gender, which could as easily be female and thereby present a sapphic idyll of the female erotic, perhaps as a radical alternative to the compulsory heterosexuality Blake configures for Oothoon. Thus when the speaker urges the lady to 'join my rapt'rous song' (l. 4), 'trace with me the opening flowers' (l. 15), and be superior to the frowns of Nature (l. 18), the 'heavenly song of liberty' (l. 20) might be sapphic love. Similarly, in the 'Song' that follows, 'Through springtime walks with flowers perfumed, / I chased a wild capricious fair' (ll. 1–2), Cristall rewrites Blake's usual depiction of the cruel courtship game. Here an unmarked speaker pursues an elusive female through spring, summer, autumn, and winter, until 'Tis now too cold to rove around; / The

Christmas game, the playful dance, / Incline her heart to glee – / Mutual we glow, and kindling love / Draws every wish to me' (ll. 28–32), an image of sapphic domesticity as alternative to the golden cage.

If Cristall's title serves as homage to Blake, it offers curious tribute in pointing to an episode in Blake's experience fraught with failure, certainly financial and possibly personal. Set up as a project to initiate Blake's poetic career, *Poetical Sketches* was privately printed at the expense of Revd A. Mathews and John Flaxman in a limited edition intended for sale. But according to G.E. Bentley, Blake 'never seems to have shown much interest in the little volume' (29), or at least in selling it. Critics have speculated that Blake's reluctance stemmed from the belittling anonymous preface, which labels Blake as an 'untutored youth . . . deprived of the leisure requisite to such a revisal of these sheets, as might have rendered them less unfit to meet the public eye. Conscious of the irregularities and defects to be found in almost every page, his friends have still believed that they possessed a poetic originality' (E 846). Untutored, unfit, irregular, defective. It is telling to see Cristall (ix) transform the terms that contain Blake's achievement into positive attributes that empower her voice as wild and irregular in her preface:

> From among my juvenile productions I have principally selected for the volume some poetical tales and unconnected sketches, which a love for the beauties of nature inspired. The versification is wild, and still incorrect, though I have taken much pains to reduce it to some degree of order; they were written without the knowledge of any rules; of which their irregularity is the natural consequence.

Paula Feldman suggests 'Cristall's modesty far exceeds what was customary' (*BWP* 213), but such excess leads to a palace of wisdom: Cristall is utterly successful in acquiring subscribers, making sales, and achieving critical success. Indeed her pre-emptive acknowledgment of 'wild' and 'incorrect' versification, 'written without the knowledge of any rules', may be what enables her to push a little harder on the gender boundaries of Blake's sexual machine.

I turn from Cristall to Smith, who offers a considerably less flattering response to Blake in a series of letters to Sarah and Samuel Rose (Blake's trial lawyer) that express professional and personal jealousy over Blake's relationship with William Hayley, an irony that truly begs the Tirzah question 'Then what have I to do with thee?' Whereas Blake depicted Hayley's patronage in destructive terms, Smith saw Hayley as an enabler of her career. She took it upon herself to acquire his patronage in April 1784: she sent him a manuscript copy of *Elegiac Sonnets*, asked permission to dedicate it to him if published, and thereby managed to publish her first book with a 'famous name for her Dedication' (Fletcher, 65). That same April Flaxman sent Blake's

Poetical Sketches to Hayley: 'I have left a *Pamphlet of Poems* with Mr. Long which he will transmit to Eartham; they are the writings of a Mr. BLAKE you have heard me mention, his education will plead sufficient excuse to your Liberal mind for the defects of his work' (Bentley, 31). Ten years would pass before Hayley pursued a relationship with Blake, during which time Smith enjoyed Hayley's friendship; Smith's letters reflect how Hayley began to withdraw his attention from 1794 on, when he met Blake and became 'consumed with this new friendship' (Stanton, xviii). In 1803 she tries to restore Hayley's attention by asking Samuel Rose whether Hayley might recommend an artist to produce drawings for her *Conversations Introducing Poetry*, perhaps like the 'ingenious engraver' who worked on Hayley's *Designs to a Series of Ballads*, namely Blake: 'I am afraid of addressing myself to Mr Hayley now on any subject whatever. I have not been favord with any answer to the Letter I took the liberty to address to him . . . My present purpose is to enquire whether there is not an ingenious Engraver who executed certain plates for a small work of Mr Hayley's relating to Animals. I know not what it is as I have never seen it' (9 February 1803; Stanton, 532–3). A year and a half later Smith names Blake directly as her competitor in a letter to Sarah Rose, which castigates Hayley for the uncomfortable situation he has put her in by pointedly repeating a remark Mrs Sargent made:

> Before I would venture to send him my little book, I wrote to know if it would be acceptable, for notwithstanding he has begun a Poetical Buffon himself to assist his worthy friend Mr Blake, I was afraid mine would be deem'd *too puerile*. I wishd to have seen that number of his fables – or whatever they are calld which told some extraordinary *feats* perform'd by a certain Eagle who carried away a child & then served as Monture to the Mamma – because a remark of Mrs Sargents amused me extremely; when having read this fable, she said, 'Dear Mr Hayley, how *could* you think of telling such a thing – really you *do love* to put Women in the *most extraordinary situations!*'
>
> (10 September 1804; Stanton, 661–2)

During the next year and a half Smith displays her jealousy and anger so freely that she needs to reassure Sarah Rose she has no intention of '*attacking* Mr H –' in her next volume of poems:

> [T]ho I have sufferd myself in writing confidentially to you to smile at our friend . . . at his strange tho benevolent fancy of writing such very sad doggrell, for the purpose of serving a Man, who might be any thing rather than an engraver – Yet I never went *beyond* such a laugh between ourselves. . . . [My last letter to him] threw out an hint how much I *wanted a friend* who could & would correct the work I have now in hand.
>
> (20 March 1806; Stanton, 723–4)

One would like to imagine Smith evincing a charitable thought about Blake as a poet and artist when she says he might be anything but an engraver rather than providing another cut; but of course the ultimate irony comes in her desire for the very aid that proves so devastating to Blake.

Unlike Smith and Cristall, Tighe needed no assistance to publish her work: a member of a wealthy, well-connected family, she printed 50 copies of her epic poem *Psyche; or, the Legend of Love* in 1805 to distribute to friends and relations. Requiring neither subscribers (like Cristall) nor patrons (like Smith), she actually declined an opportunity to publish a volume for the public (despite being urged to do so by her literary circle, which included Thomas Moore and Joseph Cooper Walker). Of all the poet-daughters of Zelophehad under review, Tighe seems likeliest to provoke the Tirzah line, given her status as a beauty – more a Vala than an Enitharmon – whose lived experience as a member of society seems so remote from Blake's. But *Psyche* explores the psychological and moral ramifications of admiration, desire, and female identity in a series of visionary tableaus that invite comparison with the scenarios Blake constructs for Thel, Oothoon, and several female figures in the *Songs*, an invitation Tighe extended to two special readers, Eleanor Butler and Sarah Ponsonby (the Ladies of Llangollen), who received an 1803 manuscript copy of *Psyche* that concludes the poem with the illumination shown in Figure 15.1 (*L* 51).

Figure 15.1   Mary Tighe, watercolour sketch for the final page of 1803 manuscript copy of her *Psyche*, prepared for the Ladies of Llangollen (National Library of Wales, Aberystwyth/Llyfrgell Genedlaethol, Cymru)

Illumination rather than illustration because this stunning image performs work analogous to the images that cap *Thel* and *Visions* in so far as Tighe and Blake signal the liberating potential of visionary experience to controvert the problematic endings of their poems (for women, that is). Unlike Thel, who runs shrieking from the land unknown back to Har, or Oothoon, who remains locked in debate with Theotormon, Psyche merges with Cupid in the penultimate stanza of the poem and thereby loses her distinct identity: 'she enraptured lives in his dear eye' (6: 1, *L* 151). After Psyche merges with Cupid, Tighe represents herself as a disconnected daughter of Albion who can no longer experience visions of Psyche: 'Ah no! her smiles no longer can illume / The path my Psyche treads no more for me; / Consigned to dark oblivion's tomb / The visionary scenes no more I see, / Fast from the fading lines the vivid colours flee!' (6: 536–40, *L* 151). The illumination counters the negation by offering the vision of Tighe communing with Psyche, like the children riding the serpent at the end of *Thel*, or Oothoon flying above/towards the daughters at the end of *Visions*. While Tighe makes no overt references to Blake in letters or journals, her image visually references several significant Blake illuminations: 'The Sick Rose', where a female emerges from a blown rose; the title-page to *Thel*, where Thel observes a female emerging from a rose as a male grasps her; plate two of *Thel*, where the Lilly bows to Thel; and, best of all, 'The Argument' of *Visions*, where Oothoon kisses the flower-nymph Leutha. Could Tighe have known these images? Yes: she had several means of access to Blake's work as she visited the members of her social circle (such as Thomas Johnes of Hafod, who owned a copy of *Songs*), but perhaps most intriguing in terms of aesthetic representation of the female entails her connection with George Romney, who painted her portrait in 1794–95, and had acquired several Blake books by 1795, including *Visions* (Bentley, 31). She sat in his studio at least seven times and would have had ample opportunity to examine his copies of Blake's illuminated texts and ponder the seductive nature of admiration even as Romney captured her image for posterity.

Whereas Cristall, Smith and Tighe respond to Blake during his lifetime, via poems, letters or sketches that alternately position him as influence, competitor, or parallel visionary, Hemans and Hooper offer posthumous, legacy-building responses to Blake, notably informed by Allen Cunningham's 1830 memoir. In 1832 Hemans deploys Cunningham's account of Blake's final days to shape her poem on 'The Painter's Last Work – A Scene', which artfully delineates a dying painter's final sketch of his loving wife through an extravagant ekphrasis that constitutes half of the poem's 93 lines. Lest anyone miss the reference to William and Catherine Blake in the poem's two characters, Francesco and Teresa, Hemans's note to the title explains that the poem was 'Suggested by the closing scene in the life of the painter Blake; as beautifully related by Allan Cunningham.' Cunningham's version of that closing scene is a short paragraph with two sentences on how Blake finishes a copy of 'The Ancient of Days' followed by one sentence on his final drawing of Catherine Blake: 'He saw his wife in tears – she felt this was to be the last of his works – "Stay, Kate! (cried Blake) keep just as you are – I will draw your portrait – for you have ever been an angel to me" – she obeyed, and the dying artist made a fine likeness' (Bentley, 655). By contrast, Hemans's visionary artist Francesco focuses his dying energies exclusively on Teresa; even though Teresa urges him to see how the sunset has made 'the lake one sea of gold!' (l. 6), he insists on producing 'one last work!' (l. 22) to stand as testament to their love, a picture of Teresa. From line 47 on, Hemans's Francesco luxuriantly describes the image he is sketching, which not only glorifies his angelic wife but the artistic process through which her verbal-visual portrait is constructed (by the painter and, more importantly, by Hemans):

> Stand with thy meek hands folded on thy breast,
> And eyes half veil'd, in thine own soul absorb'd,
> As in thy watchings, ere I sink to sleep;
> And I will give the bending flower-like grace
> Of that soft form, and the still sweetness throned
> On that pale brow, and in that quivering smile
> Of voiceless love, a life that shall outlast
> Their delicate earthly being. . . . The dear work grows
> Beneath my hand – the last! Each faintest line
> With treasured memories fraught.
>
> (ll. 53–60, 85–87)

Feldman suggests that Hemans's sympathetic representation of Blake as Francesco foregrounds Blake's accomplishment as poet as well as painter, given the achievement of the 'verbal tribute' (*BQ*, 71). What seems particularly interesting here in terms of Blake's legacy for women poets and the Tirzah line is how advantageously Hemans uses an episode in Blake's life to fire her own imaginative work, to produce the verbal portrait Blake did not compose about an image she had not seen, as she transforms William and Catherine Blake into the objects of her vision.

Like Hemans, the American poet Lucy Hooper used an episode in Cunningham's memoir to generate her 1833 poem on 'The Fairy's Funeral', which acknowledges Blake's provenance in the opening epigraph: 'It was one among the many visionary fancies of the painter Blake, that he once saw a fairy's funeral, as here described.' According to Cunningham, Blake shared his vision of the fairy's funeral with 'a lady, who happened to sit by him in company':

'Did you ever see a fairy's funeral, madam?' he once said to a lady, who happened to sit by him in company. 'Never, sir!' was the answer. 'I have,' said Blake, 'but not before last night. I was walking alone in my garden, there was great stillness among the branches and flowers and more than common sweetness in the air; I heard a low and pleasant sound, and I knew not whence it came. At last I saw the broad leaf of a flower move, and underneath I saw a procession of creatures of the size and colour of green and gray grasshoppers, bearing a body laid out on a rose leaf, which they buried with songs, and then disappeared. It was a fairy funeral.'

(Cunningham, 640–1)

Surely in deliberate contrast to that proper lady, Hooper lets herself imagine the fairy funeral vicariously, transforming Blake into a visionary interlocutor who enables her to script his poem (using metrical innovation to recreate the unheard sound of the funeral dirge in a mimetic move comparable to Hemans's sly ekphrasis). Hooper casts Blake as a 'dreamer' who walks in the garden at sunset, hears thrilling music, and witnesses a throng of fairies burying not just any body but, tellingly, that of their queen:

> Beneath that folded leaf,
>   He saw a moving throng,
> And listened to their music's breath,
>   As the fairies stole along;
> A bright and sparkling crowd, I ween,
> But where in that array, the queen?
>   On a rose leaf bed
>   Reposed the dead,
>   The tone of song
>   From her lips has gone,
> And the crown from her lovely head;
> But those who wept her, by her side
> Had placed her fairy wand of pride.

(ll. 21–33)

When the funeral ends, 'the dreamer' walks away with 'gentle memories and song' (l. 46), but not Hooper's weening 'I', neither proper lady nor fairy queen, who poignantly concludes 'Sweet dreamer! Would such thoughts could come / To soothe me when I muse alone' (ll. 48–9). Set out as an imperfect couplet, these last two lines speak volumes as they simultaneously align Hooper with and distinguish her from a Blake whose 'Opposition is true Friendship' (E 42) because she can use his vehicular imagination to open the doors of perception and provide the locus for her poem. Her complex expression of affinity presents a fitting reply to Blake's Tirzah question: while she signals her ability to connect with Blake through their shared outsider status, she adverts to the crucial difference his insider status as male visionary artist effects. That duality makes Hooper's invocation of Blake as her muse even more surprising and powerful.

Hooper, Hemans, Cristall, Smith, Tighe: one could add names like Caroline Bowles, Lady Caroline Lamb, and Elizabeth Barrett Browning to this short list of contemporary Romantic-era women poets who read and responded to Blake as a 'Sweet dreamer!' or 'ingenious engraver' of visions, poems, and images that provided unexpected inspiration, who saw him as an influence, competitor, parallel visionary or source; not yet the patronising Miltonic father but *Jerusalem*'s 'brother and friend' (E 146), with all the attendant complications of nineteenth-century sibling rivalry, where brothers possess the cultural freedom to go where sisters could only vicariously imagine. If Blake's outsider status enabled connection, in Hooper's analysis, Blake's outsider status also prompted the estranging jealousy that Smith so painfully articulates about men on the fringe in her 1797 sonnet 'On Being Cautioned against Walking on an Headland Overlooking the Sea, Because It Was Frequented by a Lunatic': 'In moody sadness, on the giddy brink, / I see him more with envy than with fear; / *He* has no *nice felicities* that shrink / From giant horrors' (ll. 9–12). The Blake who displayed his 'Giant forms to the Public' (E 145) might well have asked these new poet-daughters of Zelophehad 'Then what have I to do with thee?' and they might well have answered 'everything' as they struggled to demonstrate their right to own their poetic visions, to produce their own emanations.

References

Bentley G.E. Jr, *Blake Records*, 2nd edn (New Haven and London: Yale University Press, 2004).

Cristall, Ann Batten, *Poetical Sketches* (London: Joseph Johnson, 1795).

Cunningham, Allen, *The Lives of the Most Eminent British Painters, Sculptors and Architects*, 6 vols, 2nd edn (London: John Murray, 1830), II, 143–88; reprinted in Bentley (627–60).

Curran, Stuart, 'Something Evermore About To Be: Teaching and Textbases', in Stephen C. Behrendt and Harriet Kramer Linkin (eds), *Approaches to Teaching British Women Poets of the Romantic Period* (New York: MLA, 1997), pp. 25–31.

Feldman, Paula R., *British Women Poets of the Romantic Era: an Anthology* (Baltimore and London: Johns Hopkins University Press, 1997).

Feldman, Paula R., 'Felicia Hemans and the Mythologizing of Blake's Death', *BQ*, 27:3 (Winter 1993/94), 69–72.

Fletcher, Loraine, *Charlotte Smith: a Critical Biography* (New York: Palgrave, 2001).

Hampsey, John C., 'Innocence . . . and Irony?: the Poetry of Jane Taylor', *European Romantic Review*, 8:3 (Summer 1997), 262–73.

Hemans, Felicia, 'The Painter's Last Work – A Scene', *Blackwood's Edinburgh Magazine* (February 1832); reprinted in Feldman, 1997: 320–3.

Hooper, Lucy, *Poetical Remains of the Late Lucy Hooper*, ed. John Keese (New York: Colman, 1842).

McGann, Jerome, *The Poetics of Sensibility: a Revolution in Literary Style* (New York: Oxford University Press, 1996).

Mellor, Anne K., 'Blake, the Apocalypse and Romantic Women Writers', in Tim Fulford (ed.), *Romanticism and Millenarianism* (New York: Palgrave, 2002), pp. 139–52.

Smith, Charlotte, *Elegiac Sonnets*, 2 vols (London: Cadell and Davies, 1797).

Stanton, Judith Phillips, *The Collected Letters of Charlotte Smith* (Bloomington: Indiana University Press, 2003).

Tighe, Mary, *The Collected Poems and Journals of Mary Tighe*, ed. Harriet Kramer Linkin (Lexington: University Press of Kentucky, 2005).

Wu, Duncan, *Romantic Women Poets: an Anthology* (Oxford: Blackwell, 1997).

Zimmerman, Sarah M., 'Charlotte Smith's Lessons', in Stephen C. Behrendt and Harriet Kramer Linkin (eds), *Approaches to Teaching British Women Poets of the Romantic Period* (New York: MLA, 1997), pp. 121–8.

16

'Endless Their Labour': Women in Blake's Illuminated Works and in the British Workforce

Catherine L. McClenahan

> And one Daughter of Los sat at the fiery Reel & another
> Sat at the Shining Loom with her Sisters attending round
> Terrible their distress & their sorrow cannot be utterd
> And another Daughter of Los sat at the Spinning Wheel
> Endless their labour, with bitter food. void of sleep,
> Tho hungry they labour. . . .
>
> (*J*, 59; E 209)

This oft-quoted example of Blake's depiction of working women's labour in his material and historical world raises the question of how his depictions of labouring women in the illuminated works correspond to the occupations of women in the labouring classes between 1750–1830.[1] A closer look at women's labour in Blake's work demonstrates that Blake doesn't just ground his images of female labour in material reality, but leads his audience to find the sublime in the everyday. At the same time, in illuminations such as *The Marriage of Heaven and Hell* (*MHH*) 3, *Europe* 9, or *Jerusalem* 100, Blake's images of women often defy ideas about women's lack of power or proper behaviour, especially in the working classes, that were widely accepted in his culture (BA *MHH* Copy D, Pl. 3, Copy E, Pl. 11, *J*, Copy E, Pl. 100).

Modern economic historians debate the nature of working women's employment, how much jobs changed because of the industrial revolution, and in what ways. Employment evidence from the eighteenth century is missing or patchy, while some areas of Great Britain are under-researched (Vickery, 312). The kinds of work that women could get, working conditions, and wages varied widely even within the same industry, from one industry to another, and from one region to another.

By 'official' definitions of 'work' for wages in 1811, about 33 per cent of women workers were in domestic service, 'about the same' percentage in textile production and garment making together (a huge category involving dozens of trades), and 7.7 per cent in heavy agricultural jobs, such as dairywomen (Rule, *Labouring* 14). Much women's work wasn't officially counted because it was unpaid, performed to help husbands or other heads of household. In other cases, women were hardly likely, for instance, to report that they lived by prostitution and theft (Earle, 124). Despite the lack of specific numbers, it is clear nonetheless that women's labour formed a vital and public part of the national workforce.

Two lists of working women's occupations amplify Rule's observations, bracketing a period 20–30 years larger than Blake's lifetime. Table 16.1 is derived from Peter Earle's study on 'The female labour market in London in the late seventeenth and early eighteenth centuries', based on women's depositions in the London church courts 1695–1725. In Earle's sample of 613 women, mostly poor, the top three occupations were domestic service, making or mending clothing, and charring or laundry work (Earle, 123, table 5.10, 132). Table 16.2 adapts Ivy Pinchbeck's Appendix to *Women Workers and the Industrial Revolution 1750–1850*, which lists the most frequent jobs of women in the 1841 Census (317). Here women's most common waged occupations were domestic servants, milliners or dressmakers or seamstresses, and cotton manufacturing jobs. Despite the different sources used, the results are remarkably similar. In Table 16.2, adding category 3 (milliner/ dressmaker) to category 6 (seamstress), results in a category that would equate to Earle's 'making/mending clothes', and which would also be in second place. The difference in third place (cotton manufacturing) reflects the particular conditions of London's urban environment. So agricultural work (category 5 in Table 16.2) doesn't appear on Earle's list of London occupations, unless perhaps in his undefined final category of 'hard labour/daywork'. Because London's population was 'dominated by immigrants', however, many of Earle's deponents probably did agricultural work before they came to London (Earle, 126). As both tables show, domestic service was 'a life-cycle stage' for most working women (Sharpe, 128–9). In

Table 16.1   Occupations of London women, 1695–1725 (%)

1. Domestic service	25.4
2. Making/mending clothes	20.2
3. Charring/laundry	11.1
4. Nursing/medicine	9.1
5. Catering/victualling	8.7
6. Shopkeeping	7.7
7. Hawking/carrying	7.2
8. Textile manufacture	4.6
9. Misc. services	2.9
10. Misc. manufacture	2.0
11. Hard labour/daywork	1.1

Table 16.2 Occupations of women in the UK, 1841

1. Domestic servant	692,493
2. Cotton manuf. jobs	115,425
3. Milliner, dressmaker	89,079
4. Laundry	45,019
5. Agricultural labourer	35,262
6. Seamstress	37,946
7. Silk manuf. jobs	29,833
8. Weaver	26,311
9. Wool/cloth manuf. jobs	22,938
10. Lace manuf. jobs	20,046
11. Charwoman	18,284
12. Farmer/grazier	15,392
13. Nurse	12,993
14. Worsted/wool manuf.	12,142
15. Other labourer	11,155

short, women's work in the eighteenth century typically focused on the domestic demands of others' families as much as or more than one's own.

While the nature of women's work changed little during the first half of the nineteenth century, its remuneration in real terms declined, resulting in widespread and deepening female poverty. Employment opportunities for women were already narrow in 1700, and if more women worked for a living in the seventeenth and early eighteenth centuries, it was 'probably because more of them were poor' (Earle, 134). Women in the eighteenth century were more likely to be in need of parish relief than in the seventeenth century, but getting less of it (see below).[2] Most historians agree that many mill and factory owners hired women and children because they were adaptable, dextrous, docile, and cheap. The relative wages of women declined about 50 per cent over the eighteenth century (Sharpe, 1996: 149); even worse, by the end of the century, 'the poverty of women met with the profound disapproval of those who earlier in the century had praised their industriousness' (Honeyman, 139), despite the fact that the kingdom's economy depended on their contributions. 'They are mockd, by every one that passes by. they regard not / Their labour . . . ', Blake notes in *Jerusalem* (E 209).

Against this background, it is easy to see that many of the century's most common female occupations did not appear directly in Blake's work, even as symbols. Some occupations seem to suggest a whole class, however, as nurses may do for domestic servants. Blake's roster of women's occupations adds work that is not on any official list: the family roles of brides and wives, mothers, teachers, and children's nurses – but also prostitutes, vagrants, and slaves. Blake represents agricultural work by female sowers and reapers, harvesters (wine-treaders or harvesters of human heads in *The Gates of Paradise*; BA Copy D, Pl. 3), and tending animals. Visual and verbal images of rural butchery work shade into the literally unlikely roles of torturers, priestesses, or executioners in *Milton* and *Jerusalem*.[3] Most Blake readers know how common the spinners, winders, weavers, garment-makers and seamstresses are in the major prophecies. *Jerusalem* also alludes to women's work in 'Mills' and perhaps in mines (see below).

Blake also depicts women in other real-world occupations not listed in the 1841 Census, such as women musicians[4] in the illumination to *M* (BA Copy C, Pl. 17) and the text of *J* (68:56; Erdman 222), and female 'secretaries', for example Milton's daughters (E 110) or the illumination to *MHH* 10 (BA Copy D, Pl. 10). Erdman sees Catherine Blake working with William as a painter on the right side of the illumination on *J* (36[40]; Erdman 315; BA Copy E, Pl. 40), and a woman seems to be drawing or writing on a tablet in 'There is No Natural Religion' (BA Copy G, Pl. 3). The Shadowy Daughter of Urthona is a jailer armed with bow and quivers (E 51), like Elynittria (E 99). The Sons *and* Daughters of Los not only weave but 'build' the Looms of Generation and the City of Golgonooza (E 97), and the Daughters of Albion 'builded Jerusalem as a City & a Temple' (or tried to), though 'here we build Babylon . . . compelld' (E 243), while women in Blake's time assisted masons and bricklayers and were brickyard workers. In the jobs women did, Pinchbeck notes, no task was considered too heavy or distasteful' (2). The greater the contrast between real-world occupations or work conditions and Blake's images of women's work, the more Blake seems to honour the labour of women by suggesting its difficulty while representing it as sublimely significant.

Blake's use of pastoral imagery, then, is not nostalgia for an imaginary bucolic past but calls attention to the labours of many working women. Women's agricultural jobs made a crucial contribution to rural family wages until the agricultural depression that began in 1814 (Pinchbeck, 67). Since many women had several occupations at once before industrialisation (Honeyman, 139), the availability of agricultural work correlates with the numbers of women in the textile or fashion trades, in domestic service – and to rates of prostitution and vagrancy. Certain kinds of work were only seasonal or were more available during wartime, only to disappear later. As farm enclosures progressed, traditional sources of income for rural women, such as commonland for crops and grazing, gathering berries, firewood or seafood, and especially gleaning were increasingly defined by landowners as theft or trespassing (Sharpe, 82–5). When new farming crops and methods created a need for additional workers, more women did agricultural work such as setting crops by hand, hoeing, weeding, cleaning crops, doing various kinds of work during harvest, and gathering stones or 'dressing' meadows (Pinchbeck, 54–62) and haymaking (Sharpe, 74). In Blake's

London during the 1790s, the fruit and vegetable gardens in Kensington, Hammersmith, Twickenham and other sites covered 3000 acres where a 'whole army of women' worked: many walked to London from North Wales every spring. They worked in the garden daily, then walked the 4–7 miles to London to sell their produce and back *twice* a day, sometimes for as little as 6d. a day (Pinchbeck, 61–2).

Blake could easily have seen women working at these and other rural tasks in his rambles. For example, women sowing or planting appear in illuminations to *Songs of Innocence and of Experience* (BA Copy AA, Pl. 4, side vignette on the right), to *MHH*, where a figure with a dibble stick makes holes for seeds (BA Copy F, Pl. 7), and *J* 20, where she sows 'star seeds' and floats behind the harrow (BA Copy E, Pl. 20). Women also tend flocks in the text and illuminations to *Thel* (E 3, BA Copy H, Pl. 3) and *J* 9 (BA Copy E, Pl. 9). Texts and designs thus pay tribute to otherwise unlauded but vital contributions of women rural labourers.

Agricultural and textile labourers in Blake's work demonstrate some of the heavy, exhausting work that women and children endured in other occupations, too. Elynittria and Leutha tend the Horses of the Plow in *Milton* (E 105–6), and while Leutha may fail for mental or spiritual reasons, Pinchbeck calls this once common job of women 'one of the most unpleasant and wearisome of all farm tasks' (109). The woman in the illumination to *J* 8 (BA Copy E, Pl. 8) is harnessed to a moon like a draft animal herself. This illumination also suggests other jobs that women did: for instance, the less common but terrible work of women and children in the mines, outlawed in 1842. During Blake's lifetime, women and children worked in the smaller pits of some areas as 'hurriers': ' "chained, belted, harnessed, like dogs in a go-cart . . . more than half -naked" ', as they hauled coal from the workings to the bottom of the shaft or the horse carts (Pinchbeck, 249 and ch. 11 generally, quoting a Parliamentary Paper, *Report on Mines*, 1842, xvii, p. 74). Erdman also thinks that the trapped and frantic-looking female figure in the illumination to *M* 10 (BA Copy D, Pl. 10) seems to be 'in a cellar or mine' (Erdman 227), a reminder of the very unhealthy work of female cotton weavers who had to work in damp and often-flooded cellars because cotton had to be woven damp (Pinchbeck, 181). The Daughters and Sons of Luvah tread grapes in Los's Wine Press in *M* 27 (E 124), although 'many fall oerwearied' (l. 4). This harvest, however, 'is call'd War on Earth' (l. 8), and 'in the Wine-presses the Human grapes sing not, nor dance' (l. 30).

These 'Human grapes', then, include female agricultural workers, who worked long hours at backbreaking work for very little pay.[5] Like women's work in other industries, agricultural work was seasonal and intermittent: as little as 86–185 days per year (Pinchbeck, 64). Changes in the poor laws made bad economic conditions even worse for women. Until the 1780s, women often collected parish relief in kind as well as money, but many parishes thereafter took up the Speenhamland System of 1783: a scale to supplement men's earnings in relation to the cost of bread and the size of his family. Not only did this lower the amount of financial help that widows, single women with children, and unmarried women could get, but employers also used the new system as an excuse to cut wages (Pinchbeck, 68–79). Parish officials saved money by pushing women into marriage, into certain trades, or to move to London (Sharpe, 138, 150): 'They compel the Poor to live upon a crust of bread', Blake points out angrily in *Jerusalem*, 'then give with pomp & ceremony' (E 193).

As for spinning, weaving and garment-making work of women in the texts and illuminations after 1797, the historical picture is complex and the reasons for the distress of the women at the Reel and Looms in passages such as *J* 59: 26–55 (E 209) are many; the women in the illumination seem frantic and fearful (BA Copy E, Pl. 59). While spinners and weavers in cotton and wool had periods of relative prosperity, jobs and wages would decrease in the nineteenth century (Pinchbeck, 155–6), causing great distress.[6] Blake's verbal and visual representations of working women's occupations thus mirror the economic realities of working women in the British Isles struggling to cope with the violent swings of the 'boom and bust' cotton industry, the steady decline of work in agriculture and the wool industry, or even the seemingly protected and high-paid but limited economy of London silk weavers. Although a few women among the Spitalfields weavers could earn men's wages, this was a rare exception. Commonly, less-skilled work was sent from London to parish workhouses in counties such as Essex, where little girls worked in mills from 5 a.m. to after 6 p.m. (Sharpe, 44–46).

These literal labours of working women, devalued and mocked by those who demand the products of their work, look sublime – terrible – or even beautiful to Blake's imaginative vision, which builds on the assumption that 'every thing that lives is holy' (E 54). The spinners and weavers of *Jerusalem* 59 are from one angle the epitome of the mental and physical degradations of alienated labour. When Blake describes them as taking an 'intoxicating delight' in their work that 'Obliterates every other evil' (E 209), their condition is close to the literal meaning of 'intoxicated': poisoned, being deprived of the ordinary use of the senses or reason, and corrupted morally or spiritually (*OED*). They are 'dulled and deluded', as Jerusalem says 'by the turning mills' (E 211), by lack of education, by terrible working conditions and wages, and often by malnutrition and hunger more than alcohol. In Blake's vision, human beings are meant to be 'Every one a translucent wonder: a Universe within' (E 158), yet most of these labouring women were unable to recognise, develop or use their gifts of body or especially of mind, in ways that they themselves might choose and profit by. Few women got much education, especially the poor, even in dame schools, where they learned only the alphabet and the duties of their class and sex (Smith, 12): their earnings were needed by their families. 'Lace schools', industrial set-ups, simply exploited children, packing as many as 30 girls in a 12-foot-square room with no fire in winter (Pinchbeck, 233–4). The contrast between Blake's vision and economic reality sheds a bleak light on the sheer waste of people who might perform 'wonders' with better education and opportunities. Instead, they work 'In sorrowful drudgery, to obtain a scanty pittance of bread: / In ignorance to view a small portion & think that All, / . . . blind to all the simple rules of life' (E 216).

Blake shows the wasted human potential of women's work most starkly in the lowest of low positions, vagrants and prostitutes. Enitharmon appears in this world of Generation as 'an aged Woman raving along the streets' in the text and perhaps the illumination of *Milton* 10(11) (E 104; BA Copy C, Pl. 10); Enion wanders 'like a creeping inarticulate voice' (E 113). Albion's Children call Jerusalem 'Liberty' (E 203), but in a counter-revolutionary and warlike England, Albion's Sons call her 'The Shadow of delusions! / The Harlot daughter!' for embodying 'dishonourable forgiveness', or 'hateful peace & love' (E 163).

The historical counterparts of these Emanations became 'harlots' and vagrants for many reasons. Some women didn't marry because it had become expensive (Clark, 233); others were forced into it by parish officials. Cohabiting men or husbands increasingly abandoned families for the military, or simply because they couldn't earn enough to provide for families. Women found it harder to find employment or survival wages. Between 1780–1820, unemployment forced more women into unstable domestic service, the loss of which forced many into prostitution or 'increased [the] numbers of lawless unemployed poor women' who haunted cities with textile mills or soldiers (Sharpe, 129–31).

For Blake, the most important work for human beings of either sex, however, is not on any official list. For his dramatic characters, for the poet/artist himself, for the audience he envisioned, the essential human/ humane work is paying attention to the work of others who support your existence and your pleasures. This work is thinking, learning, and revising your assumptions and conclusions. Human(e) work is having compassion for others' suffering and combining that with anger when cruelty and injustice are the cause. The anger has to work with vision and hope to become action, however. This work is protesting, arguing, persuading – but also being persuadable. It's using your particular gifts 'to build up Jerusalem' (E 231–2). So even the literal work of the Daughters spinning and weaving in *J* 59 becomes a 'most grievous work of pity & compassion':

> Men understand not the distress & the labour & sorrow
> That in the Interior Worlds is carried on in fear & trembling
> Weaving the shuddering fears & loves of Albions Families. . . .

(E 209)

In the illuminated books, this work can begin just by looking and listening, as the Daughters of Albion do in the illuminations to *Visions of the Daughters of Albion* (BA Copy J, Pl. 10, 11), or the woman studying in the illumination to *America* (BA Copy E, Pl. 2). The work is often to lament, though there are gradations.[7] The self-absorbed Ahania is only a formless voice 'weeping upon the void' (E 88). More often, female characters passionately denounce the oppression of others in some of Blake's most powerful poetry. The Shadowy Female, for example, 'howls in articulate howlings' of protest against the suffering of the poor:

> I will lament over Milton in the lamentations of the afflicted
> My Garments shall be woven of sighs & heart broken lamentations
> The misery of unhappy Families shall be drawn out into its border
> Wrought with the needle with dire sufferings poverty pain & woe
> Along the rocky Island & thence throughout the whole Earth
> There shall be the sick Father & his starving Family! There
> The Prisoner in the stone Dungeon & the Slave at the Mill
>
> (E 111)

Like some other female voices in Blake's work, the Shadowy Female may have no hope or solution as she laments, but she implies clear moral and ethical standards by which to denounce the results of Albion's blend of war and commerce. This in itself is hardly the female modesty, the docile and silent assent to male opinion, that the middle classes were enjoining on 'respectable' women. Alone, the Shadowy Female can do little. If she can awaken the conscience of her listeners, however, dramatic results can ensue, as we see with Leutha (E 106–7), Ololon (E 134–5) or Britannia (E 254).

A violent, powerful, threatening figure such as Vala, Rahab, or Tirzah is not simply 'repulsive' but 'superb in the eloquence of her defiance': 'large, strong, vocal, angry, violent and out of control' (Sturrock, 341) even when she revels in her power within Albion's world and endorses his precepts. At the same time, however, defiant voices like Vala's just as often turn to lamenting indictments of how badly the present system serves their desires and interests. While Vala laments to Albion, for instance, that 'thy terrors have surrounded me / Thy Sons have naild me on the Gates piercing my hands and feet', while 'my morn & evening food were prepared in Battles of Men': 'All Love is lost! terror succeeds & Hatred instead of Love / And stern demands of Right & Duty instead of Liberty' (E 167), she begins to articulate what she could be as Jerusalem, even if she can't find reason to hope for that change.

Arguing with Vala, Jerusalem explains a way to move beyond despair if one can recognise errors, such as those of a crudely capitalistic and materialistic society: 'O Vala . . . What is Sin but a little / Error & fault that is soon forgiven, but mercy is not a Sin / Nor pity nor love nor kind forgiveness!' (E 165). One incarnation of Jerusalem, the 'Aged Pensive Woman' Erin is the most powerful and innovative female artist/thinker in all the prophecies, shaping time and space themselves 'in labours / Of sublime mercy'; she revises an ethic of 'Sacrifice of Enemies' to forgiveness or acts where 'Friends Die for each other', not just literally but as a 'Divine Analogy' of re-vision and change that Los will subsequently use (E 197–9).

Blake's point is that women didn't need to be Mary Wollstonecrafts to do this work, or even the readers of like-minded writers. Most working women of the lower classes would have had little access even to such publications as these, or the education to read them, let alone access to Blake's relatively expensive illuminated works. Blake's essential 'Human' work could be a simple matter of everyday choices made by plebian women. Resisting the pressures of magistrates, parish officials and growing public opinion to adopt bourgeois standards of female sexual and social behaviour, many women chose not to mock or ignore the 'harlots' who failed those standards. Such women risked their reputations by choosing their own definitions and values, deciding that friendship, being a good neighbour, having compassion, or honouring kinship ties mattered more than definitions of chastity created by the more fortunate. It took only a little attention and imagination for a labouring woman to see herself in the same desperate straits (Clark, 235–36). Such small 'Seeds' of community exemplify the advice Jesus gives to the awakened Albion at the end of *Jerusalem* – 'every kindness to another is a little Death / In the Divine Image' (E 256) – or that the narrator gives to his audience: 'I know of no other Christianity and of no other Gospel than the liberty both of body and mind to exercise the Divine Arts of Imagination' (E 231).

It's a sad irony, then, that Blake's work could only reach so small an audience for so long; similarly, that his own solution to finding work of his choice, which developed his particular talents and whose profits he controlled, was available to so few workers of this time, and to hardly any women. The work sometimes barely kept the Blakes alive, even with the contributions of Catherine's unwaged work, not least because of Blake's stubborn refusal to play to his market. Los says that 'Sexes' or systems of gender division 'must vanish & cease' in a truly awakened Albion (E 252), but the early nineteenth century was not the time for the range of women's occupations to expand significantly or be more greatly valued. Even when debate about women's position and roles surfaced in the political discourse of working people during the Chartist movement of the 1830s and 1840s, traditional male values and fears of competition from low-waged women workers triumphed when poorer people adopted middle-class ideas that women were and should be 'home-centred' (Rule, 1986:

393). Despite this historical trend, Blake's sublime representations of his labouring women, even the Daughters of Albion at their most sinister, offer them what he asks for himself in *Jerusalem*: respect and love for the 'energetic exertion of . . . talent', and a readiness to forgive errors, beginning with one's own.

Notes

1. Many thanks to Professor Lynn Botelho of the History Department at Indiana University of Pennsylvania for her perceptive comments on drafts of this chapter.
2. Rule (1986: 181) claims that 'Only exceptional groups like mill girls had the opportunity to earn wages sufficient to support themselves.'
3. See Sturrock (1998) on Blake's representations of the Daughters of Albion versus depictions of female violence to represent The Terror in the 1790s.
4. The 1841 Census lists only 261 women as 'Artist (Fine Arts)' (Pinchbeck, 1969: 317).
5. Farm labourers in southern England earned 8 shillings a week at best, but had to spend about 9s 6d, so even women's low wages were critical. Compare, Pinchbeck (1969: 145) on the parish poor.
6. London trades with 'apprenticeships' (milliners, mantua-makers, and stay- and bodice-makers) were merely a way to hire half-pay workers (*Labouring* 118).
7. See Hilton's (1983: ch. 3) categories of lamentation.

References

Clark, Anna, 'Whores and Gossips: Sexual Reputation in London 1770–1825', in Arina Angerman et al. (eds), *Current Issues in Women's History* (London: Routledge, 1989), pp. 231–48.

Earle, Peter, 'The Female Labour Market in London in the Late Seventeenth and Early Eighteenth Centuries', in Pamela Sharpe (ed.), *Women's Work: the English Experience 1650–1914* (London: Arnold, 1998), pp. 121–49.

Erdman, David V. (ed.), *The Illuminated Blake* (Garden City, NY: Anchor Press/ Doubleday, 1974).

Hilton, Nelson, *Literal Imagination: Blake's Vision of Words* (Berkeley: University of California Press, 1983).

Honeyman, Katrina, *Women, Gender and Industrialisation in England 1700–1870* (London: Palgrave Macmillan, 2000).

Pinchbeck, Ivy, *Women Workers and the Industrial Revolution 1750–1850* (1930, Preface Ivy Pinchbeck) (New York: Augustus M. Kelley Publishers, 1969).

Rule, John, *The Experience of Labour in Eighteenth-Century English Industry* (New York: St Martins Press, 1981).

Rule, John, *The Labouring Classes in Early Industrial England, 1750–1850* (London: Longman, 1986).

Sharpe, Pamela, *Adapting to Capitalism: Working Women in the English Economy 1700– 1850* (New York: St Martin's Press, 1996).

Smith, Olivia, *The Politics of Language 1791–1819* (Oxford: Clarendon, 1984).

Sturrock, June, 'Maenads, Young Ladies, and the Lovely Daughters of Albion', in Jackie DiSalvo et al. (eds), *Blake, Politics, and History* (New York: Garland Publishing, Inc. 1998), pp. 339–49.

Vickery, Amanda, 'Golden Age to Separate Spheres? A Review of the Categories and Chronology of English Women's History', in Pamela Sharpe (ed.), *Women's Work: the English Experience 1650–1914* (London: Arnold, 1998), pp. 294–331.

17
Sentiment, Motherhood and the Sea in Gillray and Blake

Cindy McCreery

Introduction

The sea has long shaped Britain's cultural and political as well as economic identity. In the late eighteenth and early nineteenth centuries, the sea provided protection from foreign invasion as well as the means for trade.[1] The contemporary importance of the sea was demonstrated most clearly perhaps during the Napoleonic Wars (1793–1815). This conflict led to spectacular and decisive naval battles and severe economic hardship and social dislocation. A combination of poor harvests and Napoleon's economic blockade led to food shortages and high prices in Britain, and thousands of men joined the Navy to support their families as well as to serve their country.[2] Britons who remained at home observed the different moods of the sea, a source of both wonder and terror, and prayed for the safe and speedy return of loved ones. Shipwreck was a common occurrence, and indeed posed a greater danger to seafarers than naval battle.[3]

Disasters at sea fascinated many, and shipwreck narratives became a well-established genre in Britain.[4] So too, poems such as William Falconer's *The Shipwreck*, first published in 1762 and reissued in numerous editions over the next century and a half, impressed readers with their combination of technical detail and pathos.[5] Rapid social and economic change contributed to a sentimental turn in literature in the last decades of the eighteenth century. Sentiment was particularly popular in cultural products which catered to a female audience, such as novels and poems, as well as in engravings designed for consumption and display within the home. Such engravings often focused on scenes of human suffering, and on individuals' struggles against the forces of nature, for example shipwrecks. Many sentimental engravings depicted the unfortunate mother, who protected her children as best she could from an often cruel and unsympathetic world. Often this woman was herself alone, usually abandoned by the death or desertion of her lover. While many of these images were intended to appeal to female viewers, male viewers were not forgotten. Numerous engravings represented scenes of feminine distress in an aesthetically pleasing and even sexually suggestive manner.[6]

James Gillray and William Blake both addressed the terrors of shipwreck and the vulnerability of unfortunate mothers in their art. Yet as much of the existing scholarship emphasises what separates Gillray and Blake from their fellow artists – that is, what makes their work distinctive – their use of these popular themes remains unexplored. Nor has there been much comparison of the artists' lives and careers. This is odd, given that they were almost exact contemporaries (Gillray 1756–1815, Blake 1757–1827) who spent most of their lives in London. Both demonstrated artistic promise at a young age and studied at the Royal Academy Schools, and both rejected many of the Academy's artistic conventions in their subsequent careers as artist/engravers. Both were fiercely independent individuals, who struggled for recognition and financial security during their lifetimes. Most importantly, Gillray and Blake are today regarded as giants of what was in many ways the 'golden age' of British graphic design.[7]

While Gillray's political satire and Blake's mystical poetry and imagery display highly individual styles and treat somewhat abstract subject matter, both artists also produced more conventional engravings. By examining two examples, namely Gillray's *The Nancy Packet* and Blake's *Little Tom the Sailor*, we will learn more about how these artists interpreted popular contemporary themes, as well as the extent to which they depended on patrons and the public for their livelihood. Both engravings reflect the limits of their creators' engagement with popular culture, and help explain why both Gillray and Blake made their names, if not necessarily their fortunes, with more idiosyncratic designs.

The Nancy Packet

James Gillray's line engraving *The Nancy Packet* was published on 19 October 1784 by Robert Wilkinson in London (Figure 17.1).[8] Gillray produced the engraving not long after the end of the American War of Independence, at a time when he was trying to establish his career in 'high' art, rather than relying on the caricatures that later made him famous and relatively prosperous. At this time portraiture, genre scenes and above all history painting were more highly esteemed and, for the successful artist, better remunerated than caricature. *The Nancy Packet* depicted a recent historical event, the loss of an East India ship with all hands off the Scilly Isles eight months earlier, on (or about) 25 February 1784. Given that there were apparently neither survivors nor witnesses, the description of the wreck was largely the creation of the artist's imagination, as informed by reports of its discovery.[9] Gillray, like the writers of the news reports, chose to depict the suffering of the passengers and crew in a lifeboat as they approached their death. The print's caption reflects the melodramatic tone of his design:

Figure 17.1   James Gillray, *The Nancy Packet* (British Museum, London)

The Nancy Packet wrecked off Scilly in a storm, on the night of the 25th of Feb.ry 1784, by which the whole of the Crew, together with several Ladies & Gentlemen passengers on board, then on their return from India, all unhappily perished: a part of the Crew having with some of the passengers embarked in the Boat, in hopes of reaching the neighbouring Island, but not being able to clear the Rocks, the whole company, were by an amazing swell of the sea, all buried in one common Grave. – among other persons of note, on board was Mrs Cargill the celebrated actress, who having, in her shift, escaped with the rest of the boats company from the vessel just before it foundered, was while clasping the Infant of 16 Months old to her breast, swallowed up by the merciless ocean. . .

Mrs Cargill, 'the celebrated actress', was singled out for attention because her story would appeal to both male and female viewers. Popular actresses were celebrities in eighteenth-century England, and their private life was often given as much attention as their public performances.[10] Ann Cargill was well known for her lively acting style and scandalous personal life. Even her circumstances aboard ship invited controversy –

such as the rumour that she was having an affair with the captain.[11] While this was not mentioned in the print's caption, it did observe that she was wearing only her 'shift' at her death, which no doubt heightened the story's appeal to lascivious as well as sympathetic male viewers. Perhaps for the same reason, the *London Chronicle* noted her corpse's beauty as well as its injuries: 'Mrs Cargill's body was one of the first that came on shore; which looked extremely well, except that one of her breasts was shockingly torn.'[12]

Yet it was not just Mrs Cargill's status as a beautiful actress that explains her prominence in both the written and visual accounts of the wreck. Rather, it was her tragic final role as a mother that fascinated the public. Thus Gillray places mother and child in the centre of his design. Mrs Cargill clasps her baby to her breast, and, although she is clearly terrified by her ordeal, she displays a calm demeanour that suggests Christian acceptance of her fate. Despite her apparent awareness of her imminent death, she refuses to abandon her helpless infant. By contrast, the other occupants of the lifeboat struggle helplessly, indicating both their sheer terror and their lack of Christian fortitude. While two sailors try to save a woman who has fallen overboard, for the most part the passengers and crew appear concerned only for their own survival.

This role as saintly mother may not accurately represent Cargill's last moments (not least because the infant supposedly found in her arms was apparently not her child), but it satisfied popular expectations of good maternal behaviour.[13] Perhaps because they gave reassurance in a time of great uncertainty, such sentimental images of unfortunate mothers protecting their babies were common in Britain at this time.[14] Viewers could sympathise with such images because they reflected real-life hardships. Moreover, elegant renderings of beautiful tragic mothers allowed viewers to combine pity for their fate with pleasure in their appearance.

Little Tom the Sailor

Sixteen years after *The Nancy Packet* was published, William Blake described the terrors of the sea, and their impact on innocent men, women and children, in his 1800 broadside *Little Tom the Sailor* (Figure 17.2).[15] Like *The Nancy Packet*, *Little Tom* is a type of history painting. Where the former depicts an accident that occurred after the end of the recent American War of Independence, the latter illustrates a case of hardship that, at least indirectly, was caused by the ongoing Napoleonic Wars. Thus *Little Tom*'s depiction of human suffering would have had particular resonance for contemporary viewers.

Little Tom also reflects Blake's engagement with the commercial art world. Certainly Blake despised London publishers' greed and underhanded behaviour, and he warmly endorsed a fellow artist's decision to pursue art for art's sake rather than commercial gain.[16] Yet financial necessity dictated

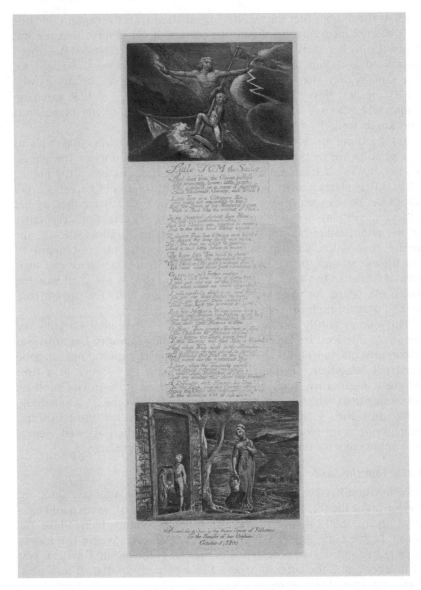

Figure 17.2 William Blake, *Little Tom the Sailor* (British Museum, London)

that Blake, much more often than Gillray, engrave other people's designs. Furthermore, Blake illustrated the work of other authors as well as his own literary compositions. Such commissions formed an important aspect of Blake's career, and supported him through many lean times.[17] For example, when Blake's patron William Hayley wrote a biography of the painter George Romney, he commissioned Blake to engrave several of Romney's works, including a *Scene of Shipwreck*.[18]

Yet Blake was no mere hired hack, passively following his master's orders. In 1804 he thanked Hayley warmly for an illustrated edition of Falconer's poem *The Shipwreck*, and described how it had inspired his engraving of Romney's picture.[19] So too, while it was Hayley's idea that Blake illustrate his ballad 'Little Tom the Sailor', Blake's own fascination with both the perils of the sea and the spiritual significance of children informed the resulting design.

Hayley's ballad, which was based on a true story, recounts the tale of 'Little Tom'.[20] Tom, a 'Cottagers Son; His years not amounting to ten', looks after his helpless younger siblings while his mother travels to his dying father. When his father dies, leaving the family impoverished, Tom's mother sends her son to sea to earn an income. Tom again demonstrates his maturity and courage, and proves himself a worthy replacement for his father. While, as in *The Nancy Packet*, the mother's relationship with her child is important, in *Little Tom* it is the child who keeps the family together. This focus on the virtue of the child is typical of Blake, just as it is more typical of Gillray to focus on the charms of the mother.

Blake's *Little Tom* illustrates the most poignant aspects of the accompanying text. The image is composed of two plates (1 and 3) in a four-plate broadside, and the use of woodcut and relief etching give it a rougher, bolder appearance than Gillray's elegant line engraving. Plate 1 depicts Tom bidding farewell to his mother as she leaves to care for her sick husband. Unlike the beautiful Mrs Cargill, who cradles her baby protectively, Tom's downcast mother looks to her son for reassurance. Tom gestures to the cottage interior, where a little child stands near an infant in a cradle. The message is clear – he will care for his young siblings with as much maternal devotion as their own mother. In Plate 3, Tom clutches the mast of a storm-tossed ship, as lightning illuminates the scene. His position echoes that of a figure in *The Nancy Packet*, who struggles to remain upright on an overturned lifeboat. But unlike this figure, who seems terrified, Tom, like Mrs Cargill, appears calm. Nor is he completely alone. Above him the head and torso of a human figure stretches out his arms.

The apparition may represent God, or the spirit of Tom's father. Blake believed in the spirits of loved ones maintaining a presence in people's lives, and in a letter to Hayley he movingly described the great comfort that he received from the presence of his dead brother Robert.[21] Blake's description of an enduring bond between family members beyond the grave would have had special significance for Hayley. He had recently lost his son, Thomas Alphonso, and was so distraught that he couldn't attend the funeral. Indeed Hayley's ballad 'Little Tom' creates an image of family devotion which the author found difficult to achieve in his own life. Thomas Alphonso was illegitimate, and both of Hayley's marriages proved unhappy.[22] Whatever the intended link between Thomas Alphonso and 'Little Tom', the bond between these boys and their fathers transcends death. So too Tom's empathy with his mother provides an idealised example of the mother-son relationship.

While 'Little Tom' is based on Hayley's direct experience of family life, it also draws attention to the hardships that many contemporary British families faced. Orphan children and fractured families were commonplace during the Napoleonic Wars, when economic pressures as well as the demand for soldiers and sailors forced many British men and boys to leave their families for long periods. In this way 'Little Tom' resembles other contemporary ballads, and engravings such as *Yo Heave Ho* (1799) which depicts a loyal sailor who goes to sea in order to defend his family's way of life. Such patriotic texts and images present a picture of brave British manhood sacrificing their own comfort to safeguard the future of both their families and the nation.[23]

Rather than just an individual tale of heroism, then, 'Little Tom' describes the courage and loyalty of the British people during the Napoleonic Wars. Indeed, the ballad suggests that Tom's heroic qualities, namely 'Tenderness, Courage, and Truth', are exactly those required by the nation. Britain needs men who will defend their nation as Tom has defended his family:

> A Defender, with Honour his Due!
> In the Man, may his Country admire!
> Since the Child was a Guardian so true
> To the desolate Cot of his Sire.

While these are Hayley's words, Blake's depiction boosts the patriotic elements of the tale. Patriotism may not be a quality we immediately associate with Blake. Yet at times this radical could be passionate in his advocacy of British interests, for example in his letter to his friend George Cumberland warmly endorsing Cumberland's efforts to establish a national gallery of art.[24] For Blake, it was important that Britain champion the arts, not just for the sake of art, but for that of national glory as well. Of course Blake did not endorse the political and economic conditions which made Tom's sacrifice necessary, and he was certainly no fan of war. Perhaps the best summary of Blake's position is that he praised the resilience and courage of the common people of Britain, including children, during wartime, yet lamented the hardships they faced.

Blake and Gillray compared

Little Tom the Sailor reflects Blake's and Hayley's complex responses to the sea. The print was created when Blake was staying near Hayley in a cottage in Felpham, on the Sussex coast.[25] Here Hayley and Blake would have encountered many people who depended upon the sea for their survival. Hayley's awareness of the hardships they faced may explain his interest in Widow Spicer, the inspiration for and beneficiary of his ballad. Blake, too, was moved by the sea. He refers to the sea in his letters as displaying both a terrifying and wondrous character: 'My Wife & Sister are both very well & courting Neptune for an Embrace, whose terrors this morning made them afraid but whose mildness is often Equal to his terrors.'[26] In the sea, as elsewhere in the natural world, Blake detected a divine presence which is made manifest in his engraving of *Little Tom*.

So, too, in Gillray's *The Nancy Packet*, the sea is represented as both fearsome and beautiful. The majesty of the waves breaking over the lifeboat is awesome to behold. Although not as strong as in *Little Tom*, there are hints here of a divine presence. If Gillray and Blake responded to the sea in similar ways, they presented two very different views of sailors. In *The Nancy Packet*, the sailors appear as ineffectual, almost foolish creatures. Indeed, as a recent commentator has noted, their disappearing posteriors are reminiscent of Gillray's devastating caricatures of the Duke of Clarence, who was often represented as a sailor (he had a long association with the Navy) pursuing sex with his mistress the actress Dorothy Jordan.[27] In short, Gillray's depiction has much in common with the standard caricature view of sailors ashore: rather dim, vain men who think only of themselves. This reflects the artist's own cynical view of human nature.

By contrast, Blake's view of sailors accords with the contemporary sentimental view made popular by ballads and mezzotint engravings such as *Yo Heave Ho*: sailors are selfless family men, who go to sea to support not only their loved ones but the entire nation. In a letter to Hayley, Blake expresses his hope that his engraved black-and-white impressions of *Little Tom*, 'tho' they are rough like rough sailors' 'will be no less favour'd' than the coloured impressions.[28] His affectionate, paternalistic attitude to his engravings matches his view of 'rough sailors'. Rather than laughing at such men, viewers are encouraged to sympathise with their struggles and to support the families they leave behind. Such was the explicit intention of *Little Tom the Sailor*, whose publication line reads: 'Printed for & sold by the Widow Spicer of Folkstone for the Benefit of her Orphans'.

Despite their shared appeal to the contemporary taste for sentiment and melodrama, it is unclear whether either Gillray's or Blake's engraving succeeded financially. *Little Tom the Sailor*, which sold for threepence, was unlikely to have made Widow Spicer much of a profit (though Hayley claimed that it did provide useful assistance), and indeed its rarity suggests that relatively few impressions were ultimately printed.[29] While this project did not mark the end of Blake's relationship with Hayley, Blake eventually left his patron to pursue his own, often more innovative projects. Although *The Nancy Packet*, as befitted its more elaborate design, would have sold for a higher price, perhaps several shillings, it also seems to have made little commercial impact. This disappointment helps explain why, frustrated in his attempt to succeed as an engraver of conventional images, Gillray returned to graphic satire. Like Blake, he succeeded most when he defied 'high' artistic conventions rather than emulated them.

Conclusion

Although *The Nancy Packet* and *Little Tom the Sailor* must ultimately be seen as minor works in the oeuvres of James Gillray and William Blake, they provide useful insight into these artists' careers. While the two engravings share many features, they also reflect the differences in their artists and audiences. *Little Tom the Sailor* was a cheap broadside created for a charitable purpose. Its simple, rather rough design reflects Blake's role as an engraver hired to create an image around his patron's ballad. Yet Blake's sympathetic portrayal of the subject matter conveys his own deep empathy with children as well as his fascination with the power of the sea. In contrast, *The Nancy Packet* was a relatively expensive object. Gillray's elegant, highly stylised design reflects elite viewers' demand for images of beautiful women as well as pathetic scenes of human suffering. So while Gillray had more control than Blake over the subject matter of his design, his choice seems to indicate more what he thought potential customers wanted to see than his own interests. The tendency to caricature his subjects expresses Gillray's true genius. *The Nancy Packet* and *Little Tom the Sailor* thus reveal some of the constraints on Gillray's and Blake's careers, and remind us that these artists operated within a commercial art market that was influenced by both academic conventions and popular tastes.

Indeed, these engravings demonstrate how, far from always ignoring popular culture, Gillray, and in particular Blake, did engage with fashionable themes such as shipwreck and unfortunate mothers. So too these artists' use of sentiment and melodrama reflects the popularity of these genres in a nation struggling with war and economic crisis. Thus, *The Nancy Packet* and *Little Tom the Sailor* reflect not only Gillray's and Blake's individual responses to their society, but the contemporary British fascination with sentiment, motherhood and the sea.

Notes

1. N.A.M. Rodger, *The Wooden World: an Anatomy of the Georgian Navy* (London: Collins, 1986).

2. D. Hay and N. Rogers, *Eighteenth-Century English Society: Shuttles and Swords* (Oxford: Oxford University Press, 1997), ch. 10.

3. A. Corbin, *The Lure of the Sea: the Discovery of the Seaside in the Western World 1750–1840*, trans J. Phelps (London: Polity Press, 1994), 1–18.

4. M. Lincoln, 'Shipwreck Narratives of the Eighteenth and Early Nineteenth Centuries: Indicators of Culture and Identity', *British Journal for Eighteenth-Century Studies*, 20: 2 (1997), 155–72.

5. W. Falconer, *The Shipwreck, a poem, in three cantos. By a Sailor* (London, 1762); W.R. Jones, 'Falconer, William (*bap.* 1732, *d.* 1770)', *Oxford Dictionary of National Biography*, OUP, 2004, http://www.oxforddnb.com/view/article/9117.

6. For example, *The Neglected Daughter – An Affecting Tale*, pub. Laurie & Whittle, 2 July 1804, col. etching (Library of Congress, British Cartoon Collection, PC3–1804, A size), in C. McCreery, *The Satirical Gaze: Prints of Women in Late Eighteenth-Century England* (Oxford: Oxford University Press, 2004), pp. 205–10.

7. For Gillray, see D. Hill, *Mr. Gillray. The Caricaturist. A Biography* (London: Phaidon Press, 1965). For Blake see R.R. Easson and R.N. Essick, *William Blake: Book Illustrator: a Bibliography and Catalogue of the Commercial Engravings*, vol. 1, Plates Designed and Engraved by Blake (Normal, Illinois: The American Blake Foundation at Illinois State University, 1972), vii. For information on engraving in eighteenth-century Britain, see T. Clayton, *The English Print 1688–1802* (New Haven and London: Yale University Press, 1997).

8. J. Gillray, *The Nancy Packet*, line engraving, etching and stipple, 44.2 × 56.2 cm, published 19 October 1784 by R. Wilkinson, No 58 Cornhill, London (The British Museum, object number 1862, 0712.296) (Figure 17.1). See *James Gillray: the Art of Caricature*, R. Godfrey with an Essay by M. Hallett (London: Tate Publishing, 2001), 76, from which much of the information that follows is drawn.

9. The *London Chronicle* first reported that no one survived the wreck, and one day later claimed that one person had survived; see *London Chronicle*, 8 March and 9 March 1784.

10. See K. Crouch, 'The Public Life of Actresses: Prostitutes or Ladies?', in H. Barker and E. Chalus (eds), *Gender in Eighteenth-Century England*, (Harlow, Essex: Addison Wesley Longman, 1997), pp. 58–78.

11. O. Baldwin and T. Wilson, 'Cargill, Ann (*c.*1760–1784)', *Oxford Dictionary of National Biography*, OUP, 2004, http://www.oxforddnb.com/view/article/4660.

12. *London Chronicle*, 10 March 1784.

13. Ibid.

14. McCreery, *Satirical Gaze*, 205–7.

15. W. Blake, *Little Tom the Sailor*, broadside consisting of four plates printed on one sheet: woodcut and pewter (Pls. 1 and 3) and relief etching (Pls. 2 and 4), 47.4 × 16.1 cm, hand-coloured impression, 'Printed for & sold by the Widow Spicer of Folkstone for the Benefit of her Orphans October 5, 1800' (The British Museum, object number 1868, 0808.13497) (Figure 17.2).

16. Blake to W. Hayley, 28 September 1804 (E 755).

17. R.N. Essick, 'Blake, William (1757–1827)', *Oxford Dictionary of National Biography*, OUP, 2004, http://www.oxforddnb.com/view/article/2585.

18. Blake to Hayley, 22 June 1804 (E 752–3); Blake to Hayley, 28 September 1804 (E 755).

19. Blake to Hayley, 4 May 1804 (E 748–9).

20. G. Keynes, *Blake Studies* (Oxford: Clarendon, 2nd edn, 1971), 105–6.

21. Blake to Hayley, 6 May 1800 (E 705).
22. V.W. Painting, 'Hayley, William (1745–1820)', *Oxford Dictionary of National Biography*, OUP, 2004, http://www.oxforddnb.com/view/article/12769.
23. *Yo Heave Ho*, pub. Laurie & Whittle (24 April 1799), col. mezzotint (NMM PAF4013), 148–50 in C. McCreery, 'True Blue and *Black, Brown and Fair*: Prints of British Sailors and their Women during the Revolutionary and Napoleonic Wars', *British Journal for Eighteenth-Century Studies*, 23: 2 (2000), 135–52.
24. Blake to G. Cumberland, 2 July 1800 (E 706–7).
25. Blake to T. Butts, 23 September 1800 (E 711).
26. Ibid.
27. *James Gillray*, 76.
28. Blake to Hayley, 26 November 1800 (E 714–5).
29. Keynes, *Blake Studies*, 106.

18
Framing Eve: Reading Blake's Illustrations

Jennifer Davis Michael

> Tyger Tyger, burning bright,
> In the forests of the night:
> What immortal hand or eye,
> Could frame thy fearful symmetry?
> (William Blake, E 24)

> Eve was framed out of a rib of Adam.
> (Sir Thomas Browne[1])

To frame is at once to shape and to contain within boundaries. Much of William Blake's work is concerned with framing the framer: comprehending the act of creation. Blake's own use of the verb *to frame* tends to have negative overtones, as in his awestruck yet horrified description of the Tyger's maker.[2] The Spectre, he tells us, 'frames Laws & Moralities / To destroy Imagination!' (E 229). Yet he uses the noun *frame* in a positive way to refer to the human form, a 'golden frame' (E 325). This seeming contradiction reflects Blake's larger ambivalence toward creation, especially the creation of the human body and the division of the sexes.

Because delineating is also binding, creation and fall are synonymous, or at least simultaneous, in much of Blake's work. Lately I have been interested in Blake's attempts to picture Paradise, to frame the prelapsarian existence of human beings and, in doing so, to (re)create the space of Eden. The same frame that allows us to 'see' this state or place also sets us apart from it, creating both a sense of 'hereness' and a sense of 'thereness'.[3] While Blake is just one of many artists who have tried to open windows on to Paradise, his efforts are particularly intriguing when juxtaposed with his own mythology of human origins and the self-consciousness with which he approaches his own creation. He seems peculiarly aware that the making of art is at once a divine and a fallen act, and that the same birth that animates a body also contains a spirit within mortal bounds. Framing, in other words, is a richly nuanced word and action, not merely an abstract concept, in respect to Blake.[4]

Blake literally draws frames around his illuminations in late copies of the *Songs*, many of whose plates also employ framelike devices within the image. Several of the *Paradise Lost* watercolours similarly feature a frame through which a fragile Eden may be glimpsed. Such frames open spaces in the texts that speak of Paradise: sometimes welcoming bowers, sometimes gaping holes. These frames rearticulate the static space of pastoral tradition, which holds its subjects at a safe distance, as a more fluid, translucent space. We are invited into that space through its instability, its indeterminacy. In considering *frame* not as a noun but as a verb, as it pertains to the creation and re-creation of Eve, this chapter will explore the relationship between her creation and her fall. I shall draw examples from the *Paradise Lost* series of watercolours, completed in 1808, and from an earlier series of biblical illustrations that Blake made for Thomas Butts (1799–1805). In each illustration, the space around Eve's figure is as important as the figure itself. She is born not into a void but into a world contrived not only by God, but also by Blake, Milton, and the Genesis author(s) in the stories that they tell. So when Blake depicts Eve's creation, he is both framing (creating) her and offering an interpretive frame for her origin and her fall.

Complicating matters, the scene that Blake frames is itself already a textual or verbal representation. Blake's illuminations of his own poems suggest that the graphic frame not only contains but opens the text to visual perception. The same is true of his illustration of Milton and the Bible: even where text is not literally incorporated on the page, the text is being framed (held, opened) through the image. Illumination and text thus form a double frame for an act that cannot literally be seen: an event that pre-dates human memory.

In Old English, *frame* is related to *from*. Hence, to *frame* is not only to create but also to derive the source of, to find where something comes *from*, just as to *trace* can mean to delineate or to find the source of. It is no accident, then, that Blake uses *frame* to describe the tyger's making, nor that he uses visual framing devices to represent primal acts of creation. *Frame* in Old English meant 'to be helpful or profitable, to make progress'. By 1250 it meant 'to prepare', which gave rise to a more specialized meaning, 'to prepare (timber) for building'. Only in the sixteenth century did it take on the more general meanings 'to shape, fashion, form', 'to make, construct'. Soon after, however, it came to mean 'to utter' or 'to fabricate with words' (as in 'to frame a story'), further reinforcing the link between verbal and visual representation. And from 1597 it has meant 'to imagine', as in 'to frame to oneself'. Framing not only occurs around a work of art, it constitutes the work itself. And herein lies a difficulty.

Kant classified the frame of a work of art as a *parergon*, not a 'constituent' but an 'addendum' to the representation (the word *parergon* meaning 'something subordinate or incidental').[5] Derrida expanded and challenged Kant's definition, calling the frame 'an outside which is called to the inside of the inside in order to constitute it as an inside'.[6] Properly speaking, however, the frame is neither inside nor outside the work. Similarly, when Blake frames Eden and the stories of Eden, he and we are neither inside the scene nor entirely outside it. His way of framing it calls attention to our distance from it, just as Milton first presents Adam and Eve to us through Satan's eyes. By re-framing the *hortus conclusus* of Eden, Blake opens it to the outside and also invites us to reconsider what the 'inside' and 'outside' are.

The other current definition of *frame*, pertaining to false accusation (as in 'frame-up'), which my title takes advantage of, does not appear until the late nineteenth century. The late twentieth century brought the bumper sticker, 'Eve Was Framed'. Yet, as quoted in my epigraph, Sir Thomas Browne referred to Eve's framing in 1646, and his word choice reinforces the conflation of creating and enclosing. My point, as well as Blake's, as I read it, is not to assign blame for Eve's sin, or to exonerate her, but to analyse this emphasis on her making as different from Adam's. Whereas he is moulded out of clay, she is framed out of a part of his body, a fragment. As Lynda Nead puts it, 'woman was created to fill Adam's own insufficiency . . . her existence always testifies to the original lack in Adam'.[7] This idea of filling a lack, an emptiness, appears vividly in Blake's illustrations.

Creation

The creation of Eve seems to be a more compelling event for Blake than that of Adam, because her creation represents the division of humanity into two sexes, thus engendering what Blake calls 'the torments of Love & Jealousy' (E 300). However, both pictures of the creation of Eve differ dramatically from the agonising division of sexes in *The Book of Los*, *The Four Zoas*, and in this passage from *The Book of Urizen*:

> The globe of life blood trembled
> Branching out into roots;
> Fib'rous, writhing upon the winds;
> Fibres of blood, milk and tears;
> In pangs, eternity on eternity.
> At length in tears & cries imbodied
> A female form trembling and pale
> Waves before his deathy face
>
> All Eternity shudderd at sight
> At the first female form now separate

(E78)

In place of such violent and painful separation, the pictures of Eve's creation are scenes of gentleness in which Eve is led by the hand to Adam or levitated from his side. It could be that Blake is being scrupulously faithful to Milton and to Genesis, rather than offering his own 'Bible of Hell' as he does elsewhere. Yet Blake is not known for his deference to the authors he illustrates.

The *Paradise Lost* watercolours[8] have received copious commentary, but not always in relation to Blake's other illustrations of the opening books of Genesis.[9] In *The Creation of Eve* (Figure 18.1), an almost rectangular frame is produced by the arrangement of bodies. The figures, that is, form their own frame rather than being set inside one. The act of framing (making) Eve is represented further as a framing of empty space: Dunbar suggests that the space around the figures conveys 'primordial emptiness'.[10] Or is it? Meyer Schapiro points out that we take for granted the 'smooth prepared field' of a painting,[11] which is itself a contrivance; it did not exist for the cave painters of Lascaux. Blake is painting over the surface of Milton's narrative as well as the Genesis narrative. Although Eve looks as though she could be descending from heaven, the text describes her being physically wrenched from Adam's body:

> Abstract as in a trance methought I saw,
> Though sleeping, where I lay, and saw the shape
> Still glorious before whom awake I stood;
> Who stooping op'n'd my left side, and took
> From thence a Rib, with cordial spirits warm,
> And Life-blood streaming fresh; wide was the wound,
> But suddenly with flesh fill'd up and heal'd
> The Rib he form'd and fashion'd with his hands;
> Under his forming hands a Creature grew. . . .
>
> (*Paradise Lost*, 8.462–70)[12]

In the painting, Eve's near-perpendicular angle to Adam is matched by Christ's posture.[13] In arranging these three figures – man, woman, and God – Blake is providing a window through which we see the 'natural' landscape beyond them. In so doing, he reminds us that the window itself is a work of art – as is the invisible window through which he allows us to see the figures.

Sleeping below Eve, Adam appears as a third party – certainly a passive one – in the tableau between Eve and Christ. The ethereal quality of the scene reinforces the sense that Adam dreams Eve into being. Perhaps it would be a stretch to say that she takes solid form only when she falls, but her fall is inextricably linked with the body and its appetites. Such an interpretation would be borne out by Blake's repudiation of 'fleshly desires'

Figure 18.1 William Blake, *The Creation of Eve* (Museum of Fine Arts, Boston)

in his preface 'To the Christians' (E 231), though of course he celebrates such desires in *The Marriage of Heaven and Hell*. In Milton's narrative, Eve's desire for self-determination is what leads her to sin: at no point is she more separate from Adam than in the moments after she eats the fruit. That separateness, however, frightens her so much that she begs him to join her.

Here, she rises from his side as an expression of his desire, but also to help fill the vast space of the page, of which Adam occupies very little, testifying to the 'lack' Lynda Nead mentioned. Similarly, the serpent convinces Eve that something is lacking in their existence in Eden. That lack produces desire, which leads her to taste the fruit. No sooner has she done so than she desires something else: Adam.

The space in the painting, in other words, testifies to the restlessness of desire: first Adam's, then Eve's, and finally the artist's and the viewer's. Even before Adam's desire is God's: the artist replicates God's expression of desire in creating humanity. We frame what we desire; we create a space and fill it. As Theseus says in *A Midsummer Night's Dream*, 'Such tricks hath strong imagination / That if it would but apprehend some joy / It comprehends some bringer of that joy'.[14] 'To frame [something] to oneself', as in the *OED* example, is to imagine it, to bring it into being *for* oneself, out of desire. Eve's hovering figure in this picture shows her poised between the two male figures who are both agents and objects of desire: they desire her into being, and she desires them as well.

A watercolour from the Butts series, *The Creation of Eve: And She shall be called Woman* (Figure 18.2),[15] shows Eve being brought to Adam by the white-bearded God as if descending from clouds. Adam is half-lying on the ground, as if just awakened from sleep. Here, it is Adam who is being raised. As the Father holds both of their right hands, he seems to be giving them to each other in marriage. Interestingly, God's gesture of joining is frozen at a moment when his own figure separates them. In the *Paradise Lost* painting, Eve is already a part of Adam; her perpendicular relation to him is matched by the L-shaped form of Christ's body, even as Christ's action draws her forth. In the Butts painting, Adam and Eve are joined only through the intervention of the divine figure, who dwarfs them physically just as he dominates the composition. Thus, although both illustrations emphasise the spiritual nature of Eve's 'birth', only the later one has her emerging from the space of Adam's body into a space of her own in which she is – for a moment – face-to-face with Christ.

Temptation

Early plates in the *Paradise Lost* series show Adam and Eve together, often 'framed' by vegetation or other structures and observed by angels or Satan. Beginning with the Fall, there is always some figure (angel, cross, or tree) dividing them and displacing them from the centre of the frame. The creation of Eve therefore initiates a physical separation, but as we have seen, the space at the centre of that plate is empty: framed by the human figures, joined by Christ's body. The spiritual division requires another figure, that of Satan. Eve's role in this displacement also bears close examination.

Figure 18.2 William Blake, *The Creation of Eve: 'And She shall be called Woman'* (Metropolitan Museum of Art, New York)

In the well-known *Temptation and Fall of Eve*, the snake coils around Eve's body, not only touching but covering her pubic region, suggesting simultaneously the carnal appetite that causes the Fall and the shame that follows it. This image repeats the autoerotic pose of Satan with the serpent in an earlier scene, which foreshadowed Satan's absorption into the serpent. Eve's embrace by the serpent, then, implies that she too becomes one with evil:

her bodily frame is now entirely comprehended, delimited, by the tight coils that surround her. The snake thus becomes a frame for her frame. Whereas the creation paintings raised her ethereally from a dream – hers, or Adam's – these bind her to death, to the earth.

In the Butts' tempera *Eve Tempted by the Serpent* (Figure 18.3), the snake only encircles her feet. The rest of its coiled, upright form creates a background as well as a frame for her. Perhaps she doesn't even see it. The frame is completed by the huge tree at the left with its overhanging branches, making an arch typical of Blake's illuminated plates. This time, the tree, as Behrendt points out, is 'massive', occupying roughly the left third of the picture.[16] The vines twisting round it suggest the coils of the snake, as well as echoing Satan's account in *Paradise Lost* of climbing the tree to reach the fruit. The snake's neck arches over Eve's head so that its head hovers directly above hers and nearly meets her uplifted hand, framing her head like an oval portrait. The composition here is closer to the creation scene from *Paradise Lost*: the postures of Eve and Adam are similar, with Adam again asleep, as though this too is his dream (or nightmare). Again, Eve is being lifted up and away from Adam in an L-shape, but here, she raises her right arm toward the fruit rather than folding her hands in prayer. The separation of her hands indicates her divided attraction: one stretches toward Adam, the other toward the tree. Furthermore, the hand toward Adam is palm

Figure 18.3   William Blake, *Eve Tempted by the Serpent* (Victoria and Albert Museum, London)

down, as if willing him to stay asleep, while the upraised hand opens toward the snake's head. Indeed, Eve's figure here is positioned more like that of Christ in *The Creation*, where his right hand elevates her and his left hangs down toward Adam. This correspondence suggests that Eve believes she is creating herself, distancing herself from her physical source (Adam) and mimicking her own levitation, when in fact it is the serpent that stretches her body upward through its rising coils.

The moon, which is directly above Eve's head in the creation watercolour, is here displaced to the right side of the tempera; in fact, we may follow the snake's coils from its head (above Eve's), around her feet, alongside Adam's body, and finally up toward the moon. This displacement is significant in light of the moon's association in Blake with love, Luvah, and the 'married land' of Beulah. According to Damon, 'The original place for the Moon was in Man's heart, or center, but when Man was divided, the Moon became separated.'[17] *The Creation of Eve* shows almost a straight line from Adam's heart through Eve's body toward the moon. In *Eve Tempted*, Eve's vertical connection is only to the snake and the tree, and her conjugal link to Adam, under the auspices of the moon, has become serpentine.

In the *Paradise Lost* watercolour *Temptation*, Eve and Adam are both engaged in their own separate dramas, divided by the tree and separately framed by jagged thorns or lightning bolts signifying the new disorder in nature. In the tempera, however, the same coils encircling Eve's feet stretch past Adam's sleeping head, and his entire body lies within their sinuous frame. Both illustrations make it clear that Adam will fall with Eve, yet the tempera implies that he may be framing Eve's fall out of his imagination, spawning from his own brain the serpent that ensnares them both.

Eve's serpentine self-creation in *Eve Tempted* forms a not-quite-closed frame, similar to that in the creation picture, but substituting an oval for a rectangle. The rectangle has open space in the centre, but is shaped by three figures: Christ, man, and woman. The oval, a more organic form, that of an egg, is formed by Eve's curved arm, curved like the coils of the serpent, and her face is its focus (though not its centre). The image Eve has created, with Satan's help, is the illusion of separateness, in which she is both framer and framed. By leaving the frame slightly 'ajar', Blake invites us to see it as incomplete, and also to observe the larger frame in which it operates, encompassing the tree, the snake, Adam, the moon, and the rest of the Edenic landscape.

Conversely, the frame of Eve's creation is also 'ajar', with gaps above her head and below her feet. She does not fully make contact with Adam or with Christ. Perhaps, then, this illusion of separateness, also known as the Fall, *is* inherent in her creation. Ironically, however, the illusion is achieved only through the agency of another: in rising from Adam's side with the help of Christ, she also rises toward the forbidden tree with the help of Satan. And, we might add, with Blake's help, and ours.

Blake's images of Eve not only frame the Miltonic and biblical texts, they are inevitably framed by them. More important, our own readings of each picture are framed by our knowledge of these texts and, in turn, our interpretations of the texts. The fragmentary origin of Eve (in Adam's rib) carries over to these frames in which we see her: no image, by itself, tells the whole story. The desire that draws her forth – and *draws* her – leads her, in turn, to draw her own frame, which she believes to be complete and separate, but it too is only a fragment. So, to return to Derrida's question for Kant, where does the frame end and the 'true work' begin? I suggest that Blake deliberately leaves the frame open, just as in these two images, to allow the image to enter our world, and to allow us to enter the world of the image. The work, in the ongoing sense – the work of framing – is never complete, because desire, by its very nature, always leaves a space for more.

Notes

1. Sir Thomas Browne, *Selected Writings*, ed. Sir Geoffrey Keynes (Chicago: University of Chicago Press, 1968), 348.
2. An early draft of 'The Tyger' had the word *form*, which Blake later changed to *frame* (E 795).
3. Gordon Cullen, *Townscape* (New York: Reinhold Publishing, 1961), 182–3.
4. Much of the work on framing in Blake deals with the relationship between visual and verbal art. See, for example, W.J.T. Mitchell, *Blake's Composite Art: a Study of the Illuminated Poetry* (Princeton: Princeton University Press, 1978); David L. Clark, 'Against Theological Technology: Blake's "Equivocal Worlds"', in David L. Clark and Donald C. Goellnicht (eds), *New Romanticisms: Theory and Critical Practice* (Toronto: University of Toronto Press, 1994); and Kathleen Lundeen, *Knight of the Living Dead: William Blake and the Problem of Ontology* (Selinsgrove: Susquehanna University Press, 2000).
5. Kant, *Critique of the Power of Judgment*, ed. Paul Guyer, trans. Paul Guyer and Eric Matthews (Cambridge: Cambridge University Press, 2000), 110 and n.
6. Jacques Derrida, *The Truth in Painting* (Chicago: University of Chicago Press, 1987), 63.
7. Lynda Nead, *The Female Nude* (London and New York: Routledge, 1992), 18.
8. I regret that space constraints prevent the inclusion of more than three illustrations. All the watercolours in the *Paradise Lost* series may be seen online at http://www.mfa.org/collections/.
9. See, for example, Stephen Behrendt, *The Moment of Explosion: Blake and the Illustration of Milton* (Lincoln: University of Nebraska Press, 1983); J.M.Q. Davies, *Blake's Milton Designs: the Dynamics of Meaning* (West Cornwall, CT: Locust Hill, 1993); Pamela Dunbar, *William Blake's Illustrations to the Poetry of Milton* (Oxford: Clarendon, 1980); James Treadwell, 'Blake, John Martin, and the Illustration of Paradise Lost', *Word and Image: a Journal of Verbal Visual Enquiry*, 9:4 (October–December 1993), 363–82; and Bette Charlene Werner, *Blake's Vision of the Poetry of Milton* (Lewisburg: Bucknell University Press, 1986).
10. Dunbar, 73.
11. Meyer Schapiro, *Theory and Philosophy of Art: Style, Artist, and Society* (New York: George Braziller, 1994), 1. On the frame as surface, see also Louis Marin, *On*

Representation, trans. Catherine Porter (Stanford: Stanford University Press, 2001), 356.

12. John Milton, *Complete Poems and Major Prose,* ed. Merritt Y. Hughes (New York: Macmillan, 1957), 373.

13. Werner points out that the curve of Eve's body derives from her origin as a bent rib (84); yet Blake offsets the 'sinister' element of her creation by having Christ raise her with his right hand, after originally sketching it with the left.

14. Blake alludes to this speech in *Milton,* plate 28 (30) (E 125).

15. Metropolitan Museum of Art, New York (06.1322.2).

16. Behrendt, 162.

17. Damon, *A Blake Dictionary,* rev. edn (Hanover, NH: Brown University Press/ University Press of New England, 1988), 285.

19
Lucid Dreaming/Lucid Reading: Notes on Sleepers in Blake's *Songs*

Gerda S. Norvig

Dreams permeate much of Blake's poetic and pictorial world. Some dreams are large and visionary, as in his experimental epic *The Four Zoas: a Dream in Nine Nights*, others small and pointed, as in the last line of the epilogue to *The Gates of Paradise: For the Sexes* where Satan is epitomised as 'The lost Traveller's Dream under the Hill' (E 269). Dreams also appear in his illustrations to the works of other writers, for example the watercolour of the youthful poet dreaming which is meant to represent the speaker of Milton's 'L'Allegro', or the first design of Blake's twenty-eight plate pictorial interpretation of John Bunyan's *The Pilgrim's Progress*, 'delivered under the similitude of a dream'.[1]

Often in Blake's work the line separating the depiction of a waking vision or imagined scene from the rendering of an actual sleeping dream is thin, even absent, at times deliberately so. And clearly the frequent exhortation to 'arise' (used 77 times) and 'awake' (used 63 times),[2] expressed both literally and metaphorically throughout Blake's illuminated canon, invites characters and readers alike to emerge from their habitual 'sleep of Ulro' (E 4) by way of conscious recognition that their experiences are occurring in a fantasy state mistaken for reality. It is in this sense, then, that I am regarding the evocations of sleepers and dreamers in *Songs* as a form of what has come to be known in dream research as the art of lucid dreaming.

Learned commentary on lucid dreaming, defined as the capacity to attain waking consciousness within one's dreams, has a long history. One of the chief contemporary investigators of the phenomenon, Stephen LaBerge of Stanford's Sleep Research Center, provides an overview of historical accounts that range from descriptions of such abilities by Aristotle and Aquinas, to appreciative statements on the process from figures such as Nietzsche and Freud, to the psychological writings of Dutch psychiatrist, Frederik Willem van Eeden, who invented the term 'lucid dreaming' in 1913, to the empirical studies of contemporary scientists based on data from sleep lab experiments.[3] LaBerge's own summary of the condition, representing it as an exercise in transcendence, is adequate to our purpose here. 'The phenomenon of dreaming while being fully conscious', he writes, meaning more precisely becoming fully conscious while dreaming, consists of our 'recognizing' on the spot that 'what we are actually "doing"' in our dream is not simply undergoing a set of behaviors that are happening 'to' us in a pre-ordained dream plot.[4] Rather, the lucid dreamer suddenly comprehends that what is really happening is that he or she is creating an imaginative process which simultaneously involves his or her enactment *of* and *in* it. As we shall see, Blake's narrative focus on such dual consciousness does not always follow this formula. Often it seems a topsy-turvy version of conventional lucid dreaming as when an individual speaker's supposed waking consciousness turns out to be the product rather than the producer of a dream.

Songs of Innocence and of Experience (hereafter *Songs*) is a good primer of such differences because there is a general shift from the attitudes of dreamers and sleepers toward their experiences in *Innocence* to the attitudes expressed by sleepers and dreamers in *Experience*. To begin with, in *Songs of Innocence* there are two fictional situations in which the double presence of the power of imagining and the experience of being imagined takes centre stage. The first example, the song entitled 'Introduction', involves a 'vision' or hallucination rather than a sleeping dream, but it is paradigmatic of the seamless relationship between conscious and unconscious states as they occur in *Innocence*. In the text of this song, a piper protagonist speaks in the first person of an event in his past when he suddenly 'saw a child' on a cloud. The child functions like a muse, instructing the piper to transform the instrument of his music into vocal and then written form. At that point the child vanishes from the piper's 'sight', and the piper performs the translation of song into script – or we might say into (Blakean) scripture. Key here is the intercession of ocular vision. The piper did not dream, neither did he imagine the presence of the child. He simply saw him and then stopped seeing him. Left ambiguous is whether the child's disappearance was initiated by the speaker or by the child himself. What is lucid, however, is the cooperation of the content of the vision and the will of the piper. Everyday consciousness is presumed by the piper to have brought these two together: the visionary experience that simultaneously shapes and is shaped by the speaker is not regarded as a special mental state separate from his normal waking state.

A similar situation occurs in 'The Chimney Sweeper' of *Innocence*. Here, however, the narrative is a twice-told tale. The speaker exclaims that his little protégé, Tom Dacre, experienced a miraculous 'sight' while sleeping. He then he goes on to describe the sight in a way that does not distinguish it from a clinically interpretable wish-fulfilling dream in which the young sweeps are unlocked from the coffins of their servitude and welcomed by an angel to a realm in the clouds where they are promised repatriation and adoption by a protecting 'father'. At this point the 'sight' becomes a sort of lucid dream, not for the dreamer, Tom, but for the speaker, retelling what he was told in what Freud might call, instead, a tertiary revision of the actual dream event.[5] We cannot know how much of the content of the 'sight' that is revealed in the text by the utterance of the song's speaker is meant to be a manipulated account. But the very telling of it remains significant to him, as we see in the end when the narrative concludes with a proverb of his own making ('if all do their duty they need not fear harm') that recapitulates the advice of the dream's major character, the angel who 'told Tom if he'd be a good boy / He'd have God for his father and never want joy'. Furthermore, the dream is recited by the speaker half in the past tense, as a bygone event, and half in the present tense as if it were still an ongoing lucid experience for him.

Two other repeated references to sleep and dreams among the songs of *Innocence*, those in 'Night' and 'A Cradle Song', also have angelic intercessors. Like the child of 'Introduction', these angels contribute to the sense that the state of sleep is nurtured by visitations from another realm of consciousness. To put it a different way, angelic presences become analogues of a waking consciousness that illuminates or makes lucid the dreams of sleep. In 'Night', the speaker, who announces himself in the fourth stanza of the text, creates a metaphoric relationship between the moon and 'the feet of angels bright' (l. 12). Silent and unseen (except by the consciousness of the speaker), these bright essences visit every nook and cranny of the natural world and transform whatever waking sorrow they find among sentient beings into the peace and pleasure of sleep. Only if the angels find them in mortal jeopardy, as sheep that are being hunted down by wolves, does this sleep become the sleep of the afterlife, which is then figured as an awakening into 'our immortal day'. 'Night' ends with the unexpected disclosure that the speaker is, or has become wholly identified with, the king of the beasts – a lion who, however, can now enact the vision of Isaiah and lie down to sleep beside the lamb, Christ's avatar. Claiming this identity, this act of conversion, the speaker enlarges his role in his waking imagination and states that he will behave like the angels and 'guard o'er the fold' instead of performing his natural function as a beast of prey. Transmutations of identity connected with sleep are supported here and elsewhere in *Innocence* less by the powers of lucid dreaming or its analogues, and more by the power of a lucid conviction that the paradigm of Christ's journey from incarnation to resurrection applies everywhere and is being perpetually re-enacted, whether we are awake or asleep.

Leaving aside the two cradle songs, one in *Innocence* and one in *Experience* as pieces that involve sleep and dreams in too prototypically antithetical and obligatory ways to forward my exploration of the lucid dreaming/lucid reading theme, I turn next to 'The Angel', from *Songs of Experience*. Here the distinction between the perceptual and cognitive functions of speakers in the two states, Innocence and Experience, is made clear. For instance, contrary to Tom in 'The Chimney Sweeper' of *Innocence* who is said by the speaker to have experienced his sleeping dream as a 'sight' apparently undifferentiated from sights of waking consciousness, the speaker of 'The Angel' in *Experience* expresses bewilderment and dissociation from both the content and psychological state of his or her dream. 'I dreamt a dream! What can it mean?' So reads the first line of the text. The speaker then goes on to tell the plot of the dream as a story about the past. In it, he/she was 'a maiden Queen / Guarded by an Angel mild' who behaved like a reluctant Psyche unwilling to enjoy her clandestine betrothal to Amor. The angel attempted to soothe the maiden, but her 'Witless woe was ne'er beguil'd'. The dreamer disconnects this statement, however, from the experience of a human subject, omitting the pronoun 'her' – or 'his', for that matter – so that no one, neither maiden nor angel, is given ownership of the foolishness or the woes. In the first line of the ensuing stanza, the location of the story becomes momentarily ambiguous as well. The dreamer, speaking in the first person, declares that he/she 'wept both night and day', but we do not know at first whether this occurred within the dream or after awakening from it. Again, in the third stanza, when the angel 'took his wings and fled' and 'the morn blush'd rosy red', the end of dreaming is suggested by the imagery of disappearance and dawn. But in the last stanza as the dreamer reports that 'Soon my Angel came again', the time *of* the dream and the time *in* it are confused. The lapse expressed as 'soon' seems to refer to a short break in the action of the dream narrative, while the proleptic event described (the chronological transformation of the maiden into an old maid) sums up the distant result of a long life of ageing and resistance.

Several times I have referred to the speaker of this song as 'he/she'. The deliberate effacement of the actual dreamer's sex lends the song a special quality not only of uncertainty, but also of possibility. If the dreamer is male, the opening question about the dream's signification ('What can it mean?') would imply that the dream raises for the speaker questions about the ontology of gender and might be read as an unconscious sympathy and lament for socially determined behaviours of female repression, what Blake later will disparage as 'the Female Will'.[6] On the other hand, a man dreaming that he is a woman could express the man's psychic identification with his inner feminine – Jung's 'anima'.[7] In any case, the dreaming here is expressly un-lucid: the dreamer never wakes up to his/her situation in the dream, a situation which leaves that function to the willing lucid reader.

Investigation of the complexity of adult female consciousness, such as profiled in 'The Angel', is one of the many conceptual markers of *Songs of Experience*, issued first in 1794. I will turn now to a trio of songs that Blake deported across the border from his stash of 1789 *Innocence* impressions to the *Experience* volume that he was creating at that time. One of these went over by default and only temporarily, but the other pair was exiled permanently and has a sort of emblematic status as an indication of the dialectical tilt the combined *Songs of Innocence and of Experience*, 'shewing the two contrary states of the human soul', was designed to take. In an early issue of *Songs*, the first poem of the trio in question, titled 'A Dream', appeared along with the second two, the so-called Lyca poems, titled 'The Little Girl Lost' and 'The Little Girl Found' (hereafter 'LGLF'). The Lyca poems are unique among Blake's songs in that they are literally inseparable, having been engraved on a triptych of three plates with the middle plate containing both the end of the 'Lost' poem and the beginning of the 'Found'. In a large printing edition of *Songs of Innocence*, *c*. 1789, which left Blake with extra, unbound stock, the four plates of 'A Dream' and 'LGLF' had been printed together, recto/verso, recto/verso, on two consecutively bound leaves. Thus when Blake decided to move LGLF into his new *Experience* volume, he simply inserted unused impressions of the Lyca poems from the old printing edition of *Innocence* into the pages of his newly engraved designs for one of the first issues of *Songs of Experience*. Because of the recto/verso format, however, 'A Dream' appeared along with 'LGLF' as an unavoidable tag-along.[8] Some critics have ignored the technical inadvertence of this move and so have interpreted 'A Dream' as a deliberate reflection of the *Experience* world view. And while this reading is not supported by Blake's decision to place the song back in *Innocence* when he stopped using the recto/verso format, there are tantalising links between 'A Dream', 'The Angel' of *Experience*, and the variously placed 'LGLF'.

'A Dream' is a song that begins by framing itself twice.[9] The first frame, the dreamer's 'angel-guarded bed', is described as being overshadowed by the second frame, the artifact of the dream: 'Once a dream did weave a shade / O'er my Angel-guarded bed'. The two coverings seem to permit dissociation with all its reverberating but unacknowledged and muffled reflections on the personality of the dreamer. However, the dream content concerns an ant lost in the same grass on which the dreamer/speaker 'thought' he/she lay: 'That an emmet lost its way / Where on grass methought I lay'. Whether this thought was an event within the dream or was part of the waking analysis (Freud's 'secondary revision' stage of dream recall) is ambiguous. If it occurred within the dream it would be a low-level sign of lucid dreaming, a characteristic hedge of *Innocence* against the dissociative tendencies so evident in *Experience*, but if it is a post-dream, analeptic observation, it could be a sign of low-level lucid reading on the speaker's part. In either case, relevant to the question of agency is the fact that the dream is represented as self-generated, able to weave itself into existence – the opposite of the stance in 'The Angel' where the dreamer claims origination: 'I had a dream!'

The continuation of the speaker's narration of the dream in the second stanza then begins a series of multiple overlapping identifications. Here, six adjectives float through four lines before the pronoun they are attached to appears. Even then, the descriptors (troubled, bewildered, forlorn, dark-benighted, travel-worn, and heart-broke), following on the announcement of the dreamer's presence on the grass, seem at first to apply to the dreaming subject rather than to the dreamed of object (the emmet) both referred to in the sentence's predicate: '*I* heard *her* say'. Again in the opening of the fourth stanza, after the dream emmet voices lament for her children and husband whom she imagines as distraught, the lines that begin 'Pitying I drop'd a tear' are grammatically and syntactically attributable to either the dreamer or the ant. And in the last two stanzas of this song, as a third dream character, named a glow-worm, speaks its part, identity ambiguities (including gender equivocation) mount. The glow-worm states: 'What wailing wight / Calls the watchman of the night. / I am set to light the ground, / While the beetle goes his round: / Follow now the beetle's hum, / Little wanderer, hie thee home'. Most critics participate in the confounding of identities in these verses, regarding watchman, glow-worm and beetle as one figure. But what is more likely is that there is a chain of command here, involving at least two intercessors. First of all, the word 'watchman', besides signifying the ubiquitous night crier of Blake's day, was used by some old-style clergy as a way of referring to one's guardian angel, and this somewhat outdated allusion in the text seems signalled by the archaicism of the expression 'wailing wight'.[10] Secondly, 'watchman' was frequently applied as well to the common dung or dor beetle which makes a droning sound when it flies and in some forms tends to cohabit with ants in their nests.[11] Entomologically, the glow-worm is also classed as a beetle: the two insects share an order (*Coleoptera*) but are of different families. In addition, like Blake's glow-worm in 'A Dream', the female of the species is wingless and moves 'grublike' across the ground as it emits a 'soft, bright light, quite delightful and amazing to see'.[12]

All these layered meanings, overdetermined identities and equivocal gender assignments (specifically the sex of the narrator and the glow-worm) belong to the rhetoric of dreams as they are recalled by the consciousness of adults after awakening. Such adult narrators are rare in *Innocence*, common in *Experience*, but in either case the rational dissociation of the narrator from the actual dream event mars the lucidity of connections that the children of *Innocence* normally see and express. For instance, in 'The Lamb', (not a dream song) where the child speaker spells out the commonality between child, lamb and Christ, the knowledge of that commonality is relational and so is not confused with a merger of identities such as occurs in 'A Dream'. Thus, despite the accidental nature of the shift of this dream song from *Innocence* to *Experience*, and despite Blake's decision to move it back to *Innocence* when he stopped using the recto/verso production format, a number of its ingredients regarding the relationship between conscious and unconscious perception mark it as liminally situated between these two states of the human soul. Furthermore, the original attachment of 'A Dream' to 'LGLF' also seems relevant as a propaedeutic to reading 'LGLF' and so brings me to the following concluding observations on what I have called lucid dreaming and lucid reading in the combined *Songs*.

Among those characters who sleep, dream or are said to have entered either of those states in *Songs*, none is a longer or more deliberate sleeper than Lyca, the 'heroine' of 'LGLF'. Following the example of 'A Dream', 'LGLF' begins with a frame, but the frame in this case consists of a two-stanza pronouncement delivered by an unnamed speaker claiming a lucid, prophetic vision: 'In futurity / I prophetic see / That the earth from sleep / (Grave the sentence deep) / Shall arise and seek / For her maker meek; / And the desart wild / Become a garden mild'. Awakening from sleep, presented as a metaphor of human regeneration, is the theme of this little sermon. But the story it introduces presents a contrary parable that unfolds along the lines of a paradoxical epic simile. The main protagonist is Lyca, one whose very name is 'like a' simile.[13] She is already lying down in the second line of her story, and her main action throughout the narrative of the double song is to fall asleep and stay asleep. Once she closes her eyes, things are represented as happening to her but she no longer exhibits consciousness of these events. For all intents and purposes, the rest of the text represents her dream, one from which she is dissociated, a mere object for others to manipulate and regard as projections of their own designs and desire. In this way, sleeping in her sleep, she is at the extreme opposite pole of a lucid dreamer.

Features that we have already observed as hallmarks of identity confusion in 'A Dream' proliferate here. Ambiguous pronoun and syntax usage bear the brunt of such diluted subjectivity in the first of the linked songs. While Lyca bemoans her fate, and like the lost ant in 'A Dream' identifies with her imagined grieving family at home, she soliloquises: 'How can Lyca sleep / If her mother weep. / If her heart does ake, / Then let Lyca wake'. In this speech, Lyca's self-awareness has become melded with her mother's so that she even calls herself by the name her mother uses for her, and because of the ambiguous pronoun 'her', the aching heart evoked may belong grammatically to either female. Two stanzas later, after the beasts of prey arrive, they are said to have 'View'd the maid asleep', which again has two overlapping meanings: either Lyca was asleep when viewed by the beasts, or the beasts were asleep when viewing her. In the latter case we would be facing a situation in which the beasts were dreaming inside Lyca's dream. This is an imbrication that actually occurs later in the second, 'found', part of the narrative when Lyca's (dreamed of) parents dream of her. In this first part, however, the equivocal placement of the act of looking is repeated in the lines that read 'The kingly lion stood / And the virgin view'd' where ambiguous syntax allows us to imagine either that the lion viewed the virgin or that the virgin viewed the lion.

These overdetermined statements and the Chinese-box structure of dreams within dreams together defeat the expression of subjective lucidity on the part of the characters in 'LGLF'. As suggested earlier, this is a quintessential quality of *Experience* and balances out the antithetical attitude germane to speakers in *Innocence*. But dreaming is really only a special case of how the subjects in the contrary states of the soul both condition and are conditioned by the way they see the world. Subjective lucidity in *Innocence* goes along with an experience of relationship that seeks neither to usurp nor obliterate the Other. At the same time, however, it tends to leave the individual submissive, as the chimney-sweep narrator exemplifies, to whatever harm their socioeconomic system may inflict on them. In *Experience*, individuality dominates over connectedness and permits clear-eyed social outrage. But the trade-off is a weakening of empathic relatedness and an overdeveloped narcissism ratcheted up in sleep and dreams to the point where every face and figure is a dissociated simulacrum of the autonomous ego.

In the end, the more lucid speakers and dreamers of *Innocence* often leave the reader with a sense of inadequate purchase on the subtle heft of their narratives, while the ambiguous identities, the complex projections and the frequent dissociations in stories relayed by the dream narrators in *Experience* induce in the reader an interpretive desire that creates a place for a reparative lucid reading of their songs.

Notes

1. For reproductions of designs see 'The Youthful Poet's Dream', in J.M.Q. Davies, *Blake's Milton Designs* (Cornwall, CT: Locust Hill Press, 1993), fig. 60, and 'The Dreamer Dreams a Dream', in Gerda S. Norvig, *Dark Figures in the Desired Country: Blake's Illustrations to the Pilgrim's Progress* (Berkeley and Los Angeles: University of California Press, 1993), Plate 1.
2. Blake's word use frequency is given in David V. Erdman (ed.), *A Concordance to the Writings of William Blake*, Vol. II (Ithaca, NY: Cornell University Press, 1967), 2181–249.
3. Stephen LaBerge, *Lucid Dreaming* (New York: Ballantine Books, 1985), 3.
4. Ibid., 7.
5. Sigmund Freud, *The Interpretation of Dreams* (New York: Avon Books, 1965), ch. VI.
6. The term 'female will' appears in Blake's *Jerusalem* (E 661, 688) and elsewhere.
7. See C.G. Jung, 'The Syzygy: Anima and Animus', in *The Portable Jung*, ed. Joseph Campbell (New York: Viking, 1971), pp. 148–62.
8. For precise details see Joseph Viscomi, *Blake and the Idea of the Book* (Princeton, NJ: Princeton University Press, 1985), ch. 28.
9. Heather Glen notes the opening double frame of 'A Dream' but sees different implications, *Vision and Disenchantment: Blake's Songs and Wordsworth's Lyrical Ballads* (Cambridge: Cambridge University Press, 1983), 184–5.
10. See 'watchman', *OED*, entry 3b.
11. Ibid., entry 6; see also John C. Pallister, 'Insects and other Invertebrates', in Frederick Dimmer (ed.), *The Animal Kingdom*, Vol. III (Garden City, New York: Doubleday, 1954), 1874.

12. Pallister, 1855.
13. The likeness of 'Lyca' to 'like' is mentioned by Nelson Hilton, 'Blake's Early Work', *The Cambridge Companion to William Blake*, ed. Morris Eaves (Cambridge: Cambridge University Press, 2003), 196, and is explored further by me in a forthcoming essay, 'The Movable Text and Blake's Utopic Imagination in *Songs*: the Case of "The Little Girl Lost/Found"'.

20
Valkyries and Sibyls: Old Norse Voices of Female Authority in Blake's Prophetic Books

Heather O'Donoghue

The influence of Old Norse mythology on Blake's poetry has not been overlooked. If anything, it has been rather grandly overstated – as in Harold Bloom's sweeping declaration that Blake's 'own true Sublime comes in . . . a Northern [mode] . . . in the tradition of the Icelandic Eddas'.[1] Northrop Frye has similarly pronounced that 'Eddic myths' are 'integral to Blake's symbolism', claiming that 'we cannot understand Blake' without understanding how to read the Prose Edda, 'at least as he read [it]'.[2] More recently, De Luca has compared what he understands to be the characteristic form of individual Eddaic poems – 'dramatic exchanges between characters in conflict . . . [which are] usually mere pretexts for long expository accounts chronicling divine history and escatology, cataloguing mythic names, and mapping out supernatural geography' – with Blake's own work: 'One might be describing the typical features of *Jerusalem* itself.'[3] But these male voices of authority are tellingly unspecific about what it was, precisely, that Blake read, and in what forms it is found in his poetry.[4]

Then again, when Margaret Omberg, in a tantalisingly brief account of Old Norse influence on Blake's work, argues that Frye's faith in Eddaic influence 'remains largely a matter of interpretation', we might respond, how could it be otherwise?[5] Particular effects of the fashion for Old Norse poetry which dominated literary society in Britain in the latter part of the eighteenth century may be impossible to pin down. However, I will examine two specific forms in which Blake would have encountered Norse mythology: Thomas Gray's Norse Odes, and the work of Paul-Henri Mallet, translated and re-worked by Thomas Percy as *Northern Antiquities*.[6] I will focus on one aspect of this mythology: the voice of female authority.

Thomas Gray wrote his two Norse Odes – 'The Fatal Sisters' and 'The Descent of Odin' – in 1761, as part of a plan to produce 'A History of English Poetry', tracing its roots back to Celtic, Saxon and Old Norse.[7] His major sources for the Old Norse (Icelandic) originals were two seventeenth-century Latin treatises by Scandinavians: the Icelander Thormod Torfason's *Orcades*, a collection of texts relating to the Orkney Islands,[8] and Thomas Bartholin's

Antiquitatum Danicarum.[9] Both works included Old Norse poems with Latin translations, and Gray based his odes on the Latin. Blake was commissioned, in 1797, to illustrate Gray's *Poems*, and used pages from a disbound copy of the 1790 edition as the basis for his plates.[10] Blake must have absorbed in a concentrated way these poems based on Norse mythology, revealing his understanding and interpretation of them in the illustrations.

Paul-Henri Mallet's work on the history of Denmark was published in English in 1770. The first of the resulting two volumes recounts the prehistory of Denmark, and more generally, Scandinavia, including such chapters as 'A general idea of the Ancient Religion of the Northern Nations', or 'Of the Customs and Manners of the ancient Northern Nations'. The second volume of *Northern Antiquities* is different: it consists of an annotated translation of the *Edda* of Snorri Sturluson, a thirteenth-century Icelandic historian and mythographer. This *Edda* is a prose *ars poetica*, ostensibly written to explain the mythological references in Old Norse poetry. Snorri's *Edda* is not, therefore, an authentic pagan source; it is Christian retelling of Norse mythology. But Snorri's primary source was Old Norse poetry (much of it later collected in an anthology confusingly known as the *Poetic Edda*), and he also quotes substantial amounts of this poetry in his narrative – quotations retained, in translation, by Mallet/Percy. If we assume, with Omberg, that Blake could not read Latin, then 'his acquaintance with northern mythology . . . was almost certainly made through *Northern Antiquities*'.[11]

These, then, are the two sources I want to work with; and specifically, how their representations of valkyries and sibyls, authoritative female speakers, can be traced in Blake's works.

Thomas Gray's poem 'The Fatal Sisters' was first printed in 1768. But he dates a transcript of the poem in his Commonplace Book to 1761, giving it there the title 'The Song of the Valkyries'.[12] This poem – now known as *Darraðarljóð* – is found in the thirteenth-century Old Norse *Njáls saga*. According to the saga, a man called Dörruðr had a horrific vision, in Caithness, on the morning of the Irish battle of Clontarf, of women weaving: 'men's heads were used as the loomweights, and the weft and warp were men's intestines. The beater was a sword, and the pin-beater, an arrow.'[13] As the women weave, they speak verses, quoted in the saga. The poem almost certainly does not belong in the context the saga describes: it is probably not even about Clontarf, and the man Dörruðr may be no more than the result of a linguistic back formation from the difficult phrase *vefr darraðar* (web of ?pennants/?spear) which is repeated in the poem.[14]

But it is evident that these women are valkyries – 'choosers of the slain', as verse 6 makes clear:

> let us not permit
> his life to be lost;
> the Valkyries have
> their choice of the slain.[15]

In Mallet, Odin's valkyries are subordinate creatures: 'their business is to wait upon [the heroes in Valhalla], and they are called VALKERIES. Odin employs them to chuse in battle those who are to perish, and to make the victory incline to whatever side he pleases'.[16] Their role as heavenly stewardesses is elaborated in the second volume of *Northern Antiquities*: 'there are . . . a great many virgins who officiate in Valhall, pouring out BEER and ALE for the heroes, and talking care of the cups, and whatever belongs to the table . . . These goddesses are called *Valkyries'*.[17] However, in the poem *Darraðarljóð*, the women weaving are not merely mimicking the action of the battle, but producing, or directing, it, and Gray's poem stresses their power:

> We the reins to slaughter give
> Ours to kill and ours to spare.

> (ll. 33–4)

Important here is the double function, almost an oxymoronic one: both protective and destructive.

Given the violent power and drama invested in Blake's illustrations to 'The Fatal Sisters', Blake's image of valkyries was evidently more of controlling destinies than of Mallet's heroic waitresses. Further, as Irene Tayler points out, Blake 'almost always pictures the sisters as three, perhaps conflating them in his mind with the three Norns, or Fates'.[18] It is, I think, striking that in the face of Gray's clear reference in the preface to the poem (Blake's plate 4) to twelve women, and the poem's mention of five valkyrie names, Blake repeatedly pictures three women. It may be that the poem's new title, 'The Fatal Sisters', suggested the classical Fates to Blake, but it is interesting that in Old Norse mythology itself, three Norns, often confused with valkyries, are figured as creating or determining the fates of human beings and, indeed, of the gods themselves. According to the Old Norse poem *Völuspá*, for instance, three maidens, 'deep in knowledge . . . laid down laws, / they chose out lives / for mankind's children, / men's destinies'.[19]

Blake's debt to 'The Fatal Sisters' has been carefully documented by Paul Miner[20] and Morton Paley.[21] As Paley notes, in Blake's work after 1797, 'the imagery of weaving suddenly assumed a major importance'.[22] Weaving is identified with the production or controlling of destiny, and Enitharmon weaves spectres in *The Four Zoas* (including the spectre of Tharmas).[23] In

Milton, she is 'weaving the Web of Life' (*M*, 6.28; E 100). And this weaving/creation is invariably accompanied by song, 'lulling cadences' (*M*, 6.6; E 99).

But as we have seen, the action can be either protective or destructive, and this dark side is represented too in Blake's poetry. In *Milton*, for instance, the sisters of Tirzah recall the bloody valkyries. As they 'weave the black Woof of Death' (*M*, 29 [31]. 56; E 128),

> The stamping feet of Zelophehads Daughters are covered with
>   Human gore
> Upon the treddles of the Loom, they sing to the winged shuttle

> (*M*, 29 [31]. 58–9; E 128)

In *Jerusalem*, Cambel and Gwendolen 'wove webs of war' (*J*, 7.44; E 150), a precise echo of the refrain in 'The Fatal Sisters', 'Weave the crimson web of war' (1.25; 36).

Perhaps the clearest allusions to the Old Norse occur when Blake imagines the weaving, or its product, the web, with its many negative connotations in his work, being spun from the bowels of the weavers, a disturbing variation on the 'texture' which is 'of human entrails made' (1.10) in Gray:

> The Daughters of Enitharmon weave the ovarium & the integument
> In soft silk drawn from their own bowels in lascivious delight
> With songs of sweetest cadence

> (*FZ* VIII: 209–11; E 376)

Tirzah and her sisters sit within a monstrous 'Polypus', 'Spinning it from their bowels with songs of amorous delight' (*M*, 34 [38]. 28; E 134). In the work known as 'The Circle of Life' or 'The Arlington Court Picture',[24] S. Foster Damon identifies the figure at the foot of the picture, holding 'a phallic hank of rope, the line of material life, which the Three Fates . . . grasp', as Tharmas.[25] One of these fates is about to cut the rope; it's not clear whether Tharmas is the spinner or the spun. But there is one final, strange connection to be made with Old Norse before we move on. The threads on the fatal sisters' hideous loom are made, as we have seen, out of men's intestines.It seems unlikely that Gray knew much Old Norse, and still less likely that Blake had access to the original, as quoted in Bartholin and Torfaeus. But it is a curious coincidence that the Old Norse word used for intestines is, in its plural form, 'tharmar'.[26]

What could *Northern Antiquities* tell Blake about the sibyl, the foremost female voice of authority in Old Norse? Describing the Germanic culture of ancient Denmark, Mallet quotes Tacitus as his authority for the respect with which this voice was treated: 'The Germans suppose some divine and prophetic quality resident in their women, and are careful neither to disregard their admonitions, nor to neglect their answers.'[27] This follows Mallet's (somewhat comic) contention, that 'Nothing was formerly more common in the North than to meet with women who delivered oracular information.'[28] Mallet's brief summary of the Old Norse poem *Völuspá* – the prophecy of the sibyl, and the fundamental source for Old Norse creation and apocalypse myths – is striking:

> The Prophetess having imposed silence on all intellectual beings declares, that she is going to reveal the decrees of the Father of Nature, the actions and operations of the Gods which no person ever knew before herself. She then begins with a description of the chaos; and proceeds to the formation of the world, and of that of its various species of inhabitants, Giants, Men and Dwarfs. She then explains the employment of the Fairies or Destinies; the functions of the Gods, their most remarkable adventures, their quarrels with Loke, and the vengeance that ensued. At last, she concludes with a long description of the final state of the universe, its desolation and conflagration: the battle of the inferior Deities and the Evil Beings: the restoration of the world; the happy lot of the good, and the punishment of the wicked.[29]

This is massive intellectual authority: wisdom unparalleled in its range and profundity. This female voice has absolute command of the sum of human – and, even more significantly, divine – knowledge. Gray's poem 'The Descent of Odin', based on the Old Norse poem *Baldrs Draumar* (Baldr's dreams) also features an Old Norse prophetess, or *völva*, whom the pre-eminent god Odin has to consult about the fate of his own son Baldr, pleading with her to yield up her transcendent knowledge of the future.[30] Gray shows Odin conjuring up a 'prophetic maid' (l. 20), but when she angrily realises his hitherto concealed identity, he slanders her in turn, denying her virginal status:

> No boding maid of skill divine
> Art thou, nor prophetess of good;
> But mother of a giant-brood!
>
> (l. 84–6)

Blake's illustration of the first appearance of the sibyl shows a stern and sorrowful mature woman, face heavily lined, and lips parted, about to speak – a stark contrast to the blank, unlined faces of his Fatal Sisters.

Two of Blake's early prophecies, *America* and *Europe*, feature a dramatic female voice. In *America* (A), the 'shadowy daughter of Urthona' (A1.1; E 51) is silent until her violent sexual encounter with Orc, when she is suddenly delivered of an unexpectedly peremptory and authoritative declaration: 'I know thee, I have found thee, & I will not let thee go' (A2.7; E 52). In the preludium to *Europe*, the same 'shadowy female' also raises her voice – but in lament for the burdens of childbearing (E 60–1). But she is completely distinct from the post-sexual prophetesses figured in *The Book of Los* and, most importantly, *Vala, or the Four Zoas*, which are, as we shall see, plainly derived from the Old Norse *völva*.

The *Book of Los* (BL) opens with 'Eno' the 'aged Mother', a monumental figure who has been 'Since the day of thunders in old time / Sitting beneath the eternal Oak' (E 90). Unlike the sibyl, who is associated with the great ash tree Yggdrasill, the Old Norse world tree, Eno is 'sitting beneath the eternal oak', apparently a druidic association.[31] But everything else about Eno – the chariot she guides, the tree which is associated with the shaking of the earth, and even the mention of thunder – is unmistakably Norse. In *Völuspá*, as quoted in Mallet, the shaking of the great ash tree presages the coming violent apocalypse, and throughout *Northern Antiquities*, Thor is identified as the god of thunder, who rides a chariot. And like the sibyl in *Völuspá*, who can look back to a time before the world was created, Eno too commands an immeasurable span of time; she looks back eons,[32] to a golden age in 'Times remote' (BL3.7; E 90), before moving on, like her Old Norse counterpart, to a creation myth.

In *Northern Antiquities*, following Snorri's work, this creation myth is recounted, in prose, by a trinity of mysterious interlocutors, Har, Jafnhar and Thridi (in the original text, their names translate as High, Just-as-High and Third). Their account is closely based on the poem *Völuspá*, the prophecy of the sibyl. To begin with, Har explains, 'All was one vast abyss'. Thridi takes over to describe a burning world, 'luminous, glowing' and Har and Jafnhar speak of a corresponding world of ice in which 'many strata of congealed vapours . . . were formed, one above another, in the vast abyss'. Thridi concludes:

> And as to that part of the abyss which lay between the two extremes; it was light and serene like the air in a calm. A breath of heat then spreading itself over gelid vapours, they melted into drops; and of these drops were formed a man . . . This man was named YMIR . . . From him are descended all the families of the Giants.[33]

There are suggestive echoes of this creation myth – so very unlike Genesis – in Chapter I of *The Book of Los*: the begetting of the giant race and the void between two great realms (E 91) in which Los takes shape. Just as Eno resembles the Old Norse sibyl, so the creation myth which follows her exordium closely resembles the sibyl's vision.

A cancelled opening line to *The Four Zoas* once read 'This is the dirge of Eno' (E 819). But this was replaced by 'The Song of the Aged Mother which shook the heavens with wrath' (*FZ* I: 1; E 300) – clearly our female prophetess – and the third line, with its reference to 'the day of Intellectual Battle'

(*FZ* I: 3; E 300) vividly recalls Mallet's sibyl who 'imposed silence on all intellectual beings'. A little further on, we are told that Urthona 'his Emanations propagated' (*FZ* I: 18; E 301); in *Northern Antiquities* too we are told that 'from [the] supreme god were sprung (as it were emanations of his divinity) an infinite number of subaltern deities and genii'.[34] Blake's conception of the universal man is also strongly suggestive of the fate of Ymir: in the Norse, the gods:

> dragged the body of Ymir into the middle of the abyss, and of it formed the earth. The water and the sea were composed of his blood; the mountains of his bones; the rocks of his teeth; and of his hollow bones, mingled with the blood that ran from his wounds, they made the vast ocean.[35]

But throughout the whole poem, whatever Blake's original intentions might have been, the figure called Vala is portrayed not as a speaking authority, but as a character – an evil one – in the psychomachia. It has still seemed axiomatic to some critics that, in name at least, Vala is derived from the Old Norse sibyl, or *völva*. But others have scorned this identification – for instance, Margoliouth, who notes tersely: 'This is a mistake. The name Blake could have found in Mallet's *Northern Antiquities* (1770 ii 202) is not Vala but Vola.'[36] However, it was standard practice among British writers to anglicise this form as 'Vala'. William Herbert, for instance, one of the first to translate Old Norse poetry into English directly from the original (and not via Latin), calls his version of *Völuspá* 'The Song of Vala'.[37] And Thomas Gray, in his Commonplace Book list of books on Old Norse, calls it 'The Oracles of Vala'.

It is clear that, like *Völuspá* – the sibyl's prophecy itself – Blake's poem is an account of creation and apocalypse. And nowhere are Blake's debts to Old Norse myth more evident than in its final section, 'Night the Ninth, Being the Last Judgement' (E 386).

Blake's Night the Ninth opens with Los and his wife Enitharmon weeping over the body of Christ crucified, just as the Old Norse gods weep at the death of Baldr, the radiant young son of Odin, perhaps, like Christ, sacrificed by his own father in the hope of resurrection. In Old Norse, the death of Baldr is the final act before Ragnarök, the doom of the gods. The first cosmic loss in the ensuing cataclysm is the disappearance of sun and moon, just as in *The Four Zoas* Los's first action wrenches the sun and moon from the sky. And while in *The Four Zoas*:

> With thunderous noise & dreadful shakings rocking to & fro
> The heavens are shaken & the Earth removed from its place
> The foundations of the Eternal hills discoverd

> (*FZ* IX: 15–17; E 387)

so at Ragnarök, in Percy's translation, 'the earth and the mountain shall be seen violently agitated; the trees torn up from the earth by the roots, the tottering hills to tumble headlong from their foundations';[38] similarly, Los is described as 'cracking the heavens across' (*FZ* IX: 9; E 386), just as in the Norse, 'the heaven shall cleave asunder'.[39]

Of course, much of this imagery is echoed in biblical sources, especially the Book of Revelation (in fact Percy's note in *Northern Antiquities* draws attention to the similarities, quoting at length from Revelation).[40] But the verbal correspondences with the text of *Northern Antiquities* are very close. There, the gods and the giant monsters engage in battle: the Great Serpent bears down on Thor and all the time 'the great ash Tree of Ygrasil is shaken'[41] – recalling 'the serpent Orc' and 'The tree of Mystery' (*FZ* IX: 69–70; E 388).

In both *The Four Zoas* and *Northern Antiquities* a new world is born from a great conflagration. Again, we must take account of parallels in Revelation (especially 'And I see a new heaven and a new earth'). But the pastoral images of regeneration in Blake are clearly influenced by Mallet/Percy: compare, 'The sun arises from his dewy bed & the fresh airs / Play in his smiling beams, giving the seeds of life to grow' (*FZ* IX: 846–7; E 407) with, 'There will arise out of the sea, another earth most lovely and delightful; covered it will be with verdure and pleasant fields; there grain shall spring forth and grow of itself, without cultivation';[42] or, 'And Man walks forth from the midst of the fires, and evil is all consumd' (*FZ* IX: 828; E 406) with 'While the fire devoured all things, two persons of the human race ... lay concealed ... They feed on the dew.'[43]

At the end of the poem, Blake's 'spectre of prophecy', his 'delusive phantom' (*FZ* IX: 851; E 407), disappears. So too, at the end of the prose Edda, as in Percy/Mallet: 'Gangler heard a terrible noise all around him; he looked every way, but could discern nothing, except a vast, extended plain ...'[44] All, in the end, is immaterial discourse. But it is a discourse originally articulated by wise and powerful women.

Notes

I am very grateful to Sebastian Kalhat Pocicovic, University College, Oxford, for his expert advice on Blake.

1. Harold Bloom, 'William Blake', in *The Oxford Anthology of English Literature*, eds Frank Kermode and John Hollander, Vol. II (New York and London: Oxford University Press, 1973), pp. 10–14, 12.
2. Northrop Frye, *Fearful Symmetry* (Princeton, NJ: Princeton University Press, 1947; 4th printing 1974), 418.
3. Vincent Arthur De Luca, *Words of Eternity* (Princeton, NJ: Princeton University Press, 1991), 131.
4. De Luca's footnote to this remark makes the vague assertion that Blake 'presumably' would not have had access to the poems themselves.

5. Margaret Omberg, *Scandinavian Themes in English Poetry 1760–1800* (Uppsala: Almqvist & Wiksell International, 1976), 127.

6. Thomas Percy, *Northern Antiquities, or, A Description of the Manners, Customs Religion and Laws of the Ancient Danes* (London: T. Carnan and Co., 1770).

7. H.W. Starr and J.R. Hendrickson (eds), *The Complete Poems of Thomas Gray* (Oxford: Clarendon, 1966), 27. All references to Gray's Norse Odes are to this edition.

8. Thormodus Torfaeus, *Orcades* (Hafniae, 1697).

9. Thomas Bartholin, *Antiquitatum Danicarum de Causis Contemptæ a Danis adhuc Gentilibus Mortis* (*Danish Antiquities on the Pagan Danes' Disdain for Death*) (Hafniae: Joh. Phil. Bockenhoffer, 1689).

10. See David Bindman, *Blake as an Artist* (Oxford: Phaidon, 1977), 113.

11. Omberg, 126. See also Jason Whittaker's note on the verbal correspondences between *Jerusalem* and *Northern Antiquities, William Blake and the Myths of Britain* (Basingstoke: Macmillan, 1999), 28.

12. Starr and Hendrickson, 29.

13. *Brennu-Njáls saga*, ed. Einar Ól. Sveinsson, Íslenzk fornrit XII (Reykjavík: Hið Islenzka Fornritafélag, 1954), ch. 157. Translated by Robert Cook as *Njal's saga* (London: Penguin, 2001).

14. See Russell Poole, *Viking Poems on War and Peace* (Toronto: University of Toronto Press, 1991), 119 ff., esp. 125.

15. Ibid., 117.

16. *Northern Antiquities*, Vol. I, 102.

17. *Northern Antiquities*, Vol. II, 98–9.

18. Irene Tayler, *Blake's Illustrations to the Poems of Gray* (Princeton, NJ: Princeton University Press, 1971), 111. Tayler suggests that the plate illustrating the beginning of the poem (plate 5) may show more than three figures, but I am inclined to disagree.

19. Ursula Dronke (ed. and trans), *The Poetic Edda*, Vol. II (Oxford: Clarendon, 1997), stanza 20, 12.

20. Paul Miner, 'Two Notes on Sources', in *Bulletin of the New York Public Library*, LXII (1958), 203–7.

21. Morton Paley, 'The Figure of the Garment in *The Four Zoas, Milton*, and *Jerusalem*', in Stuart Curran and Joseph Wittreich (eds), *Blake's Sublime Allegory* (Madison, WI and London: University of Wisconsin Press, 1973), pp. 119–39.

22. Ibid., 121. Paley also notes that Blake does not use the word 'loom' before *The Four Zoas*.

23. For instance, *FZ* VIII: 51–3 (E 372) and *FZ* VIII: 182–5 (E 376); see Paley, 127. Enitharmon and Los are, repeatedly, twin creators: 'Enitharmon's Looms & Los's Forges' (E 376).

24. S. Foster Damon, *A Blake Dictionary* (London: Thames and Hudson, 1973), plate IV. See also Martin Butlin, *William Blake* (London: Tate Gallery, 1978), 142 (plate 307).

25. *A Blake Dictionary*, 400–1 (entry under 'Tharmas').

26. Bartholin, 617.

27. *Northern Antiquities*, I, 317.

28. Ibid., 316–17.

29. *Northern Antiquities*, II, 204.

30. Margaret Clunies Ross notes that both 'The Descent of Odin' and 'The Fatal Sisters' feature what she calls 'vatic' speech by female figures, and claims it was

Mallet's remarks about Germanic prophetesses which led to 'eighteenth-century translators' fondness for vatic poetry either delivered by female speakers or verses in which they are shown playing a prominent part' (*The Norse Muse in Britain 1750–1820* (Trieste: Parnaso, 1998), 46).

31. W.H. Stevenson suggests that the oak may be understood as being distinct from the 'pernicious trees of the druids', but then goes on to claim that 'Eno speaks as a prophetic female bard', *Blake: the Complete Poems* (London and New York: Longman and Norton, 1989), 279 n.4. I cannot find any contemporary source which allows the possibility of female druids (see A.L. Owen, *The Famous Druids*, Oxford, 1962).

32. See *A Blake Dictionary* (under Eno).

33. *Northern Antiquities*, II, 14–15.

34. Ibid., I, 79.

35. See, for instance, E 328, or *FZ* VII: 283–6 (E 359), where veins are figured as rivers.

36. H.M. Margoliouth, *William Blake's* Vala (Oxford: Clarendon, 1956), xviii.

37. William Herbert, *Select Icelandic Poetry, Translated from the Original with Notes* (London: T. Reynolds, 1804).

38. *Northern Antiquities*, II, 160.

39. Ibid., 161.

40. Ibid., 176–7.

41. Ibid., 162.

42. Ibid., 165.

43. Ibid., 166.

44. Ibid., 167.

21

Re-Deeming Scripture: My William Blake Revisited

Alicia Ostriker

The story until now. Close to twenty years ago in a talk called 'The Road of Excess: My William Blake', I said this:

> I fall in love with the man, I fall deeper in love the better I know him, he fails me, I reject him and walk out, I forgive him and renew my fondness while keeping my distance. Perhaps I love him better at a distance. Or, more truly: Blake to me has been hero, lover and ally, has been standard-bearer and courage-bringer, has been the chosen teacher to whom I attributed all wisdom, has been an antagonist in that mental fight in which opposition is true friendship, and has latterly become the paternal figure from whom I most gratefully deviate.[1]

I had been asked to speak at a conference on 'The Romantics and Us', and wished to explore what Blake meant to me not only as a scholar but as a whole person: a feminist, a poet, a woman. So I began by describing how as a student I was thrilled by Blake's full-court press audacity about sex, society, and religion, and how the fusion of meaning and form in his poems was for me the essence of poetry. Then I described writing *Vision and Verse in William Blake* on Blake's prosody; editing the Penguin edition of his complete poems with two hundred pages of notes so that nobody would ever again have to cope with the irritating mystification of Harold Bloom's notes; seeing Blake as a proto-feminist in his scorching analysis of patriarchy, then discovering that he was also a misogynist with a gynophobic streak a mile wide.[2] I wanted to explain, to others and to myself, both the Blake who was my friend and ally and the Blake who was my enemy. Lastly I wanted to look at some aspects of my work as a woman poet that I felt to be extensions of Blake's work. For standing behind many of my poems I could see a fiery William Blake, urging me along a path that was not identical with his road of excess but lay in the same general direction.

Since that time I am less certain of exactly how Blake has influenced me. I believe that I remain his daughter, perhaps more than ever, although the bloodlines may be difficult to discern. Blake late in life asks a rhetorical question whose answer appears obvious to him: 'Are not Religion and Politics the Same Thing?' (*J*, 57.10; E 207). In much of my work I have pursued a path in which religion and politics are indistinguishable, the path of re-reading and re-imagining the Bible. For me as for Blake, the work oscillates between despair and hope. Like Blake I write in a time of war, and like Blake I try to imagine alternatives.

I

Nobody needed to teach William Blake that the personal is the political, and that sex is where it all begins. 'The Garden of Love', where Law replaces Love and tombstones replace flowers, indicts religion as a source of sexual repression. 'London' attacks the hypocritical and oppressive alliance of Church and State against the poor. 'God & his Priest & King' (E 23) afflict the helpless chimney-sweeper coughing himself to death in the streets of London and the hapless soldier about to be sent to fight in France. The marriage hearse enforced by Church and State is the cause, not the cure, of prostitution and venereal disease.

Yet in 'All Religions are One', Blake has already declared that 'the Jewish & Christian Testaments' derive from 'the Poetic Genius', and that religions differ with 'each Nation's different reception of the Poetic Genius' (E 1). In 'The Marriage of Heaven and Hell', Blake at first ridicules 'all Bibles or sacred codes' for their dualistic moral laws, then describes reading the Bible 'in its Diabolical sense which the world shall have if they behave well' (E 44). What would that sense be? What is 'the Bible of Hell' he promises to produce? In *Milton* he sees the Bible not simply as a pillar of the temple of tyranny but as a nonpareil work of imagination. 'The Stolen and Perverted Writings of Homer & Ovid: of Plato & Cicero. which all Men ought to contemn: are set up by artifice against the Sublime of the Bible' (E 95).[3] Late in life he quips, 'Both read the Bible day & night/ But thou readst black where I read white' ('Everlasting Gospel', E 524).

Anticipating what literary critics will say of the Bible a century or so later, Blake sees it as 'the Great Code of Art' ('Laocoon', E 274), a single text containing contradictory meanings, a source both of oppression and of liberation.[4] Throughout his career he struggles with and against it, re-imagining the ancient text from his perspective in time present, seeing it as dynamic not static, in a state of growth and change, pulses of a living entity that is ultimately divine. Locating it in the context of the prophetic craving for social justice, he wishes to re-deem scripture as a story of the liberation of imagination itself.

This has been my wish as well. At the time that I wrote 'The Road of Excess', I had already begun writing midrash.[5] I too have wrestled with the Bible, attempting like Jacob with the angel to wrestle a blessing out of it.

Blake wrote as a Christian man, I write as a Jewish woman. Of my encounter with the Bible and Jewish tradition three books have been born. Each is radically feminist, yet the seed of each is a Blakean seed.

Blake insists that the God of the Bible is an egotist and a tyrant. He calls this figure 'Nobodaddy' when he is joking, and 'Urizen' throughout his prophecies. Urizen is 'your reason' and 'horizon'; he represents calculation, limitation, the rule of authority over feeling and imagination. Moral Law is his doing. So are 'War & Princedom & Victory & Blood' (*FZ*, 1. 11.24; E 306). Like Blake I believe that Urizenic tyranny is a defence against anxiety – the pain of a being sundered from its original wholeness. How is that wholeness to be re-imagined? How is it to be recovered by and for our fragmented selves? Blake spent a lifetime hammering out answers, which grow increasingly arcane and complex. As for me, I come late to the game. My own answers, like his, keep returning to the split between male and female. Keep fumbling for a way to heal it.

My *Feminist Revision and the Bible* (1992) tracks a repeating plot feature in biblical narrative: women are significant and active at the outset of stories, dead or disappeared by the close. Looking at the figures of Sarah in Genesis and Miriam in the Exodus narrative, I claim that the pattern encodes what Gerda Lerner in *The Creation of Patriarchy* describes as the thousand year process whereby goddess worship throughout the ancient world was replaced first by polytheism, then, gradually, by male monotheism:

> The observable pattern is: first, the demotion of the Mother-Goddess figure and the ascendance and later dominance of her male consort/ son; then his merging with a storm-god into a male Creator-God, who heads the pantheon of gods and goddesses. Wherever such changes occur, the power of creation and of fertility is transferred from the Goddess to the God.[6]

In story after biblical story, the disappearance of a strong female coincides with the establishment (or re-establishment after a rupture) of an exclusively male covenant. Eve, Sarah, Rebecca, Rachel, Leah, Dina, Tamar, Potiphar's wife, the unnamed mother of Samson, and Hannah the mother of Samuel, are all examples of such females. In the narrative of Exodus we have the midwives, the mother of Moses, his sister Miriam, and the daughter of Pharaoh, all conspiring to save the life of the future liberator of Israel. The strong female is Bathsheba in the David narrative, Sheba in the Solomon story. Often she is a trickster figure. But the heroes of the stories are men. Men move biblical history forward, men carry out the will of God. The news of three thousand years ago is very like this morning's news. I argue that the process can never be complete because the goddess is the repressed that keeps returning, even if she keeps being re-absorbed into the male narrative just as, in Blake, Emanations must be re-absorbed into their Zoas.

The biblical woman typically represents Desire, or what Blake centuries later called Female Will. Blake fears her power. I as a feminist cherish this power as a trace of what has been imperfectly destroyed. Yet our shared quest is for a world free of the mind-forged manacles of power relations, a world whose ordering principle is not hierarchy but unity in multiplicity, a world that doesn't worship the phallus. I feel that Blake inspires and teaches me, much as Milton inspired and taught him. Without contraries there is no progression. So is Blake of the woman's party without knowing it? I imagine that if he were alive today he might concur not only with my analysis of God the Father, but with my concluding speculation about the voice of biblical narrative:

> How well we know that voice, whose tremendous verbal sublimity becomes at its most sublime the voice of a male God who demands over and over, across the texts and across the centuries, that we have no other Gods but Him, and has been able to make that command stick, more or less, for at least two thousand years. 'I thy God am a jealous God.' We recognize it all too well. But who is this God so anxious about his dominance that he requires absolute obedience like any common tyrant? . . . Is it possible that the whole story of canonicity, the whole story of authority in our culture, is intimately bound up with the repressed mother, shimmering and struggling at the liminal threshold of consciousness, against whom the Father must anxiously defend himself?[7]

II

The Nakedness of the Fathers: Biblical Visions and Revisions (1994) is my rewriting of what Christians call the Old Testament and Jews call, simply, the Bible, or Torah. In writing it I depended on the conviction that the men and women of the Bible were my mothers and fathers, and that the God was my God, whether I liked him or not. The story was *mine*, and almost nobody but men had interpreted it for two millennia.

Blake leads me here as the visionary who perceives that all gods are projections of the human imagination, and who envisions the rewriting of sacred history as the poet's 'great task' (*J*, 5.17; E 147). A combination of midrash and autobiography, poetry and prose, *Nakedness* follows the trajectory of the Hebrew Bible from the Garden to the Book of Job and beyond, retelling the compelling tales of the patriarchs, warriors, judges and kings that have played such a governing role in western history and culture, along with those secondary beings, their sisters, wives, mothers. In each episode I see the biblical story as both deeply archaic and utterly contemporary, and attempt to discern its relevance to the world of violence and vision, passion and politics I live in – and to my own personal life. From time to time I lift a particular strategy from Blake, and spin it my way. In my version of the meeting between King Solomon and the Queen of Sheba, for example, Sheba recites a set of her own Proverbs. Blake readers will recognise the spirit of the Proverbs of Hell in lines like 'Does God reward the virtuous? Do frogs love flies?' A poem in the voice of Joshua deals with the subject of genocide. A prose piece on the Book of Judges takes place in a women's crisis centre and dramatises the ways war interfaces with gender war. Ultimately, like Blake, I attempt to imagine a more liveable future.

Nakedness suggests at the outset that God the Father swallowed God the Mother in prehistory:

> God was originally a female who gave birth to a male companion. He refused to live in a state of equality with her, and so he ate her. Swallowed her whole. Regretting this act when it was too late, he created the universe . . .[8]

The metaphor of swallowing should recall the story of the wolf swallowing grandmother in Red Riding Hood, as well as Blake's conflict of the Prolific and the Devourer. Like the grandmother, God the Mother did not die. She remains in the belly of the beast. Biblical scholars have long known that the biblical text includes traces of Sumerian, Babylonian, Canaanite sources. *Nakedness* puts it this way: 'Inside the oldest stories are older stories, not destroyed but hidden. Swallowed. Mouth songs . . . The texts retain traces, leakages, lacunae, curious figures of speech, jagged irruptions.' (*N* 15)

When we see traces of female power in the scriptural text, I propose that we are seeing the goddess kick. Her presence all but disappears in the Bible after the tales of the patriarchs in Genesis. In the establishment of Law as the guiding principle of Torah, woman becomes property. A daughter is the possession of her father, who may sell her if he wishes; a wife is the property of her husband. Yet something of her energy survives. We may see her also in the gendered aspect of the Hebrew language, where key terms are feminine and over the centuries often become personified as females in rabbinic literature:

> if *hokhmah*, wisdom, is a woman; if *rachmanes*, God's attribute of compassion, derives from the mother's womb; if the Sabbath is a bride; if the *shekhinah* is daughter, bride, mother . . . and if *Torah* herself is the king's child, who shows herself little by little to her lovers – then it is *inside the language*, the place of interpretation, the place of dialogue, interrogation, commentary, laughter, the place of holy disobedience, the site of persistent stubbornness, wrestling and the demand for blessing . . . here in the place of metaphor is where she waits.

(*N* 141)

To say that she waits is to say that God is pregnant. Not dead, not dying, though in pain – in pain and labouring to be delivered of the female self he has incorporated, repressed and denied for millennia. Think what discomfort she causes, in her roles as whore, femme fatale, discontented wife, demanding bitch. Understand that our pain, as human beings ensnared by dysfunctional sexual dynamics, is also God's pain. Remember Blake crying out in the midst of the Napoleonic wars that 'the Whole Creation Groans to be deliverd' (*Vision of the Last Judgement*, E 554). The penultimate section of *The Nakedness of the Fathers* takes place in an intensive care room, where a crowd of journalists and paparazzi harangue what appears to be a dying deity. Two female reporters, Chloe and Olivia, whom I have lifted from Virginia Woolf's *A Room of One's Own*, retire to the hospital cafeteria in disgust. It is they who are struck by the possibility that God is pregnant and in labour. 'Believe that?' says Olivia. 'I believe because it is absurd', replies Chloe, quoting Tertullian. 'Well, burn my bush', says Olivia (*N* 251).

As Woolf at the end of *A Room of One's Own* urges her audience of young women to work toward the rebirth of the genius she calls Shakespeare's sister, so I would exhort my audience to be midwives of the Goddess. 'If we have the habit of freedom and the courage to write exactly what we think', says Woolf, 'the dead poet who was Shakespeare's sister will put on the body which she has so often lain down.'[9] She will be born, says Woolf, when the collective work of women has made the conditions for her birth possible. I believe the same of the Goddess. For to say that she is trapped, undigested and struggling within the being we call God the Father, is also to say that she is present as the repressed divine energy within each of us. 'All deities reside in the human breast' (*Marriage* 11; E 38) and are brought into living existence through the collective labours of the human imagination.

It is varied labour, since the Goddess has many names. In Judaism, her name is 'Shekhinah', a term drawn from a Hebrew word for 'dwelling', used in the Bible to signify God's presence in the world. Because the term is feminine in gender, the tradition of Kabbalah – Jewish mysticism – came to personify it as the feminine aspect of God, who at the moment of creation is disastrously divided from him and hidden within the material world. Hers is, in our terms, a divinity of immanence rather than transcendence, while God the Father remains ineffably transcendant. The goal of history in Lurianic Kabbalah is the reunification of God and his Shekhinah, toward which we humans contribute whenever we perform good deeds. *Tikkun olam*, the repair of the world, depends upon us.[10]

Having hinted at God's pregnancy, I close *The Nakedness of the Fathers* with a 'Prayer to the Shekhinah' that invokes her waking from her long repose in us, wiping the nightmare of history from her eyes, returning from exile, shaking her breasts and hips and playing her timbrels, and causing tyranny to vanish from the earth. The idea that history is a sleep from which we will ultimately awake is Blake's idea. The image of divine and human reunification as erotic is Blake's image. My language is the language of Jewish liturgy, but with an erotic twist:

When she and he meet
When they behold each other face to face
When they become naked and not ashamed
On that day will our God be One
And their name One.

(*N* 254)

III

After finishing *Nakedness*, I thought my next task as a writer was to invoke
the Shekhinah herself. To imagine her. To begin to participate in the collective labour of birthing the Divine Female. I wanted, in other words, to
have some equivalent of a Blakean vision. Instead I suffered a three-year
writing block during which I was unable to produce essays, book reviews –
anything that required a brain. Anything that required a soul was out of
reach. One can be receptive but not receive; one can have a concept without
conceiving. William Blake, in response to a young disciple asking if he ever
suffered artists' block, turned to Catherine. 'What do we do, Catherine,
when the visions do not come?' 'We kneel down and pray, Mister Blake',
she is supposed to have replied. I too knelt and prayed, stood and begged.

The book that ultimately came of my begging and praying is *The Volcano
Sequence* (2002; hereafter *V*[11]). The voice of these poems addresses a slippery
'you' that is sometimes God, sometimes my mother. The poems exploded
initially from a state of despair, and were essentially 'dictated', as Blake
would put it (*J*, 4.5; E 146); that is, received in states of meditation in which
my role as poet was that of aperture. I had promised the poems that if they
agreed to keep arriving, I agreed not to tell them what to say.

The poems to God are poems of anger and longing. Here is a section of
a 'psalm':

I am not lyric any more
I will not play the harp
for your pleasure

I will not make a joyful
noise to you, neither
will I lament

for I know you drink
lamentation, too,
like wine

so I dully repeat
you hurt me
I hate you

(*V* 13)

At times the poet-as-woman expresses a desire for reconciliation and is unsatisfactorily answered by the god-as-male. She pleads:

> I am named *k'dsha*, harlot, whore, abomination
> while you are named *kaddosh*, holy, separate or apart

He responds:

> *I said Let us reason together I said I hate your sacrifices I said feed*
> * the hungry*
> *I said clothe the naked I said do justice, love mercy, I said keep my law*

> (*V* 23)

In this dialogue of the deaf, while the poet attempts to draw closer through a play on language as pun, God's response in terms of language as law has much in common with Blake's Urizen proposing '*Laws* of peace, of love, of unity' (italics mine, E 72), laws ostensibly benign yet impossible to keep and by their very nature tyrannical. The god of *Volcano* is responsible for creation but also destruction: for war, for conquest, for oppression, for the righteousness of true believers:

> One of these days
> oh one of these days
> will be a festival and a judgment
>
> and our enemies will be thrown
> into the pit while we rejoice
> and sing hymns

> (*V* 34)

The parallel poems addressing my mother are both generic and auto-biographical; Mother is Nature, composing and decomposing, rendered destitute by humans who 'bite whatever they need' (*V* 21). She is also 'mistress of futility' (*V* 22), what Blake would call 'an ever-weeping melancholy Shadow' (*J*, 53.26; E 203), that which we reject and wish to escape. Here I draw, of course, on a whole body of feminist work on mother-daughter relations within patriarchal society, but also on my own experience:

> for fifty years
> it has tortured me that I cannot save you from madness
> and that I do not love you enough . . .
> nothing is enough

> (*V* 20)

And what of the Shekhinah? In *Volcano* she remains exiled, amnesiac, mute, inaccessible. The very gates of the mystical texts that invoke her are closed to her. She is like Blake's Ahania, cast out by Urizen, weeping in the void.

Toward the close of the book the tyrant-God is seen as paradox, as 'exquisite/joke . . . absent presence . . . good evil . . . perfect nothing' (*V* 91), but also 'the quarrel in my art', while the pathos of the rejected mother ultimately yields to a memory of her as 'my mother, my queen', inverting the invocation of liturgy that addresses 'our father, our king'. Most significant, it becomes clear that the unimaginable Shekhinah is closer than we think. Blake's Saviour assures his alter ego Albion, 'I am not a God afar off, I am a brother and friend / within your bosoms I reside and you reside in me' (*J*, 4:18–19; E 146). In *Volcano*, the repressed explodes into consciousness. Immanent within the material world, the Shekhinah is inaccessible to us precisely because we reject our biological mothers while seeking spiritual ones:

> they cannot say *seek me*
> they teach us cooking clothing craftiness
> they tell us their own stories of power and shame
>
> and even if it is she who speaks through their mouths
> and has crawled through ten thousand wombs until this day
> we cannot listen
>
> their words fall like spilled face powder

(V 64)

I have come to believe that the collective task of becoming midwives to the Mother involves (among many other things) ceasing to flee our actual lower-case mothers, the women of flesh and blood, fault and shame, who bore us and humiliate us. My belief seems to be confirmed by the fact that whenever I suggest to intellectual women, feminists, poets, women involved in women's spirituality movements, that they may need to turn and face their own mothers, they look at me with horror. No, not that, is the implicit reply. Too difficult. But is it not obvious that here is where we need to look, precisely because it is so difficult?

> when she comes it will not be from heaven, it will be up from the
>   cunts and breasts
> it will be from our insane sad fecund obscure mothers
> it will be from our fat scrawny pious wild ancestresses their claws
>   their fur and their rags

(V 109)

I do not suppose that the task will be easily accomplished. Still, it can be begun. If 'everything that lives is Holy' (E 45) we ought to be able to seek holiness in the actual – not simply the theoretical – maternal beings who are closest to us, with all their awful minute particulars. Blake believed that a 'Last Judgement' passes over any individual who 'Rejects Error & Embraces Truth' (*Vision of the Last Judgement*, E 562). We can but try.

IV

'If the doors of perception were cleansed every thing would appear to man as it is: infinite' (E 39). So it would appear to woman also. To be a daughter of Blake is to maintain a faith that the human imagination transforms us through fits and starts, cycle after cycle, throughout history, away from tyranny and toward liberty, equality, and re-entry to the garden of love. The process is necessarily collective. The task of awakening the human imagination in all human beings is the task of the artist, but the artist must first awaken it in herself. Like Blake, I have attempted to understand where and how the structures of oppressive authority work within culture, and to hear the clanking of the mind-forged manacles inside my own head. Part of what I take from Blake is a double stance toward tradition, an awareness of its duplicitous sources and possibilities, a willingness to find in it both prison and liberation. Part is an urgent wish to cleanse the doors of my own clouded perception. If I were able to perceive experientially what I conceive theoretically – that the parallel lines of God, my mother and the Shekhina converge at an infinity that is also here and now – I would feel closer to the garden. At present I can but wait, and wish good luck to anyone engaged in a similar quest. May we all learn to melt apparent surfaces away, and display the infinite that was hid.

Notes

1. 'The Road of Excess: My William Blake', in Gene W. Ruoff (ed.), *The Romantics and Us* (New Brunswick, NJ: Rutgers University Press, 1990), pp. 67–88.
2. See my *Vision and Verse in William Blake* (Madison: University of Wisconsin Press, 1965); *William Blake: the Complete Poems*, editor (New York: Penguin Books, 1977); 'Desire Gratified and Ungratified; Blake and Sexuality', *BQ*, 16: 3 (winter 1982), 156–65.
3. Later in *Milton* he calls the Bible 'the Woof of Six thousand years' (E 143). Compare Davis M. Baulch, 'The Sublime of the Bible', *Romanticism on the Net*, 3 (August 1996), http://users.ox.ac.uk/~scat0385/sublime.html.
4. See Northrop Frye, *The Great Code: the Bible and Literature* (New York: Harcourt, 1983) but also more modern work stimulated by biblical self-contradiction – what Roland Barthes calls 'the abrasive frictions, the breaks, the discontinuities of readability' in the biblical text, 'The Struggle with the Angel', *Image, Music, Text*, essays selected and translated by Stephen Heath (New York: Hill and Wang, 1977), pp. 125–41, 140, or what Geoffrey Hartmann calls 'a fusion of hetero-

geneous stories', 'The Struggle for the Text', in Geoffrey Hartmann and Sanford Budick (eds), *Midrash and Literature* (New Haven: Yale University Press, 1986), pp. 3–18, 11–13 (and see note 5 for a definition of 'midrash'). Feminist criticism tends to look beyond the Bible's dominant androcentrism to its prophetic-messianic tradition as rejecting 'every elevation of one group against others as image and agent of God, every use of God to justify social domination and subordination'. See Rosemary Reuther, *Sexism and God-Talk: Toward a Feminist Theology* (Boston: Beacon Press, 1983), 117–19.

5. The term 'midrash' (pl. midrashim) derives from a Hebrew term meaning search or investigate. Originally a genre of rabbinic discourse, it refers to stories that re-tell biblical stories, filling in their gaps, explaining their contradictions, making them morally and spiritually meaningful to ongoing generations. Traditional midrashim may be theological, psychological, moralising, comic, or wildly imaginative. The same is the case with contemporary midrash. In the renaissance of midrashic writing in America today, women writers seem to be taking the lead.

Gerald Bruns, 'We take the text in relation to ourselves, understanding ourselves in its light, even as our situation throws its light upon the text, allowing it to disclose itself differently, perhaps in unheard-of ways', 'Midrash and Allegory: the Beginning of Scriptural Interpretation', in Robert Alter and Frank Kermode (eds), *The Literary Guide to the Bible* (Cambridge, MA: Harvard University Press, 1987), pp. 625–46, 633.

6. Gerda Lerner, *The Creation of Patriarchy* (New York and Oxford: Oxford University Press, 1986), 145.

7. Alicia Ostriker, *Feminist Revision and the Bible* (Cambridge, MA: Blackwell Publishers, 1993), 50.

8. Alicia Ostriker, *The Nakedness of the Fathers* (New Brunswick, NJ: Rutgers University Press, 1994), 30. Hereafter *N*.

9. Virginia Woolf, *A Room of One's Own* (New York and London: Harcourt Brace Jovanovich, 1957), 117–18.

10. I oversimplify vastly, of course. For more scholarly accounts of the changing roles of the Shekhinah in Jewish mysticism, see Raphael Patai, *The Hebrew Goddess* (New York: Avon, 1978), Gershom Scholem, *Major Trends in Jewish Mysticism* (New York: Schocken Books, 1971) and Scholem, *On the Kabbalah and its Symbolism*, trans. Ralph Mannheim (New York: Schocken, 1965). For a study of the ways in which Blake absorbed and adapted Christianised versions of Lurianic Kabbalah, available in England, see Sheila A. Spector, *'Wonders Divine!': the Development of Blake's Kabbalistic Myth* (Lewisburg, PA: Bucknell University Press, 2001).

11. Alicia Ostriker, *The Volcano Sequence* (Pittsburgh: University of Pittsburgh Press, 2002).

22
The Gender of Los(s): Blake's Work in the 1790s

Tilottama Rajan

As a student in the early seventies at a university which many outsiders associated with one of the most influential figures in Blake studies, I avoided taking a class with Frye or confronting the metastasis of literature's fearful symmetry in Blake. For whatever reason, my undergraduate professor (and later, supervisor) Milton Wilson did likewise, paying lip-service to the *Songs* in the very last week, and informing us that Blake was really in 'the eighteenth century'. By the early seventies Toronto – unlike some other Canadian universities – was no longer quite the bastion of Christian Humanism associated with Frye, A.S.P. Woodhouse, and Arthur Barker that Ross Woodman describes in his account of his lifelong agon with Frye. It had become sufficiently large and characterless, sufficiently broken up by Americans trained in the New Criticism, that such gestures of avoidance were safely inconspicuous. I did not have to confront Blake until I started teaching in the late seventies, at a university which, unlike Toronto, had compulsory syllabi, often developed by faculty trained at Toronto in the fifties. The full-year undergraduate course in Romanticism did not cover *Milton* and *Jerusalem*, because of their length, but rather included *Thel*, *Visions of the Daughters of Albion* and *The (First) Book of Urizen*, classified in Frye's Modern Library edition as 'minor prophecies' so as to maintain their synecdochic and typological subordination to the later texts whose monumentality allowed them to be simulacra of completion. I found myself profoundly uncomfortable with the subl(im)ation of these strange texts from the 1790s into this completeness, and if nothing else the New Criticism allowed me to read them closely and without ideological presuppositions. Urizen seemed less the villain of an allegorical psychomachia than an (in)humanisation of, and thus a way of not dealing with, a series of traumatic and incomprehensible effects. Indeed who or what 'Urizen' is is radically unclear. The name seems to describe both a series of obscure geological mutations, 'rifts' and 'perturbations', in the prehistory of the world, and the (distinctly human) response to these effects: a response that is at once formative of the human and the cause of its deformity. It designates something uncertainly inside or outside, before or within man, an ontological and a psychological problem. Perhaps Urizen, as the response to what Urizen is, is what Melanie Klein would later recognise as the constitutive role of the paranoid-schizoid and depressive positions in creativity. For it is not clear that one can be without Urizen or the melancholia over what he is. Urizen, in other words, is the paranoid response to not being able to see the void except as 'abominable' (3.3; E 70). But before this Urizen is another Urizen described in the first chapter, which is precisely this void and 'vacuum', what Levinas calls the *il y à*, the inhuman (57–60). Abjecting as Urizen what he cannot understand, Blake probes the very foundations of his defensive mythology, in asking 'what Demon' has 'form'd . . . this soul-shudd'ring vacuum'. He replies, calling into question his own anthropomorphisms, that 'Some sa[y]' it is Urizen, but that the 'dark power', whose power may be a haunting rather than an agency, remains 'unknown' and 'abstracted' (3.3–8; E 70).

Quite differently, Blake's females also seemed to resist the systematisations imposed on them by an omniscient critical voice at odds with the pathos of the poems' inside views. It seemed too easy to dismiss Thel's flight from experience as immature (even easier given her gender), when the ungendered rhetoric of redemption projected through clouds and flowers might equally constitute a retreat into the imaginary. The then-dominant reading (Bloom, 51–62; Frye, 232–3) ignored the unbridgeable difference between humans and plants that nineteenth-century philosophy of science from Hegel onwards marked in making individuality – selfhood in Hegel's term – and death the factors distinguishing animal from vegetable organisms. This difference is momentarily confronted by the poem when Thel's existential questioning takes her to the worm, but then elided when the worm's nudity is covered over by the Christian comfort of the clod. Perhaps, then, the poem really forces us up against a double bind: the impossibility of going back to the vales of Har, but, given the sheer obscenity of experience in the poem's climax, the impossibility of going forward and of models of *Bildung* that require us to do so. The same problem arises with Oothoon, who is often praised for taking the step Thel avoids, but one has to wonder at what cost. In the frontispiece Oothoon remains bound to Bromion with Theotormon looking on. Some versions of the plate are coloured so as to show the sun rising but in some the sun's disk is not filled in and the sky remains dark. In one version, moreover, this plate moves to the end, giving the poem a cyclic rather than progressive form. For it is by no means clear that Oothoon's advocacy of free love, which is bravely revolutionary to begin with, like that of Sibella in Eliza Fenwick's *Secresy*, is not finally a defiantly masochistic submission to the law of the father that functions as a form of death-drive. Slavoj Žižek discusses this assumption of the death-drive, with reference to characters such as Antigone and Carmen, as woman's refusal to cede her desire. Žižek argues that woman becomes a subject 'when she finally becomes an object *for herself'*, by making herself a victim so as to 'confront the utter nullity of [her] narcissistic pretensions' (63–4). Yet this is not subjectification as self-consciousness, since it relies on an abjection of interiority. To see Oothoon as surviving what Thel fails to confront, and then to make her a figure of prophetic liberation, thus seemed to repeat Bromion's rape as the violence of prophetic writing: the silencing of her voice by her use as a mere 'figure' in an allegorical schema. Oothoon, after all, achieves mastery over her experience by offering to procure women for Theotormon. That her liberation can only take this form is surely the trauma of prophecy.

My readings of *Thel* and *Visions* in the seventies, which did not emerge from the privacy of the classroom till 1988 and into print till 1990 (*Supplement*, 238–52), could be seen as a variant of so-called images of women criticism. A variant in the sense that they did not take up the representation of women *in* Blake, but rather the way such representations functioned as the institutional support for a construction of Blake and Romantic 'prophecy' that avoided what Ross Woodman has called Blake's 'madness'. Blake's madness is his excessive and tormented relationship, traumatic as much as transgressive, to the allegorisations of experience into which he and his interpreters alike have bound him. Gender was a particularly poignant site of this avoidance, since to execute the interpretive programmes of Frye, Bloom and Damon was, for a woman reader, to be forced to identify against herself. These programmes and their filing of Blake under the genre of prophecy cast Romanticism in the mode of self-certainty rather than self-doubt. Yet the texts from the 1790s are less prophecies than poems of crisis, or the crisis of prophecy. Blake did not refer to them as prophecies, except for *Europe* and *America*. These two texts, moreover, are visibly, spatially divided between tortured preludia spoken by women, and the actual prophecies, which in *America* have only male actors, and in *Europe* involve a demonisation of the female. It would seem that prophecy is possible only through the bounding off of the female within a crisis pushed back into prehistory. Yet in *Europe* this boundary is troubled by Enitharmon's presence in the prophecy section, which plunges prophecy back into the dark space of family romance. That Enitharmon has been put to sleep, curiously absented from the history of which she is said to be the cause, is a sign that this crisis has not been worked through: Enitharmon's sleep is narrativised as her oblivion but is just as much a hiatus or syncope in Blake's own consciousness. And in *Visions*, where the characters' speeches grow progressively less distinguishable, this boundary between a crisis gendered as female and the male voice of prophecy collapses entirely.

For in *Visions*, despite thematic reminders of the distinct gender positions of the speakers, Bromion, Oothoon and Theotormon are tonally indistinguishable. Rhythmically, syntactically, in the rising crescendo of questions and the torrent of opaque images whose affect exceeds their aphoristic condensation, the poem from Plate 3 onwards is spoken by an amorphously hysterical voice struggling to divide itself in three. This voice dislocates and cannibalises Blake's own rhetoric from the 'Proverbs of Hell'. Oothoon's anguish is harnessed by a prophetic ecstasy that cannot separate itself from the trauma of its violence, because the prophetic voice cannot be separated from those of Bromion and Theotormon, who fall into the same cadences as Oothoon. This ecstasy, moreover, has no readable content, and can be felt as ecstasy only if we allow ourselves to be mesmerised by the sheer sound of the poem. Blake thematises the oblivion of sound in *Europe* through Enitharmon's song, which continues in the Imaginary, as Enitharmon sleeps through western history, sleeping through a song that she sings but does not hear, cut off from the reality that is cast out of language into the visual plates. Blake projects through Enitharmon, as the mesmerised displacement of the tormented but still articulate shadowy female, something of this inability to hear his own song. Listening to this song in *Visions* involves opening oneself up to what Julia Kristeva calls 'affects that involve the presence of nonknowledge': 'the unsignifiable which we confront in the analysand's discourse as an inhibition, or symptom', as a space or gap, or 'the possibility of condensation or displacement', 'as articulations' (35–7). In *America* and *Europe* Blake tries to leave behind this 'torment' (*America*, 2.17; E 51) of nonknowledge by casting it as energy: something that can be harnessed, and thus the preludium to activity rather than listening. But in *Visions*, the necessity of listening is marked by the daughters of Albion. The poem's choral form, moreover, generates an affect that Nietzsche was later to analyse by linking lyric and tragedy not to *katharsis*, but to music as the space of an 'original Oneness', 'pain and contradiction' (38), the exposure of beings to one another.

Yet, as this history of how I came to Blake suggests, gender is only one particularly charged point in a network of discrepancies between language and affect, the system and its characters, or (in *Urizen*) the visionary text and its traumatic visual remainders. For me, then, the issues it raises are complex: they proceed from how Blake represents female figures, to how gender forms part of the figural economy of reading, to how it might inform and deform writing itself at an *archaeological* level – in Foucault's terms – by opening up the very conceptualisation of art and systematicity. These multiple figural effects of gender obviously have implications that go beyond Blake to the place of gender in literary studies generally. Jean-François Lyotard distinguishes three levels of figure: the image-figure, the form-figure, and the matrix figure, each progressively more removed from the visibility or perceivable form associated with the word figure. The image-figure is the most concrete form of the figure, while the form-figure 'sustains the visible without being seen' but can be made visible through a figure. At the farthest distance from visibility, the matrix-figure does not belong 'to plastic' or 'textual space' at all, and is 'no more visible than readable', being instead the general condition of possibility for a kind of figuration (277–8; translation mine). From this perspective Blake's actual images of women are a point of access to a more archaeological level at which the very nature of form and imaginative work is constituted and put in question. It is *both* constituted and questioned because Blake's female figures, at least in the 1790s, are at once symbolically encoded and released, by being given their own voice, from the 'solid form' with which they have been 'stamp[ed]' (*Europe*, 2.8; E 61). Thus one cannot speak of images of women in the sense of stereotypes; rather Blake's images of women are already deeply conflicted, whether they are symbolically deformed like Enitharmon, or allowed to cry out against the identities thrust on them like Oothoon and the nameless shadowy female of *Europe*. As such, Blake's females at the level of the image-figure are correlated with a profound crisis at a more archaeological level where gender forms part of a matrix from which the very space of literature is generated. This space has conventionally been configured in Blake criticism as systematic, which is to say fully organised, or as illuminated: the space of the illuminated book where seeing and saying coincide. And these ways of configuring literature, needless to say, are invisibly masculine since they involve a certain mastery: illuminated space, as Levinas says, 'collects about a mind which possesses it' and 'is already like the product of a synthesis' (48).

We can trace the matrix of gender through Blake's use of the word 'labour' to describe his own work. Blake uses the word constantly, from *Europe* to *Jerusalem*, to suggest an immensely arduous and perhaps endless process. In so far as this labour is not specified, it connotes simply the *form* that activity takes, as when Urizen is described as being 'In enormous labours occupied' (*Urizen*, 3: 23; E 71). Here it is unclear whether the activity is physical or mental; indeed given that Blake later writes of Los, 'Incessant the falling Mind labour'd / Organizing itself' (*Book of Los*, 4: 49–60; E 92), labour may even be a form of (in)activity, the mind endlessly revolving within itself. When this labour is specified in an image-figure, it is sometimes as routinised toil done by men or women: labouring in the mill or the fields. Most often it is imaged as the specifically masculine *agon* of Los labouring at 'his resolute Anvil' or 'labouring in the furnaces of Golgonooza' (*M*, 3.7, 31.26; E 96, 130). Sometimes it is associated with harvesting and the vintage (25.16; E 121), at which point labour becomes fruitful work. Yet labour is not always masculine or shared work. It is also the labour of gestation and birth, as when *Europe's* shadowy female wraps her 'turban of thick clouds around [her] lab'ring head', and brings forth 'howling terrors' (1.12, 2.4; E 61). Or it may be the labour of *being* born, as when this same shadowy female describes how her 'fruits in earth beneath / Surge, foam, and labour into life' (1.8–9; E 60).

But as conspicuous as this passage's association of labour with childbirth is its confused, surreal quality: like her precursor in *America*, the shadowy female in *Europe* gives birth, but her womb is her head, or her head is a womb. In a further dis-figuration of both the masculine activity of Los as prophet/engraver and the female activity of childbirth, this female 'sieze[s]' (sic) the 'burning power', mating with herself to give birth not to children but to a 'progeny of fires' we associate with Los's furnace (2: 3–5,8; E 61). The female is cross-gendered as Orc/Los, coupling with herself to produce 'howling terrors' that may be the fires of prophecy or the pangs of child-birth. Nor is this fusion a transcendence of gender roles: rather, masculine prophecy is afflicted with the torment of being gendered female, even as the preludium also wrenches the female away from the traditionally sub-servient role of muse, and allows her to speak her pain at the way the system stamps 'with a signet' her 'vig'rous progeny of fires'. Moreover, the union of Orc and *America*'s female, despite the disturbing violence of the rape that causes the bard to break his harp, could still be allegorised to produce the story of fire joining with earth to give birth to the prophecy that follows. But in *Europe*'s preludium the dialectic of production and reproduction is tied up in a knot of uncertainty about what or who is produced: the proph-ecy or the female herself. For at one point she produces a child (2: 14), but earlier it is she herself who is born, as she describes her fruits surging and labouring into life and asks: 'Then why shouldst thou accursed mother bring me into life?' The profoundly uprooted nature of this creativity that is at once giving birth and being born is marked in the description of the female as a tree turning into an ocean, her roots 'brandish'd in the heavens' and her 'fruits in earth beneath' (1: 1.8–11; E 60).

Europe provides one of the few instances of specifically female labour listed in the Blake Concordance. Yet labour as birth is a motif that runs through the last four Lambeth books, dis-figuring prophecy through the catachrestic figure of a globe or disk that may be a world, a womb, an embryo, an orb of vision or a globule of blood. The figure occurs thrice in *Urizen*'s designs and twice in those of *The Song of Los*. It also appears in the text of *Urizen* as 'the dark globe of Urizen' over which Los keeps watch (5: 38; E 73), the 'red/Round globe hot burning deep' which drops from Uri-zen's spine (11: 2–3; E 75), and the round globe of blood that drops from Los (13: 58; E 77), becoming a 'globe of life' that turns into 'the first female form now separate' (18: 1,15; E 78). Blake writes in *Jerusalem* that there is a 'Void, outside of Existence, which if enterd into / Englobes itself & becomes a Womb' (1: 1–2; E 144). But what is a globe, a world, a self-contained system, if it closes around itself to become a womb that seems to bleed and miscarry? Or, if having given birth, it is once again left 'void as death' (*Europe*, 2: 11; E 61)? In *Urizen* the title character constructs such a world: a 'roof, vast petrific around /. . . fram'd: like a womb'. Within this womb he constructs as though he is outside it, Urizen himself emerges, as in an ectopic pregnancy, as a 'human heart strugling & beating', inside what he is creating, as the poem is claustrophobically inside its own womb

(5: 28–9,36; E 93). Yet one cannot refer to 'he', as 'he' is a body in bits and pieces, a body without mind, that is all organs, all affect, the body of the poem itself as body rather than book or system.

The Book of Los too conflates male and female labour, so that the creative mind cannot break free of the processes by which it creates. For as Los labours to shape Urizen in his furnace, Los himself falls into the void where he flails around 'like the babe/New born into our world', then producing Urizen through 'Many ages of groans', not as an illuminated book but as a human body that emerges in 'Branchy forms', its organs 'like roots / Shooting out from the seed' (4: 38–9, 43–4, 64–5; E 92–3). The furnace, which is also an ocean (4: 60), is also Los's own body in which Urizen is produced as 'The lungs heave incessant' (4: 54). I speak of Los producing Urizen, but the two are impossible to separate in their endlessly drawn out birth-pangs, all the more because of the suppression of proper names. Not only is Los 'born' in Chapter II, but then while Urizen emerges as an outgrowth of Los and is organised 'Into finite inflexible organs', Los's falling mind also 'labour[s] / Organizing itself' (4: 45–50; E 92). Indeed Urizen's grotesque form picks up the way contemporary science constructs the vegetable, particularly the polypus, as the traumatic site of a failure in individuation that the prophetic voice needs, despite Blake's critique of selfhood (Hegel, 342–3, 363; Coleridge, 71–2). Then in Chapter III, although the 'Human' has already emerged as the vegetable psyche of Urizen, this body/psyche must once again struggle into life, coming (or not coming) to form inside Los. Yet it is not clear who is coming into being here, nor where the boundary between inside and outside, body and psyche, or self and other, lies. The lungs of the furnace, in heaving, may produce Urizen, if one assumes someone to be labouring at the furnace to create something, as Los had earlier struggled to break form out of black marble, succeeding only in rending the marble into 'innumerable fragments' (4: 21–4; E 92), like the bard breaking his harp. But perhaps it is Los himself who is described in Chapter III, his lungs heaving, while 'as yet . . . all other parts [are] formless', and the 'unformed part' pulls the entire body back into a 'stifling black' amniotic 'fluid' (4: 55–6, 59–62; E 93). Perhaps Los, whose 'fury and hot indignation' in the first chapter are at least virile (3: 48; E 91), is sucked back, in the course of the poem, into the female space of his own birth. In Chapter IV, Los does indeed hammer Urizen into a separate being, the separated shape of his own pain; but it is as though the same process of creation, which produces nothing except the history of itself, happens in each chapter, only with an increasingly bleak and rigid clarity.

The Book of Los is the reflexive coda to a series of Lambeth books that increasingly 'roll inwards' to confront the bases of creativity. In these books the dialectic of production is progressively halted. The very metaphor of work is dis-figured: this metaphor, which should seamlessly yield the idea of Los labouring on his spectre and beating it into shape as prophecy, fails to do so because masculine work falls back into the female labour it would rather forget. But female labour itself is dis-figured, wrenched out of a metaphoric system in which its process is subordinated to its product, so that biological reproduction can serve the purposes of familial and cultural reproduction.[1] For female labour in these books also resists its traditional encoding as fruitful, producing only its pain. In the 'Printing House' section of *The Marriage of Heaven and Hell* Blake mocks the industrial streamlining of production, which neatly divides labour into stages handled by different people, but he does not give up the idea of a process with discrete stages leading to a final product as the model for his own work. Yet in the Lambeth books the sequence similarly projected onto birth is profoundly disturbed: the embryo that forms inside the womb takes form again in the same way after its birth; birth is not the culmination of gestation but comes in the midst of a process that continues endlessly. Or when Los's furnaces, after 'endur[ing] / The chained Orb in their infinite wombs' for 'Nine ages', finally produce Urizen, the poem that Blake-as-Los produces is still-born, its life calcified and abjected in the 'Form' he has 'completed' (*Book of Los*, 5.39–41, 55–6; E 94).

Blake's tortured figuring of labour in the Lambeth books drives his work back into in its own primary processes, as the characters his critics will arrange in a systematic grid are cast out into the expanse and often abandoned. These characters – Fuzon, Orc, even Los himself – remain names for unnamed forms, and fail to separate, fail to come to birth. This focus on labour also halts the work's *r*eproduction, the conversion of the primal scenes of myth into a 'literature' that is 'arranged in libraries' (*Marriage* 15; E 40) and becomes part of the reproduction of culture. Labour instead configures literature as traversed by what Kristeva calls the semiotic, which exposes writing as not yet worked out, compelling us to unwork its symbolic positions, even those thought to be revolutionary. Los struggles against this 'unform'd part', and by the end has separated himself from it, at the cost of creating 'Urizen'. Urizen is the 'Illusion' of mastery produced when the 'slough' of body parts and affects is allegorically bound to landscape to create the 'Form' critics call Blake's system (*Book of Los*, 5: 53–6; E 94). Blake's disaffection with this is evident in his calling it Urizen. This 'Urizen' covers over an 'unform'd/Dark vacuity' where an earlier 'Urizen' lies in 'fierce torments' an 'immense Orb of fire / Flowing down into the night' (5: 49–56; E 94). Arguably Blake could not live with this trauma, cocooning it deep within a redemptive narrative and becoming Los to produce masculine work in *Milton* and *Jerusalem*. But in 1795 he contemplates Los with melancholy irony, knowing that his labour has produced no illumination (5: 48; E 94): an absence reflected in the austerity of this text with almost no designs. *The Book of Los* is a taking stock, and in this last of the series Blake abandons the paranoid-schizoid position of prophetic fury to expose a very different form of writing where the work of art is the experience of los(s), the black sun or perhaps the black hole disclosed when poetry becomes the abyss it seeks to abject.

Note

1. On the various meanings of 'reproduction' at the time see Rajan, 'Dis-Figuring Reproduction', 216–23.

References

Bloom, Harold, *Blake's Mythmaking: a Study in Poetic Argument* (Ithaca: Cornell University Press, 1970).

Coleridge, Samuel Taylor, *Hints Towards the Formation of a More Comprehensive Theory of Life*, ed. Seth B. Watson (London: John Churchill, 1848).

Damon, S. Foster, *A Blake Dictionary: the Ideas and Symbols of William Blake* (Boulder: Shambhala, 1979; reprinted 1965).

Frye, Northrop, *Fearful Symmetry: a Study of William Blake* (Princeton, NJ: Princeton University Press, 1947).

Hegel, G.W.F., *The Philosophy of Nature*, trans. A.V. Miller (Oxford: Clarendon, 1970).

Kristeva, Julia, 'Within the Microcosm of "The Talking Cure"', in Joseph H. Smith and William Kerrigan (eds), *Interpreting Lacan* (New Haven: Yale University Press, 1983), pp. 33–48.

Levinas, Emmanuel, *Existence and Existents*, trans. Alphonso Lingis (Hague: Martinus Nijhoff, 1978).

Lyotard, Jean-François, *Discours, figure* (Paris: Klincksieck, 1971; reprinted 2002).

Nietzsche, Friedrich, *The Birth of Tragedy*, in *The Birth of Tragedy and the Genealogy of Morals*, trans. Francis Golffing (New York: Doubleday, 1956), 1–146.

Rajan, Tilottama, *The Supplement of Reading: Figures of Understanding in Romantic Theory and Practice* (Ithaca: Cornell University Press, 1990).

Rajan, Tilottama, '(Dis)figuring the System: Vision, History, and Trauma in Blake's Lambeth Books', in *William Blake: Images and Texts* (San Marino: Huntington Library, 1997), pp. 107–36.

Rajan, Tilottama, 'Dis-Figuring Reproduction: Natural History, Community, and the 1790s Novel', *CR: The New Centennial Review*, 2:3 (2002), 211–52.

Woodman, Ross, *Sanity, Madness, Transformation: the Psyche in Romanticism* (Toronto: University of Toronto Press, 2005).

Žižek, Slavoj, *Looking Awry: an Introduction to Jacques Lacan through Popular Culture* (Cambridge, MA: MIT Press, 1992).

23

The 'Secret' and the 'Gift': Recovering the Suppressed Religious Heritage of William Blake and Hilda Doolittle

Marsha Keith Schuchard

In 1941, as German bombers set much of London in flames, the expatriate American poet Hilda Doolittle (H.D.) feared that the fires would destroy all records of the historical 'Secret' of her own psychic 'Gift' – a secret once preserved within the inner sanctum of the eighteenth-century Moravian church.[1] An admirer of William Blake's most radical and visionary poetry, H.D. did not know that the Nazi planes came perilously close to destroying the only evidence of his mother's Moravian background, when they destroyed the Fetter Lane Chapel where Catherine Armitage Blake worshipped in the 1740s and 1750s. Frustrated by two centuries of official, church-sponsored suppression of the esoteric-erotic theology of her maternal ancestors, H.D. searched for the historical roots of her inherited capacity for visionary eros and artistic expression. Though she did not know that Blake shared a similar background, she would have been pleased to learn that it was his Moravian mother who nurtured his imaginative and creative 'Gift'.

Unfortunately, the recovery of their lost religious heritage is made difficult by the censorship and destruction of their most radically mystical and erotic works. William Michael Rossetti lamented that Blake's pious executor made 'a holocaust' of them, burning 'Notebooks, poems, designs, in lavish quantities: a gag (as it were) thrust into the piteous mouth of Blake's corpse'.[2]

Blake's uninhibited expressions were deemed 'heretical' and 'dangerous to those poor dear "unprotected females" Religion and Morals'. Censorship of H.D.'s expression began in her adolescence, when her father burned her love letters to and from Ezra Pound, and it continued after her death. As Susan Friedman observes, the publication history of H.D.'s prose oeuvre is 'the story of partial revelation, endless deferral, fragmentation, destruction, and suppression'.[3]

When the German bombing began, H.D. was shocked into action at the prospect that not only her work but the secret history of the Moravian church would be lost. Thus, she determined to locate and save evidence of the ecumenical, pacifist, and mystical teachings of the 'Sifting Time' (*c.* 1743–56), the most creative and controversial period in the history of the *Unitas Fratrum*. In the process, she amazingly intuited the true nature of that turbulent time, when the Moravian leader Count Nicolaus Ludwig von Zinzendorf and his charismatic son Christian Renatus implemented a programme of daring sexual, spiritual, and racial liberation. As H.D. read Blake's *Marriage of Heaven and Hell*, she must have sensed a kindred spirit, for both their mothers were heirs to Zinzendorfian teachings about visionary art and eroticised spirituality.

In June 2001 I discovered in the Moravian Church Library at Muswell Hill, London, letters from Catherine and Thomas Armitage, Blake's mother and her first husband, and from John Blake, arguably William's paternal uncle, which revealed their immersion in the spiritual ethos of the Sifting Time.[4] These letters and other documents lend a new credibility to the long-ignored claim made by William Muir, the nineteenth-century Blake facsimilist, that Blake's parents (his mother and second husband, James Blake) attended Moravian services at Fetter Lane, before moving on to Swedenborgianism. Moreover, the Armitages and Blakes may even have met Emanuel Swedenborg, who also attended Fetter Lane services and imbibed Moravian notions of the 'mystical marriage'.[5] When Swedenborg eventually rejected the antinomianism and alleged promiscuity of the radical Moravians, he elaborated their 'marriage theology' into a more Kabbalistic version of 'conjugial love', which extended sexuality from earth into heaven. Thus, it is possible that the nineteenth-century tradition that Blake learned Swedenborgianism 'at his father's knee' is accurate, but it was a Swedenborgianism developed out of earlier Moravian themes.[6]

Until recently, the factual realities of the Sifting Time were euphemised and rationalised by church historians into inaccurate and misleading accounts. With a new generation of open-minded Moravian historians and feminist critics bringing to the surface much of that buried history, a clarifying and sometimes startling light can be shed on the possible sources of Blake's and H.D.'s most outré beliefs.[7] And those beliefs were grounded in Zinzendorf's 'religion of the heart' (*Herzensreligion*), based on the Jewish perception of the heart (*Lev* in Hebrew) as a fully sensating and even phallic organ of 'beatific vision'. Members of the inner Moravian congregation were gradually initiated – according to their spiritual and imaginative capacity – into techniques of psychoerotic meditation, which drew on Jesuit, Kabbalistic, and Yogic rituals.

Espousing a theology of 'sex, blood, and wounds', Zinzendorf preached that Jesus was fully humanised and that he experienced all the feelings, desires, and pains of ordinary mortals – both male and female. Urging the Moravians to visualise 'from head to toe' Jesus' tortured body on the cross, he helped them achieve a psychoerotic marriage with the suffering Bridegroom. While the Moravians concentrated intensely on the centurion's phallic spear, which penetrated the vaginal side wound, they could experience a psychic orgasm, as new souls were birthed in the gushing of blood. In their humble or aristocratic bedrooms, the married Brothers and Sisters re-enacted this 'holy joining' in conjugal intercourse. The achievement of the mystical marriage was facilitated by the viewing of vivid paintings and singing of passionate hymns. Unlike most British Dissenting sects, which scorned the visual arts and instrumental music, the Moravians valued painting, music, and poetry as the most effective means of achieving the gift of spiritual vision.

From the surviving documents at Muswell Hill, it is clear that Blake's mother responded passionately to the themes of the Sifting Time. She apparently passed on to her son William the Moravians' love of the arts, as well as Zinzendorf's moral antinomianism and psychoeroticism. However, in the wake of a barrage of hostile publications that accused Zinzendorf and his inner circle of scandalous and deceptive behaviour, the more conservative Moravians began a public withdrawal from his reckless heterodoxy, a withdrawal that became a full-fledged retreat after the count's death in 1760. Blake's parents evidently moved away from this white-washed form of Moravianism. As H.D. would learn, the subsequent rewriting of Moravian history meant that the precious Secret and Gift were lost for generations of her own family.

Before that loss, their Moravian ancestors were privy to a spiritual and artistic movement whose closest historical analogue was the 'Summer of Love' in San Francisco in 1968. As Craig Atwood stresses, Count Zinzendorf and his radical son Christian Renatus led what was essentially 'a youth movement', in which their more daring followers experimented with uninhibited sexual behaviour, egalitarian social relations, mystical meditation, and alchemical transmutation.[8] Assimilating Kabbalistic notions of the male-female dynamics of cosmic emanations (the *Sephiroth*), Zinzendorf urged the Moravians to break through the bonds of conventional trinitarian religion and to visualise a heterosexual divine family, in which the female Holy Spirit functioned as the wife of God and mother of the God-Man (Jesus as a Christianised version of the Kabbalists' Adam Kadmon).[9] In his passionate sermons and hymns, Zinzendorf praised the human genitals – penis and vagina – as emblems of the 'humanation' of Jesus, who took on the full range of human nature and thus sanctified not only the spirit but the body of men and women.

To the Fetter Lane congregation, Zinzendorf proclaimed, 'Ye holy Matrons, who as Wives are about Vice-Christs, you honour that precious Sign (*Membrum Virile*) by which they most resemble Christ, with the utmost Veneration . . . Member full of Mystery, which holily gives and chastely receives the conjugal Ointments for Jesus's sake.'[10] The Moravians should visualise the circumcision wound on Jesus's penis, because 'by that Rite' he was 'authentically declared a Boy: a Male that had open'd the Womb'.[11]

Referring to the Kabbalists' reverence for the *Shekhinah*, the female potency within God, Zinzendorf argued that 'the Womb of Woman is no more to be deem'd shameful, but the most awful among the Members, it having become the happy Tabernacle, which the Holy Ghost both could and would overshadow, and wherein his *Schechinah* did lodge, and quicken a divine Babe'. The vagina-womb was deliberately formed as a chapel for worship so that 'we may become Saviours in this World, Saviours of the Member of that Body . . . of that little Model of a Chappel of God'.[12] Four decades later, Blake echoed Zinzendorf's sexual theosophy when he sketched a naked woman, whose genitalia has been transformed into a chapel, 'with an erect penis forming a kind of holy statue at the centre'.[13] H.D. similarly affirmed that under the phallic, 'carved superstructure' of every church there is an earlier 'dark cave or grotto' dedicated to the divine female.[14]

Most controversial of Zinzendorf's themes was his bold antinomianism, based on his belief that the total salvation given by the crucified Jesus rendered useless all attempts at 'moral behaviour'. Affirming that 'a person regenerated enjoys a great Liberty', he argued that he is responsible only to what his heart senses is the Saviour's will; moreover, Christ 'can make Laws and abrogate them; he can make that to be moral which is against Nature; the greatest Virtue to be the most villainous Action, and the most virtuous Thoughts to be the most criminal'.[15] Blake re-affirmed this paradox when he proclaimed, 'What are called vices in the natural world are the highest sublimities in the spiritual world'.[16] To the horror of his orthodox critics, Zinzendorf preached that the commandment against adultery 'could oblige us no more in the New Testament, because it was at a time, when one Man had five or six wives'.[17] Again, Blake seemed to echo Zinzendorf when he advocated free love, polygamy, and concubinage.[18] H.D., who practised 'open marriage', argued that injunctions against adultery applied only to the visionary imagination: 'Thou shalt not adulterate inspiration with doubt nor joy with do-nots.'[19]

Though this brief sketch of the themes of the Sifting Time makes them seem rather lurid and perverse, they were actually the fuel for a bursting forth of great creativity in the arts, fertile innovations in theology, and pre-Freudian liberation and sublimation of repressed sexuality. From a modern standpoint, Zinzendorf seems a brilliant and courageous explorer of the spiritual and erotic imaginations of men and women, in both Western and Eastern guise. Moreover, his influence on Swedenborg's access to Kabbalistic-Tantric meditation techniques led to the latter's subsequent development of a theosophy of visionary sexuality, which later attracted William Blake and his wife Catherine. For the Swedenborgian Blake, 'the most religious' are 'the most voluptuous of men', for they embody 'True Christian Philosophy' (E 591).

A major reviver of 'voluptuous' religion was H.D., whose mother and maternal grandparents infused her with the passionate language, artistic sensibility, and mystical tendencies of Zinzendorf's *Unitas Fratrum*. However, she often felt that they were keeping something secret from her, perhaps because her father was not a Moravian but a rationalist astronomy professor from a Puritanical family. As a child, she sensed that 'there were things under things, as well as things inside things'.[20] She occasionally experienced 'supernormal' and visionary states, which were not encouraged by her modern schooling in Philadelphia. As an ardent and rebellious teenager, H.D. fell in love with Ezra Pound, who stimulated her powerful sexual drive and encouraged her reading of esoteric-erotic writers. Their intense relationship defined much of her later life, for she remained 'frozen in this moment' of adolescent passion and spiritual yearning: 'First kisses? In the woods, in the winter – what did one expect? Not this. Electric, magnetic, they do not so much warm, they magnetize, vitalize.'[21] Her language echoed the ardent lyrics of early Moravian hymns, as well as Blake's praise of 'The moment of desire!' when 'The virgin / That pines for man shall awaken her womb to enormous joys' (E 50).

A delighted Pound reinforced her sense of mystical eroticism when he brought her Swedenborg's theosophical treatise *Heaven and Hell*, Blake's anti-New Church satire *The Marriage of Heaven and Hell*, Balzac's mystical Swedenborgian novel *Seraphita*, and 'a series of Yogi books, too'.[22] For H.D., the frontispiece of Blake's *Marriage*, which features a nude woman with flames issuing from her genitals, would become an emblem of her own belief in 'vision of the womb'. She long remembered how her father's sudden intrusion prevented a sexual consummation with Pound:

> I was hiding myself and Ezra, standing before my father, caught 'in the very act' you might say. For no 'act' afterwards, though biologically fulfilled, had the significance of the first *demi-vierge* embraces. The significance of 'first love' can not be overestimated. If the 'first love' is an uncoordinated entity, Angel-Devil – or Angel Daemon or Daimon, Séraphitus-Séraphita – what then? Find a coordinated convention, Man-Hero, who will compensate, complete the picture. By what miracle does the *marriage du ciel et del terre* find consummation? It filled my fantasies and dreams, my prose and poetry for ten years.[23]

Sensing that she was connected to a suppressed psychic tradition and chafing at her parents' opposition to her engagement to Pound, H.D. moved to England and threw herself into affairs with women and men, always searching for the lost connection between sexuality and vision. In *Notes on Thought and Vision* (drafted in 1919), she echoed the erotic theosophy of Zinzendorf and Swedenborg when she affirmed that 'the body of a man' can be a vehicle for visionary ecstasy:

> The lines of the human body may be used as an approach to the over-mind or universal mind ... The body consumed with love gives off

heat . . . It may burn out simply as heat or physical love. That may be good. But it is also interesting to understand the process by which the heat of the physical body is transmuted to this other, this different form, concentrated, ethereal, which we refer to in common speech as spirit.[24]

For Blake, it was the fifth sense of touch and sexuality that enabled one to 'pass out what time he please' into visions of 'the eternal world that ever groweth' (E 60). Thus, love should be 'Lawless wing'd & unconfind' in order to break 'all chains from every mind' (E 472).

Zinzendorf urged the Moravians to cultivate their gift of vision in order to experience the 'mystical marriage', while Swedenborg recorded his psychoerotic achievement of 'the marriage bed of the mind'. Proud of his own 'gift of Vision', Blake affirmed that all men partake of it, but 'it is lost by not being cultivated' and, drawing on Swedenborg's theories, he trained his wife to see visions.[25] Believing that man and woman can share a state of mutual visualisation, Swedenborg wrote that 'partner sees partner in mind . . . so that each partner has the other in himself . . . and they thus cohabit in their inmosts'.[26] Blake described a similar meditative state: 'Two but one, each in the other sweet reflected; these / Are our three Heavens beneath the shades of Beulah' (E 113). Like her predecessors, H.D. connected the capacity for shared vision with the potency of sexual desire and arousal:

> We must be 'in love' before we can understand the mysteries of vision . . . The minds of the two lovers merge, interact in sympathy of thought. The brain, inflamed and excited by this interchange of ideas, takes on its character of over-mind . . . The love-region is excited by the appearance or beauty of the loved one, its energy not dissipated in physical relation, takes on the character of mind. The love-brain and over-brain are both capable of thought. This thought is vision. All men have possibilities of developing this vision.[27]

Zinzendorf's notions of visionary eros were influenced by his contacts with Jewish Kabbalists and Asian Yogis, but Swedenborg developed them further through his scientific studies of the physiology of the male and female genitals, which helped him understand the breathing and muscular (cremasteric) techniques used during their meditation rituals. The male learns how to maintain a prolonged erection, so that the 'increase in potency according to the interiors of the mind' facilitates the 'reception of spiritual truths'.[28] Impressed by the Moravians' valorisation of female sexual energy, Swedenborg revealed that the wife can also attain the state of erotic illumination: 'Conjugial love has communication with heaven, and the organs of generation have correspondence with the third heaven, especially the womb.'[29]

Zinzendorf's missionaries tried to penetrate into the hidden kingdom of Ethiopia, which influenced Swedenborg's belief that these African natives possessed the sexual energy necessary for spiritual illumination. In one of Blake's erotic illustrations to the *Ethiopian Book of Enoch*, he portrayed a naked angelic Watcher descending headlong, with outstretched arms reaching for the woman's vulva. From this genital contact, she will receive the forbidden knowledge of 'sorcery, incantations' and so on.[30] In another design, he showed a nude woman poised between 'two enormous, light-giving phalli', while she – with 'carefully emphasized' vulva – touches one phallus and gazes fixedly at the other. For the aroused women, the 'divinity' of the angelic messengers 'lies in their organs of generation'. H.D. similarly believed that the arousal of visionary womb and brain provided access to cosmic perceptions:

> Into that over-mind, thoughts pass and are visible like fish swimming under clear water. The swing from normal consciousness to abnormal consciousness is accompanied by grinding discomfort of mental agony . . . I first realized this state of consciousness in my head. I visualize it just as well, now, centered in the love-region of the body . . . In vision of the brain, the region of consciousness is above and about the head; when the centre of consciousness shifts . . . we have vision of the womb or love-vision.[31]

In 1933–34 H.D. underwent psychoanalysis with Sigmund Freud in Vienna, in order to recover lost memories of her childhood and to prepare herself for the coming war, which she clairvoyantly predicted. Like Blake, who viewed military 'Glory & Victory' as 'a phallic Whip', she interpreted German aggression as a perversion of the sexual drive (E 811). Though she did not agree with Freud's rationalist dismissal of her visionary experiences as symptoms of neurosis, she utilised his techniques to bring up from the subconscious her vaguely intuited, inherited 'Gift'. Like the eighteenth-century Moravians, who projected candlelight through vividly coloured, transparent paintings in order to emphasise the Passion of Christ and the passion of his devotées, H.D. regained confidence in the importance of her visions. In her *Tribute to Freud* (1944), she remembered their sessions in the light of her recent researches into Moravian history:

> We travel far in thought, in imagination, or in the realm of memory . . . here and there a memory or a fragment of a dream-picture is actual, is real, is like a work of art or is a work of art. I have spoken of two scenes with my brother as remaining set apart, like transparencies in a dark room, set before lighted candles. Those memories, visions, dreams, reveries – or what you will – are different . . . They are healing. They are real . . . But we cannot prove that they are real.[32]

These scenes could have come straight from the Fetter Lane chapel in the 1740s and 1750s, when Blake's mother viewed such painted and illuminated transparencies, which were used to stimulate the spiritual imagination of the congregants.

H.D. studied the euphemistic official histories of the *Unitas Fratrum*, but she found more attractive and authentic the sensational exposés published by Zinzendorf's enemies. Drawing further on Kabbalistic, Rosicrucian, and Masonic literature, she constructed a new history of Moravianism in her autobiographical novel, *The Gift*, in which she contextualised 'vision of the womb and vision of the brain' within her maternal heritage. In the text, her grandmother Mamalie expresses the fear that 'they might burn us all up', including 'the papers', for Mamalie's husband had 'left the Secret with me. I was afraid the Secret would be lost.' In a semi-trance, the elderly woman repeated to the child Hilda his account of the Island of Wounds, where a mystical group of Moravians and American Indians worshipped the Divine Mother and Father and prayed for world peace.

Like the pacifist Moravians, Blake connected sexual repression with military violence, in which the Warrior cries, 'I am drunk with unsatiated love / I must rush again to War: for the Virgin has frownd & refusd' (E 222). By recovering her Gift, H.D. achieved a visionary refuge from the Nazi bombing: 'At the height of the terror, I could let images and pictures flow through me . . . I saw how young Christian Renatus, an artist and a poet, had indeed perceived clearly the secret of the lost church.'[33] And this hidden 'Church of Love', which survived underground for centuries, was that of the Kabbalists and Tantrists, who could visualise the reintegration of the God-Man's female potency into his androgynous body, and thus re-enact in blissful trance the *hieros gamos*. H.D. learned that beneath (or within) every outward temple, an earlier shrine to the Mother existed. Did Blake make a similar discovery in 1807, when he was in contact with two liberal and artistic Moravians and changed the title of *Vala*, his psychoerotic prophecy, to *The Four Zoas*?[34] In a beloved Moravian hymn to the Mother (*Te Matrem*), 'the Four Zoa' sing praises for her creative, generative, and visionary role.[35]

Notes

1. The 'Secret' and 'Gift' are the main themes of H.D.'s first Moravian novel (1941–43), published in severely truncated editions in 1982 and 1984; see *The Gift by H.D.: the Complete Text*, ed. Jane Augustine (Gainesville: Florida University Press, 1998). Her second Moravian novel, *The Mystery* (1949–51), is still unpublished.
2. William Michael Rossetti, *The Poetical Works of William Blake* (London: G. Bell, 1874), lvii.

3. Susan Stanford Friedman, *Penelope's Web: Gender, Modernity, and H.D.'s Fiction* (Cambridge: Cambridge University Press, 1990), 23.
4. Keri Davies and Marsha Keith Schuchard, 'Recovering the Lost Moravian History of Blake's Family', *BQ*, 38 (2004), 36–43.
5. Marsha Keith Schuchard, 'Why Mrs. Blake Cried: Swedenborg, Blake, and the Sexual Basis of Spiritual Vision', *Esoterica: the Journal of Esoteric Studies*, 2 (2000), 45–93, http://www.esoteric.msu. The following discussion of Zinzendorfian-Swedenborgian sexual and visionary beliefs draws on the detailed documentation in my book, *Why Mrs. Blake Cried: William Blake and the Sexual Basis of Spiritual Vision* (London: Random House/Century, 2006).
6. Nancy Bogen, 'The Problem of William Blake's Early Religion', *The Personalist*, 49 (1968), 509.
7. Colin Podmore, *The Moravian Church in England, 1728–1760* (Cambridge: Cambridge University Press, 1998).
8. Craig Atwood, *Community of the Cross: Moravian Piety in Colonial Bethlehem* (University Park: Pennsylvania State University Press, 2004), 17 n.57, 90.
9. Christiane Dithmar, *Zinzendorfs Nonkonformistische Haltung zum Judentum* (Heidelberg: C. Winter, 2000).
10. Henry Rimius, *A Candid Narrative of the Rise and Progress of the Herrnhutters* (London: A. Linde, 1753), 19–20.
11. Nicolaus Ludwig von Zinzendorf, *Maxims, Theological Ideas, and Sentences*, ed. J. Gambold (London: J. Beecroft, 1751), 228.
12. Rimius, *Candid*, 63.
13. Peter Ackroyd, *Blake* (New York: Alfred Knopf, 1996), 281.
14. H.D., *Gift*, 114.
15. Rimius, *Candid*, 52–3.
16. Arthur Symons, *William Blake* (London:Archibald Constable, 1904), 74–5.
17. Rimius, *Candid*, 5.
18. Edwin John Ellis and William Butler Yeats, *The Works of William Blake* (1893; reprinted New York: AMS, 1967), I, 42.
19. Janice Robinson, *H.D. The Life and Work of an American Poet* (Boston: Houghton Mifflin, 1982), 320.
20. H.D., *Tribute to Freud* (New York:Pantheon, 1956), 29.
21. Ibid., 3–4.
22. H.D., *End to Torment: a Memoir of Ezra Pound*, ed. Norman Holmes Pearson (New York: New Directions, 1979), 23.
23. Ibid., 18–19.
24. H.D., *Notes on Thought and Vision and the Wise Sappho by H.D.*, introd. Albert Gelpi (San Francisco: City Lights, 1982), 46–8.
25. Symons, *Blake*, 261.
26. Emanuel Swedenborg, *The Spiritual Diary*, trans. Alfred Acton (1962; reprinted London: Swedenborg Society, 1977), 4408.
27. H.D., *Notes*, 22–3.
28. Emanuel Swedenborg, *Posthumous Theological Works*, trans. John Whitehead (1914; New York: Swedenborg Foundation, 1978), II, 523–4, 551.
29. Ibid., II, 440–2.
30. Gerald Bentley, 'A Jewel in an Ethiop's Ear: the Book of Enoch as Inspiration for William Blake, John Flaxman, Thomas Moore, and Richard Westall', in Robert Essick and Donald Pierce (eds), *Blake in His Time* (Bloomington: Indiana University Press, 1978), pp. 213–40.

31. H.D., *Notes*, 19–20.
32. H.D., *Tribute*, 51.
33. H.D., *Gift*, 212–13.
34. In 1807 Blake was in contact with Jonathan Spilsbury and James Montgomery, who revived the creative and ecumenical spirit of the Sifting Time.
35. *A Collection of Hymns for the Children of All Ages* (London, 1754), II, 297–8.

24
A Kabbalistic Reading of *Jerusalem*'s Prose Plates

Sheila A. Spector

During the years I have been working on Blake and Kabbalism, I have been accused of doing a number of things that not only did I not intend to do, but in many cases, that I assiduously avoided doing. Among these, I have been erroneously faulted for imputing, and then failing to demonstrate a direct influence of Jewish mysticism on the Christian visionary; for denying, or at least ignoring the possibility that Blake might have been influenced by alternate systems of the occult; for asserting that he knew, or at least that he wished to know, normative Hebrew; or conversely, for rejecting normative Hebrew, and relying on linguistic distortions produced by contemporary Christian Hebraists; and most insidious, for being oblivious to anti-Semitic references sprinkled throughout the corpus. While each of these criticisms can be explained as a projection of a particular critic's own preconceptions, together they have had the effect of obscuring what I believe to be the real value of approaching Blake from the Kabbalistic perspective. Therefore, rather than addressing my critics directly, I thought it would prove more useful if I took this opportunity to provide a 'Kabbalistic' reading of the four prose plates of *Jerusalem*, as a way of illustrating the methodology and the value of the approach.

To a visionary like Blake, Kabbalism's primary advantage is that it provides an alternate approach to externality, one that accounts for and articulates non-material modes of thought, that is, mental experiences beyond the range of conventional language. Historically, material language systems evolved as the means of accommodating the laws of physical existence, predicated on two basic assumptions: lack of motivation and binary opposition. The first, the assertion that language is unmotivated, effectively *demystifies* the system by severing any imputed connection between the material sign and its referent in external reality (for example, between the word *tree* and the idea of *tree-ness* in the phenomenal world). Thus, communication is based on a consensus about the conventional relationship between signifier and signified. The second principle has to do with the binary structure of language. Because definitions are constructed negatively, each sign being differentiated from all of the others, ultimately there can be no positive definition of a term. In other words, we know the value of *x* because it is not *a*, *b*, *c*, and so on. Carried to its logical conclusion, this means that each entity can be reduced to the formula of *x* and *not-x*, a sign and everything else. However, this reduction implies that the signifier has no positive value in itself, only its difference from everything else.

This kind of dualism structures thought processes in the west, the Christian myth projecting the 'wish-fulfilment dream' of a romance in which a messianic hero, the *good*, defeats *evil*, which is thereby consigned to eternal hell, the binary opposite of the eternal life postulated for the *good*. This version of Christianity foreshortens eternity both temporally and spatially, limiting existence primarily to the material cosmos, and confining time and space to the expanse between the creation of our world and the apocalyptic New Jerusalem.[1] Although obviously necessary for everyday communication, this mode of thought yields what Blake called 'mind-forg'd manacles', a dualistic thought process that imprisons the mind within its own materiality.[2] As Blake says in *There is No Natural Religion* [*a*], 'The desires & perceptions of man untaught by any thing but organs of sense, must be limited to objects of sense' (E 2), the result being that those whose thought remains on the empirical level find themselves 'unable to do other than repeat the same dull round over again' (E 3).

As a visionary who believed himself to be a prophet, Blake required a vehicle through which the material limitations of conventional English could be transcended. As he says in *Jerusalem*:

(I call them by their English names: English, the rough basement.
Los built the stubborn structure of the Language, acting against
Albions melancholy, who must else have been a Dumb despair.)

(36[40]: 58–60; E 183)

As indicated by this parenthetical remark, Blake recognised that he was restricted to and therefore constricted by English, the 'rough basement' that serves as the material base required for verbal communication. However, in order to expand that base, Los, the prophetic faculty, strove to develop a medium through which Albion, humanity in the fallen world, might transcend its limitations.

To help fulfil that goal, Blake created a Kabbalistic-like system, an esoteric mode of thought through which he recontextualised the English language and myth into the central phases of a larger universal cycle.[3] The advantage of this kind of system is that it subverts both of the premises upon which conventional language is predicated. Believing that Hebrew is the Holy Tongue, Kabbalists assume first, that all aspects of their language are fully motivated, connected to some kind of referent in essential reality, the mind of God. If this is true, then the concept of binary opposition is obviated. Because God is One, and 'In the beginning was the Word', then all signs in this fully motivated system must be facets of the One, and rather than cancelling each other out, they share a complementary relationship in which they all coalesce. The purpose of this re-mystified form of language is not to differentiate signs from each other, but to explore the ways in which together, they reflect the Godhead. From this perspective, Blake would have seen his task as the transformation of English from a material sign system into a spiritual mode of thought that facilitated apprehension of the One.

Consistent with language, Christian Kabbalists developed a myth that transcended the physical limitations of materialism. Projecting a cyclical, as opposed to linear, structure, they postulated a four-part process in which biblical history was reduced to the middle two phases, and humanity was given a more active role in the process of restoration. The first phase, the Primordial Institution, denotes the original intention of the Godhead; and the second, the State of Destitution, is the totality of the Fall, beginning with the primordial fault and culminating in Adam's disobedience. In the third phase, the Modern Constitution, our existence in the corporeal cosmos is reconfigured from the penalty of Adam into the opportunity to compensate for Adam's sin as we help prepare for the final phase, the Supreme Restitution, when the cosmos will be restored to its purely spiritual state. To articulate the myth, both Blake and the Kabbalists developed a four-tiered hierarchical cosmos: the World of Emanations – Eden; the World of Spiritual Creation – Beulah; the World of Archetypal Formation – Ulro; and the World of Fact – Generation. Each of these planes of existence is controlled by a specific psychological faculty: the Immortal Soul – Urthona; the Spiritual Soul – Luvah; the Rational Soul – Urizen; and the Animal Soul – Tharmas. When placed within this context, the four chapters of *Jerusalem* can be seen to correspond to the four phases of the Kabbalistic myth, and each of the four prose plates – 'To the Public,' 'To the Jews', 'To the Deists' and 'To the Christians' – relates the chapter's theme to contemporary religion.

'To the Public' (plate 3, E 145–6), Blake's preface to his universal epic, corresponds to the Primordial Institution, the original intention of creation. According to the Kabbalistic myth, the Godhead emanated a succession of divine hypostases that produced the four worlds in succession: the World of Emanations contained the Divine Idea; the World of Creation, the actualisation of the Idea on the spiritual plane; the World of Formation, the archetypes; and the World of Fact, the actualisation of the archetypes in our world. Although the Godhead intended all four worlds to be purely spiritual, the initial fault caused a separation between the World of Emanations and the three subsequent strata, all of which were lowered a degree, making our World of Fact corporeal. Correspondingly, in 'To the Public', Blake traces the intellectual process of composition in terms that parallel the emanative process of creation before the separation.

The first paragraph is conventionally read metaphorically, either as a reference to Blake's stay with his patron William Hayley, or else to the printing process. But it could also be read Kabbalistically, as a reference to Blake's experience of the highest of the four levels, his apprehension of his divine vision of *Jerusalem*, 'My former Giants & Fairies' signifying the spiritual beings in the World of Emanations. If so, the assertion that his earlier works had 'reciev'd [sic] the highest reward possible: the [*love*] and [*friendship*] of those with whom to be connected, is to be [*blessed*]', could mean those 'friends in Eternity' about whom he speaks elsewhere, as well.[4] It is in these friends that Blake places his confidence: 'I cannot doubt that this more consolidated & extended Work, will be as kindly recieved [sic]' (E 145).

By definition, the second level is the place where the creative idea is consolidated on the spiritual plane. Similarly, what remains of the next paragraph focuses on Blake's conception of spirituality, the religion of 'Jesus our Lord, who is the God . . . and Lord . . . to whom the Ancients look'd and saw his day afar off, with trembling & amazement'. Excised from the plate are discussions of the gods of ancient religions, and the specific designation of Jesus as 'the God [*of Fire*] and Lord [*of Love*]', all references to the manifestation of religion in the World of Fact, as opposed to the spiritual Idea. While we cannot know why Blake revised the plate as he did, it is certainly provocative to note that the erasures unify the paragraph around the purely spiritual plane.

The third level down is the World of Archetypal Formation, that is, the spiritual idea manifested as the archetype that will be actualised in the World of Fact. Here, in the third paragraph, the love of Jesus is defined in terms of 'continual forgiveness of Sin: he who waits to be righteous before he enters into the Saviours kingdom, the Divine Body; will never enter there'. By delineating Christianity in terms of forgiveness, Blake implies a dynamic process that is part of the larger scheme: the true Christian, rather than damn man into the stasis of a binary opposition between good and evil, will actualise the archetypal process outlined on the third level. As he says in the first two lines of the prophecy itself: 'Of the Sleep of Ulro! and of the passage through / Eternal Death! and of the awaking to Eternal Life' (4: 1–2; E 146), Ulro being his equivalent of the World of Archetypal Formation.

Finally, the poem addressed to his 'Reader! [*lover*] of books! [*lover*] of heaven' actualises the archetypal structure. Differentiating this audience from 'those with whom it be connected, is to be [*blessed*]', here Blake addresses those corporeal Englishmen who believe in the God who 'speaks in thunder and in fire! / Thunder of Thought, & flames of fierce desire', and who will read Blake's composite art: 'Therefore I print; nor vain my types shall be: / Heaven, Earth & Hell, henceforth shall live in harmony'.

Having thus imaginatively descended through the four planes of existence, Blake locates himself specifically in the World of Fact – 'Heaven, Earth & Hell'. In the final section, he projects art as the means by which the reader can effect restoration, concluding with a discussion 'Of the Measure, in which / the following Poem is written', an explanation of his use of poetics in the prophecy. Although speaking from the corporeal World of Fact, Blake asserts that even the most basic physical needs are intertwined with the spiritual component – 'We who dwell on Earth can do nothing of ourselves, every thing is conducted by Spirits, no less than Digestion or Sleep.' He then indicates that we can gain access to that spiritual component by using our intellects in the act of creation: 'When this Verse was first dictated to me I consider'd a Monotonous Cadence.' Although 'dictation' and 'consideration' might seem to be contradictory activities, they make mystical sense, dictation implying inspiration on the spiritual plane, and consideration referring to the choices the biographical Blake made on the corporeal. Therefore, as he continues, he chose to vary his metre, not only to avoid monotony but to accommodate the different intellectual levels of his audience, as implied by various styles found in the prophecy: 'Every word and every letter is studied and put into its fit place.' Coalescing sound and sense, Blake also indicates how we might elevate our own levels of thought: 'The Primeval State of Man, was Wisdom, Art, and Science.'

The second prose plate, 'To the Jews' (plate 27, E 171–4), corresponds to the State of Destitution, the Kabbalistic explanation for the Fall. In contrast to the conventional Christian interpretation, Kabbalists do not define the Fall in terms of an *agon* between *good* and *evil*, but as the introduction of negation – the force that caused the initial fragmentation and now prevents cosmic restoration – into the cosmos. In this plate, Blake coalesces the Kabbalistic and Anglo-Israelite myths to project the Jews, not as the stereotype of evil, but as the spirit of negation that prevents the reintegration of the cosmos.

As with 'To the Public', this plate, too, descends through the four strata, demonstrating how negation caused the initial fragmentation. The first section, corresponding to the Divine Intention, establishes the mythic basis for *Jerusalem*: by redefining 'The Religion of Jesus: [as] the most Ancient, the Eternal: & the Everlasting Gospel'; by identifying Jerusalem as the symbol of divine imminence, 'the Emanation of the Giant Albion'; and by establishing Britain as the Holy Land, 'the Primitive Seat of the Patriarchal Religion'. Thus are the British distinguished as the chosen people: 'All things Begin & End in Albions Ancient Druid Rocky Shore.' Although the Everlasting Gospel is available to all, still, 'The Wicked will turn it to Wickedness, the Righteous to Righteousness', that is, we have free will and must freely choose the Religion of Jesus.

The second section, corresponding to the World of Spiritual Creation, indicates what Blake considers to be the source of the pre-Adamic fault, the Jews' refusal to accept Christ. Tracing history backwards from Abraham,

Blake superimposes the Anglo-Israelite belief – that the British were the true descendants of Noah – onto biblical history: 'Your Ancestors derived their origin from Abraham, Heber, Shem, and Noah, who were Druids: as the Druid Temples (which are the Patriarchal Pillars & Oak Groves) over the whole Earth witness to this day.' He then uses the Kabbalistic doctrine that pre-lapsarian Adam contained within himself all souls to project the fragmentation of prototypical man as the spiritual manifestation of the fragmentation of the cosmos: 'But now the Starry Heavens are fled from the mighty limbs of Albion.'

The archetypal plane is suggested by Albion's 'Chaotic State of Sleep', in which he dreams that 'Satan & Adam & the whole World was Created by the Elohim'; and then the poem occupying the central portion of the plate articulates the dream. Conflating Britain and Jerusalem, Blake structures the poem in terms of the Kabbalistic myth, substituting fragmentation and negation for biblical sin and punishment. The poem opens with the pastoral image of Jerusalem and the Lamb – 'And every English Child is seen, / Children of Jesus & his Bride' (ll. 19–20) – and then projects the threat not as an evil Satan intending to seduce Eve, but as organised religion, the system that perpetuates the duality of good and evil: 'With Moral & Self-righteous Law / Should Crucify in Satans Synagogue!' (ll. 23–4). Thus, the poem redefines Adam's sin from being the cause of man's fall to the effect of a primordial fault, now identified as the rejection of the religion of forgiveness. Once Albion turns his back on the Divine Vision, he is subjected to the duality of good and evil, thereby consolidating negation: 'Satan his name: in flames of fire / He stretch'd his Druid Pillars far' (ll. 39–40). At that point, the spirit of immanence, Jerusalem, is exiled; man becomes corporeal; and Jesus' sacrifice becomes necessary. Had Albion rejected the religion of retribution, then the catastrophe could have been avoided.

The plate ends with a final paragraph addressed to the Jews in the World of Fact. Exhorting them to 'Take up the Cross O Israel & follow Jesus', Blake cites their rejection of this distorted version of Christianity as his basis for identifying the Jews as the true Christians – 'If Humility is Christianity; you O Jews are the true Christians.' Not the conventional evangelical appeal, Blake pleads with the Jews to stop being an impediment, and to help restore the cosmos: 'The Return of Israel is a Return to Mental Sacrifice & War.'

Kabbalists view the third phase, the Modern Constitution, as the arena in which negation is to be consolidated so that it can be neutralised, in preparation for the Supreme Restitution. In the third prose plate, 'To the Deists' (plate 52, E 200–2), Blake condemns the materialism of religion as the source of negation in our world. The label for all of what he considers to be the fallacies of materialism is Rahab. Likely derived from the proper noun found in both the Old and New Testaments, Blake seems to have taken the name back to its Hebrew root, 'breadth', 'width', 'extent' – 'space'. Implying the physical dimensions of the corporeal cosmos, Rahab, as Blake explains at the top left of the plate, 'is an Eternal State'; however, as he continues on the top right, 'The Spiritual States of the Soul are all Eternal Distinguish between the Man, & his present State.' Thus, Rahab, like the Modern Constitution, is not *evil* in a binary opposition between *good* and *evil*; rather, it symbolises the positive opportunity to consolidate negation so that it might be put off: 'He is in the State named Rahab: which State must be put off before he can be the Friend of Man.'

The real negation in the Modern Constitution is the *agon* between organised Christianity and Deism, their opposition doing little more than prolonging our existence in the 'State named Rahab'. It must be emphasised here that Blake is not condemning any religion in particular: he is not saying that because organised Christianity gets it wrong, then its contrary, natural religion, must have it right. Rather, he is saying that the two are mirror images of each other, both predicated on foreshortened perspectives, and therefore, each providing a flawed interpretation of morality:

> Every Religion that Preaches Vengeance for Sin is the Religion of the Enemy & Avenger; and not the Forgiver of Sin, and their God is Satan, Named by the Divine Name Your religion O Deists: Deism, is the Worship of the God of this World by the means of what you call Natural Religion and Natural Philosophy, and of Natural Morality or Self-Righteousness, the Selfish Virtues of the Natural Heart. This was the Religion of the Pharisees who murderd Jesus. Deism is the same & ends the same.

Because organised religions are mirror images of each other, it is hypocritical for one to condemn the sinners found in any other; rather, the entire system of condemnation must be replaced by the true Christianity.

The poem that concludes the plate uses the conflict between Catholicism and Deism to depict the consolidation of the false dualistic religion:

> When Satan first the black bow bent
> And the Moral Law from the Gospel rent
> He forgd the Law into a Sword
> And spilld the blood of mercys Lord.

(ll. 17–20)

But it also projects the means by which the negation can be put off, intellectual warfare:

> For a Tear is an Intellectual thing;
> And a Sigh is the Sword of an Angel King
> And the bitter groan of a Martyrs woe
> Is an Arrow from the Almighties Bow!

(ll. 25–8)

At the end of the plate devoted to the State of Destitution, Blake had urged the Jews towards 'Mental Sacrifice & War'; here, at the conclusion of his Modern Constitution, he explains how that might be achieved in our world.

Finally, 'To the Christians' (plate 77, E 231–3) projects the Supreme Restitution, the rejection of the false systems of Christianity for the true. The top of the plate contains a visual rendition of the theme articulated by the four prose plates. Beneath the title 'To the Christians' is the epigraph:

> I give you the end of a golden string,
>   Only wind it into a ball:
> It will lead you in at Heavens gate,
>   Built in Jerusalems wall.

At the top right of the plate is a figure who follows the golden string that extends across the plate, encompasses the quatrain and then crosses diagonally to the top left corner, thereby excluding the negation:

> Devils are
> False Religions
>   'Saul Saul'
> 'Why persecutest thou me.'

The rest of the plate explains, first in prose and then in verse, what Blake perceives to be the true Christianity: 'I know of no other Christianity and of no other Gospel than the liberty both of body & mind to exercize the Divine Arts of Imagination.' Identifying organized religion as the impediment to the true Christianity – 'It is the Wheel of Religion / . . . Jesus died because he strove / Against the current of this Wheel' – Blake concludes the plate by calling on Englishmen to help bring about the Supreme Restitution:

> And now the time returns again:
>   Our souls exult & Londons towers,
> Receive the Lamb of God to dwell
>   In Englands green & pleasant bowers.

The point of this reading is not to insist that Blake deliberately modelled his prose plates after any particular recension of Christian Kabbalism. Rather, it is to suggest a new mode of reading that provides some plausible explanations for a few of the conundrums surrounding Blake's most enigmatic prophecy. While various scholars have been able to rationalise individual passages found on the prose plates, none has been able to explain why Blake selected these particular audiences, or why he placed them in this specific order. The advantage of the Kabbalistic context is that it provides an alternate mode of thought to which Blake was at least sympathetic. Beyond that, it also helps explain contradictions in Blake's apparent denunciations of various forms of religion, as well as the puzzling turn to philo-Semitism so late in his life. From our perspective, the Kabbalistic model helps us transcend our own preconceptions; and the Kabbalistic terminology and assumptions help release us from the prison house of our own language. Therefore, instead of questioning whether or not Blake intended to use a Kabbalistic model, what his source(s) might have been, whether or not he might have used other antithetical systems, or why, given his earlier anti-Semitism, he would exploit Jewish materials; we should focus on how the Kabbalistic model helps open the composite books up to different and possibly more fruitful explanations.

Notes

1. Northrop Frye associates the 'wish-fulfilment' of romance with the Christian myth in 'The Mythos of Summer: Romance', in *Anatomy of Criticism: Four Essays* (Princeton, NJ: Princeton University Press, 1957), 186–206.
2. 'London', *Songs of Innocence and of Experience* (E 27).
3. The summaries of Kabbalism and Blake's development of his own Kabbalistic-like system are from my *'Glorious incomprehensible': the Development of Blake's Kabbalistic Language* and *'Wonders Divine': the Development of Blake's Kabbalistic Myth* (both were published by Bucknell University Press in 2001). I provide a Kabbalistic reading of the plate structure in *Jerusalem* in my 'A Numerological Analysis of *Jerusalem*', in Alexander S. Gourlay (ed.), *Prophetical Character: Essays on William Blake in Honor of John E. Grant* (Cornwall, CT: Locust Hill Press, 2002), pp. 327–49.
4. See, for example, the letters to Butts of 25 April and 6 July 1803 (E 728–9).

25
Brittannia Counter Britannia: How *Jerusalem* Revises Patriotism

June Sturrock

> Fee Fi Fo Fum
> I smell the blood of an Englishman
> Be he alive or be he dead
> I'll grind his bones to make my bread!

But of course, the 'Englishman', Jack, defeats the rhyming giant, sending him crashing headfirst down the beanstalk (Tatar, 144). Jack's giant – and his brothers – walks again in *Jerusalem*:

> Hark! Hear the Giants of Albion cry at night
> We smell the blood of the English! We delight in their blood on
>   our Altars!
> The living and the dead shall be ground in our rumbling Mills
> For bread of the Sons of Albion.

> (*J*, 38.47–50: E 185)

Fee fi fo fum indeed. The British war machine, which ground away from 1793–1815, becomes the cannibalistic folktale giant: English institutions survive on 'the blood of the English' – ordinary English people like Jack.[1] The quintessential popular English narrative – popular then in oral form and in chapbooks, popular now in print and as pantomime[2] – becomes a commentary on a division in England's national consciousness, a division that is among the central concerns of *Jerusalem*. In his very use of the popular (non-elite) form of the national folk-tale, Blake ranges himself with Jack the Englishman rather than the giants of Albion.[3]

Clearly a poem called *Jerusalem The Emanation of The Giant Albion*, that begins with the Saviour calling on Albion to awake, and can end only after 'England who is Brittannia awoke from Death on Albions bosom' (*J*, 94.20: E 254), is deeply involved with ideas of England's nationhood: the best-known lines in all Blake's work flaunt a fierce dedication to 'England's green & pleasant land' (*M*, 1.16: E 96). But in England, during the years in which

228

Jerusalem was written, patriotism – and the emblematic figures of Albion and Britannia[4] – had been taken over by Jack's giant, the anti-Gallican, pro-war faction. One of Blake's tasks in writing *Jerusalem* was to rescue Britannia, to find a different version of patriotism. Ideas of nation are intricately involved with those of gender, and it is through narratives involving gender, and especially through female personages – Jerusalem, Mary, Erin, Dinah, all calumniated women in various ways – that Blake disputes entrenched assumptions about British nationhood. He 'rouzes the faculties to act' (E 702), here in *Jerusalem*, as elsewhere, through using common social constructs and reversing their values. The chaste and modest woman, celebrated in the fiction and conduct literature of the period, appears in *Jerusalem* as a vengeful warmonger, as I have already shown.[5] Here I discuss female figures who are the objects not of celebration but of calumny and whose narratives hinge on ideas of forgiveness and acceptance rather than revenge. During the Revolutionary and Napoleonic wars, in every kind of popular discourse, Britain defined itself in opposition to France, in an intensification of a long-established Francophobia. *Jerusalem* struggles towards a shift from this rigidly oppositional and self-righteously punitive stance, replacing the machinery of revenge with the dynamics of forgiveness and the practice of the arts: it is this struggle that is seen in the narratives of the major female personages of *Jerusalem*.

'The intellectual historian, seeking to define the basic facts of British mental life in the opening years of the nineteenth century, might well begin with Britain's intense consciousness of France', according to Gerald Newman (397). This consciousness involved fear and hatred of 'our foes the base French', as one war song of 1804 put it,[6] and of their homeland, 'a pestilential den of degenerating equality', in the words of the anti-Jacobin Charles Lucas.[7] Contempt for the French became the defining point of British nationalism at the period, as if the nation only knew what it was by contrasting itself against another: 'What's a Frenchman? – *Slavery's fool.* / What's a Briton? – *Freedom's tool,* / Form'd to curb *despotic* rule.'[8] Francophobia was of course well-established in the British psyche long before the French Revolution. 'Long Live his Most Excellent Britannic Majesty King George the Third, or Down with the Devil, Pope, French King, and Pretender', reads the caption of an engraving of 1760, but hatred of the French was already an old story (Carretta, 44). It is not surprising that a patriotic poem of 1803 refers proudly to English victories over France at the battles of Agincourt (1415) and 'Cressy' (1346).[9] This long-established hatred intensified during the years of the Revolutionary and Napoleonic wars, when, as Shirley Dent and Jason Whittaker observe, national pride 'was polluted by . . . xenophobia and intolerance' (68). Patriotism had become, as it readily does, associated with hatred of the outsider, the other. Blake represents the 'soft Family Love' of 'the Spectre of Albion' as in fact 'cruel Patriarchal pride

/ Planting thy Family alone / Destroying all the World beside' (*J*, 27. 74–81: E 173), an image of Britain's global and imperial stance that is well-founded on historical reality. At the period when Blake was writing *Jerusalem*, he saw his Albion as 'possess'd by the War of Blood' (*J*, 50.8: E 199), in 'a World in which Man is by his Nature the Enemy of Man' (*J*, 38.52: E 185).[10]

The twelve Sons of Albion – most of whom are named, significantly, from the adversarial professions, the law and the army, on the basis of Blake's 1804 treason trial – embody this view of man as enemy of man. Their attack on Jerusalem, however, also articulates a contrary position:

> Cast ye Jerusalem forth! . . .
> The Harlot daughter! Mother of pity and dishonourable forgiveness
> . . .
> No more the sinful delights
> Of age and youth and boy and girl
> . . .
> But War and deadly contention, Between
> Father and Son, and light & love! All bold asperities
> Of Haters met in deadly strife
>
> (*J*, 18.11–22: E 163)

The Sons of Albion, that is, oppose 'deadly contention' with 'dishonourable forgiveness', and though Jerusalem's values are the reverse of theirs, she, too, counterpoises war against forgiveness.[11] Blake gives her a voice that is characteristically tentative in contrast to the 'bold asperities' praised by the Sons of Albion, as she asks:

> Why should Punishment Weave the Veil with Iron Wheels of War
> When Forgiveness might it Weave with Wings of Cherubim.
>
> (*J*, 22.34–5: E 168)

Forgiveness – 'dear Mutual Forgiveness' (*J*, 49.29: E 198) – is not only opposed to war throughout this poem but also associated with sexuality, from the superscription to Chapter 1 – Μονοσ ο Ιεσουσ ('only Jesus', John 8:9) – onwards. As Morton Paley points out in his edition of *Jerusalem*, the context of these words in St John's Gospel (8.9) is the story of the woman taken in adultery and thus they relate to one of the 'central themes in *Jerusalem*: the continual forgiveness of sins by Jesus' (135), and, significantly, also to a specifically sexual offence. Jerusalem dispenses forgiveness; she also needs it, in so far as the narrative places her as 'Harlot daughter' as well as 'Mother of . . . dishonourable forgiveness' in the eyes of the Sons of Albion. Blake adopts the many biblical narratives in which Israel or Jerusalem is castigated as a whore, in a metaphor of the Jewish attraction towards the religions of neighbouring groups, 'a-whoring after other gods' (Judges 2:17).[12] Ezekiel, for instance, in a passage that Blake uses in *Jerusalem*,[13] accuses God's unworthy bride, Jerusalem, in these words: 'thou didst trust in thine own beauty and playedst the harlot . . . and pouredst out thy fornications on every one that passed by' (16.15). Jerusalem here betrays the god of her nation by her openness to other nations. Retaining the biblical association between fornication and differing views of religion and nation, Blake reverses the biblical values of this association, so that fornication becomes associated with the joy of forgiveness and inclusion, while the condemnation of fornication is associated with cruelty, error, and exclusion. Mary's story in Blake's unorthodox version adds a New Testament narrative of forgiveness to that of Jerusalem, as she rejoices over the act that will produce Jesus:

> O Forgiveness & Pity & Compassion! If I were Pure I should never
> Have known Thee; if I were Unpolluted I should never have
> Glorified thy Holiness or rejoiced in thy great Salvation

> (*J*, 61.44–6: E 212)

The reiterated opposition between war and forgiveness in this text ensures that narratives of sexual lapse and forgiveness bear a political weight beyond their obvious personal and religious meanings. Their implications relate specifically to Blake's own war-torn England as well as to 'corporeal war' in general.

Like the biblical authors he knew so well, Blake associates sexual transgression with female figures. This association is not merely a matter of following his sources or adopting the gender conventions of his society: no doubt these elements are present, but it has in addition strong political implications. Part of England's sense of national identity at this period, as represented in cartoons, novels, and political commentaries, is related to the idea of the chaste Englishwoman and the happy and secure English home, while in the inevitable and persistent contrast, the French were seen as sexually immoral and lacking in 'family values':[14]

> With the Jacobins of France vague intercourse is without reproach: marriage is reduced to the vilest concubinage; children are encouraged to cut the throats of their parents; mothers are taught that tenderness is no part of their character; and to demonstrate their attachment to their party they ought to make no scruple to rake with their bloody hands in the bowels of those who came from their own.

> (Burke, 245)

This is Edmund Burke, writing in 1796, but the association between sexual licence, domestic discord, and the French certainly extended well into the years in which Blake was at work on *Jerusalem*.[15] Maria Edgeworth's novel of 1806, *Leonora*, for example, ends with these resounding words: 'England is not the place for women of her [adulterous] character. Happy the climate in which no venomous creature can exist. More happy the country under whose salutary laws and opinions no exotic vice can flourish' (2. 290–1). Olivia, the aforesaid 'venomous creature', meanwhile, is represented as complaining to a French friend: 'You have no idea of the miserable force of prejudice that still prevails here [in England]' (1. 100–1) – referring, of course, to sexual prejudice. Linda Colley, discussing 'the coming together of Francophobia and preconceptions about sexual roles', argues that 'there was a sense at this time . . . in which the British conceived of themselves as an essentially "masculine" culture . . . caught up in an eternal rivalry with an essentially "effeminate" France' (252). If Blake accedes to the British feminisation of France, as he seems to in representing 'Shiloh the Masculine Emanation' (*J*, 49.47: E 199) as related to France in the same way that Jerusalem is related to Albion, he condemns other aspects of sexualised national roles. His approach to the 'eternal rivalry' between the two countries is through narratives of calumniated women, narratives that depend on an idea of forgiveness politicised through a repeated opposition with war.[16] The sexual values of middle-class Britain are reversed: Brittannia awakening 'from Death on Albions bosom', remembers with horror her 'Dreams of Chastity & Moral Law' (*J*, 94 20–3: E 254). It is her awakening from this dream of death that arouses Albion: with his awakening, corporeal wars can become transformed into 'Wars of mutual Benevolence Wars of Love' (*J*, 97.14: E 256). Through narratives of female sexuality, a concept of nation as exclusive is replaced by a concept of nation as both inclusive and interactive.

Like Mary and Jerusalem, Erin and Dinah are among the calumniated women that figure so largely and, paradoxically, so powerfully in this poem. However, the narratives of Erin and Dinah function somewhat differently from those of Mary and Jerusalem, focusing on national rather than merely sexual interactions.[17] My discussion of Erin and Dinah is brief, partly because space in this volume is limited, and partly because Catherine McClenahan has written so well of these narratives, though with a rather different emphasis.[18]

Both Erin and Dinah can be regarded as 'consorting with the enemy'. Dinah (who appears only once in *Jerusalem*, as 'the youthful form of Erin'; *J*, 74.54: E 230) is Jacob's daughter, who goes out to visit 'the women of the land' – Hivite and not Israelite women, that is – strangers and outsiders. After the Hivite prince, Shechem, who has raped her, falls in love with Dinah, his father, Hamor, proposes intermarriage and trade relations between the two groups. Dinah's brothers, perceiving the Hivites as the enemy, trick and then slaughter them, motivated by concern not so much for their sister as for the honour of the group: '[Shechem] has wrought folly in Israel in lying with Jacob's daughter, which thing ought not to be done', they say (Genesis 34:7).[19]

Dinah, then, is connected with the possibility of interaction between apparent enemies, a possibility that is frustrated by an automatic (male) hostility towards the outsider. As McClenahan says, 'from one perspective, Dinah's "going out" and the efforts of Hamor and Shechem to join the two communities are the kind of "exchanges," of refusing narrow and rigid definitions of identity and community, which Blake endorses throughout *Jerusalem*' (159). Erin, as the old woman who traditionally represents Ireland – the Shan Van Vocht – bears the same associations, for the Irish were too commonly regarded in this period as 'a disaffected part of the people, governed by French Principles' (*Beauties of the AntiJacobin*, 11).[20] The United Irishmen working for reform in Ireland hoped for military support from France in their 1798 uprising, and indeed a French invasion of Ireland in 1796 had been averted only by tremendous storms in Bantry Bay.[21] Erin, then, like Dinah, promotes intercourse with the enemy: she represents an idea of nation that is open to difference and interaction, just like Jerusalem and Mary in their different ways. Accordingly, in her speech to the Daughters of Beulah, like Jerusalem, she praises 'dear Mutual Forgiveness' (*J*, 49.29: E 198) and opposes 'the War of Blood' (*J*, 50.8: E 199).

Erin has a further resonance. Not only does she speak to the Daughters of Beulah, she also merges with them, in that she voices words repeatedly associated with the Daughters – the words of Martha to Jesus before the raising of Lazarus: 'Lord, if thou hadst been here my brother would not have died' (John 11:21).[22] Now the Daughters of Beulah are, for Blake, the 'Muses who inspire the Poets Song!' (*M*, 2.1: E 96). This implicit association between Erin and the arts adds an important colouring to Blake's versions of national identity, for in *Jerusalem*, as elsewhere, Blake counters corporeal war, associated with an idea of nationhood that he entirely rejected, with warfare through the arts – intellectual war. Indeed, Blake's deliberate retention of the image of war in poems that bitterly oppose war is perhaps the most disturbing aspect of the later work to readers like myself whose earliest memories include bombs falling and families shattered beyond repair.[23]

The war Blake celebrates is fought through the arts and learning. 'Poetry Fetter'd, Fetters the Human Race! Nations are Destroy'd, or Flourish, in proportion as Their Poetry Painting and Music, are Destroy'd or Flourish! The Primeval State of Man, was Wisdom, Art & Science' (*J*, 3: E 146). In his Public Address of 1809–10 he associates 'Love to My Art & Zeal for my Country' (E 574), thus claiming art as the proper expression of national identity. As Paley writes, 'if Blake's Jerusalem is built in England's green and pleasant land, it is through the practice of art and poetry' (132). More specifically, Blake supported the campaign to establish Britain's reputation as a home of the visual arts that was currently being fought by such artists and writers as his friend James Barry, Prince Hoare, George Cumberland, and John Opie.[24] All these men regarded the support and encouragement of art – through such schemes as patriotic memorials, extended arts education, and a National Gallery – as a primary responsibility of any healthy nation. Blake, aligning himself with these activities, represents the 'Wars of mutual Benevolence' waged by an awakened Albion as fought through 'Wisdom, Art & Science.' And the awakening of Albion to these responsibilities and to intellectual life from his/its mechanical rivalries and complacent moralism is in large part expressed through the female personages of the poem.

Notes

1. Like Blake, Simone Weil perceived that 'the war of one state against another is immediately transformed into a war of the state . . . against its own army' (241).
2. Tatar calls this 'the quintessential British folktale' (131).
3. Blake writes in the period in which the significance of the folk-tale, and its connection with nationalist movements, were becoming recognised throughout Europe. The Brothers Grimm first published their *Children's and Household Tales* in 1812: their collections were inspired partly by their concern with German unification.
4. Examples include Wordsworth's 'Occasioned by the Battle of Waterloo' (253: l.1), or the following patriotic lyrics: 'A Tear for Albion – 1808', where Albion is a 'daughter', 'Thoughts Suggested by the Approach of a Regiment of Soldiers', 'Serious Advice to Bonaparte', 'Epicedium on the Death of Lord Nelson' (Bennett, 432, 452, 312, 354).
5. In 'Maenads, Young Ladies, and the Lovely Daughters of Albion'.
6. 'The Voice of the British Isles', from *The European Magazine*, 44 (1803) (Bennett, 294).
7. *The Infernal Quixote*, 1. 169. For Charles Lucas (1769–1754), see Grenby's introduction.
8. 'The Oracle Consulted' from *The Gentleman's Magazine*, 73 (1803) (Bennett, 293). Colley, among others, writes of the British tendency to confirm its identity by comparison with France (5). 'The Contrast', a much-discussed cartoon of 1792 is a case in point: see, for instance, Ellison (174) and Hertz (161–2).
9. See Bennett (291). Mee notes, 'Blake's early fragment *King Edward the Third* represents the Hundred Years War against France as the disastrous result of royal ambition and pride' (135).
10. In Erin's speech, Luvah, like Albion, enters 'A World where Man is by Nature the Enemy of Man' (*J*, 49.69: E 199).
11. Moskal places Blake's concept of forgiveness in the context of recent works on the ethics of character, describing him as 'an ethical bricoleur' (2).
12. Biblical texts often use images of harlotry in representing irreligion. Hosea's narrative of the unfaithful wife is presented as parallel to Israel's faithlessness to God. Ezekiel speaks of his people as 'whoring after their idols' (6:9). In Jeremiah 3:6–20, Israel is a harlot (6), commits adultery (8), and God complains of her treachery (20). See also Nahum 3:4.
13. Mary, describing herself as cast out to the loathing of her person (*J*, 61.40), quotes directly from Ezekiel 16:5.
14. Colley writes of a new insistence on ' "public probity," regular church-going and conventional sexual morality' in reaction to Jacobinism (188–9).

15. Anti-Jacobin sentiments were voiced long after 1800: '*The Progress of the Pilgrim Good-Intent* subtitled *In Jacobinical Times* was no less out of sync with the age it professed itself to concern itself with in 1822 when it reached its tenth edition than it had been when originally published in 1800' Grenby (2001, 10). Some Blake scholars have been reluctant to recognise that the historical context of *Jerusalem* includes an anti-Jacobinism that stretches far beyond the 1790s.

16. Blake uses other narratives of forgiveness: Moskal describes *Jerusalem 99* as reminiscent of representations of the return of the Prodigal Son, referring to Samuel Palmer's account of the ageing Blake as unable to finish reading this story through his tears (177). Paley's edition notes Blunt's comment that this plate is 'striking similar to that of the main figures in an engraving of the story of the Prodigal Son by Martin de Vos' (296). Tannenbaum discusses Blake's versions of the story of Cain and Abel in relation to Blake's horror of revenge (23).

17. Dinah's significance also involves her sexual position: 'as a "fallen woman" in the eyes of her own family/nation, Dinah is a type of Jerusalem, everywhere denounced by Albion's forces as a treasonous harlot, for the crime of desiring liberty and independence' (McClenahan, 160).

18. See also Erdman (444–7).

19. For a sensitive discussion of Dinah's story, see Sternberg (445–75).

20. This is part of a 'Letter to Lord Moira' who in a speech to the House of Lords in 1797 denounced the regime in Ireland. He was frequently attacked in the anti-Jacobin press.

21. Grenby's introduction to *The Infernal Quixote* provides a useful summary of the events of 1797–98 (22–31). There was a further rising in 1803, under Robert Emmett: neither the 1800 Act of Union, nor the 1801 suspension of the Habeas Corpus act ameliorated the situation.

22. Compare *FZ*, 4.56.1.

23. Aers makes a similar point (264).

24. For Blake's support for Cumberland's proposal of a National Gallery, see Essick and Paley.

References

Aers, David, 'Representations of Revolution: From *The French Revolution* to *The Four Zoas*', in Dan Miller et al. (eds), *Critical Paths: Blake and the Argument of Method* (Durham, NC: Duke University Press, 1987), pp. 244–70.

Barry, James, *An Inquiry into the Real and Imaginary Obstructions to the Acquisition of the Arts in England* (London: printed for T. Becket 1775).

Barry, James, *Letter to the Dilettanti Society . . . the improvement of PUBLIC TASTE and for accomplishing the original Views of the ROYAL ACADEMY OF GREAT BRITAIN* (London: J. Walker, 1798).

The Beauties of the AntiJacobin or Weekly Examiner (London: J. Plymsell at the AntiJacobin Press, 1799).

Bennett, Betty (ed.), *British War Songs of the Age of Romanticism, 1793–1815* (New York: Garland, 1976).

Blake, William, *Jerusalem The Emanation of The Giant Albion*, ed. Morton D. Paley (Princeton, NJ: Princeton University Press, 1991).

Burke, Edmund, 'First Letter on a Regicide Peace', *Writings & Speeches*, IX, ed. R.B. McDowell (Oxford: Clarendon, 1991), 187–263.

Carretta, Vincent, *George III and the Satirists from Hogarth to Byron* (Athens, GA: University of Georgia Press, 1990).

Colley, Linda, *Britons: Forging the Nation* (New Haven: Yale University Press, 1992).

Dent, Shirley and Jason Whittaker, *Radical Blake: Influence and Afterlife* (New York: Palgrave, 2002).

Edgeworth, Maria, *Leonora*, 2 vols (London: Joseph Johnson, 1806).

Ellison, Julie, *Delicate Subjects – Racism, Gender, and the Ethics of Understanding* (Cornell: Cornell University Press, 1990).

Erdman, David V., *Blake, Prophet against Empire: a Poet's Interpretation of the History of his own Time* (Princeton, NJ: Princeton University Press, 1954).

Essick, Robert and Morton D. Paley, ' "Dear Generous Cumberland": a Newly Discovered Letter and Poem by William Blake', *BQ* (1998), 4–13.

Grenby, M.O., *The Anti-Jacobin Novel* (Cambridge: Cambridge University Press, 2001).

Grenby, M.O., 'Introduction', *The Infernal Quixote, Charles Lucas* (Peterborough, Ont.: Broadview, 2002).

Hertz, Neil, *The End of the Line: Essays on Psychoanalysis and the Sublime* (New York: Columbia University Press, 1985).

Hoare, Prince, *An Inquiry into the Requisite Cultivation and Present State of the Arts of Design in England* (London: Richard Phillips, 1806).

Lucas, Charles, *The Infernal Quixote: a Tale of the Day* (London: Minerva Press, 1801).

McClenahan, Catherine L., 'Blake's Erin, the United Irish, and "Sexual Machines" ', in Alexander S. Gourlay (ed.), *Prophetic Character: Essays on William Blake in Honor of John E. Grant* (West Cornwall, CT: Locust Hill Press, 2002), pp. 149–70.

Mee, Jon, 'Blake's Politics in History', in Morris Eaves (ed.), *The Cambridge Companion to Blake* (Cambridge: Cambridge University Press, 2003), pp. 133–49.

Moskal, Jeanne, *Blake, Ethics, and Forgiveness* (Tuscaloosa: University of Alabama Press, 1994).

Newman, Gerald, 'Anti-French Propaganda and British Liberal Nationalism in the Early Nineteenth Century: Suggestions toward a General Interpretation', *Victorian Studies* (1975), 385–418.

Opie, John, *Lectures on Paintings . . . with a letter on the Proposal for a Public Memorial to the Naval Glory of Great Britain . . .* (London: Longman, Hurst, Rees, Orme, 1809).

Paley, Morton D., *The Continuing City: Blake's Jerusalem* (Oxford: Clarendon, 1983).

Sternberg, Meier, *The Poetics of Biblical Narrative: Ideological Literature and the Drama of Reading* (Bloomington: Indiana University Press, 1987).

Sturrock, June, 'Maenads, Young Ladies, and the Lovely Daughters of Albion', in Jackie Di Salvo et al. (eds), *Blake, Politics, History* (New York: Garland, 1998), pp. 339–50.

Tannenbaum, Leslie, 'Blake and the Iconography of Cain', in Robert Essick and Donald Pearce (eds), *Blake in His Time* (Bloomington: Indiana University Press, 1978), pp. 23–34.

Tatar, Maria, *The Annotated Classic Fairy Tales* (New York: Norton, 2002).

Weil, Simone, *Formative Writings, 1929–1941* (Amherst: University of Massachusetts Press, 1987).

Wordsworth, William, *Poetical Works*, ed. T. Hutchinson (London: Oxford University Press, 1965).

26

Blake: Sex and Selfhood

Irene Tayler

Feminists have a problem with Blake. Without a doubt he understood sexual oppression and loathed its effects on both men and women. Yet his works bristle with sexist comments voiced with what sounds like a highly personal sense of male grievance.

Half a lifetime ago, in an essay named for Blake's sardonic little notebook poem 'The Woman Scaly',[1] I tried to understand this phenomenon and concluded that for Blake gender division, like class or ethnic or role division of any kind, was evidence of the Fall and an invitation to jealous power-grabbing mutual hostility. His prophecies make it clear that redemption requires of both men and women a leap of selflessness, as in joyous sexual union and ultimately in the loving 'self-annihilations' of Eternity.

Today I find myself revisiting the question of Blake's views concerning sex and gender because I am newly struck by how personal his struggles with these issues seem to have been, how key problems he faced in himself are addressed through his visionary engagements with Selfhoods, Spectres, and the broad range of female Emanations. I have come to think that his prophetic vision was skewed by two ancient and related habits of thought concerning the sexes, and that he sensed this and struggled against it, with mixed success.

The first disturbing habit of thought concerns the derivative or secondary status of women, as in the biblical story of Eve born from Adam's rib and in Blake's assumption that his mythic female characters, being 'Emanations', should eventually be reabsorbed into the male counterparts that were their source.

Such views were validated in ordinary society by the time-honoured laws of coverture. In the words of Sir William Blackstone's *Commentaries of the Laws of England*, 'The husband and wife are one person in law; that is, the very being or legal existence of the woman is suspended during marriage, or at least is incorporated and consolidated into that of the husband: under whose wing, protection, and *cover*, she performs everything.' As one wag quipped, 'My wife and I are one and I am he.'[2]

It should not surprise anyone that Blake shared the common assumption that the primary human form is male, or that for him the 'second' sex embodied the very idea of separation and fragmentation. Indeed the surprise lies elsewhere. Throughout much of world history men have treated women as commodities for ownership and trade and so demanded of them the 'virtues' of chastity, docility, and reverence for the male. We see vestiges of this practice in wedding ceremonies today where the veiled bride is transferred from father ('Who gives this woman . . . ?') to husband, whom she promises to love, to honour, and in the traditional language, to obey. To his enormous credit Blake – as visionary artist and as married man – fought against any suggestion that men own women and indeed against the exploitation of sexuality under any circumstances. I think his engagement with this issue was central to his life's work. Still – despite all this – much of that work is coloured by a flattering assumption of male entitlement, and I will argue that this was a key element in the Selfhood he sought to overcome.

The second disturbing habit of thought derives from the concept that 'to know' is to penetrate a veil, such as the 'veil' of Nature, Truth, or Allegory. Revelation and Apocalypse both literally mean 'unveiling'.

As a social convention men are almost never veiled. But the veiling of women is older than writing. Women are veiled in Homer, the Bible, and *The Gilgamesh Epic*. Indeed Mesopotamian laws requiring the veiling of married women were rooted in cultural traditions that probably reach well back into the third millennium BCE. And the veil as metaphor must be at least as old. Odysseus, held so long in Calypso's arms, is captive to a woman whose very name means veil or cover. His escape from Calypso is an apocalypse, a literal dis/covering that releases him for his journey home.

In a related way, though to somewhat different metaphorical effect, the ark of the Hebrew desert Tabernacle, and later the Temple, was hung with a veil or curtain. Its function was to close off the Holy of Holies, which might be entered only by the High Priest. Blake enjoyed the sexual suggestiveness of the image, and parodied it by noting that in Eternity 'Embraces are Cominglings: from the Head even to the Feet; / And not a pompous High Priest entering by a Secret Place' (E 223). In *FZ* he wickedly illustrates his critique by depicting a woman whose pubic area is a cathedral with a rather toothy-looking door.

The root concept here is that to see is to know. Thus veiled female figures regularly represent some hidden knowledge desired by the implicitly male eye/I. The verb 'to know' has always retained something of its ancient connotations of carnal knowledge, the sexual penetration of that bodily veil, the hymen: Adam knew Eve. Perhaps this helps explain why Blake insisted so passionately that the doors of perception are opened 'by an improvement of sensual enjoyment' (E 39), why the passage to reunion in Eternity requires freely offered love – which is death to the insular Selfhood – and why he so honoured the naked body and the 'lineaments of Gratified Desire' (E 474–5).

This concept of veiling and unveiling was central to Blake's myth, based as it is on *vision*. Among his 'eternal forms' are the two great females Vala and Jerusalem. Vala figures the natural world of our bodily senses and the reductive rationalism that derives from them. With her 'Veil of Moral Virtue, woven for Cruel Laws' (E 168), she is associated with 'the Caverns of the Grave & places of Human Seed' (E 329), and accordingly with the dark mental prison that results from sexual jealousy, religious mystery, and the anxious fear of death. Vala's name connects her with 'veil' and 'vale' – both the covering that hides and the secret valleys that lie hidden.[3]

Jerusalem – 'called Liberty among the Children of Albion' (E 203) – is the divine liberty of the visionary imagination, open always and to all people through the power of true art.

Jerusalem's name and meaning derive from a pair of biblical passages based squarely on the implications of veiling and vision. In II Corinthians 3 Paul takes the curious veil Moses wore in descending from God's presence as a figure for the Israelites' mental blindness: 'for until this day remaineth the same vail untaken away in the reading of the old testament; which vail is done away in Christ'.[4] The mental veil is lifted 'in Christ', Paul explains, because 'where the spirit of the Lord is, there is liberty'. Liberty is neither gendered nor personified in this coupling with the 'spirit of the Lord', but *Revelation* provides both gender and person in the marriage of 'the Spirit and the Bride' – that is, God's presence pervading the holy city Jerusalem.

This contrast between mental blindness and liberty is vividly pictured in Blake's *Jerusalem 32*:[5] to the left, facing inward, stands Vala, alienated, menacing, and darkly veiled; to the right are Jerusalem and her vigorous daughters, fully visible and radiantly naked. Blake had drawn a similar contrast between spiritual liberty and stunted selfhood years before: 'He who sees the Infinite in all things, sees God. He who sees the Ratio only sees himself only' (E 3).

Since the late 1790s Blake had been at work on *Vala, or the Death and Judgment of the Ancient Man*. This Man is Albion, the people of England (and by extension all Mankind), currently 'asleep' in his fallen state. As work progressed Blake dropped Vala's name and changed his title to *The Four Zoas: The torments of Love & Jealousy in The Death and Judgment of Albion the Ancient Man*, implicitly locating the battle less in Albion's struggle with Vala than in the stormy world of his own psyche – those quarrelsome Zoas (beings) who conduct 'every thing' we do, even 'Digestion or Sleep' (E 145). At every stage the work deplores the torments of love and jealousy, and its hand-drawn pages burn with depictions of sexual exploitation and rage.

But suddenly in October of 1804 Blake experienced a life-altering spiritual crisis and victory. In a letter to William Hayley he exulted, 'For now! O

Glory! And O Delight! I have entirely reduced that spectrous Fiend to his station, whose annoyance has been the ruin of my labors for the last passed twenty years of my life. He is the enemy of conjugal love and is the Jupiter of the Greeks, an iron-hearted tyrant' (E 756). That Jovian fiend is Blake's Selfhood, and in his Notebook Blake tells how Jupiter, in fathering the daughters of Memory (*not* Inspiration), caused Reality to be forgotten and 'the Vanities of Time & Space only Remember'd & calld Reality' (E 555). This ersatz 'Reality' is Vala – the veiled condition personified.

And why the enemy of conjugal love? Clearly this 'tyrant' undermined the Blakes in their workplace. 'O the distress I have undergone, and my poor wife with me. Incessantly laboring and incessantly spoiling what I had done well . . . it shall be so no longer.' In reducing 'that spectrous Fiend to his station' Blake seems to suggest that he has achieved some radical, liberating victory of self-insight.

In *Milton* Blake was to condemn the Spectre as 'a Selfhood, which must be put off & annihilated' (E 229); that is, we must purge from our spirit the rigid and power-hungry 'self' we have learned in the school of worldly life. In *Jerusalem* he would further explain that 'The Spectre is the Reasoning Power in Man; & when separated / From Imagination, and closing itself as in steel, in a Ratio / Of the Things of Memory. It thence frames Laws & Moralities / To destroy Imagination! the Divine Body, by Martyrdoms & Wars' (E 229). Blake wrote in his 1804 letter that his marriage and his work had suffered from this 'spectrous' enemy for twenty years: that is, since the onset of both his marriage and his poetic career. One might say ever since he had become a grown man.

Blake's victory had come in one great flash. In that 1804 letter he says 'Suddenly, on the day after visiting the Truchsessian Gallery of pictures, I was again enlightened with the light I enjoyed in my youth . . . I am really drunk with intellectual vision.' The crisis may have resulted from Blake's visit to the gallery, or the visit may have served merely to date it. In either case it delivered a tremendous rush of artistic confidence and spiritual energy: a heady taste of Jerusalem.

I think this 'taste' was what brought Blake to abandon his unfinished *Vala* and envision the grand prophecies *Milton* and *Jerusalem*, both of which take as their prophetic goal the overcoming of Selfhood. *Milton* emphasises the individual journey, *Jerusalem* the universal one. Significantly both title pages are dated '1804'.

Blake's three-year stay near Hayley in Felpham (1800–03) was made arduous by Hayley's patronising intrusiveness as well as by a charge of sedition brought by a drunken soldier whom Blake had expelled from his garden. But there had also been extensive and gratifying new work on Milton, whose poetry Blake had revered since childhood. Evidently the total Felpham experience had prepared Blake for this crisis of 1804. In his letter to Hayley, Blake thanks Felpham, 'parent of Immortal Friendship', for 'the strength I now enjoy'. On the evidence of *Milton* the Immortal Friend was Los, divine poetic Imagination: Los 'enter'd into my soul' and 'I became One Man with him arising in my strength' (E 117).

Blake's task in *Milton* is to lead his poetic progenitor to purge the fallen aspects of his self and doctrine, and recover his fully human state 'Lest the Last Judgment come & find me unannihilate / And I be seiz'd & giv'n into the hands of my own Selfhood' (E 108). This stormy purgation will permit Milton to meet and reunite with his sixfold emanation Ololon, his much-tried three wives and three daughters, similarly purged. That's the 'plot' of the prophecy.

But its Preface sings a ringing song of war. Denouncing in one breath carnal war, commodified art, and Memory as opposed to Inspiration, Blake undertakes through *Milton* to build or re-build Jerusalem. *Milton* opens with the famous poem in which Blake asks for his 'Bow of burning gold' and 'Arrows of desire' so that by 'mental fight' he may 'build Jerusalem / In England's green & pleasant Land' (E 95). Then, in Miltonic tradition, he turns to his muse to provide the poetic argument: 'Say first! What mov'd Milton' to redeem his 'Sixfold Emanation . . . & himself perish?' The answer is 'A Bard's prophetic Song!' which Blake then offers verbatim over ten closely engraved plates that march to the refrain: 'Mark well my words! They are of your eternal salvation.' The Bard's Song is the story of Blake's 'mental fight' in Felpham, raised to universal prophetic proportions.

In *Milton* Blake uses his renewed 'strength I now enjoy' to imagine Milton's ensuing descent and his renunciation of 'Satan! My Spectre!' (E 139). Meanwhile Ololon, learning of Milton's self-sacrifice, decides to match him: 'Let us descend also, and let us give / Ourselves to death.' Jesus himself unites 'in one with Ololon', encouraging her to 'Watch over this World, and with your brooding wings, / Renew it to Eternal Life' (E 116). Divine forces are at work in both sexes to annihilate Selfhood and thus effect the vast spiritual apocalypse that Blake's prophecy records.

Blake wrote often about his battles with his own Selfhood or Spectre – which was clearly a fearsome and imperious power. One way of understanding his crisis of 1804 is to suppose that as he worked on *Milton* at Felpham, the older poet's errors stirred Blake to some fresh but as yet unwitting awareness of his own, and that the crisis itself was a delayed explosion of self-recognition and release. This process may be depicted in *Milton* when, in prophetic idiom, Milton himself drops from the sky over Felpham like a falling star and plunges into Blake's left foot. 'But I knew not that it was Milton, for man cannot know / What passes in his members till periods of Space & Time/Reveal the secrets of Eternity' (E 115).

Blake's fullest, most apocalyptic vision of Eternity appears in the closing plates of *Jerusalem*: 'Self was lost', the sexual garments have been cast away, and the wholly liberated Human Forms converse 'in Visionary forms dramatic . . . & every Word & Every Character/Was Human' (E 256–8). Not much in *Jerusalem* prepares us for this apocalyptic moment. But beginning some dozen plates earlier (pl. 86–) there is a telling point of pivot that I read as an extended and dramatised version of what led up to the 1804 crisis. Despite its momentous implications, this pointedly domestic igniting scene has a decidedly comic edge.

As Albion prepares to awaken from his long sleep of death, Enitharmon divides from Los and they begin to quarrel like Milton's Adam and Eve, Los scolding Enitharmon for refusing 'my Fibres of dominion' and she responding with some hauteur, 'This is Woman's World'. Los's Spectre looks on approvingly. 'Knowing himself the author of their divisions & shrinkings, gratified / At their contentions, he wiped his tears, he wash'd his visage', and he laid out his programme for the enhancement of 'Family feuds'. 'Thus joy'd the Spectre . . . eyeing Enitharmon . . . While Los stood at his anvil in wrath' (E 246–7).

This is wonderful theatre, and if we allow ourselves to imagine its relevance to the Blake household, we may recognise the three characters as William and Catherine Blake, with William's own 'spectrous Fiend', that 'iron-hearted tyrant' and 'enemy of conjugal love', provoking serious marital trouble.

But here comedy ends and apocalypse begins with a terrifying vision of consolidated error: 'no more the Masculine mingles / With the Feminine'; instead the (male) Sublime builds 'walls of separation' and the (female) Pathos weaves 'curtains of hiding secrecy'. Los thunders at his Spectre, who is 'a Fiend of Righteousness', and propounds Blake's own belief that each person is 'a Divine Member of the Divine Jesus'. The Spectre resists violently, building stupendous errors, but Los, 'undaunted furious', hammers them down until 'all [the Spectre's] pyramids were grains / Of sand & his pillars: dust on the flys wing'.

Seeing this, Enitharmon is filled with jealous foreboding: she fears she will be annihilated and 'Then thou wilt Create another Female according to thy Will.' But Los has no such thought. Having subdued the Spectre '& every Ratio of his Reason', he foresees an utterly different next step: 'Sexes must vanish & cease / To be, when Albion arises from his dread repose O lovely Enitharmon' (E 249–52).

We move quickly now. 'Time was Finished!' First Brittannia (England) awakes 'from Death on Albion's bosom'. Thinking she has murdered him, she cries guiltily 'behold ye the Jealous Wife!' But then Albion too wakes and arises 'speaking the Words of Eternity in Human Forms, in direful / Revolutions of Action & Passion'. Angrily he drives the misbehaving Zoas back to their proper roles and recalls the strayed Brittannia, who 'enter'd Albion's bosom rejoicing / Rejoicing in his indignation, adoring his wrathful rebuke' (E 254–5).

Given this moment of joint awakening into Eternity, both adoration and rebuke seem startlingly out of place. One would assume that Sexes would 'vanish & cease' by mutual self-abnegation, not by dominance and submission. But Blake's old Selfhood is still lurking here and can't quite let go the thought that even in Eternity reunion is a rightful victory of angry husband over jealous wife. In this spirit Blake adds the line 'She who adores not your frowns will only loathe your smiles.'

This line is familiar from Blake's marital grumblings elsewhere. 'The Woman that does not love your Frowns / Will never embrace your smiles' appears in a scratched-over and revised Notebook poem (E 475–7), probably written in 1803, the year Blake returned from Felpham. The opening stanza sets the scene: 'My Spectre around me night & day / Like a Wild beast guards my way. / My Emanation far within / Weeps incessantly for my sin.' And the rest of the lines describe a rousing fight, with the husband accusing the wife of jealously destroying his 'loves', and the wife vowing never to return to him unless she can have him all to herself.

In terms of Blake family feuds, we might think of the Spectre in this case as William's impulse to denounce Catherine's jealousy and extol his own masculine righteousness. But he knows this is a bad mistake, the work of that 'Wild beast', his Spectre.

This Notebook poem must reflect some period of sharp inner turmoil that preceded the crisis of 1804; Blake returned to its formulations in *Milton*, too. Just as the Spectre of the Notebook poem 'follows' the wife and 'scents thy footsteps in the snow / . . . Thro' the wintry hail and rain', so Milton follows his Emanation and 'hunts her footsteps thro' the snow & the wintry hail & rain' (E 131). But Blake's great lesson in *Milton* is that Milton *can* overcome his 'cruel' Spectre by an act of willing self-annihilation: 'her to redeem & himself perish'. We can trace a mental path here, running from the Notebook poem where the 'wild Beast' hovers around Blake 'night & day', to the crisis in 1804 when Blake 'entirely reduced' the 'tyrant', and then into the argument and even the texts of both *Milton* and *Jerusalem*. It culminates now with the awakening of Albion and Brittannia in the company of what looks like Blake's old Selfhood, which will surely have to be annihilated if Jerusalem is to be built.

Blake's Selfhood seems closely tied to sexuality. In the early 1790s Blake had famously argued that the doors of perception are opened by an improvement of sensual enjoyment. But two stanzas from 'My Spectre around me' argue explicitly for giving up 'Love'. In the first of these stanzas the husband says that until he turns from 'Female Love' he shall 'never worthy be / To Step into Eternity'. In the second he addresses his wife: 'Let us agree to give up Love / . . . Then shall we . . . see / The worlds of happy Eternity'. Nowhere here is 'Love' a liberating force; rather it enroots one in 'the Infernal Grove'. On the Notebook sheet Blake used to draft this poem, his stanzas encircle a drawing of Daphne metamorphosing into a tree.

Already in 'The Clod & the Pebble' (E 19) of the early 1790s Blake had observed that 'Love' can build either a Hell or a Heaven, depending on whether (as hard pebble) it 'seeketh only Self to please' or (as flexible clod) 'for another gives its ease'. I think Blake saw 'self-annihilation' as an ongoing process of loving 'ease'-giving that was both initiated and rewarded by visionary glimpses of Jerusalem. 'Love! Free as the mountain wind' (E 50) had once been the route to liberty; but by 1804 Blake had found that road pebble-bestrewn with the 'torments of Love & Jealousy' and dominated by the tyrannous Spectre.

Contributing to Blake's entanglement with self-seeking 'Love', I think, were those two related habits of thought I mentioned at the outset: the ones whereby men see women as some divided-off part of themselves (Adam's rib), and 'woman' as an object for man's possessive unveiling/apocalypse. I have argued that these habits occluded his vision. But never underestimate Blake.

Back in *Jerusalem*, the reunion of Albion and Brittannia – indignant husband and adoring wife – bodes ill for Eternity. No mutuality of annihilation or forgiveness: only the Emanation Brittannia might be said to offer self-sacrifice, whereas Albion's wrath is framed in the very words of 'My Spectre Around Me'. The building of Jerusalem seems badly stalled.

But 'O Glory! And O Delight!', as in Blake's crisis of 1804, Vision springs miraculously to the rescue. At the moment Brittannia enters Albion's bosom, Jesus appears 'in the likeness & similitude of Los' and Albion immediately confesses his flaw: 'O Lord what can I do! My Selfhood cruel / Marches against thee'. Jesus replies 'Fear not Albion', and explains the meaning of self-sacrifice: 'Man is Love: / As God is Love: every kindness to another is a little Death / In the Divine Image'. Profoundly moved, and at last fearing 'not for himself but for his Friend/Divine' – Albion chooses self-annihilation and throws himself 'into the Furnaces of affliction'.

This act of selflessness is utterly transformative, ushering in Blake's visionary four-fold Eternity as Albion sets about building Jerusalem in England's green and pleasant land: 'Awake, Awake Jerusalem! . . . For lo! The Night of Death is past and the Eternal Day / Appears upon our Hills'. Albion reaches into Infinitude and takes his bow, 'And the Bow is a Male & Female', and his arrows – those 'arrows of desire' from *Milton*, now renamed 'Arrows of Love'. Jerusalem indeed! Now the 'Spectre was Annihilate' and the sexual body's 'Husk & Covering' evaporated, 'revealing the lineaments of Man' (E 255–7).

In his letter of 1804 Blake had rejoiced at regaining 'the light I enjoyed in my youth', and in a beautiful passage of *Jerusalem* he amplified his concept of visionary light: in Eternity 'every particular Form gives forth or Emanates / Its own peculiar Light, & the Form is the Divine Vision / And the Light is his Garment. This is Jerusalem in every Man / A Tent & Tabernacle of Mutual Forgiveness Male & Female Clothings. / And Jerusalem is called Liberty among the Children of Albion' (E 203).

Jerusalem is the liberty to see 'the Infinite in all things' through garments that are actually 'Light' emanating from all the myriad human forms. What a lovely figure for a visionary universe: all lit from within, open to every human mind, protected (not enclosed) by a Tabernacle that hides no secret place of religion or sex but is rather a timeless shelter of Mutual Forgiveness.

I take 'Man' here to mean complete human, as when Blake grieves that 'The Feminine separates from the Masculine' and both from 'Man' (E 249). Still the concept of gender does remain, implicitly in the maleness of Jesus and explicitly in the bow that is 'a Male & Female', and of course in the male and female clothing. But the eternal forms are not 'men' or 'women'; they are human. There are no Emanations in the sense of female extrusions from the male (only light 'emanates'), nor is there sex in the mundane sense of 'pompous' penetration. Of course there is no Selfhood. Speech is not by words or (veiled) fictions or allegories, but by 'visionary forms dramatic'. Time and Space are not functions of Jupiter, but are created 'according to the wonders divine / Of Human Imagination'. Even 'Tree, Metal, Earth & Stone' are 'Human Forms identified . . . / Awakening into [Jesus'] Bosom in the Life of Immortality'. With this grand vista of shining, gender-free human forms, Blake's prophecy concludes: 'And I heard the Name of their Emanations: they are named Jerusalem.'

I want to believe that some strong version of this luminous vision was vouchsafed to Blake after his visit to the Truchsessian Gallery in 1804, when he 'was again enlightened' with the light of his youth and was 'really drunk with intellectual vision'. Certainly Blake came at this time to regard his Selfhood as the enemy of creative work and generous love, and strove both to act on this insight and to communicate it to the world through the twin labours of *Milton* and *Jerusalem*. Indeed, it was with these two prophecies – both, we recall, taking 1804 as their point of departure – that the word 'Selfhood' first entered Blake's poetic vocabulary.

Yet even if I am correct in thinking Blake's conjugal relations were implicated in his concept of Selfhood, I doubt that in 1804 he and Catherine gave up (sexual) 'Love' in the interests of Eternity. Yet just by confronting the 'pebble'-like tyrant and naming it 'Selfhood', he may have improved their marital peace. In a remarkable passage of self-revelation early in *Jerusalem*, Blake describes himself 'Trembling' at his prophetic task: 'O Saviour', he prays, 'Pour upon me thy spirit of meekness & love: / Annihilate the Selfhood in me' (E 147).

Notes

1. First printed in *Bulletin of the Midwest Language Association*, 6 (Spring 1973), 74–87.

2. Blackstone passage is from Book the First (Oxford, 1765), 442. Quip is Ray [Rachel] Strachey's, *The Cause* (London, 1928), 15.
3. See Nelson Hilton's ground-breaking study, *Literal Imagination: Blake's Vision of Words* (Berkeley: University of California Press, 1983), 127–46.
4. Biblical quotations follow the King James translation.
5. See BA:J. copy E, pl. 32.

27

Blake Moments

Janet Warner

There are moments in life, when, on reflection, you realise – *just then you were changed*. James Joyce may have called them *epiphanies*, but I call them 'Blake Moments', because with me they had to do with William Blake and my life as an academic and writer.

The first one occurred in my first year at university. I went to see my English professor to discuss an essay. He sat at his desk below the picture of an old, bearded man in a circle of light, who bent down while lightning forked from his fingers. I can still remember the way my heart seemed to stop. It was my idea of God (I was then devout).

'What is that picture?' I asked.

'That is the Ancient of Days. William Blake', said my professor. He seemed to expect me to know who Blake was, so I pretended I did. I went to my textbooks and looked up William Blake, but found only poems, no pictures. I could not understand a word of the longer poems, but the image of the Ancient of Days was burned into my mind.

It was a few years before I encountered Blake's art again. In the meantime, I had married, moved, and begun graduate studies. I was working on the modern novel. My English husband was interested in art. He took me to London to meet his parents and to see the museums and galleries.

London in the fall of 1957 was at its smoggiest. At the end of the day, fingernails would be grimy. Fogs were so dense one of our bus drivers had to ask a pedestrian to find the curb. London's great buildings, like St Paul's or the British Museum, were still coal black. They must have looked the same in Victorian times. The floors of the British Museum's manuscript room, where I went to see *Beowulf* and *The Canterbury Tales*, were highly polished and smelled of beeswax. However, it was at that extraordinary house of treasures, the Victoria and Albert Museum, that I had my second Blake Moment. Here was a small but powerful exhibition of work by Blake. And there was the Ancient of Days again. Suddenly I wanted to know more about William Blake.

I compiled a list of critical reading, and consulted a copy of Sir Geoffrey Keynes's text, just published by the Nonesuch Press. I was not up to the task. I needed a teacher.

Six years and two children later, a teacher presented himself. I had resumed my abandoned graduate studies and enrolled at the University of Toronto. There I took Northrop Frye's course on William Blake, and my education began in earnest.

Shy and bespectacled, Frye had a distinctive way of teaching. He would ask a question and wait for an answer. And wait. And wait some more. The suspense would be unbearable, but he would not speak. Eventually, someone would respond, just to break the silence. No matter how trivial the reply, Frye could make something of it. (I once tried this technique in a seminar but could not hold out long enough.)

We had to write a paper and were encouraged to look at the Blake facsimiles in the library. This, I think, was the turning point of my academic life. I held in my hands the Trianon Press Facsimile of *America*. I opened it and felt elated. The colours, the designs, the rhythm of the swirling lines were like music. I decided to write on the designs of *America*, relating them to the text. Of course, I looked at all the other available facsimiles. (In the months and years to follow, I saw original copies of Blake's Illuminated Books in most of the world's great museums and libraries, yet the thrill of seeing for the first time that facsimile of *America* was unforgettable.)

My paper on *America* raised questions in my mind that influenced the path of my subsequent career in Blake studies. Why did Blake repeat his motifs so often? Why did he imitate the poses of Greek art? Why did he and other artists 'borrow'? Grappling with these questions resulted in the research, travels, conferences and publications that made up my career as an academic. I remain convinced that Blake used his repeated visual images for symbolic meanings, though I probably would not be so adamant these days.

I was fortunate that the late David V. Erdman, noted American scholar and editor, took an interest in my work and gave me by correspondence what amounted to a short course in editing. There were no e-mails or computers in those days (unless someone in your university was very advanced in new technology). I used an electric typewriter, carbons, and did much cutting and pasting with scissors and sticky tape. When I could afford it, I hired a typist for a final draft.

Erdman and John E. Grant edited *Blake's Visionary Forms Dramatic* (1970), a collection devoted to Blake's pictorial language. Here my first published article 'Blake's Use of Gesture' appeared. Was seeing the publication a Blake Moment? No, the moment occurred months before, while I was preparing the essay. Both Erdman and Grant wielded wicked pens when they criticised. Perhaps they were harder on women than men, I was never sure.

They told me my organisation was all wrong. Chronological would not do. I had to organise in categories. I had about four days to get the manuscript mailed back to them.

The only solution was to move away from my husband and young children and seclude myself in an absent friend's apartment. Here I worked uninterrupted (bliss for a young mother) around the clock for three days, drinking coffee and eating tomato sandwiches. I re-typed, cut and pasted. There was not time to type a clean final draft. The mailed manuscript looked like a collage.

Erdman wrote, 'What a mess! But it is very fine now.' That was a Blake Moment.

I was in Cambridge in 1973 at the start of my first sabbatical, when I was invited to Peterhouse to attend a dinner in honour of Sir Geoffrey Keynes. (I had contributed an article to a Festschrift for Keynes, edited by Morton D. Paley and Michael Phillips, 1973.)

Sir Geoffrey was eminent in medicine, bibliography, and editing. He was a famous surgeon who had pioneered the use of blood transfusion and rational surgery for breast cancer. He was younger brother of John Maynard Keynes, the economist, had climbed with Mallory (before Everest), and had lodged with Virginia Stephen (Woolf) and her brother Adrian, saving her life after a suicide attempt. He had served in two wars, becoming a Senior Surgeon at Bart's and Acting Air Vice-Marshall, eventually knighted for surgical distinction. On top of all this, he published a Blake bibliography in 1921 and a three-volume edition of Blake's writings in 1925, pioneering the rediscovery of Blake for the twentieth century. He had known all the Bloomsbury group and many prominent writers and artists of the early twentieth century, including Rupert Brooke.

A formal dinner at a Cambridge College for such a man was an exciting event for me. I had been ill just before I came and was very thin, so what to wear was important. I chose a long gown with a pattern of red and cream flowers and small cape sleeves – I can see it still – and a silk fringed shawl, so popular in the seventies. The Tudor dining-hall was dimly lit, and four wine glasses sparkled at each table setting. The company was as heady as the wine: here I met Sir Geoffrey and members of his family, members of the Board of The William Blake Trust, and British scholars and curators whose work I had read. Seated next to me was a charming, white-haired man, Dr A.N.L. Munby, Librarian of King's. He told me gossip about Virginia and Leonard Woolf, and invited me to see King's copy of the *Songs of Innocence and of Experience*, which had belonged to E.M Forster, whom he called Morgan.

It was another Blake Moment. This is the copy with gold leaf designs around each poem. Each page glows. I was moved many years later when one of its designs was chosen as the cover of my novel on William and Catherine, *Other Sorrows, Other Joys* (St Martin's Press, 2003).

Dr Munby became my friend. He showed me other treasures of King's library, including the notebook of Sir Isaac Newton. Blake would have appreciated that irony.

One day, Dr Munby said to me, 'Geoffrey Keynes would like to see you at Lammas House.'

I was all nerves. I had been introduced at the Peterhouse dinner, but this was different. Tea at Lammas House! It was a lovely, apricot coloured house near Cambridge.

It was full of threadbare Persian carpets, worn chintz sofas and shining hardwood floors. Paintings by Vanessa Bell and Duncan Grant hung on the walls.

Sir Geoffrey liked to give people little tests. His library held a large oak cabinet, with narrow drawers for storing prints. From a drawer, he drew a large engraving.

'What do you think this is?' he asked. I can't remember my response, but the answer was not important to him. He knew no one was going to get it right. I had been warned by David Erdman that Sir Geoffrey was competitive: one had better not beat him at croquet on his own lawn.

Sir Geoffrey was a tall, distinguished-looking man, still handsome at eighty-six. His wife, Margaret, was a Darwin. She must have grown weary making tea for the stream of Blake scholars who made their way to Lammas House. I was to visit twice more over the years.

Was it Margaret who put me in mind of Catherine Blake? On the wall of the entrance hall in Lammas House was a framed tapestry called *Two Hares in Long Grass*. Margaret said it was done by Catherine for Mrs Butts. I wondered then, and for many years after, what it must have been like to be the wife of such a singular man. When I came to write my novel about Blake and his wife, I had read many impressions of Kate, all written by men. How could anyone have been such a paragon? The perfect wife, according to the Victorian critics. Then why all that poetry about the anguish of jealousy, I wondered. And so a character, not at all the perfect wife, emerged in my mind, and the novel took shape. I had to retire, however, before I wrote it.

Perhaps I can call the decision to sit down and write the first paragraphs of this novel a Blake Moment. I had taken early retirement and we had moved to rural British Columbia from Toronto, Ontario, where I had taught at Glendon College, York University for 23 years. I found it a challenge to fulfil the roles of wife and mother and still manage an academic career. The writing of poetry or fiction was not possible for me while I produced scholarly articles: it seemed to use the same energy. In retirement, however, I had the room of my own and the 'unearned' income that Virginia Woolf so clearly saw as necessary for women to write fiction.

I am also of the generation of women liberated by Betty Friedan. When I was a graduate student, an eminent Shakespeare professor said to me, 'Why aren't you home looking after your husband?' Earlier, the Dean of

Women at another university had told me, 'A woman should not expect to get anywhere in academic life.' *Well*, I thought, *you did!* Now I realise what she had to endure, and what she gave up – marriage, motherhood – to get where she was. In my own case, I had that six-year pause for marriage and motherhood before I resumed graduate studies. I was one of the first 'mature students', as we were called, at the University of Toronto, though becoming a female academic (and the challenges of departmental life) is not my subject here.

What a liberation a novel was! I tried hard to get most details right – but, well, why not invent a lover for Kate and one for William? Why not give her a few feminist ideas she may have garnered from Mary Wollstonecraft? Why not give Mr and Mrs Butts some children? It is a novel.

However, is fictional biography quite ethical? 'Parasitical', one male critic said (*San Francisco Chronicle*, December 2003). It interests me that the two harshest critics I have had are men. (I do not mean to imply that men have not been also encouraging and admiring.) Women reviewers are often enthusiastic and see the story as I intended – the examination of the role of a spirited eighteenth-century woman in a marriage to a difficult man (for example Bernadette Murphy, *The Los Angeles Times*, March 2004). One American male reviewer was outraged, 'Too much Janet Warner and not enough Catherine Blake!' he stormed, reviewing the book as if it were a real biography and plenty of information existed on Catherine Blake (*Books in Canada*, April/May 2004). It was a wilful misreading, and I had run into this sort of thing before, in academe (for example, Robert Gleckner's review of my *William Blake and the Language of Art*, *BQ*, 1987). Sometimes there is a tone, a kind of condescension, in the criticism of a male critic towards a female writer. Not for nothing did J.K. Rowling use her initials when submitting her Harry Potter proposals, even in the modern age. If I had it to do over again, I would have been J.A. Warner.

Back to Blake Moments. A long time ago in a small office in the Metropolitan Museum of Art, overlooking Central Park, I held the only coloured copy of *Jerusalem* in my hands, turning its magical gilded pages. It was on exhibit there, before Paul Mellon gave it to Yale, and I was a friend of the young curator who allowed me to study it. He took *Jerusalem* from the showcase just for me. This was a different experience from the time I examined *Milton* at the New York Public Library, and the curator would not let me turn the pages myself, but did so for me with white-gloved hands.

I recall, too, the three weeks I spent one summer in the Print Room of the British Museum, daily going through large red leather boxes of Blake's watercolour designs for Edward Young's *Night Thoughts*. In those days, the pages were not encased in plastic. Not too many people had even seen them. So much Blake in such a short time makes one a little dizzy.

There was something dizzying, too, about the sixties and seventies as a time to be studying and teaching Blake.

'Blake Power' said a little plastic badge I acquired – which managed to convey the literary message and also remind one of the civil rights movement in the United States. The Beatles were abroad in the land, Allen Ginsberg's *Howl* (1956) and *America* provided Blakean background for the summer of love in 1967, when young people felt they were watching the dawning of a new age.

Imagination and liberty (political and sexual) were on our minds: the Romantic poets were In – especially Blake, who must surely have been on *something*, like Coleridge and De Quincy? Young men who objected to the war in Vietnam came to study at Canadian universities, and called their professors by their first names. Women's skirts were either mini or flowing and both women and men wore long hair. Hair was In, as the musical will still remind us. I remember my friend the young Blake bibliographer, G.E. Bentley Jr, striding across the University of Toronto campus, long fair hair and black cape billowing in the wind. His petite wife, Beth (now Dr E.B. Bentley) always wore a flower in her hair.

Odd memories collect over the years – snapshots to enjoy in my mind's eye of the road not taken. A sign in a village on the Isle of Wight read: *Blake and Sons, Printers*. I always meant to call in. Blake's cottage in Felpham, Sussex, is still lived in, well-kept. I did not have the courage to knock on the door. There was a tiny print shop near Leicester Square, going out of business, where I bought for a few shillings an old engraving of the likeness of John Milton, not, alas, by Blake.

The last time I visited Lammas House, in 1980, Margaret Keynes had died and Sir Geoffrey was in his nineties, still energetic and hospitable. As I stood up to take my leave, he asked me suddenly, 'May I kiss you goodbye?'

Do you know the poem by Leigh Hunt, *Jenny Kissed Me?*

> Jenny kissed me when we met,
> Jumping from the chair she sat in:
> Time, you thief, who love to get
> Sweets into your list, put that in:
> Say I'm weary, say I'm sad,
> Say that health and wealth have missed me,
> Say I'm growing old, but add,
> Jenny kissed me.

Well, Geoffrey kissed me!
I call that a Blake Moment.

Like Blake's golden thread, my Blake Moments lead me to reflections on what it meant to be a female scholar in the seventies and eighties. At the time, a woman did not always realise a patriarchal system was influencing her life, but the kindness of (male) department heads, or supervising professors, or periodical editors, or eminent scholars, was central to her success. When I was an undergraduate, there were no female professors in the English Department at the University of British Columbia. Later, there were few female role models in the Blake world, except perhaps Kathleen Raine, a lone genius. One had to seek approval or acceptance from male colleagues: some were father figures, some were younger than yourself.

One had the feminine wish to please, and the contradictory impulse to independence. Sometimes you knew in your heart the criticism of an editor was based on his attitude to you as a woman, and not your work. There might be jealousy involved – or quite the opposite, sexual attraction. In the most complicated case, you might be married to a fellow scholar – what a tightrope that was! Probably it still is.

However, there has been a wonderful change, and patriarchal attitudes have at least been brought to consciousness, and real efforts have been made in the institutions – at least in North America – to set things right. Women like me can see with some satisfaction that the field is a little clearer now for younger players.

28
Blake, Sex and Women Revisited

Brenda Webster

When Helen asked me to write something about Blake for her new anthology, I was reluctant; I had been away from the field too long – 25 years. Then I read a draft of Addie Stephen's fascinating essay about what happened when she tried to live out Blake's visions of sexual sharing. Her essay could have been written to illustrate my belief that Blake is a dangerous sexual prophet for women. It made me think that there might be good reasons for revisiting Blake's attitudes towards women and sexuality – a subject I had written about at length in my 1983 book *Blake's Prophetic Psychology*.

Visions of the Daughters of Albion could be called the Ur text of sexual generosity. It is easy to see why it might appeal to a feminist critic. The chief woman character, Oothoon, is very strong and preaches what seems to be a doctrine of mutually free love to her wimpy lover. However, what is really involved is a one-sided male fantasy. Oothoon offers to net girls of 'furious gold' and 'mild silver' and watch him while he enjoys them 'in lovely copulation' (E 49). There is no suggestion of reciprocity. Theotormon, the semi-impotent hero, is furiously jealous and rages at Oothoon abusively after she has been raped. Generosity is all on one side: hers.

Still critics at the time I was writing persisted in seeing the poem as somehow in favour of women's rights. One of the most influential Blake scholars, David Erdman, thought the poem's argument derived from Mary Wollstonecraft's *Vindication of the Rights of Woman* (1792) – and therefore was implicitly feminist.[1] But the emotional force of the two works is entirely different. Blake pictures Oothoon as completely benevolent and totally available. Wollstonecraft points out that 'the end, the grand end of [women's] exertions should be to unfold their own faculties'.[2] Far from seeing woman as devoted to Blake's ideal of 'happy, happy love' (E 49), she wanted to substitute equality based on reason for women's 'sexual character' as a gratifier of man.

Blake's fantasy of sexual gratification in *Visions* is vital to understanding his attitude towards woman on yet another level. The sexually gratifying

254

woman is imagined as a sexually permissive mother. This is important, not to prove a Freudian point, but because his attitude towards women seems saturated with conflicted feelings toward a mothering figure. He is interested in his female characters primarily for their role in triangular situations reminiscent of the Oedipal triangle of mother, father, son. In *Visions*, Oothoon is raped by an older man while on her way to give herself to a young lover. Though she is not literally Blake's mother or sister, Blake suggests the mother-son relationship in several ways. One of the clearest of these is in his opening illustrations.

The opening illustration of Oothoon is developed from an engraving by Vien of a procuress holding a small cupid by the wings. Blake adapts the figures but gives them an opposite meaning. His naked woman lifting full breasts and kissing a small male figure leaping from a flower suggests both the maternal nature and the special non-possessive quality of Oothoon's love, which combines generosity and lack of restraint. The next illustration replaces the idealised view of mother and child with sexual fantasies. The mother-son theme continues in the image of a small, naked male angel standing in the lap of a woman riding a cloud horse. The sexual nature of the embrace between woman and small angel is clearly shown by the penis and testicles Blake has drawn emerging between the woman's legs where we should expect the neck and head of her cloud mount. In some versions, Blake has added a beak or bill to the penis, which seems equivalent to biting teeth in its potential to injure the maternal body.

In the illustration, Blake's images of mother and child are untroubled by any hint of a rival. The fantasy seems to be of undisputed possession of the mother. Blake's description of Oothoon raped by a paternal tyrant fits such an assumption of the mother's resistance to the father. However, Theotormon struggles in the poem with the fact that Oothoon doesn't regret the rape. Moreover she is aroused by it. Her arousal represents the side of parental love-making that the child denies because it signifies the mother's unfaithfulness to him. This idea of unfaithfulness makes emotional sense of Theotormon's (the other man's) extreme jealousy and his angry wish to punish Oothoon which is expressed in sexualised imagery. Blake makes Oothoon collaborate in Theotormon's ambivalent wish to punish and possess her by having her writhe naked, calling on his eagles to penetrate her flesh.

Blake doesn't just use visual images to suggest a young boy's fantasies about his mother and sexuality. In presenting Theotormon's reaction to the rape, Blake uses imagery that suggests a young child soiling his pants in a situation that arouses impotent rage. Theotormon's first act after the rape is to surround Oothoon and Bromion with 'black jealous waters' (E 45). If this isn't quite clear in context, it becomes clearer if we remember Blake's earlier portrayal of the serpent Envy, who expresses its jealousy by discharging a river of filth. From Blake's imagery one might infer his own repressed memory of such a reaction, but whatever the source of his insight, as an artist Blake is able to connect Theotormon's childishly ineffectual rage with the imagery that best expresses it.

Blake's imagery not only evokes a young child's reactions to parental sex at a time when his only weapon is his own excrement, but he also connects this reaction to other psychological themes typical of the child's perceptions. For instance, the rape's violent sadism suggests a child's perception of intercourse. Blake depicts Theotormon as being caught in the emotions of this stage, (hating the sadistic Bromion) but unable to fight back successfully, Theotormon turns his anger against himself (in one illustration he whips himself) and against Oothoon. Oothoon urges him to give up his anger and masochism and enjoy her. Like a mother choosing her son's wife, she reminds him she would gladly procure women for his pleasure. In a series of monologues she acts like a psychoanalyst encouraging him to dredge up his forbidden sexual desires – the forbidden 'joys of old', here again the imagery turns to childhood as she reminds him of 'Infancy, fearless, lustful, happy! Nestling for delight / in laps of pleasure' (E 48). But instead of helping him give up his incestuous wishes like a psychoanalyst, she urges him to act on them and free himself from his sense of failure. Is this really such a good idea?

What Blake seems to be doing is evoking a set of early experiences of despair and rivalry and then imagining the woman – in the past, the mother – who could, by her total generosity, make up for what he had suffered. When this is understood, it is easy to see how far Blake is from portraying equality between the sexes. His male characters are no more capable of mature love than a man in real life jealously fixated on his mother.

Subsequent prophecies reinforce the interpretation of Oedipal drama in *Visions* and show what a pervasive and haunting theme it was for Blake. In *America*, the hero Orc rapes his sister – committing the incest that Theotormon failed to do – while young patriots overthrow the paternal tyrant. In still later prophecies, we read how Orc was originally chained to a rock by his father after he saw the boy 'embracing his bright mother' and discerned that Orc 'plotted his death' (E 340).

When I read the early revolutionary prophecies as an adolescent, I too fell under Blake's spell – the overthrowing of tyrants and freeing of sexuality was deeply appealing. Later as an adult, I found a whole other side – the objective religious and political meanings laid out by critics like Frye and Erdman. It took many years of learning about Blake's cosmologies and myth, his cycles, his system, before I was ready to go back and look at what first attracted me – his sensitivity to the emotions of the child and the outcast, his defence of free sexuality. Like the occasional feminist critic in the 1970s who mentioned Blake approvingly, I expected to find a man in favour of a truly liberated sexuality and equality.

As I struggled to make sense of his obscure and difficult Prophecies, I noticed that Blake's attitudes towards women and sex changed quite radically during his life – they became more rather than less hostile. His attitude toward woman fell into roughly two stages and a transition. In the first stage of the revolutionary prophecies, he sees women and sexuality as a source of salvation and continually imagines his heroes liberating females from paternal tyrants. Though even in this early work, where he has a more positive use for women, there is a strong undercurrent of hostility and fear which is important to recognise if you want to understand his later attitudes. In mid-life, during the decade long writing of *Vala*, he goes through a transitional phase in which he becomes increasingly negative toward sexuality. As he Christianises the work in rewriting, he comes to see woman as responsible for the Fall and in the form of 'The Female Will' he blames her for all the world's evils. His negative images of women become ever more extreme and bizarre. The only positive images of women are totally weak females sequestered in Beulah. Finally, in his late Christian prophecies, *Milton* and *Jerusalem*, he suggests that the female should cease even to exist independently and become reabsorbed into the body of man where she belongs. This is in effect Blake's final solution.

Blake's obsession with incest has an unfortunate effect on his attitude toward women. Because he is obsessed with the overthrow of paternal rivals, he feels guilty and begins to blame women for causing trouble between fathers and sons. Another reason for Blake's increasingly negative attitude is that his demands on women as nurturers and lovers are so total – it wouldn't be unfair to call them infantile – that he can't help imagining them as enraged and wanting revenge. After *Vala*, his fantasies about what bad women do to men become more and more violent and bizarre. In drafts we see him giving way to totally negative fantasies: women destroy men's bodies, unweave them on their looms, drain them in sex and appropriate their penises. Blake becomes increasingly certain that any attempt by men to satisfy basic needs for food and sex will have horrible consequences: if they want food, they are eaten, if they want sex they are castrated. In the end Blake needs Christ to help him control his imagined women. Within a Christian structure he can reintroduce his idea of a completely giving woman – one who is so totally programmed that in Beulah, she even dies smiling every winter, to be reborn as a virgin every spring. This realm is carefully separated from the male world of creation. Man drops into Beulah only temporarily for a rest cure before continuing his virile forward progress 'in the Bosom of the father' (E 130). All in all, Blake's concept of Beulah doesn't really solve anything. It seems impossible for Blake to imagine real men and women coexisting in a state of peace. Outside of Beulah, his evil women characters split off, doubling and tripling as though he can't control their rampant proliferation. Their acts are increasingly fearful. In *Jerusalem* for example, he has them dancing in the flayed skins of their victims, waving the men's severed organs.

Blake's view of male-female relationships hasn't been clear to readers partly because it is at first contradicted by his enormous sensitivity to feminine traits such as tenderness and maternal care. On the one hand they belong to the ideal Female and help her care for the Male Genius; on the other hand, the poet can incorporate and use them in creation and drawing close to other men. In this later view Blake anticipates the modern recognition of bisexuality and its importance for creativity. But Blake did not extend the right to express traits of the opposite sex to his females. When they do express them, they become threatening Female Wills and must be destroyed.

Blake's rhetoric too can distract readers from seeing the aggressive or selfish nature of his fantasies. Some early critics however, clearly picked up on his misogyny. Before it was taboo to say such things, a male critic – and I don't think it was an accident that most Blake critics were originally male – could admit satisfaction with Blake's view of women. After telling us that Blake views woman's chief attribute as 'deceit' Bernard Blackstone goes on to say that she is consoled for her loss of delight in life 'by the mysteries of religion, by the pomp and ceremonies which act so efficiently on her weaker intelligence. But man' he adds, 'has no such consolation', that is, 'if he is virile . . .'[3] His remarks are embarrassing in their forthrightness, but I think he has correctly caught Blake's anger at woman's power and his wish that she be properly subservient.

Male critics who are consciously more benign towards women may still respond to Blake's underlying fantasies without being quite aware of it. Ten years after Blackstone, Jean Hagstrum misreads the line: 'In Beulah every female delights to give her maiden to her husband', thinking that maiden here means maidenhead.[4] The point of the line is that Blake's ideal female freely provides her husband with other women as Oothoon does in *Visions*. Hagstrum concludes his essay with an odd tone of mixed apology and male congratulation, which suggests that at some level he understood very well what Blake had in mind: 'Some modern women may have much to object to in Blake's latest thought about the relation of the sexes. But it is hard to believe that *l'homme moyen sensuel* would reject the hearty bread and full-bodied wine the late Blake is offering him.'[5]

I had hoped that my attempt to deal with emotions in Blake's work would arouse some interest in the many critics using other approaches. I've always felt there was something to gain from a diversity of approaches to Blake's work. But perhaps because I spoke bluntly, didn't follow any established reading and investigated what seemed to be various critical lapses, critics were unreceptive. Then too, if Blake was really expressing hatred and fear of murderous females, where did that leave the approving critic? Morton Paley, to whose journal *Blake Studies* I submitted three of my early chapters, rejected them outright with the statement that psychoanalysis has *nothing* to teach us about Blake. I no longer believe in Freudian analysis as a cure, nor am I now a literary critic – I write novels – but I still believe that Freud has a lot to teach us about emotions. Some of the early responses to my Blake book were on the level of a marital spat. One reader suggested my interpretations derived from Blake-envy. Similarly Norman Jeffares the eminent Yeats biographer, though recommending publication of an earlier book of mine to the editor at Stanford, quipped that 'your author has sex on the brain – and that's not where a woman should have it'. As a product of the repressive fifties, I accepted being talked down to at the time. But after mid-life changes – a good, new marriage, a new career as a writer – I allowed my angry feelings to surface. I hadn't been nicely treated.

Over a decade later I heard Macmillan was putting out a Blake case book featuring writing of the last twenty years and wanted my essay, 'Blake, Sex and Women'. I was very pleased. It felt a bit as if I were being resurrected. My admittedly somewhat vindictive pleasure was all the greater when I found myself and my work placed in a context which reveals the old boy's club atmosphere in early Blake studies. The editor, David Punter, speaks of the 'protective attitude certain critics have had towards their textual "master" who is often their mentor as well'.[6] Indeed this is what one finds in the two journals, Morton Paley's *Blake Studies* and *Blake: an Illustrated Quarterly*. Punter concludes in a genteel understatement: 'It is tempting to say that the old nineteenth-century sense of a coterie remains.'[7] Punter's selection includes the diversity that wasn't in evidence in my day. There are many stimulating views: Marxist, Feminist, Structuralist – and not just one but two opposed psychoanalytic readings. However, there are still fewer women represented than men – only two out of ten. And it was disappointing to find old views resurfacing in new clothes. Jean Hagstrum – the full-bodied wine enthusiast – under cover of a psychoanalytic reading denies the misogyny I hoped I'd made evident and reintroduces the idea that Blake's attitudes towards women are benign: as Punter puts it Hagstrum believes 'there is a benevolent Blake who . . . knowingly represented perversions and problems, and was in the end if you read him right, a believer in the happy possibilities of sexual love, marriage and family'.[8] No one wishes this were true more than I do. But though I love and admire many aspects of Blake's genius, I'm afraid it simply won't work to see him as a prophet-guide to improved sexual relations. Still, it's good that the conversation continues so vigorously. For, as Blake so brilliantly put it, 'opposition is true friendship' (E 41).

Notes

1. Erdman, David V., *Blake: Prophet Against Empire* (New York: Anchor Book, 1969), 228.

2. *Vindication* . . . (Harmondsworth: Penguin, 1975), 109.
3. Blackstone, *English Blake* (Hamden, CT: Archon Books, 1966), 294.
4. Hagstrum, 'Babylon Revisited, or the Story of Luvah and Vala', in Stuart Curran and Joseph Wittreich (eds), *Blake's Sublime Allegory* (Madison: University of Wisconsin Press, 1973), 105.
5. Ibid., 118.
6. *William Blake: Contemporary Critical Essays* (Basingstoke: Macmillan, 1996), 8.
7. Ibid., 8.
8. Ibid., 9.

29
The Strange Difference of Female 'Experience'

Susan J. Wolfson

The measures of Blake in the critique of gender have swung widely, partly by force of his own conflicts, partly from the conflicting (sometimes unrecognised) investments of his critics. Modern arguments on gender are intimately tied to Blake's, in no small part, because Blake's are so extravagant. In the first blush of enthusiasm for the railer against repression and the champion of sexuality without shame, Blake was the universal liberator. Then, against the grain of a male-clubbed critical enthusiasm, feminist critics had second thoughts about some attendant sexism and misogyny. Especially in Blake's later visions, systems of male privilege and prejudice were emphatic: 'Woman is the Emanation of Man she has No Will of her own There is no such Thing in Eternity as a Female Will.'[1] Tracking her course on this road of excess, and noting the typecasting of female heroes as victims and agental females as monsters, Alicia Ostriker had to resort to an old romance strategy, splitting Blake into 'ally' and 'enemy'.[2] The sharpest polemic has issued from our convener Helen Bruder, armed from the archive of 'seriously neglected contemporary discourses' for a run at the male-dominated critical establishment.[3] Conceding this trouble, I'm interested in the emergence from 1789 to 1794 – from *Songs of Innocence* to the double-bound *Songs of Innocence and of Experience* – of female sexuality as a Blakean metafigure for the complexities, and sometimes outright contradictions, of reading 'experience'. This gendering involves ambiguities that might radiate into ironies, but which remain sufficiently indeterminate in agency and effect to abide as signs of what Blake was compelled to figure, without figuring out.

If Blake is the Poet Laureate of contraries, the crux for his readers is the recurrence of female sexual innocence as a negative figure and sexual experience as liberation. Thus the revolution-charged cries of 'free love', the visionary yearning of rape-victim Oothoon. This Blake is the celebrity of my youth, the 1960s (that happy interval of sexual freedom between the advent of birth control and the advent of AIDS). Yet it is telling that one of the strongest voices of sexual liberation back then was 'The Playboy

Philosophy'. It championed liberation (along with birth control and abortion) because it made women more available to men; and it was collated, in *Playboy* cartoon humor, with a routine misogyny about women (usually over 30) whose lust was incommensurate with their attractiveness. In Blake's version, the fearful female singer of *The Angel*, armed 'with ten thousand shields and spears', finds no takers after her hot youth.[4]

Yet in the world before birth-control, when a pregnant girl could be disowned by her family, jilted by her impregnator, and shunned by society, defence was no pathology. It was vital safety and security. When Wollstonecraft berated female 'innocence', she did not mean sexual knowledge; she meant mental development: 'when the epithet is applied to men, or women, it is but a civil term for weakness'.[5] *Innocence* is *in-noxious*, doing no harm. It's a negation of agency that to Wollstonecraft spells incapacity. Experience *ex-periri* (from the attempt) is the trial from which the self develops moral capacity and strength: and it matters that *periri* is cognate to *peril*.

And for women, the peril is equivalent to sexual experience. While STD could strike both sexes, the (frequently fatal, as for Wollstonecraft) consequence of unmarried pregnancy, and the social death sentence, is gender-specific. Free love was not free for females. Nothing spells this difference more than the tradition of *carpe diem*. 'Gather ye rosebuds while ye may / Old Time is still a-flying', was the way Herrick put it in 1648, and Marvell took that ball and ran with it 30 years later in his extravagant seduction, *To His Coy Mistress*. This suitor's use of 'coy' discredits hesitation into the art of female flirtation, to be matched with male arts of poetic argument. Like the Playboy philosophy, *carpe diem* is a man's discourse. Women don't write *carpe diem*. They tend to invocations to fidelity, because after the seized day may ensue months of pregnancy and then a life of social death, should the suitor prove false (or the real death that was the risk of childbearing).

Blake's gender marking of experience ripples the rhetorical indeterminacy of the most complex and elusive poem in the 1789 *Songs of Innocence: The Little Girl Lost*. Its two-stanza proem is the story we hear often in these songs: some lass is under a grave death sentence, and liberation will turn her desert into a garden. This is the visionary playcard – rising from the grave, from isolation to union, from barrenness to fertility – that frames the fable of lassie Lyca. The tradition-laden (especially Miltonic) signposts of *wanderd* and *wild* that mark her adventure seem posed to embarrass an experienced reader with interpretive overdrive: these are the controls on anyone's rebellion against parental, especially maternal, policing of sexuality. The mother in the head must be put to sleep so the 'virgin' can awake to something new.

But the puzzle that fissures Blake's fabling is the question of whether Lyca is lost only to maternal manacling, or is experientially lost – truly in peril. The narrative, for all its allegorical accessorising, refuses to settle the question. When 'beasts of prey / Come from caverns deep' to view 'the maid asleep', we may sense a predatory potential. And yet the beasts act less like predators than playmates: the kingly lion 'gambold round / O'er the hallowd ground' that the virgin seemingly commands; 'Leopards, tigers play'; the old lion bows and his 'eyes of flame' are transformed into jewels, 'Ruby tears'. The lioness seems a new den-mother of this veneration, undressing Lyca's former virginal life, and bringing her into a new cave home. Blake's song ultimately echoes its reader: is Lyca's danger the product of a reader's mind-forged manacling? Or does an experienced reader, as in so many of *Songs of Innocence*, discern dangers Lyca cannot? Does our literacy penetrate the charade of play and reverence in her seduction? Or, to wax psychoanalytic, are Lyca's repressed desires being discovered? *Lyca* (little she-wolf) may signify affinity with the beasts; she exercises agency (wanders, wills her sleep); 'Do father, mother weep' hovers between interrogative and imperative (do they weep? let 'em!). No wonder Blake moved this song into *Experience* – by force not just of Lyca's trial, but of the uncertain shimmer of her tale, especially in differentials of gender: is this more a trial for the female reader than the male?

Such uncertainty binds *The Book of Thel* (1789–91), where the passage from innocence to experience is marked both as a general instruction in transience and mortality, and as a gendered induction of the virgin into sexual experience and female socialisation. 'O virgin know'st thou not . . .' Thel hears, in an equation of her ignorance with sexual inexperience. Then, in the heart of her unknowing innocence, she is tutored in the foundational requirements of female self-sacrifice, all gentled as a girl's garden of verses. Where Marvell's *carpe diem* seducer darkly jokes that all other suits resisted, 'worms shall try / That long preserved virginity: / And your quaint honour turn to dust' (27–9), Blake tempers this into the eco-knowledge that everyone is 'food for worms' in nature's great cycle.

Yet even with this tempering, Blake does not hesitate to cast the fearful virgin as a hysteric, fleeing mortality, sexuality, mature life itself – and, as in *The Little Girl Lost*, allows the narrative arc to cast an interrogative rhetoric. How much does the sexual logic of *The Book of Thel* require an endorsement of culture's book of female self-sacrifice? Might Thel's hysteria be a creditable intuition? Readers who too quickly reduce Thel's problems 'to those of consciousness only', Bruder argues, discount the insight about 'the functioning of patriarchy and its justificatory ideologies'.[6] Thus Harold Bloom summarily condemns Thel by the 'law of Blake's dialectic': if 'where man is not, nature is barren', 'Thel has refused to become man'.[7] This manful critique bloomed in the liberal 1960s before the advent of (what was then called) the Women's Liberation Movement. Forty years on, it might get a feminist endorsement: Thel has refused to become what male culture prescribes.

This is the puzzle of plate 2, where a woman at the margin looks blankly at a scene of a naked man, reaching from swirling flowers at the waist of a woman: are her arms thrown up in alarm or ecstasy?[8] This is surely the crux of how to read *Thel's* fourth and last chapter. Its panorama of lurid Gothicism is usually attributed to Thel's hysteria, her mind forging 'the secrets of the land unknown' (the binary of her virginity, a hollow pit host to corpses and graves), in a vision that proves too much.[9] Yet it is at this crux that Blake's rhetoric wavers most. The cry (erased in copies I and J, but kept in N) that would level question with exclamation – 'Why a tender curb upon the youthful burning boy! / Why a little curtain of flesh on the bed of our desire?' (as if Thel herself were the enemy) – sees a protest against any dousing of youthful heat. But the discursive slide from *boy* to *our* exposes the male investment. A female answer might be unveiled in the Virgin's vision of sexual experience as a world where 'a thousand fighting men in ambush lie', of a peril for women in which male aggression (so Rajan proposes) 'might just as well refer to war as to sex'.[10]

It is brave of Blake, no less politically than rhetorically, to leave open the question of whether, for a female visionary, this reticence is pointlessly hysterical or pointedly self-protecting. *The Marriage of Heaven and Hell* (1793) stays pretty close to the man's book: in 'The Voice of the Devil' Blake proposes, 'Man has no Body distinct from his Soul' (4), with the proto-*Playboy* advisory that 'Prudence is a rich ugly old maid courted by Incapacity' (7), a misogyny scarcely tempered by the aphorism that 'The nakedness of woman is the work of God' (8). The news a few lines down that 'Joys impregnate. Sorrows bring forth' might echo a Wollstonecrafted caution, but the proverb of liberation, 'Sooner murder an Infant in its cradle than nurse unact/-ed desires' (10), would find no counsel in Wollstonecraft's critique of the sense-driven woman's neglect of maternal duty.

Wollstonecraft's argument for the male-forged character of 'woman' foregrounds the problem of gender with which *Thel* contends: female innocence and experience is at once metafigure for these contrary states and, inescapably, a synechdoche of the social relations of the 1790s.[11] In contrast to the Blakean Devil's general contempt of the governor Reason (4–6), *A Vindication of the Rights of Woman* takes pains to argue that weak reasoning is woman's oppression, and surrender to the senses and the body is her prison. Blake's Devil casts Reason as a mind-forg'd manacle and passion a liberator, but to Wollstonecraft's Vindicator, the wrongs of woman are the catalogue of male assignments of them as creatures of body; it was only by developing reason that women could resist tyranny and oppression.

If it is a stretch to save *The Marriage of Heaven and Hell* for female 'Experience', Blake's post-*Vindication* visionary epic, *Visions of the Daughters of Albion* (1793), seems to nod to Wollstonecraft by showing two men behaving badly, and by the old book: Bromion the rapist, and jealous Theotormon, who can't get over the vision of his raped beloved. The bearer of sexual experience to the woman here is no burning boy: he is a practised tyrant, for whom rape is power, male rivalry, and violent possession, analogous to the oppression of slavery and thuggish imperialism. *Thel Vindicated* is a virtual subtitle. It is against this order of experience that Blake has Oothoon cry out, 'Love! Love! happy happy Love! free as the mountain wind' (7), preceded by a linked Wollstonecrafted critique of the cultural marking of raped woman as harlot, and the institutions that would bind the burning, youthful, radically innocent desire that 'knows no fixed lot . . . / In spells of law to one she loaths', forcing her to 'drag the chain / Of life, in weary lust!' (5).

Yet all this is parallel-parked in plates 6 and 7 with a channelling of male sexual self-interest through the legitimising voice of Oothoon. In disdain of Wollstonecraft's polemic for modesty (as male and female sexual self-control), Blake has Oothoon reprise Marvell, railing against 'subtil modesty' and 'hypocrite modesty' as the enemy of 'virgin joys' of 'happy copulation' (6): 'The moment of desire! the moment of desire! The virgin / That pines for man; shall awaken her womb to enormous joys' (7). The larger containment for this selfless love (as it would be for Percy Shelley) is a licence for a free male desire, with happy female endorsement: in opposition to the 'self love that envies all' and makes a 'frozen marriage bed' (7), Oothoon pledges to spread for Theotormon 'silken nets and traps of adamant' to 'catch for thee girls of mild silver, or of furious gold; / I'll lie beside thee on a bank & view their wanton play / In lovely copulation bliss on bliss with Theotormon', free from 'jealous cloud' and 'selfish blightings' (7). In his dreams. And perhaps Blake's: this is the Beulah fantasy in *Milton*, where the wife 'shall begin to give / Her maidens to her husband: delighting in his delight / And then & then alone begins the happy Female joy' (36 [A]). Editors Eaves, Essick, and Viscomi hail this woman's 'radical contrast' to the 'jealousy, self-love, and envy' of Theotormon's pathology, and Ostriker cheers this heroine of unequalled generosity, vitality, and liberty.[12] But other readers, mostly women, are caught by the imagery of a harem procuress, her nets and traps textually (if not consciously) implicated with the 'nets & gins & traps' with which one man steals the labours of another (5) and with the 'nets' men use 'to catch virgin joy, / And brand it with the name of whore' (6).[13] Oothoon, in a fantasy of generosity, joins the system as one of its agents.

Visions thus vexes coherent configuration: do we see Oothoon trapped in the system of male tyranny after all? Is this a case of victim psychology? or of Blake's ability in the 1790s to imagine liberation only for male desire? Or is this a sly satire of how a libertine male, tendering liberty, may conscript female agency and approval? For his own part, Blake was divided between theory and practical consequences. When, stoked on Old Testament justifications for concubinage, he proposed a version of this male liberty to Catherine Blake, she wept.[14]

The pressure of female social experience lays claim to the plural *Visions* and the ambiguous grammar of *Visions of.* A female screening of epistemology, of daughters as the objects and bearers of visions, brings a sharper focus to the contradictions of universal desire and female social existence. This focus pretty much diffuses in *Songs of Experience* (1794) where the differential is not gender but a general *'two contrary states of the human soul'* that allows a reinscription of patterns of female inhibition and salutary liberation. The keynote is given in feminine 'EARTH's Answer' to the Bard of the Introduction:

> Break this heavy chain,
> That does freeze my bones around
> Selfish! vain!
> Eternal bane!
> That free Love with bondage bound.

The call of this global feminine rings out: unchain my heart! Inhibition is disease, pathology, death-in-life. At the same time, a subtler keynote in this movement from *freeze* to *free* plays in the last line's ambiguous syntax. It is at once appositive, in rhyme, syntax and sense, to 'That does free my bones around', but as a summary epigram, it lets slip a suggestion that for a female speaker in 1794, free love is bondage of some kind: if (as Rajan sums the introductory scene of reading in *Songs of Experience*) 'interpretation is engendered by cultural difference', the issue of liberation is a sharply etched site of the gender differential.[15]

This difference ripples across the 1794 *Songs*, where the female is bound not just by a grave socio-psychological sentence (call it 'inhibition') but also by systems of male desire. Reassigned to *Experience*, *The Little Girl Lost* is even transformed, since here, the alternative to 'experience' (however we gauge its calculus of peril and play) is not the restless safety of innocence, but the disease of virginity, inhibition, repression. On a single plate, *My Pretty ROSE TREE*, AH! SUN-FLOWER, and *THE LILLY* tell a tale in three chapters. In fidelity to his 'pretty rose tree', a male singer disdains an invitation to love elsewhere, but for all his faith and solicitude, 'my Rose turnd away with jealousy: / And her thorns were my only delight'. The singer of AH! SUN-FLOWER envisions a world free from the inhibitions that freeze and starve the natural desires of youth in the name of socially prized chastity. This is the longed-for clime (not socially realisable in the 1790s) 'Where the Youth pined away with desire, / And the pale Virgin shrouded in snow: / Arise from their graves'. As the sunflower trope itself signifies and the singer of THE LILLY knows, nature is no alternative to the manacles of culture: 'The modest Rose puts forth a thorn; / The humble Sheep, a threatening horn', and only the 'lilly' white, reworked from conventional semiotic binds of virginity and death, 'shall in Love delight.'

And yet this resolution poses one more puzzle: it is sheer idealism, a sweet golden clime beyond time and history, that is, Experience. And across the contradictory visions of its *Songs*, females figure not just as primary victims but also primary agents. This framing of male frustration with female pathology infuses the arresting contradiction of *London*, the youthful Harlot. The master-villains are Church and Palace, the emblematic victims, the Chimney-Sweeper and Soldier – and in the expansive social tableau, every infant, every marriage, the hopes of life itself. But in the song's starkly compressed summary, the agent of curse, blight, and plagues is female sexual experience in its most unforgiving formation: the 'youthful Harlot'. She might have qualified for outraged Blakean sympathy along with boy soldier and sweep, but (as Wollstonecraft could even feel intermittently) she is cast as the poster-girl, the epitome of social disease, the infectious broadcast of misery.

This implication of victim with agental disease infects the most infamous flower song of *Experience*, *The SICK ROSE*. In the conventions that code lily virginal, the rose is female sexuality, and it is reported across Blake's book of experience, where even a modest rose or a beloved rose tree sulks are thorny. Yet for all the declarative certainty of 'O Rose thou art sick', the diagnostic force of Blake's poetry is no less troubled than in *Thel* and *Visions*. Is the invisible worm a hidden cause or a repressed cure? For all the satanic aura around the worm, Bloom blames the rose (no less than Thel) for refusing to become man, or more fundamentally, for refusing man. He concedes the 'phallic menace', but not without adjudicating more blame to 'female-self-gratification (the rose's bed is one of "crimson joy," before the worm finds it out)'.[16] Sick if she does, sick if she doesn't.

In this conundrum of cause and cure, one clear assignment seems to be gender: the rose is *femme fatale* from the coy mistress school. But Blake's gendering may be less certain than Bloom's. In his draft, it was 'her dark secret love' not 'his dark secret love / Does thy life destroy'. In she-agency, what the rose keeps secret may be self-destroying (*thy* still refers to rose), or it may be he-destroying (*thy* shifts to worm). Even in the engraved text, can we rule out the possibility of the singer's being female, the rhetoric a self-address, an alarmed self-report? Elizabeth Langland proposes this, even suggesting that 'her dark secret love' is a she-worm's, bearing a (pregnancy immune) homosexual joy that a would-be *carpe diem* male singer 'regards with fear and horror as destructive' because of its threat to male sexual privilege.[17]

Staging the deformations of living in a culture that fears what it prizes, Blake's female figures shape general questions about innocence and experience, repression and liberation, but in terms that convey processes and prejudices that fall into drastic differentials of gender, no less then than now.[18]

Notes

1. *Vision of the Last Judgement*, 85 (E 562). For key feminist interventions, tracking a misogyny that sees women as either passive, inferior and dependent, or

monstrously aggressive and dominant, see Susan Fox, 'The Female as Metaphor in William Blake's Poetry', *Critical Inquiry*, 56 (1977), 507–20; and Anne Mellor, 'Blake's Portrayal of Women', *BQ*, 16 (1982–83), 148–55. Though we can't blame Blake for 'failure to escape the linguistic prisons of gender-inflected metaphors inherent in the literary and religious culture in which he lived', advises Mellor, 'neither should we hail him as an advocate of androgyny or sexual equality to whom contemporary [1980s] feminists might look for guidance' (154). For a succinct review of subsequent gender criticism and Blake, see Brenda S. Webster, 'Blake, Women, and Sexuality', in Dan Miller et al. (eds), *Critical Paths* (Durham, NC: Duke University Press, 1987), esp. 204–5, 209–10.

2. 'The Road of Excess: My William Blake', in Gene W. Ruoff (ed.), *The Romantics and Us* (New Brunswick, NJ: Rutgers University Press, 1990), pp. 73–5.

3. *William Blake and the Daughters of Albion* (New York: St. Martin's Press, 1997) 1.

4. Here and throughout, Blake's poetry is quoted from the illuminated plates, on view in BA, and numerous print sources.

5. *Vindication of the Rights of Woman* (London: J. Johnson, 1792), 34 (chapter 2).

6. Bruder (46). Compare the multiply begged questions in the commentary that Harold Bloom supplies for E: 'Thel's name ... from the Greek for "will" or "wish" ... is ironic, for Thel's pathetic fate is the consequence of her weakness in will ... failure of desire' (895). An unironic reading of her name would grant her a creditable hesitation about male desire and critical will.

7. *The Visionary Company: a Reading of English Romantic Poetry* (1961; 2nd edn, Ithaca, NY: Cornell University Press, 1971) 53; the motto is one of the Proverbs of Hell (*Marriage of Heaven and Hell*, plate 10).

8. See BA; also in *William Blake: the Early Illuminated Books*, ed. Morris Eaves, Robert N. Essick and Joseph Viscomi (Princeton, NJ: Princeton University Press, 1993).

9. Zachary Leader's reading is a virtual epiphenomenon of this fable: 'Thel flees back ... because she has been terrified by ... a projection of her own fears and limitations rather than any objective or independent reality': her 'tragedy is lack of vision, and we leave the poem feeling that the powers restricting her are within her control', *Reading Blake's Songs* (London: Routledge & Kegan Paul, 1981), 94–5. A resistant 'we' might invoke a social rather than a psychological test: might Thel have a tragic vision that the powers restricting her are projected from a system of male aggression not at all within her control?

10. Tilottama Rajan, *The Supplement of Reading: Figures of Understanding in Romantic Theory and Practice* (Ithaca, NY: Cornell University Press, 1990), 239.

11. I appreciate Rajan's sharp attention to the way Blake's female figures produce questions about 'the *semiotic* status of woman in the economy of mythmaking' (signifier or motivated construction?), interrupting the visionary argument with 'social and historical considerations' (*Supplement*, 243–5).

12. *Early Illuminated Books* (cited above, 228); Ostriker, 'Desire Gratified and Ungratified: William Blake and Sexuality', *BQ*, 16 (1982–83), 158.

13. For example, Webster (213), Bruder (82). Leopold Damrosch Jr paused over the 'negative connotations' of nets and traps, *Symbol and Truth in Blake's Myth* (Princeton, NJ: Princeton University Press, 1980), 197. If he didn't develop the question, he at least improved on D. Aers, who, sensing Oothoon's complicity in the system she is at pains to critique, tags this a 'forced' reading, 'William Blake and the Dialectic of Sex', *ELH: A Journal of English Literary History*, 44 (1977), 506. So

eager is Michael Ackland to celebrate the 'unselfish companionship' devoted to 'the total sexual freedom of one's partner' (172) that he discounts any design of male privilege (181 n. 8), declaring (even) that Blake's visions of female sexuality 'transcend' Wollstonecraft's conservatively snared *Rights of Woman*, 'The Embattled Sexes: Blake's Debt to Wollstonecraft', *BQ*, 16 (1982–83), 172–83.

14. Mona Wilson gives the legend in *The Life of William Blake* (New York: Jonathan Cape & Robert Ballou, 1932), 70.

15. Rajan, *Supplement*, 230.

16. *How to Read and Why* (New York: Simon and Schuster, 2000), 72.

17. 'Blake's Feminist Revision of Literary Tradition in "The SICK ROSE"', *Critical Paths* (see n. 1), 232, 239.

18. I'm grateful to my colleague Jasper Cragwall for a sharp conversation on the subject.

30
Baillie and Blake: at the Intersection of Allegory and Drama

Julia M. Wright

> the Four Faces of Humanity fronting the Four Cardinal Points
> Of Heaven going forward forward irresistible from Eternity to
> Eternity
> And they conversed together in Visionary forms dramatic.
> (J, 98.26–8; E 257–8)

> Jerusalem
> Hidden within the Covering Cherub as in a Tabernacle
> Of threefold workmanship in allegoric delusion & woe.
> (J, 89.43–5; E 249)

The allegorical dimension of William Blake's poetry has arguably been the bedrock of Blake studies, from such influential works as S. Foster Damon's *Blake Dictionary* (1965) and David Erdman's essential *Blake: Prophet Against Empire* (1954) to such critical collections as *Blake's Sublime Allegory* (1973).[1] Many of us thus began as Blake critics with assurances, such as Damon's, that 'Ahania, or Pleasure, is the Emanation of Urizen', 'Bromion is Reason', 'Enitharmon is Spiritual Beauty', 'Los is Poetry', and 'Oothoon . . . represents thwarted love'.[2] But, as Theresa Kelley has recently noted, 'Blake's resistance to allegory warrants attention'.[3] While Kelley's concern is Blake's 'shifting allegorical frames',[4] my interest here is in the different modes of characterisation in Blake's works, modes I would organise under headings from my epigraphs above: 'dramatic' and 'allegoric'. So-called 'personification allegory' is traditionally associated with static, flat characters even when it is narratively oriented. In his *Elements of Criticism* (1762), Henry Home (Lord Kames) quotes 'Lord Halifax, speaking of the ancient fabulists: "They (says he) wrote in signs, and spoke in parables; all their fables carry a double meaning; the story is one and entire; the characters the same throughout; not broken or changed, and always conformable to the nature of the creature they introduce."'[5] However, 'Of all the means for making an impression of ideal presence', writes Home, 'theatrical representation is the most powerful.'[6] I would like to sketch here some of the ways in which Blake's spectacular displays of dynamic interiority, particularly in his early female characters, are incompatible with the demands of personification allegory but consistent with contemporary dramatic theory, particularly that of Joanna Baillie whose *Plays on the Passions* (1798) traces the development of emotional states on terms derived from Enlightenment sensibility. More specifically, I would like to suggest that reconsidering the particularity of Blake's women characters in the context of dramatic extensions of sensibility, such as Baillie's, allows a revaluing of them not as secondary or corporeal but as Enlightenment subjects.

This chapter arises in part out of my long-standing interest in the ways in which Blake engages the limits of formal structures, and in part out of my attempt to grasp more fully my students' response to a classroom exercise that I developed in the mid-1990s. I wanted to defamiliarise certain popular literary assumptions for my students, particularly the well-entrenched view that poems are personal expressions tied to an individual author's life rather than rhetorical constructions with crafted speakers. I would put three poems on one page, with the authors' names removed, and distribute copies to the class. The three poems were usually Percy Bysshe Shelley's 'The Spectral Horseman', Mary Robinson's 'January, 1795', and Blake's 'Song' beginning 'My silks and fine array'. The first is a Gothic poem, the second is a political ballad, and the third is a lyric from *Poetical Sketches* addressed to a male lover. I would tell my students only that one poem was written by a lower-class man, one was written by a middle-class woman, and one was written by an aristocratic man, and then ask them to form small discussion groups and consider whether it is possible to determine who wrote which poem. The students never questioned the possibility of making such a determination and always, year after year, delivered the same answer: the political poem was written by the aristocratic man, the Gothic poem was written by the lower-class man, and the only woman wrote the lyric, a poem that they assumed is in a woman's voice.[7] I would then reveal the poets' identities. After dealing with the students' general surprise, even shock, I encouraged discussion which often revealed that the premise that the poet could be located in the poem was grounded not only in Wordsworthian ideas of poetic expression but also in unquestioned assumptions about the demographics of genre: the lower classes are drawn to the less respectable modes, such as the Gothic; upper-class men have power and education, and their writing demonstrates their stake in matters of state; women are determined by their sex and so they write about love and children. Yet the students' surprise was always focused on 'January, 1795',[8] producing my own surprise that students firmly bound to such a determinist model would be more disconcerted by the discovery that a woman wrote about politics than that a man could write – quite convincingly, apparently – in a woman's voice.

Underlying their relative ease with the idea that a man could write in a woman's voice is the same general premise that informed many treatments of gender in Blake's writings before the advent of feminist theory: men are universal and women are particular, so a man can represent a woman (politically, symbolically, poetically) but not vice versa.[9] Perhaps the most explicit instance of this thinking in Blake studies comes from Harold Bloom, who suggests that, in Blake's texts, 'every male at last represents human-kind, both male and female'.[10] This often merely implicit assumption has significant implications for allegorical readings of Blake works, reinforcing the representation of Blake's women characters as secondary figures in a larger allegorical scheme – as Emanations, for instance, or as confined to preludia. From Plato forward, western thought has tended to privilege the universal over the particular. But it is a paradox of Blake's works that he argued for the value of the particular, the individual, and the unique while writing allegorically, in universals, generalisations, and personifications.

In *Jerusalem*, Los suggests that the universal capacity for sympathy is directed towards the defence of individuals:

Humanity, who is the Only General and Universal Form
To which all Lineaments tend & seek with love & sympathy
All broad & general principles belong to benevolence
Who protects minute particulars, every one in their own identity.

(38.20–3; E 185)

In such passages, Blake clearly draws on Enlightenment moral theory in which sensibility is the foundation of communal attachment and social order – the basis for justice (David Hume), benevolence (Adam Smith), and national feeling (Home). Condemnations of false sensibility are almost coterminous with the arrival of the novel of sensibility in the 1740s, but authentic sensibility was understood to be an expression of moral judgement and so the basis for moral action, for men and women, well into the early 1800s.[11] While Mary Kelly Persyn suggests that Blake, like Mary Wollstonecraft in her *Vindications of the Rights of Woman* (1792), offers 'a critique of the culture of sensibility, which claimed that women, the more "sensitive" and feeling gender, were also more identified with embodiment and bodily process than men',[12] Wollstonecraft's critique in fact addresses specifically the flawed sensibility that arises from the faulty education of women. Thus Wollstonecraft praises the educated Catherine Macaulay because 'she writes with sober energy and argumentative closeness; yet sympathy and benevolence give an interest to her sentiments, and that vital heat to arguments, which forces the reader to weigh them'.[13] As in *Jerusalem*, 'sympathy' and 'benevolence' energise the relationship between 'general principles' and the individual (38.21–3; E 185).

Sensibility ideally offers a dynamic model of a feeling subject who sympathises with the feelings of others, rationally judges the moral implications of their situation, and then acts on the basis of sympathy modified by rational judgement, and who can improve and refine sensibility and so become more moral in both feeling and action. The literature of sensibility offered itself as a means of achieving such refinement: readers would identify with and judge characters, and so develop their sensibility.[14] Blake's contemporary, Joanna Baillie, did much to argue for drama as a means of not only refining sensibility but also of refining an understanding of the workings of the sentimental subject. As Aileen Forbes notes, Baillie understands 'sympathetic curiosity' as 'our natural propensity to observe others, to observe human nature, that draws our interest to the site of passion. For Baillie, this specular allure of passion forms the origin of theater. Passion commands our gaze; it commands an audience.'[15] In the 'Introductory Discourse' to her *Plays on the Passions*, Baillie suggests that the dramatic form is best suited to the representation of the development of a strong emotion:

> there is no mode of instruction which they will so eagerly pursue, as that which lays open before them, in a more enlarged and connected view, than their individual observations are capable of supplying, the varieties of the human mind. Above all, to be well exercised in this study will fit a man more particularly for the most important situations of life. He will prove for it the better Judge, the better Magistrate, the better Advocate; and as a ruler or conductor of men, under every occurring circumstance, he will find himself the better enabled to fulfil his duty, and accomplish his designs.[16]

In an important refinement of Aristotelian mimesis, drama becomes heuristic, giving the spectator an education in the varieties and changes of personality that can then be extrapolated to real-world situations. In her larger argument, Baillie draws on sensibility to identify passion and reason as the mainsprings of action, and sympathy with passion as the foundation of understanding. Hence, sympathy is heightened as the passion is intensified: 'If man is an object of so much attention to man, engaged in the ordinary occurrences of life, how much more does he excite his curiosity and interest when placed in extraordinary situations of difficulty and distress' (69).

This perspective not only sheds light on Wollstonecraft's characterisation of Macaulay but also puts a different valence on women's suffering in Blake's poems than that assumed by Susan Fox in her biting remark that the protagonist of *Visions of the Daughters of Albion* is a woman because Blake 'needed a chief character who could be raped and tied down'.[17] As Nancy Roberts has argued, the typical scene of the literature of sensibility is gendered in its specularity: a suffering female subject is observed by a male spectator whose moral sensibility is refined by the encounter.[18] That Theotormon does not perceive Oothoon's suffering speaks directly to Blake's refusal of a moral resolution: Theotormon's failure to see, and so sympathise with, her suffering is a failure of his moral sensibility. He cannot enter the sentimental scene, eschewing both self-development and communal obligations. Smith opens his study of sensibility with the sweeping claim, 'How selfish soever man may be supposed, there are evidently some principles in his nature, which interest him in the fortune of others, and render their happiness necessary to him, though he derives nothing from it except the pleasure of seeing it.'[19] Theotormon, eroding stone 'With secret tears' (2.6–7; E 46), 'hears [Oothoon] not' (2.37; E 47). Like the fabular characters of which Halifax complains, he is the 'same throughout', and that sameness is defined as insensible.

Conversely, the scene which has troubled so many critics, in which Oothoon offers to 'catch for [Theotormon] girls of mild silver' and 'view their wanton play / In lovely copulation bliss on bliss with Theotormon' (7.24, 7.25–6; E 50), outlines a limit case of Smith's argument that 'the pleasure of seeing it' is sufficient to motivate the desire for another's happiness: 'Oothoon shall view his dear delight, nor e'er with jealous cloud / Come in the heaven of *generous love*' (7.28–9; E 50; emphasis added). While Theotormon's insensibility prevents his further development, Oothoon's progress through the poem reaches its apex in this moment of 'generous love'. Oothoon is not only an object of violence but also a sentimental subject who responds sympathetically to those around her – particularly in her desire for 'the pleasure of seeing' Theotormon's 'happiness' – on terms that characterise her not merely as innocent but also as moral in the refined, reflective sense defined by sensibility. Considering Oothoon as an Enlightenment subject does not void the problem of the violence enacted upon her or of the insidiousness of her promise to 'catch' women, but it does shed light on the terms on which her character moves through a series of emotional states to arrive at a plea for 'generous love'. In *Visions*, Blake arguably approaches in Oothoon what Baillie sought in her dramas: the progress of passions, 'To trace them in their rise and progress in the heart' (91). Structuring the poem as what Erdman terms a 'three-sided soliloquy',[20] is, in Baillie's argument, required by such an aim: 'Soliloquy, or those overflowings of the perturbed soul, in which it unburthens itself of those thoughts, which it cannot communicate to others . . . must necessarily be often, and to considerable length, introduced' (105). The progress of Oothoon's passion, from self-loathing to 'generous love', locates her within dramatic notions of character rather than allegoric ones.

I do not stress Baillie here because I would suggest any direct influence between her and Blake; most of the Blake texts I discuss pre-date Baillie's work, and it is unlikely that Baillie would have had access to any of Blake's privately printed works. I am suggesting rather that Baillie and Blake are responding in similar ways to the impact of sensibility on understandings of human character – models that, because dynamic both internally and in relation to others, are well suited to the dialogic form of drama. Like closet dramas of the Romantic period, the Lambeth Prophecies consist of long speeches and minimal stage directions, so that 'The characters' private thoughts are always represented by publicly perceived actions, such as speeches, laughter, rejoicing, howling, and cursing, telegraphed as they would be on a stage rather than described by an omniscient narrator with full access to their interiority.'[21] Baillie not only emphasises process in her discussion of character but also explicitly critiques the static emotions of the sort amenable to medieval morality plays and other affiliates of allegory: 'one stage of passion must shew it [the passion] imperfectly', she complains, adding, 'We commonly find the characters of a tragedy affected by the passions in a transient, loose, unconnected . . . or if they are represented as under the permanent influence of the more powerful ones, they are generally introduced to our notice in the very height of their fury' (102, 91). Oothoon's progress develops a character who is not allegorical in any traditional sense but dramatically represents a shifting emotional state on terms typically denied to women characters in canonical Romantic drama by Blake's male peers.[22]

This form of characterisation is generally more closely allied with Blake's female characters than male ones. As I have argued elsewhere, the impulse to fit Blake's women characters into allegorical readings founded upon sexist notions of femaleness sometimes grates against the grain of the text and even elides the richness of Blake's ambiguity, as in the too-definite ascription of *Europe*'s prescriptive speech to Enitharmon.[23] In his discussion of personification allegory, moreover, Morton W. Bloomfield suggests that 'in dialogue the use of personifications throws emphasis on the speeches' as 'the poet is not interested in the effects of the agitation or conflict on a character but in the substance of the dispute'.[24] While this is arguably true of many of Blake's male characters, it is less so of the shadowy females, Enitharmon, Oothoon, or Ahania of the Lambeth Prophecies, in which 'the effects of the agitation or conflict on a character' are very much at the fore. Moreover, Lambeth-era depictions of Enitharmon and Ahania echo, though not on unproblematic terms, Smith's point about 'the pleasure of seeing' another's 'happiness': Ahania laments, 'I cannot touch his hand . . . / nor see his eyes / And joy' (*Book of Ahania* 4.65, 67–8; E 88–9); Enitharmon declares, 'My daughter how do I rejoice! for thy children flock around / Like the gay fishes on the wave' (*Europe* 14.2–3; E 65). These characters' actions are framed as responses to others, from Enitharmon's rejoicing at her children and weeping at their departure (*Europe* 14.36; E 66) to Ahania's lament for her loneliness and celebration of the joys of companionship and fecundity (*Book of Ahania* 4.45–5.47; E 88–90). While this might seem to reinforce women's status as the 'second sex' by making them dependent on others' emotional states, within Enlightenment moral theory these affective responses are proof of moral sensibility. Moreover, if any male character in Blake's early corpus conforms to sensibility it is Los in *The Book of Urizen*: Los 'watch'd in shuddering fear' and 'In terrors Los shrunk from his task' (9.9, 13.20; E 74, 77), but 'saw the Female & pitied' (19.10; E 79). The emphasis not only on Los's emotional changes but his watching of others' suffering ties him to the sentimental spectator of sensibility in a way that the self-involved figures of Urizen, Theotormon, and Bromion are demonstrably not.

If Blake's broadly allegorical works have a dramatic dimension that in part pulls characters out of mere personification through contemporary dramatic theory, then it is suggestive that in Blake's most formally dramatic work, the fragmentary *King Edward the III* from *Poetical Sketches* (1783), the leading male characters tend towards the allegorical. Interiority is both simplified and telegraphed, so that men weep over songs (3.163–8) and exhibit their willingness to fight in a 'fiery face' (3.157) as well as make bold declarations such as 'I hunger for another battle' (3.155). Dagworth, the observer of these men, is himself easily read and, moreover, is legible as a man of virtue whose consistency is a sign of his integrity. Chandos declares,

> That man's a hero in his closet, and more
> A hero to the servants of his house
> Then to the gaping world; he carries windows
> In that enlarged breast of his, that all
> May see what's done within.
>
> (3.184–8; E 431)

The Prince's reply, however, pitches Dagworth from heroic ideal into allegorical figure: 'He's a genuine Englishman, my Chandos, / And hath the spirit of Liberty within him' (3.189–90; E 431). Dagworth is the avatar of the national character defined in the first scene of the dramatic fragment, a passage that strongly anticipates Blake's *America*:

> Let Liberty . . . Enerve my soldiers; let Liberty
> Blaze in each countenance, and fire the battle.
> The enemy fights in chains, invisible chains, but heavy;
> Their minds are fetter'd; then how can they be free,
> While, like the mounting flame,
> We spring to battle o'er the floods of death?
>
> (1.9, 1.11–16; E 424)

Dagworth is the allegorical distillation of the best characteristics of the King, Prince, and other characters in the play – he is 'English', and animated by the 'Liberty' that the leading male characters all praise. Baillie, however, defines the playwright's interest as 'Those passions which conceal themselves from the observation of men; which cannot unbosom themselves even to the dearest friend; and can, often times, only give their fulness vent in the lonely desert, or in the darkness of midnight' (86). A 'hero in his closet', Dagworth does not have those passions which Baillie makes the proper focus of drama.

While allegory draws on universals and abstractions, the kind of drama that Baillie advocates keeps the focus on hearts and minds in struggle. Blake's works are too resistant to convention to be solved by any one conventional paradigm, and certainly this dramatic idea of character does not account for Enitharmon's final speech in *Europe* and carries with it sensibility's problematic emphasis on women's suffering. But the dramatic dimension of Blake's work, and its underpinnings in sensibility, is a compelling complication of the allegorical and its universalising impetus. Blake's women characters may not represent such ideal principles as imagination or revolution, but they have the capacity of the moral subject in Enlightenment philosophy, exhibiting a capacity for emotional response that necessitates a dynamic rather than static characterisation. We need to consider these women characters not only as allegorical distillations but also as challenges to allegory's refusal of particularity, challenges that are developed through Enlightenment ideals of moral subjectivity and 'generous love'.

Notes

I would like to thank the Canada Research Chairs program for their invaluable support of my research, and Joel Faflak and Jason Haslam for their generous responses to earlier versions of this chapter.
   1. S. Foster Damon, *A Blake Dictionary*, rev. edn (London: Brown University Press, 1988); David V. Erdman, *Blake: Prophet Against Empire*, rev. edn (Princeton, NJ: Princeton University Press, 1969); *Blake's Sublime Allegory*, ed. Stuart Curran and Joseph A. Wittreich Jr (Madison: University of Wisconsin Press, 1973).
   2. Damon, ibid., 7, 60, 124, 246, 308.
   3. Theresa M. Kelley, *Reinventing Allegory* (Cambridge: Cambridge University Press, 1997), 98.
   4. Ibid., 98.
   5. Henry Home, Lord Kames, *Elements of Criticism* (1762), intro. Robert Voitle, 3 vols (New York: Georg Olms Verlag, 1970), 3: 128.
   6. Ibid., 1: 116.
   7. Blake's 'Song' is not explicitly written in a woman's voice, but in the voice of a man's lover.
   8. One especially agitated student contended that if 'January, 1795' were really written by a woman then anthologies had 'lied' to him about women's writing.
   9. This is, of course, a standard rubric in western patriarchy. See, for instance, Ian Maclean, *The Renaissance Notion of Woman* (Cambridge: Cambridge University

Press, 1980). For further elaboration of this rubric's impact on earlier Blake studies, see Julia M. Wright, *Blake, Nationalism, and the Politics of Alienation* (Athens, OH: Ohio University Press, 2004), 195 n. 9.

10. Harold Bloom, *Blake's Apocalypse: a Study in Poetic Argument* (Garden City: Doubleday, 1963), 119.

11. On sensibility in the Romantic period, see, for example, Jerome McGann, *The Poetics of Sensibility: a Revolution in Poetic Style* (Oxford: Clarendon, 1996).

12. Mary Kelly Persyn, ' "No Human Form But Sexual": Sensibility, Chastity, and Sacrifice in Blake's *Jerusalem*', *European Romantic Review*, 10 (1999), 53–84, 56.

13. Mary Wollstonecraft, *Vindication of the Rights of Woman* (1792), ed. Miriam Brody (London: Penguin, 1985), 207.

14. See Janet Todd, *Sensibility: an Introduction* (New York: Methuen, 1986) for a very useful overview. Also see, for instance, *Sensibility in Transformation: Creative Resistance to Sentiment from the Augustans to the Romantics*, ed. Syndy McMillen Conger (Toronto: Associated Universities Presses, 1990); Markman Ellis, *The Politics of Sensibility: Race, Gender and Commerce in the Sentimental Novel* (Cambridge: Cambridge University Press, 1996); John Mullan, *Sentiment and Sociability: the Language of Feeling in the Eighteenth Century* (Oxford: Clarendon, 1988); and Ann Jessie Van Sant, *Eighteenth-Century Sensibility and the Novel: the Senses in Social Context* (Cambridge: Cambridge University Press, 1993).

15. Aileen Forbes, ' "Sympathetic Curiosity" in Joanna Baillie's Theater of the Passions', *European Romantic Review*, 14 (2003), 31–48, 33. The central scene of sensibility is a fundamentally specular one, beginning with the spectacle of suffering that Luke Gibbons has richly explored in *Edmund Burke and Ireland* (Cambridge: Cambridge University Press, 2003).

16. Joanna Baillie, 'Introductory Discourse', *Plays on the Passions* (1798), ed. Peter Duthie (Peterborough: Broadview Press, 2001), 76; hereafter cited parenthetically in the text.

17. Susan Fox, 'The Female as Metaphor in William Blake's Poetry', *Critical Inquiry*, 3 (1977), 513.

18. See Nancy Roberts, *Schools of Sympathy: Gender and Identification through the Novel* (Montreal-Kingston: McGill-Queen's University Press, 1997).

19. Adam Smith, *The Theory of Moral Sentiments* (1759), ed. D.D. Raphael and A.L. Macfie (Indianapolis: Liberty Fund, 1984), 9.

20. Erdman, *Blake*, 236.

21. Wright, *Blake*, xvii.

22. See Julie Carlson's important study, *In the Theatre of Romanticism* (Cambridge: Cambridge University Press, 1994), and its supplementation in 'Remaking Love: Remorse in the Theatre of Baillie and Inchbald', *Women in British Romantic Theatre: Drama, Performance and Society, 1790–1840*, ed. Catherine Burroughs (Cambridge: Cambridge University Press, 2000).

23. Wright, *Blake*, 68–74, 93–4.

24. Morton W. Bloomfield, 'A Grammatical Approach to Personification Allegory', *Modern Philology*, 60 (1963), 161–71, 168.

Index

Ackland, Michael, 269n
Ackroyd, Peter, 3, 217n
Adams, Hazard, 55, 90n
Aers, David, 235n, 268n
Aeschylus, 86
Aesop, 86–7
'Aesop, Abraham', 87
Albani, Francesco, 7
Alter, Robert, 199n
Aquinas, Thomas, 170
Aristotle, 170, 273
Armitage, Thomas, 210
Arnold, Dana, 52n
Ashburton, Charles Alfred, 48, 52n
Astley, John, 13
Astley, Philip, 13
Atwood, Craig, 211, 217n
Augustine, Jane, 216n
Austen, Jane, 29
Ayloffe, Joseph, 45, 51n

Bacon, Francis, 63
Baillie, Joanna, 29, 270–8
Baldrs Draumar, 183
Baldwin, Olive, 157n
Balfour, Ian, 71, 72, 74
Balzac, Honoré de, 213
Barbauld, Anna, 127
Barker, Arthur, 200
Barker, Hannah, 157n
Barlow, Francis, 87
Barrett Browning, Elizabeth, 135
Barry, James, 26, 233–4
Barthes, Roland, 198n
Bartholin, Thomas, 179, 182, 187n
Basire, James, 45
Baulch, Davis M., 198n
The Beauties of the AntiJacobin, 233
Behn, Aphra, 87
Behrendt, Stephen, 75, 166, 168n, 169n
Bell, Vanessa, 250
Bennett, Betty, 126, 234n
Bentley, E.B., 252

Bentley, G.E., Jr, 3, 13, 33n, 51n, 52n, 56, 90n, 96, 129, 217n, 252
Beowulf, 247
Berkeley, George, 63
Bhagavad Gita, 110
Bhagavat-Geeta, trans. Sir Charles Wilkins, 109, 114, 115, 117n
Bible, xvi, 36–7, 86, 110, 114, 185–6, 189–99, 224, 238, 265
  Corinthians, 88, 89, 239
  Ephesians, 58
  Exodus, 191, 192, 239
  Ezekiel, 230–1, 234n
  Genesis, 45, 81, 100, 160, 168, 184, 191, 193, 220, 221, 223–4, 232–3, 235n, 237, 238, 244
  Gospels, 100–8, 172, 210–11, 212, 230, 231, 233, 235n
  Hebrews, 58
  Hosea, 234n
  Isaiah, 57, 172
  Jeremiah, 234n
  Jonah, 75
  Judges, 193, 230–1
  Nahum, 234n
  Psalms, 102, 106
  Revelation, 56, 59, 60, 100, 186, 220, 239
  Song of Solomon, 30, 104
Bindman, David, 46, 51n, 63, 64, 100, 187n
Birch, Thomas, 60n
Blackstone, Bernard, 117n, 258, 260n
Blackstone, William, 237, 246
Blake, Catherine, 1, 12–15, 38, 64, 69, 78–90, 95, 132, 140, 145, 195, 212, 214, 240, 242–3, 245, 249, 250–1, 265
Blake, Catherine Armitage, 78, 209
Blake, James (father of William), 78, 210
Blake, James (brother of William), 10n
Blake, John, 210
Blake, Robert, 14, 47, 79, 153

Blake, William
  All Religions are One, 190
  America, 8, 55, 70, 73, 97, 119–25,
    140, 142, 144, 183–4, 202–3,
    204–5, 248, 252, 256, 276
  'The Ancient of Days', 133, 247
  Annotations to *An Apology for the
    Bible*, xv, xix
  Annotations to Lavater, 44, 80, 212
  Annotations to Swedenborg, 57
  Book of Ahania, 44, 49–50, 97, 144,
    197, 275
  Book of Enoch illustrations, 215
  Book of Los, 49, 161, 184, 204, 206–8
  Book of Thel, xix, 64, 66, 81, 82–4,
    95, 119, 131–2, 141, 200, 201–2,
    263–5, 267, 268n
  The Book of Urizen, 49, 65, 70, 161,
    196, 200–1, 203, 204, 205–6, 276
  Catherine Blake portrait, 133
  'The Circle of Life', 182
  Descriptive Catalogue, 9
  Edward and Eleanor (*Edward &
    Elenor*) illustrations, 44, 45–8
  Europe, 17, 70–7, 97, 119–25, 137,
    183–4, 202–5, 214, 275, 277
  Everlasting Gospel, 100, 105, 190
  Four Zoas, xvi, 9, 50–1, 55, 59, 62, 63,
    70, 93–4, 111, 114, 115, 159, 161,
    170, 181–2, 184–6, 187n, 188n, 191,
    216, 238, 239, 240, 244, 256, 257
  French Revolution, 59
  Gates of Paradise, 140, 170
  Genesis illustrations, 159–69
  'Glad Day', 109, 117n
  Gospel illustrations, 100–8
  Gray illustrations, 1–11, 45–6, 48, 180
  Island in the Moon, 88
  Jerusalem, xvi, xviii, xix, 10, 16,
    17–18, 47, 62, 63, 70, 83, 97, 111,
    114, 117n, 135, 137, 139, 140, 141,
    142, 143, 144–6, 159, 162–3, 170,
    177n, 179, 182, 190, 192, 195, 196,
    197, 200, 204, 205, 207, 216,
    219–27, 228–36, 238, 239, 240,
    241–3, 244–5, 251, 257–8, 270, 272
  Job illustrations, 107
  Laocoon, 190
  Letters, xvi, xviii, xxn, 1, 4, 9, 10,
    229, 239–45

  'Little Tom the Sailor', 149, 151–8
  Marriage of Heaven and Hell, 23, 39,
    64, 65, 69, 109, 110, 128, 134, 137,
    141, 162, 163, 189, 190, 193, 194,
    198, 203, 207, 210, 213, 238, 243,
    259, 263, 264, 268n
  Milton, xvi, 16, 17, 19, 20–4, 47, 62,
    70, 96, 111 114–15, 140, 141, 143,
    144, 169n, 182, 190, 198n, 200,
    204, 207, 214, 228, 240–1, 243,
    244, 245, 251, 257, 265
  Milton illustrations, 100, 159–69, 170
  Night Thoughts illustrations, 3, 9, 100,
    251
  Notebook, 4, 54–60, 66, 214, 215,
    237, 239, 240, 243
  Pickering Manuscript, xvi, 94
  Pilgrim's Progress illustrations, 170
  Poetical Sketches, 10, 26–34, 129,
    234n, 271, 276–7, 277n
  Song of Los, 128, 205
  Songs of Innocence and of Experience,
    xvi, xviii, 38, 54–7, 63, 78, 83,
    84–9, 111, 116, 127, 128, 129, 131,
    133, 134, 141, 159, 160, 168n,
    170–8, 190, 200, 220, 227n, 243–4,
    249, 261–3, 266–7
  There is No Natural Religion, 220
  Visionary Heads, 46–7
  'The Vision of Ezekiel', 111–12, 117n
  Vision of the Last Judgement, 194, 198,
    267n
  Visions of the Daughters of Albion, xvi,
    14, 19, 42, 62, 65–6, 69, 72, 73, 97,
    119–25, 128, 131–2, 144, 200,
    201–3, 244, 254–6, 258, 261,
    264–6, 267, 273–4
Blake's Sublime Allegory, 270
Blake-Varley Sketchbook, 44, 48–9, 52n
Blakey, Nicolas, 48
Bloom, Harold, 62, 63, 179, 186n, 189,
  201, 202, 263, 267, 268n, 269n,
  272, 278n
Bloomfield, Morton W., 275, 278n
Blunt, Antony, 235n
Boase, T.S.R., 52n
Bogen, Nancy, 217n
Bowker, John, 117n
Bowles, Caroline, 135
Bowyer, Robert, 48, 49, 52n

Brooke, Rupert, 249
Brown, Cynthia E., 52n
Brown, Dan, 102
Brown, Thomas, 103
Browne, Thomas, 159, 161, 168n
Bruder, Helen, xvii, xixn, 71, 73, 74, 117n, 119, 120, 121, 125n, 254, 261, 263, 268n
Bruns, Gerald, 199n
Buddha, 65
Budick, Sanford, 199n
Burke, Edmund, 60, 119, 124, 231
Burney, Fanny, 95, 120
Burns, Robert, 29
Burroughs, Catherine, 278n
Butler, Eleanor, 131
Butlin, Martin, 46, 51n, 52n, 100–8, 187n
Butts, Elizabeth, 250, 251
Butts, Thomas, 12–13, 63, 90n, 100, 102, 106, 107, 158n, 160, 227n, 251
    family of, 104

Cambridge Companion to William Blake, xvii, xxn, 178n
Campbell, Joseph, 177n
Carretta, Vincent, 229
Cargill, Ann, 150–1, 153
Carlson, Julie, 278n
Carlyle, Thomas, 35
Castle, Terry, 126n
Caxton, William, 86
Cellini, Benvenuto, 7
Chalus, Elaine, 157n
Chandler, Pamela, 38
Chapman, Edward, 35
Chapone, Hester, 95
Chaucer, Geoffrey, 247
Chetwynd, Mrs, 10n
Cicero, 190
Clark, Anna, 143, 145
Clark, David L., 168n
Clark, Steve, 33n, 125n
Clayton, Timothy, 52n, 157n
Coleridge, Samuel Taylor, 206, 252
Collection of Hymns for the Children of All Ages, 216, 218n
Colley, Linda, 232, 234n
Cook, Robert, 187n
Conger, Syndy McMillen, 278n

Corbin, Alain, 157n
Correggio, 9
Connolly, Tristanne, 51n, 81, 90n, 118
Cottle, Joseph, 49
Cotton, Nathaniel, 87
Crabb Robinson, Henry, 79, 90n
Crisman, William, 34n
Cristall, Ann Batten, 26–34, 127–9, 131, 135
Cristall, Elizabeth, 26, 128
Cristall, Joshua, 26, 28, 33n, 128
Crouch, Kimberly, 157n
Cullen, Gordon, 168n
Cumberland, George, 90n, 154, 158n, 233–4, 235n
Cunningham, Allan, 2, 5, 10n, 11n, 38, 43n, 51n, 132–4
Curnick, Thomas, 49
Curran, Stuart, 126, 127, 128, 187n, 277n

Damon, S. Foster, 62, 63, 81, 90n, 109, 117n, 167, 169n, 182, 187n, 188n, 202, 270, 277n
Damrosch, Leopold, Jr, 55, 59, 268n
Dante, 9, 63
Darwin, Erasmus, 31
Davies, J.M.Q., 168n, 177n
Davies, Keri, 33n, 217n
de Beauvoir, Simone, 95
de Groot, H.B., 43n
De Klerk, F.W., 54
de la Fontaine, Jean, 87
De Luca, Vincent Arthur, 179, 186n
De Quincey, Thomas, 252
de Rapin-Thoyras, Paul, 48, 51n, 52n
de Rougemont, Denis, 62
de Vos, Martin, 235n
Delany, Mary, 95
Dendy, Walter Copper, 51n
Denman, Maria, 4, 10n
Dennis, Charles, 87
Dent, Shirley, 35–43, 229
Derrida, Jacques, 160–1, 168, 168n
Descartes, René, 20
Di Salvo, Jackie, xxn
Dictionary of Famous Names from around the World, 91
Dimmer, Frederick, 177n
Dinnerstein, Dorothy, 62

Dithmar, Christiane, 217n
Donne, John, 62, 63
Doolittle, Hilda (H.D.), 65, 209–18
Dorrbecker, D.W., 71, 73, 74
Douglas, Mary, 62
Dronke, Ursula, 187n
Dunbar, Pamela, 162, 168n
Duthie, Peter, 278n
Dyer, George, 29

Earle, Peter, 138, 139
Easson, Roger, 157n
Eaves, Morris, 178n, 265, 268n
Edda, 180
van Eeden, Frederik Willem, 170
Edgeworth, Maria, 232
Egremont, Countess of, 10n
Eliot, T.S., 32–3, 34n
Ellis, Edwin J., 81, 90n, 217n
Ellis, Markman, 278n
Ellison, Julie, 234n
Emmett, Robert, 235
English History Delineated, 48
Erdman, David V., 54, 56, 57, 59, 62,
    125n, 140, 141, 177n, 235n, 248–9,
    250, 254, 256, 259n, 270, 274,
    277n, 278n
Erdrich, Louise, 65
Essick, Robert, 9, 28, 33n, 51n, 117n,
    157n, 217n, 235n, 265, 268n
Evans, Evan, 51n

Falconer, William, 148, 153, 157n
Faringdon, Joseph, 90n
Feibel, Juliet, 52n
Feldman, Paula R., 43n, 129, 133
Fenwick, Eliza, 201
Ferber, Michael, 72
Finch, Anne, 87
Flaxman, Ann, 1–11, 28, 45, 46,
    109
Flaxman, John, 4, 5, 8, 9, 10n, 28, 33n,
    34n, 46, 63, 90n, 109, 129
Flaxman, Maria, 4
Flaxman, Mary Ann, 6, 10n
Fletcher, Loraine, 129
Forbes, Aileen, 273, 278n
Forster, E.M., 249
Foucault, Michel, 203
Fox, Susan, 95, 96, 268n, 273, 278n

Freud, Sigmund, 62, 63, 64, 83, 170,
    172, 174, 177n, 212, 215, 255, 259
Friedan, Betty, 250
Friedman, Susan, 209, 217n
Frye, Northrop, 62, 63, 100, 179, 186n,
    198n, 200, 201, 202, 227, 248,
    256
Fulford, Tim, 51n
Fuseli, Henry, 48, 79

Gandhi, 82
Gardner, Stanley, 56
Gelpi, Albert, 217n
Gibbons, Luke, 278n
Gilchrist, Alexander, 9n, 10n, 12,
    35–40, 52n, 90n
Gilchrist, Anne, 35–43
Gilgamesh, 238
Gillray, James, 148–57
Ginsberg, Allen, 252
Gleckner, Robert F., 33n, 251
Glen, Heather, 56–7, 59–60, 177n
Godfrey, Richard T., 157n
Goellnicht, Donald C., 168n
Gough, Richard, 45, 51n
Gould, Elizabeth Porter, 43n
Granger, James, 48
Grant, John E., 248–9
Grant, Duncan, 250
Gray, Thomas, 179–88
    see also Blake, William, Gray
        illustrations
Greenberg, Mark L., 33n
Grenby, M.O., 234n, 235n
Grimm, Jacob and Wilhelm, 234n
Groom, Nick, 51n
Guyer, Paul, 168n

Haga, Noboru, 92
Hagstrum, Jean, 258, 259, 260n
Halifax, Lord, *see* Home, Henry, Lord
    Kames
Hallett, Mark, 157n
Hamilton, William, 48
Hamlyn, Robin, 12
Hampsey, John C., 127n
Hanh, Thich Nhat, 65
Harned, Thomas B., 43n
Harrison, John, 48
Hartman, Geoffrey, 33n, 198–9n

Hay, Douglas, 157n
Hayley, Thomas Alphonso, 154
Hayley, William, 4, 9, 10n, 28, 34n, 45, 60n, 63, 79, 118, 129–31, 153–6, 157n, 158n, 222, 239–41
Hayman, Francis, 48
Heath, Stephen, 198n
Hegel, G.W.F., 201, 206
Hemans, Felicia, 38, 43n, 127, 132–3, 135
Hendrickson, J.R., 187n
Heppner, Christopher, 106
Heraclitus, 65
Herbert, George, 62
Herbert, William, 185, 188n
Herrick, Robert, 262
Hertz, Neil, 234n
Hesiod, 86
Hesketh, Lady Harriet, 79
Hill, Draper, 157n
Hilton, Nelson, 30, 34n, 146n, 178n, 246n
Hindmarsh, Robert, 57
Hiratsuka, Raicho, 92
Hitopadesa, 112, 117n
Hoare, Prince, 233–4
Hogarth, Joseph, 90n
Hollander, John, 186n
Homans, Margaret, 97
Home, Henry, Lord Kames, 270–1, 272, 277n
Homer, 190, 238
Honeyman, Katrina, 139, 140
Hooper, Lucy, 127, 132, 133–5
Hori, Keiko, 97
Howard, Mrs, 95
Howitt, Mary, 38, 43n
Hughes, Merritt Y., 169n
Hume, David, 52n, 272
Hunt, Leigh, 252

Iki, Kazuko, 97
Imai, Nobuo, 92
Ingli, James G., 51n
Ireland, W.H., 49, 52n
Irigaray, Luce, 67

Jeffares, Norman, 259
Jennings, Sara, 95
Johnes, Thomas, 132

Johnson, Joseph, 26, 28, 46, 110, 127
Johnson, Mary Lynn, 51n
Jones, William, 109, 110–12, 116, 117n
Jones, William R., 157n
Jordan, Dorothy, 155
Joyce, James, 247
Jugaku, Bunsho, 92, 94–5
Jugaku, Shizu, 94
Jung, Carl, 62, 173, 177n

Kabbala, 194, 210, 211, 212, 214, 216, 219–27
Kanai, Yoshiko, 97
Kant, Immanuel, 160–1, 168, 168n
Kauffmann, Angelica, 48
Kawatsu, Masae, 97
Keats, John, 65, 97, 127
Kelley, Theresa M., 270, 277
Kermode, Frank, 186n, 199n
Keynes, Geoffrey, 1, 2–3, 157n, 158n, 168n, 248–50, 252
Keynes, John Maynard, 249
Keynes, Margaret, 250, 252
Keynes, Simon, 52n
King, James, 83, 90n
Kirkup, Seymour Stocker, 90n
Klein, Melanie, 201
Klemm, Christian, 52n
Kristeva, Julia, 203, 207

Labbe, Jacqueline, 28, 29, 30, 34n
LaBerge, Stephen, 170–1, 177n
Lamb, Caroline, 135
Lang, Cecil Y., 43n
Langland, Elizabeth, 267, 269n
Langland, William, 54
Lavater, Johann Caspar, 44–52, 63
see also Blake, William, Annotations to Lavater
Lawrence, D.H., 7
Lawson, Bruce, 72
Leader, Zachary, 268n
Lerner, Gerda, 191, 199n
Levinas, Emmanuel, 201, 204
Lincoln, Margarette, 157n
Linnell, John, 26, 81, 90n
Lloyd, Robert, 87n
Locke, John, 76
Lowery, Margaret Ruth, 5

Lucas, Charles, 229, 234n
Lundeen, Kathleen, 168
Lyotard, Jean-François, 203–4

Macaulay, Catherine, 272, 273
Macdonald, D.L., 34n
Maclean, Ian, 277–8
Macmillan, 42
Macpherson, James, 26
Magno, Cettina Tramontano, 59
Makdisi, Saree, 76
Mallet, Paul-Henri, 179–88
Mallory, George, 249
Malthus, Thomas, 81
Mandela, Nelson, 54
Margoliouth, H.M., 185, 188n
Marin, Louis, 168–9n
Marmontel, 87
Marvell, Andrew, 262, 263, 265
Mathew, Harriet, 10n, 28, 33n, 80, 109
Mathew, Revd Anthony Stephen, 28, 33n, 129
Matsuhashi, Keiko, 92, 93
Matthews, Eric, 168n
Matthews, Jane, 28
McClenahan, Catherine, 232, 233, 235n
McGann, Jerome, 128, 278n
McGowan, James, 27, 33n
Mee, Jon, 71, 75, 234n
Mellor, Anne, 46, 51n, 95, 96, 127, 268n
Michelangelo, 9
Miller, Dan, 268n
Milton, John, 12–13, 16, 18–19, 21, 22, 23, 30, 58–60, 64, 65, 72, 135, 140, 161, 162, 163, 166, 168, 169n, 170, 192, 240, 241, 252, 262
see also Blake, William, *Milton* illustrations
Miner, Paul, 181, 187n
Mitchell, W.J.T., 70, 168n
Montagu, Elizabeth, 95
Montagu, Mary Wortley, 95
Montgomery, James, 218n
Moira, Lord, 235n
Moor, Edward, 109–10, 117n
Moore, Edward, 87
Moore, Thomas, 131
More, Hannah, 95

Morganwg, Iolo, 46, 51n
Mortimer, John Hamilton, 48, 49
Moskal, Jeanne, 234n, 235n
Muir, William, 210
Mullan, John, 278n
Mulvahill, James, 76
Munby, A.N.L., 249–50
Murphy, Bernadette, 251

Nead, Lynda, 161, 164, 168n
The Neglected Daughter – An Affecting Tale, 157n
Newman, Gerald, 229
Newton, Isaac, 75, 76, 250
Nietzsche, Friedrich, 170, 203
Niimi, Hatsuko, 97
Njáls saga, 180, 187n

O'Flinn, Paul, xv, xvi
Oe, Kenzaburo, 96
Okada, Kazuda, 73
Omberg, Margaret, 179, 180, 187n
Opie, John, 233–4
Ostriker, Alicia, 62, 64, 90n, 95, 96, 261, 265, 268n
Otto, Peter, 60n
Oulton, Wally Chamberlain, 52n
Ovid, 190
Owen, A.L., 188n

Paine, Thomas, 119
Painting, Vivienne W., 158n
Paley, Morton D., 56, 57, 74, 75, 181, 187n, 230, 233, 235n, 249, 258–9
Palgrave Advances in Blake Studies, xvii, xixn, xxn
Pallister, John C., 177n, 178n
Palmer, A.H., 43n
Palmer, Samuel, 39–40, 43n, 90n, 235n
Parkhurst, John, 103
Pascoe, Judith, 122, 125n, 126n
Patai, Raphael, 199n
Pearce, Donald Ross, 51n, 217n
Pedley, Colin, xv
Pelham, Rachel, 13
Percy, Thomas, 46, 51n, 179–88
Persyn, Mary Kelly, 272, 278n
Peterfreund, Stuart, 28, 33n

Phelps, Jocelyn, 157n
Phillips, Michael, 13, 14, 28, 33n, 249
Pinchbeck, Ivy, 138, 140, 141, 142, 143, 146n
Pippen, Tina, 106
Place, Francis, 81
Plato, 190, 272
Playboy, 261–2, 264
Podmore, Colin, 217n
Ponsonby, Sarah, 131
Poole, Russell, 187n
Porter, Catherine, 168–9n
Porter, Jane, 51n
Pound, Ezra, 209, 213, 217
Poussin, Nicolas, 103
Preston, Kerrison, 81, 90n
Pughe, William Owen, 46
Punter, David, 259

Radcliffe, Ann, 128
Raine, Kathleen, 55, 56, 117n, 253
Rajan, Tillotama, 71, 264, 266, 268n, 269n
Ramayana, 110, 112
Redgrave, Richard, 33n
Redgrave, Samuel, 33n
Reni, Guido, 85
Reuther, Rosemary, 199n
Rich, Adrienne, 62, 65
Richards, I.A., 94
Richmond, George, 90n
Rigaud, John Francis, 48
Rimius, Henry, 217n
Roberts, Nancy, 273–4, 278n
Robertson, Leslie, 27, 33n
Robertson, W. Graham, 100
Robinson, Janice, 217n
Robinson, Mary, 118–26, 128, 271
Rodger, N.A.M., 156n
Rogers, Nicholas, 157n
Roget, John Lewis, 33n
Romney, George, 13, 132, 153
Rose, Samuel, 129–31
Rose, Sarah, 129–31
Rosenwald, Lessing, 64
Ross, Margaret Clunies, 187–8n
Rossetti, Dante Gabriel, 35, 39, 43n
Rossetti, William Michael, 35, 36, 39, 40–1, 42, 43n, 92, 209, 216n
Rowling, J.K., 251

Rule, John, 137–8, 145–6, 146n
Ruoff, Gene W., 198n, 268n
Ruskin, John, 39, 43n

Saito, Takeshi, 93
Sampson, John, 92
Sargent, Mrs, 130
Schapiro, Meyer, 162, 168n
Scherf, Kathleen, 34n
Schiller, Gertrud, 103
Scholem, Gershom, 199n
Sennett, Richard, 38, 43n
Setzer, Sharon, 125–6n
Sha, Richard, 26, 33n, 34n
Shakespeare, William, xvi, 6, 49, 164
Sharpe, Pamela, 138, 140, 142
Shelley, Percy, 265, 271
Siddons, Sarah, 95
Smiles, Samuel, 10n, 77
Smith, Adam, 272, 274, 275, 278n
Smith, Olivia, 142–3
Smith, Charlotte, 118–26, 127, 128, 129–31, 135
Smith, J.T., 28, 81, 90n
Smollett, Tobias, 48
Snyder, Christopher A., 52n
Southcott, Joanna, 127
Southey, Robert, 34n
Spector, Sheila A., 199n
Spenser, Edmund, 58–9
Spicer, Widow, 155, 157n
Spilsbury, Jonathan, 218n
Stanton, Judith Phillips, 130
Starr, H.W., 187n
Stephen, Adrian, 249
Sternberg, Meier, 235n
Stevens, Bethan, 10n
Stevenson, Warren H., 33n, 56, 188n
Strachey, Ray (Rachel), 246n
Studies in Romanticism, twentieth anniversary Blake issue (41.2), xvii, xxn
Sturluson, Snorri, 180, 184, 186
Sturrock, June, 144, 146n
Swearingen, James E., 71
Swedenborg, Emmanuel, 56–7, 63, 210, 212, 213, 214, 217n
   see also Blake, William, Annotations to Swedenborg

Swinburne, Algernon Charles, 36–7, 42, 43n, 90n
Symons, Arthur, 217n

Tacitus, 182
Talmud, 103
Tannenbaum, Leslie, 72, 235n
Tatar, Maria, 228, 234n
Tatham, Frederick, 90n
Tayler, Irene, 3, 10n, 51n, 181, 187n
Taylor, Basil, 33n
Taylor, Jane, 127
Tertullian, 194
Thompson, E.P., 55, 57
Thrale, Hester, 95
Tighe, Mary, 127, 131–2, 135
Todd, Janet, 278n
Toland, John, 60n
Torfason, Thormod, 179, 182, 187n
Treadwell, James, 168n
Trimmer, Sarah, 56
Tsuchiya, Shigeko, 96

Van Sant, Ann Jessie, 278n
Varley, John, 26, 45–7, 51n
Vaughan, Frank, 3
Vesey, Elizabeth, 95
Vickery, Amanda, 137
Vien, Joseph Marie, 255
Viscomi, Joseph, 70, 76n, 177n, 265, 268n
Vogler, Thomas, 33n
Volney, 110, 117n
Völuspà, 181, 183, 184, 185
    von Zinzendorf, Christian Renatus, 209–18
    von Zinzendorf, Nicolaus Ludwig, 209–18
Voyages of Conception: Essays in English Romanticism, 97

Wagenknecht, David, 55
Walker, Joseph Cooper, 131
Webster, Brenda, 268

Webster, David, 53
Wedgwood, Josiah, 8, 10n
Weil, Simone, 234n
Weir, David, 109, 116, 117n
Werner, Bette Charlene, 168n, 169n
Whitman, Walt, 38, 40–2, 43n, 64, 94
Whittaker, Jason, 46, 51n, 187, 229
Wicksteed, Joseph, 81, 90n
Wilkins, Charles, 109, 112, 114
Wilkinson, Robert, 149, 157n
William Blake: Contemporary Critical Essays, 259, 260n
Williams, Edward *see* Iolo Morganwg
Williams, Nicholas M., xixn
Wilson, Milton, 200
Wilson, Mona, 5, 269n
Wilson, Thelma, 157n
Wittreich, Joseph A., Jr, 16, 23, 58, 187n, 277n
Wollstonecraft, Everina, 26, 127
Wollstonecraft, Mary, 26, 32, 34n, 80, 95, 97, 119, 127, 145, 251, 254, 260n, 262, 264–5, 267, 268n, 269n, 272, 273, 278n
Wood, Polly, 79, 80
Woodhouse, A.S.P., 200
Woodman, Ross, 200, 202
Woolf, Leonard, 249
Woolf, Virginia, 95, 194, 199n, 249, 250
Wordsworth, William, 234n, 271
Worrall, David, 33n, 125n
Wright, Julia, 71, 74, 270–8
Wu, Duncan, 26, 33n, 34n, 128

Yanagi, Muneyoshi, 92–4
Yearsley, Ann, 29
Yeats, William Butler, 80, 92, 217n
Yo Heave Ho, 154, 155
Yoshida, Suzuko, 94, 95

Zimmerman, Sarah, 127
Žižek, Slavoj, 201–2